Coherence: Insights from Philosophy, Jurisprudence and Artificial Intelligence

Law and Philosophy Library

VOLUME 107

For further volumes:
http://www.springer.com/series/6210

Michał Araszkiewicz • Jaromír Šavelka
Editors

Coherence: Insights from Philosophy, Jurisprudence and Artificial Intelligence

Springer

Editors
Michał Araszkiewicz
Faculty of Law and Administration
Department of Legal Theory
Jagiellonian University
Kraków
Poland

Jaromír Šavelka
Faculty of Law
Institute of Law and Technology
Masaryk University
Brno
Czech Republic

ISSN 1572-4395
ISBN 978-94-007-6109-4 ISBN 978-94-007-6110-0 (eBook)
DOI 10.1007/978-94-007-6110-0
Springer Dordrecht Heidelberg New York London

Library of Congress Control Number: 2013934541

Printed on acid-free paper

Springer is part of Springer Science+Business Media (www.springer.com)

Introduction

What does the concept of coherence represent? What role does it play in human reasoning and in justification of beliefs in particular? Is coherence in legal reasoning necessary, sufficient, or desirable? The latter question, widely discussed by legal philosophers during the past decades, leaves no space for doubts regarding the influence of coherentism on mainstream research in the areas of legal theory, philosophy, and jurisprudence. In philosophy and cognitive sciences, coherentism is often mentioned as one of the possible candidates for a general theory of justification and a very potent explanation of how human beings make sense of the world they live in. Therefore, the topic is important not only from the point of view of legal philosophy and jurisprudence but from the standpoint of other disciplines such as cognitive science and artificial intelligence as well.

Initially, the concept of coherence became the object of interest of philosophers. Interestingly enough, the first developed accounts of this concept differ considerably in both form and content from majority of contemporary work on coherence. This is due to the fact that these early elaborations were developed by philosophers who belonged to the philosophical school of Absolute Idealism (cf., for instance, the work of F. Bradley or H. Joachim). Otto Neurath, a member of the famous Vienna Circle, coined the early conception of coherence, which is still referred to in the context of epistemology. Let us recall the famous passage from his paper "Protocol Statements" (*Erkenntnis* 1932, p. 206–209; quotation after N. Rescher, *The Coherence Theory of Truth*):

> There is no way of taking conclusively established pure protocol sentences as the starting point of the sciences. No tabula rasa exists. We are like sailors who must rebuild their ship on the open sea, never able to dismantle it in dry-dock and to reconstruct it there out of the best materials. In unified science we try to construct a non-contradictory system of protocol sentences and non-protocol sentences (including laws). When a new sentence is presented to us we compare it with the system at our disposal, and determine whether or not it conflicts with that system. If the sentence does conflict with the system, we may discard it as useless (or false) (...) One may, on the other hand, accept the sentence and so change the system that it remains consistent even after the adjunction of the new sentence. The sentence would then be called "true". The fate of being discarded may befall even a protocol sentence. No sentence enjoys the noli me tangere which Carnap ordains for protocol sentences.

The quoted passage is, undoubtedly, a manifest of anti-foundationalism. No belief or sentence should be seen as immune to revision. However, if the overall coherence of set of beliefs is responsible for acceptance or rejection of a given element of it, it seems necessary to define the concept of coherence. Although some of the authors expressed skeptical views as regards the possibility or usefulness of elaborating a more precise account of this concept (for instance, Hilary Putnam chooses this skeptical stance), the epistemologists of the twentieth (and twenty-first) century devoted much attention to make the concept more precise and understandable. Let us mention, for instance, the work of Nicholas Rescher (*The Coherence Theory of Truth*, Oxford UP 1973) or Laurence BonJour (*The Structure of Empirical Knowledge*, Harvard UP 1985). The concept of coherence has been intensively elaborated in the field of analytic epistemology since then, which has led to many interesting results, in particular in connection with the probabilistic account of coherence. Some papers included in this volume present recent results from this field of research, and they are also included because they are relevant to legally important contexts of reasoning, for instance legal fact-finding.

As regards jurisprudence, coherence has become one of the favorite topics in the last several decades. The research has been considerably influenced by general philosophical research on coherence, but the realities of juridical discourse and the juridical postulate of coherence of the legal system (be it the system of statutory norms or a series of precedents) were also an important shaping factor.

Painting with a very broad brush, it could be stated that the historical development of legal accounts of coherence may be divided into two streams: (1) the stream of Dworkinian jurisprudence, which emphasized the role of the judge in finding the right legal answer by means of interpreting the law in the context of legal principles and policies (also in the dynamic context of creating a line of judgments which can be possibly compared to writing a chain novel) and (2) the analytical stream which aimed at accounting for a proper place for coherence in a broader model of legal reasoning (Neil McCormick, *Rhetoric and the Rule of Law*, Oxford UP 2005) or at basing such model on the concept of coherence (Aleksander Peczenik, *On Law and Reason*, Springer 2008 (2nd ed). Moreover, the analysis of actual use of the so-called argument from coherence in legal reasoning creates an important context of juridical inquiry concerning this concept (for instance, Stefano Bertea, "Does Arguing from Coherence Make Sense", Argumentation 19, 2005). Of course, the present state of art as regards legal-philosophical coherence research is far more complicated, and the degree of complication is caused by many factors. We hope that this volume offers a reliable (if not complete) report concerning the plurality of present views in this context.

The concept of coherence attracts cognitive scientists and artificial intelligence researchers as well. In particular, the theory of coherence as constraint satisfaction developed by the Canadian cognitive scientist and philosopher Paul Thagard (for instance, *Coherence in Thought and Action*, MIT Press 2000) has became influential (and controversial) since the beginning of the twenty-first century in the context of application of this theory to the domain of law. A few chapters present in this volume discuss this theory of coherence in legal contexts. It should also be noted that in the field of artificial intelligence and law research, the concept of coherence proved fruitful as regards the "theory construction" approach to modeling of legal reasoning (cf. the work of Trevor Bench-Capon, Giovanni Sartor, or Jaap Hage).

Although the overview presented above is oversimplified, we believe that these three viewpoints, the general philosophical one, the legal-philosophical one, and the perspective of cognitive science and artificial intelligence research, are very relevant, or even crucial, to grasp the contemporary understanding of the concept of coherence. Of course, these three viewpoints on coherence do not exhaust the space of possible and actual research. It is also not the case that philosophical elaboration of coherence comes always first, then it is absorbed by legal philosophy, and finally implemented in formalized systems in artificial intelligence and law research. The actual picture is much more complicated. For instance, sometimes, legal philosophers offer very important contributions to the general theory of coherence, and artificial intelligence researchers may be influenced directly by philosophical account of coherence, even if they apply their results to legal domain. Sometimes, different multidirectional influences are not made explicit. Sometimes, coherentist authors working on one field are not completely aware of relevant research conducted in the neighboring field.

We are of the opinion that the interchange of views between general philosophy, legal theory, and artificial intelligence research can be very fruitful for each of these disciplines, providing mutual inspiration and increasing understanding of a given topic. Hopefully, this book realizes this aim at least to some extent, as regards the concept of coherence and the role it plays in justification in general and in legal justification in particular.

The first chapter, written by Jaap Hage, introduces the reader to the realm of coherentism by means of comparison to its competitor, foundationalism. In this chapter, three different kinds of coherentism are presented—epistemic, constructive, and integrated coherentism. It is argued that integrated coherentism should be favored against the other two kinds on the grounds it best corresponds to the principles underlying coherentism.

The second chapter, written by Stefan Schubert and Erik Olsson, addresses the general concept of coherence as well, but in the context of legal fact-finding. At this time, the reasoning of the juries becomes the center of attention. It is acknowledged that coherence reasoning is to be regularly found in the reasoning of the juries. It is argued that there exists an interesting link between coherence and reliability that is much more clear and useful than a supposed link between coherence and truth.

Similar ideas are further developed in the following chapter written by William Roche. He introduces what can be called as a probabilistic account of coherence and develops his own model which he inter alia compares to the model proposed by Olsson. He also addresses the well-known problem of justified inconsistent beliefs. Roche's chapter, like the chapter of Schubert and Olsson, is an example of the application of formal methods to the problem of coherence.

In the fourth chapter, Juan Manuel Pérez Bermejo focuses his attention on the concept of coherence in general. He introduces the reader to a large variety of coherentist literature in legal philosophy and extracts what he calls "the most meaningful and widely known metaphors." These metaphors are carefully assessed with regard to the identification of shared patterns. Bermejo argues that the patterns are concordance, cohesion, unity, and comprehensibility. Thus, he tries to achieve a substantial clarification of the concept of coherence. He does so by means of informal analysis characteristic for humanities.

Bartosz Brożek's chapter explores the role of coherence in legal interpretation. He embraces hermeneutic philosophy as the basis for further thoughts. On the one hand, he argues that interpretation plays only a limited role in legal reasoning. However, he recognizes coherence as a criterion of interpretation—perhaps the sole criterion.

In the following chapter, Giovanni B. Ratti puts the defeasible deontic logic under a very hard scrutiny. He argues that these kinds of logics have deficiencies that are often overlooked. For example, he claims that they are not capable of solving normative inconsistencies. As some formalisms, based on coherence, can be considered direct competitors to formalisms based on defeasible logic, this chapter presents a very strong *pro* coherentism argument.

Aldo Schiavello makes objectivity the principle point of his considerations. In his search for an alternative theory of objectivity to the account of natural law and positivism (opinion of majority), he embraces conventionalism. He does so despite the existing limits he introduces to the reader. Moreover, there are strong connections between conventionalism and coherence.

The next chapter, written by Kenneth Ehrenberg, works with the notions of pattern languages and institutional facts. It is a unique account of law using methods embraced by object-oriented computer programming. A parallel between this approach and Searle's theory of institutional facts is drawn. However, the main point is ease of the representation of legal rules by computer systems.

In the following chapter, Wojciech Cyrul develops an account of a textological approach. It argues legal texts greatly differ from other traditional kinds of texts in having a so-called hypertext nature. This contributes to the idea of intertextuality, which is being related to coherence in law.

Marcello Guarini offers a perspective of cognitive science for the purpose of case classification. He starts with some insights of neural network research. He suggests coherence as constraint satisfaction might possibly play a role at the level of reflective or explicit reasoning. Thus, he opens the topic of coherence as constraint satisfaction that is assessed in detail within the following chapters.

In the following chapter, Jaromír Šavelka argues that coherence as constraint satisfaction should be considered a viable candidate for judicial reasoning support mechanisms. The argumentation is opened by a brief description of the main objections against the employment of any abstract formalism into judicial reasoning. These sound objections are then transformed into a list of requirements that should be met by any formalism considered for a judicial reasoning support mechanism. Finally, it is argued that coherence as constraint satisfaction meets the requirements.

Michał Araszkiewicz considers the current model of coherence as constraint satisfaction to be a promising basis for a model of legal argumentation. However, he identifies serious deficiencies of this formalism on the technical level. He specifically points out that argumentation within coherence as constraint satisfaction framework is not structured: the nature of relations is unclear, and clear guidelines for the selection of relevant elements are missing. He suggests these issues to become the subject of future research while providing some initial solutions to the exposed problems.

In the last chapter, Amalia Amaya also focuses on coherence as constraint satisfaction. She agrees with Šavelka and Araszkiewicz in considering coherence as constraint satisfaction to be the best fitting account of coherence for the purpose of law. In general, she presents ten theses on coherence in law and discusses their details. These are mostly theses on the nature of coherentism. She is in line with Araszkiewicz by pointing out a number of issues that should be subjected to future research.

The idea to prepare this book dates back to June 2011. At that time, we held a workshop titled Artificial Intelligence, Coherence and Judicial Reasoning attached to the Thirteenth International Conference on Artificial Intelligence and Law 2011 that took place at University of Pittsburgh School of Law, Pittsburgh, Pennsylvania. At the workshop, a number of interesting addresses and following discussions convinced us that coherence has become a topic of interest for lawyers, legal theorists, philosophers but also professionals from other disciplines. Since then, we have started to communicate with other people enthusiastic about the topic, and in consequence we have been able to collect the rich materials that are now presented to the kind reader as the book he or she is currently reading.

Finally, we would like to thank Kevin Ashley, Tom van Engers, Burkhard Schäfer and Giovanni Sartor for the initial idea and encouragement to hold the Artificial Intelligence, Coherence and Judicial Reasoning workshop. Our gratitude also goes to Kevin Ashley, Tomasz Gizbert-Studnicki, Jaap Hage, L. Thorne McCarty, Radim Polčák, and Erich Schweighofer for their support during workshop preparations. We would also like to thank all the ICAIL 2011 conference organizers for providing us with the opportunity to hold the workshop, especially to Tom van Engers, Kevin Ashley, and Anne Gardner. We appreciate Hrafn Asgeirsson, Kenneth Ehrenberg, Marcello Guarini, and William Roche for taking active part in the workshop, and we also thank those who have visited the workshop and helped the speakers to further develop their initial ideas. We thank Amalia Amaya, Juan Manuel Pérez Bermejo, Bartosz Brożek, Wojciech Cyrul, Kenneth Ehrenberg, Marcello Guarini, Jaap Hage, Erik J. Olsson, Giovanni Battista Ratti, William Roche, Aldo Schiavello, and Stefan Schubert for their contributions to this book. Last but not least we would like to thank the Springer editorial team, especially Neil Olivier, for their kind support and help during the editorial process.

Michał Araszkiewicz
Jaromír Šavelka

About the Authors

Amalia Amaya

Amalia Amaya is a research fellow at the Institute for Philosophical Research at the National Autonomous University of Mexico. She holds a Ph.D. from the European University Institute (2006) and an S.J.D. from Harvard Law School (2007). Some recent publications include "Legal Justification by Optimal Coherence" (*Ratio Iuris*, v. 24, 2011), "Virtue and Reason in Law" (in *New Waves in the Philosophy of Law*, edited by M. del Mar, Palgrave, New York, 2011) as well as two books, *Law, Virtue, and Justice* (coedited with Ho Hock Lai), (Hart Publishing, 2012) and *The Tapestry of Reason: An Inquiry into the Nature of Coherence and its Role in Legal Argument* (Hart Publishing, forthcoming in 2013).

Michał Araszkiewicz

Michał Araszkiewicz is an adjunct lecturer in the Department of Legal Theory at the Jagiellonian University, Kraków (Poland). He holds a Ph.D. in law from the Jagiellonian University (2010). He is a fellow of the Ryoichi Sasakawa Young Leaders Fellowship Fund (2009) and of the Foundation for Polish Science (2011 and 2012). He is also a member of the Center for Alternative Dispute Resolution at the Jagiellonian University and admitted to practice in Poland. His research includes the theory of legal argumentation, artificial intelligence and law research, and methodology of general jurisprudence.

Juan Manuel Pérez Bermejo

Juan Manuel Pérez Bermejo is a Senior Lecturer in Jurisprudence at the University of Salamanca, Spain. He obtained his Ph.D. in 1996. During the course 98-99 he was research scholar at the London School of Economics, Department of Government. Among his different publications on coherence in law are the book *Coherencia y sistema jurídico* (Madrid, Marcial Pons, 2006) and the articles 'Alcune osservazioni sul valore della coerenza nei sistemi giuridici' (*Quaderni di Diritto & Questioni pubbliche*, 2008) and 'Principles, Conflicts and Defeats. An Approach from a Coherentist Theory' (for publication in J. Ferrer & G.B. Ratti, eds., *Essays on Legal Defeasibility*, Oxford U.P., 2012).

Bartosz Brożek
Bartosz Brożek is an associate professor in the Department of Philosophy of Law and Legal Ethics, Jagiellonian University, Kraków and Copernicus Center for Interdisciplinary Studies, Kraków. He is the author or coauthor of nine books, including *Methods of Legal Reasoning* (with Jerzy Stelmach, Springer 2006), *Rationality and Discourse. Towards a Normative Model of Applying Law* (Wolters Kluwer 2007) and *Rule-following. From Imitation to the Normative Mind*, (Copernicus Center Press 2013). His research interests include legal logic, argumentation theories in the law, the problem of normativity in the law, law and neuroscience, as well as philosophy of science, philosophy of mathematics, and philosophy of mind.

Wojciech Cyrul
Wojciech Cyrul studied law and legal theory at the Jagiellonian University of Krakow, Catholic University of Washington DC, and Katholieke University Brussels. He holds master degrees in law and legal theory (Mag.iuris, Ph.D. in Law) and in legal theory (L.L.M. and D.E.A. at the European Academy of Legal theory in Brussels). He is currently an adjunct professor at the Jagiellonian University in Krakow, a member of the Management Board of the European Association for Teaching Legal Theory, a member of the European Academy of Legal Theory, and a member of Center for Legislation, Regulation and Legisprudence (C.R.L.R.) in Brussels. He was previously an associate professor at the Katholieke Universiteit Brussels and at the University of Cardinal Wyszynski in Warsaw. He is the author of several publications dealing with the influence of ICT and IT on law and legal practice.

Kenneth Ehrenberg
Kenneth Ehrenberg is beginning as an assistant professor of philosophy and adjunct professor of law at the University of Alabama in Fall of 2012, after having served in a similar role at the University at Buffalo, SUNY. He holds a Ph.D. in philosophy from Columbia University and a J.D. from Yale Law School and writes in the areas of general jurisprudence, legal normativity and authority, and jurisprudential methodology.

Marcello Guarini
Marcello Guarini (Ph.D. from the University of Western Ontario in 1998) is an associate professor of philosophy at the University of Windsor, Canada. He is an executive director of the International Association for Computing and Philosophy (IACAP) and director for the Society for Machines and Mentality (a special interest group of IACAP). His current research is focused on similarity, analogy, and machine ethics. He is also interested in epistemology and the philosophy of mind. His research is currently funded through a Junior Research Leadership Chair at the University of Windsor.

Jaap Hage
Jaap Hage holds the chair of jurisprudence at the University of Maastricht. His research is focused on legal logic, legal epistemology, and the ontology of law, including basic legal concepts. His main publications include *Reasoning with Rules*

(Dordrecht: Kluwer 1997), *Studies in Legal Logic* (Dordrecht: Springer 2005), "Basic Concepts of European Private Law", in European Review of Private Law 1 (2007), 3–26 (together with P.W. Brouwer), and "The Method of a Truly Normative Legal Science", in Mark van Hoecke (ed.), Methodologies of Legal Research (Oxford: Hart 2011), 19–44.

Erik J. Olsson
Erik J. Olsson is chair in theoretical philosophy at Lund University, Sweden. After receiving his Ph.D. from Uppsala University in 1997, he spent six years at Constance University (Germany) as a postdoc. He was an assistant professor in Lund from 2004 to 2007 before he became full professor in 2007. His main areas of research are epistemology, philosophical logic, and philosophy of science. His recent books include *Belief Revision Meets Philosophy of Science* (Springer 2011, with S. Enqvist), *Knowledge and Inquiry: Essays on the Pragmatism of Isaac Levi* (Cambridge 2006, paperback 2011), and *Against Coherence: Truth, Probability, and Justification* (Oxford 2005, paperback 2008). Olsson has published over 80 articles, including numerous journal papers and handbook chapters. His most recent papers on coherence are "The Coherence Theory of Justification" in *Stanford Encyclopedia of Philosophy* (2012), "On the Coherence of Higher Order Beliefs" in *Southern Journal of Philosophy* (with S. Schubert), and "Coherentism" in *The Routledge Companion to Epistemology* (2010).

Giovanni Battista Ratti
Giovanni Battista Ratti is a lecturer in legal philosophy at the University of Genoa (Italy). He has been Government of Canada Research Scholar (University of Toronto, 2004–2005); Government of Spain "Juan de la Cierva" Fellow in Law (University of Girona, 2008–2011); and visiting professor at the Universities of Girona (Spain, 2006–2008), "Pompeu Fabra" of Barcelona (Spain, 2008–2009), Nacional de Mar del Plata (Argentina, 2011), and Milano "Bocconi" (Italy, 2012). Among his main publications are *The Logic of Legal Requirements*, Oxford, 2012 (with Jordi Ferrer Beltrán); *El realismo jurídico genovés*, Madrid, 2011 (with Jordi Ferrer Beltrán); *Norme, principi e logica*, Rome, 2009; and *Sistema giuridico e sistemazione del diritto*, Turin, 2008.

William Roche
William Roche is an associate professor of philosophy at Texas Christian University. He holds a Ph.D. in philosophy from Ohio State University (2006). His primary area of specialization is epistemology. His current research focuses on epistemic justification and related topics in philosophy of science and philosophy of mind. His publications include "A Weaker Condition for Transitivity in Probabilistic Support" (*European Journal for Philosophy of Science*, 2012), "Witness Agreement and the Truth-Conduciveness of Coherentist Justification" (*Southern Journal of Philosophy*, 2012), "A Reply to Cling's 'The Epistemic Regress Problem'" (*Philosophical Studies*, 2012), and "Transitivity and Intransitivity in Evidential Support: Some Further Results" (*Review of Symbolic Logic*, 2012).

Aldo Schiavello
Aldo Schiavello is a full professor of legal philosophy at the University of Palermo. He received his Ph.D. in "Analytical Philosophy and General Theory of Law" from the University of Milan in 1997 and an L.L.M. in legal theory from European Academy of Legal Theory, Bruxelles, in 1993. He is the codirector of *Diritto & Questioni pubbliche*; assistant editor of *Ragion Pratica*; advisory board member of *Ethics & Politics*; and coordinator of Ph.D. program in "Human Rights: Evolution, Protection and Limits" (University of Palermo). His research is currently focused on legal positivism, legal reasoning, and legal normativity. Besides many essays, he has published the following books: *Diritto come integrità: incubo o nobile sogno? Saggio su Ronald Dworkin* (Giappichelli, 1998); *Il positivismo giuridico dopo Herbert L.A. Hart. Un'introduzione critica* (Giappichelli, 2004); *Perché obbedire al diritto? La risposta convenzionalista ed i suoi limiti* (Ets, 2010).

Stefan Schubert
Stefan Schubert is a postdoc in theoretical philosophy at London School of Economics. He defended his thesis, *Coherence and Reliability: Studies in Bayesian Epistemology*, in 2011. His list of publications include "Coherence and Reliability: The Case of Overlapping Testimonies" (*Erkenntnis*, 2011), "Coherence Reasoning and Reliability: A Defense of the Shogenji Measure" (*Synthese*, 2012), and "Is Coherence Reliability Conducive?" (*Synthese*, 2012).

Jaromír Šavelka
Jaromír Šavelka is a research fellow and teaching assistant at the Institute of Law and Technology by Masaryk University, Czech Republic. His main research interests comprise legal aspects of computer programs, legal argumentation, and informational nature of law. His teaching activities include giving individual lectures and courses in intellectual property law, software law, media law, and legal informatics. He is also active in the area of organizing conferences such as Cyberspace and Argumentation—both held annually at the Faculty of Law, Masaryk University in Brno, Czech Republic. Last but not least, he is a deputy-editor-in-chief of Masaryk University Journal of Law and Technology which is a law journal aimed at the intersecting area of law and technology.

Contents

Chapter 1
Three Kinds of Coherentism

Jaap Hage

1.1 Introduction

Coherentism has its basis in epistemology (Bonjour 1985; Lehrer 1992, 2000; Thagard and Verbeurgt 1998; Thagard 2000; Kvanvig 2011) and ramifications into ontology (Rescher 1973; Young 2008), but has also become popular in ethical theory (Rawls 1972; Daniels 2011) and in jurisprudence (MacCormick 1978, 2005; Dworkin 1978, 1986; Peczenik 2008; Amaya 2007). Quite recently, coherentism has found its way into Artificial Intelligence and Law too (Amaya 2007; Araszkiewicz 2010). It is not at all obvious, however, that all these versions of coherentism amount to one and the same thing. In fact, I will argue in this paper that it is possible to distinguish at least three kinds of coherentism, which I will call epistemic, constructive and integrated coherentism.

My aims in this paper are manifold. First I will show what makes coherentism attractive in comparison to its main competitor, foundationalism. This is a discussion about the relative values of foundationalism and epistemic coherentism, and it is a discussion which belongs to the general field of epistemology. I will argue that what makes epistemic coherentism the most attractive of these two alternatives is also a reason to see epistemic coherentism as a holistic theory of knowledge. This a major step into the direction of integrated coherentism. I will also argue that it is attractive to see this holistic version of coherentism as a coherence theory of truth, not only

---

Jaap Hage thanks Michal Araszkiewicz, Gustavo Arosenema, Bartosz Brozek, Jaakko Husa and the (other) participants of the discussion meeting in Kraków on this paper for useful comments on a draft version. The responsibility for errors remains complete his own, or course.

J. Hage (✉)
Department of Foundations and Methods of Law, University of Maastricht, Maastricht, The Netherlands
e-mail: jaap.hage@maastrichtuniversity.nl

M. Araszkiewicz and J. Šavelka (eds.), *Coherence: Insights from Philosophy, Jurisprudence and Artificial Intelligence*, Law and Philosophy Library 107,
DOI 10.1007/978-94-007-6110-0_1,

of (the justification of) beliefs. This is an important step towards the unification of epistemic and constructivist coherentism.

Building on the foundations laid in the discussion of epistemic foundationalism, I will show how coherentism can also play a role in ethics and law. This is not at all obvious, because the issue whether an ethical theory or a theory about the contents of the law is right because it is coherent is an altogether different issue than whether a belief is justified because it is an element of a coherent belief set. The version of coherentism in the fields of ethics and law would be constructive coherentism, a version of coherentism that differs fundamentally from epistemic coherentism.

After this discussion of constructive coherentism, it is a relatively minor step towards integrated coherentism, in which epistemic and constructivist coherentism are integrated. Integrated coherentism is a truly holistic version of coherentism, in which beliefs, standards, rules, values, and everything else is seen as elements of a 'theory of everything'. Such a theory of everything would be coherent if it satisfies its own standards for a good theory.

For practical purposes, this view of coherence as a characteristic of theories of 'everything' is rather useless. Therefore I will also provide a brief indication of how such a theory might be turned into a tool that helps in improving actual theories.

To conclude, I will briefly argue why recent attempts to model coherence as a kind of constraint satisfaction (Thagard and Verbeurgt 1998; Thagard 2000; Amaya 2007, 2011; Araszkiewicz 2010) are essentially flawed as a general epistemological theory because they lack the crucial holistic aspect of coherentism.

1.2 Epistemic Coherentism

Going by our day to day experience, we are naive realists. Through our senses we obtain a 'picture' of the 'outside world' and we assume that the outside world is like we experience it. This assumption must soon be given up when we discover that our senses sometimes deceive us, and that experience might be seen as the beginning of the philosophical discipline called 'epistemology'. Epistemology addresses, amongst others, the questions what knowledge is and how claims to knowledge can be justified. (Chisholm 1989, 1; Lehrer 2000, 1). However, even when we discover that our senses sometimes deceive us, our starting points will be some form of:

1. *Ontological realism*, namely the view that the facts are somehow given, independent of our beliefs about them, and of
2. Epistemic foundationalism, namely the idea that we get our knowledge about these independent facts in the first place through our senses and that the rest of our knowledge is built on top of that.[1]

[1] Arguably, this version of foundationalism is a form of empirical foundationalism. Other forms of epistemic foundationalism are also possible, as Araszkiewicz pointed out to me.

1.2.1 *Why Epistemic Coherentism?*

Both starting points contain grounds for doubts. Epistemic foundationalism assumes that the set of our beliefs is stratified, where 'higher' layers are supported by lower layers, but not the other way round. There must be one bottom layer which contains beliefs that are not supported by other beliefs. Usually these beliefs are taken to be either self-evident or to result from sensory perception.

There is also a relation of justification between the layers, which works in the opposite direction: the beliefs of the higher layers are justified by the beliefs of the layers below because the higher beliefs can be derived from the lower ones. Only the beliefs of the bottom layer cannot be justified in this way, and then there are four possibilities (Albert 1980, 11–15):

(a) The beliefs of the bottom layer are not justified and the whole pyramid of beliefs erected upon them is not justified either.
(b) The beliefs of the bottom layer are assumed to be justified differently, that is not by means of a derivation from other beliefs. One possible way to see this is that beliefs based on sensory perception are assumed to be justified for the reason that they are based on sensory perception. This boils down to a form of dogmatising these beliefs: they do not need any justification in the form of an argument which bases these beliefs on other beliefs.
(c) The 'bottom layer' is rejected as being the bottom layer. The beliefs in it, if they are justified, must be justified by inferring them from the beliefs one or more layers below. This line of reasoning leads to an infinite regress.
(d) The chain of inference in which beliefs are derived from other beliefs is allowed to be circular or bidirectional. This gives up the idea that justification works only bottom up.

Both the fear for an infinite regress and the resistance against dogmatising the bottom layer of beliefs have caused resistance against epistemic foundationalism. The main alternative has been to accept that the direction of justification between beliefs does not have to be unidirectional. Beliefs can support each other in a holistic way and the justification of a single belief consists in its being element of a justified belief set. This still rather vague alternative for epistemic foundationalism may be called *epistemic coherentism*. It is coherentism in the broad and negative sense of not being foundationalism.

This motivation for epistemic coherentism is mainly negative. Foundationalism suffers from a number of problems—threat of an infinite regress, dogmatisation of observational beliefs—which apparently cannot be overcome well. Epistemic coherentism is then defined negatively as not being foundationalist. This means that support relation between beliefs can go both directions, and that no beliefs are exempt from criticism. But does this step towards coherentism solve all the problems? Not really. I will discuss three remaining problems:

1. Epistemic coherentism assumes that the justification of beliefs lies in the relation between these beliefs and other beliefs. However, it is in general unclear how the truth of beliefs is related to their being justified.
2. Coherence is taken to be a standard for the epistemic justification of beliefs. This means that it is implicitly assumed that beliefs in a coherent set are more likely to be true than beliefs which do not cohere. But why would the coherence of a set of beliefs make it more likely that the beliefs are true?
3. The justification of beliefs would lie in the participation of beliefs in a coherent set of beliefs. But what does it mean if a set of beliefs is coherent? What does coherence add to mere consistency?

1.2.2 Truth Connection

Epistemic coherentism as sketched here is a so-called 'doxastic' theory of knowledge. That it is doxastic means that the justification of beliefs solely consists in the relation of the justified beliefs to other *beliefs*.

Doxastic theories of knowledge are a subset of internalist theories, which take it that the justification of beliefs rests solely on the relation of the beliefs to other 'internal' states of the believer, where these internal states include not only beliefs, but for instance also perceptual states (I hear the Beach Boys playing 'Wouldn't it be nice?) and memories (I remember that I was here before). Internalist theories are to be contrasted with externalist theories, according to which the 'outside world' somehow plays a role in the justification of beliefs (Pollock and Cruz 1999, 89).

All internalist theories have a problem concerning the relation between beliefs and the 'outside world'. Epistemically justified beliefs are beliefs of which it is justified to believe that they are true. If truth is taken to be dependent on correspondence with an independent 'outside world', it is not clear how coherence of beliefs, or—more generally—of internal states, would have anything to do with their truth. Suppose that a person has formed a coherent set of beliefs and that miraculously the world changes considerably.[2] This change will presumably not affect the coherence of the belief set. In other words, the belief set remains coherent. However, even if it were approximately true before the change in the world, after the change it will hardly contain a grain of truth. How could the coherence of the beliefs justify the beliefs as being true, then?

This problem is the result of an attempt to combine two philosophical positions which are hardly compatible, namely ontological realism and epistemic internalism. Ontological realism assumes that the facts in the 'world outside' do not depend on our propositional attitudes about them.[3] For example, an ontological realist

---

[2]This example derives from Sosa (1991a).

[3]I adapted this characterisation of realism from Devitt (1991, 13–17). The adaptation consist in replacing the epistemic notions 'belief' and 'think' by the more comprehensive internalist notion

takes it that the existence of the Higgs particle does not depend on our beliefs or theories about physical reality. Somebody who is an ontological realist about morality takes it that, for instance, murder is wrong, independent of whether this is accepted or believed by human beings, individually or collectively. Somebody who is an ontological realist (Platonist) with regard to mathematics assumes that the number 438,786,592 can be divided by the number 16,892 even if nobody has ever thought about this possibility (which seems not unlikely). I have added the last two examples, because they illustrate that one can be an ontological realist with respect to some domains, while being a non-realist with respect to other domains. One can be a mathematical realist, while being a non-realist with regard to morality, or a realist about physical reality, but a non-realist about the law.

The problem with combining ontological realism and epistemic internalism is that the former detaches the world and the facts in it from our beliefs and more generally our propositional attitudes about it, while the latter detaches the justification of our beliefs from the world. As a consequence the justification of beliefs becomes independent of the facts. Where justification of beliefs is taken as being justified in holding the beliefs to be true, this is problematic.

Where the diagnosis of a problem is clear, the possible solutions can often been seen more clearly. The present problem illustrates this point. The problem of combining ontological realism and epistemic internalism can be dissolved by giving up either one of these positions.[4] Here I will assume without much argument[5] that epistemic internalism is correct, which leaves the abandonment of ontological realism as the only available option for solving the problem.

Running ahead of the discussion of integrated coherentism, I will offer here a brief account of how ontological realism can be given up, even with respect to the physical world, without completely giving up the idea that the world exists independent of our beliefs about it. The basic idea is quite simple, namely that ontological realism is a belief like any other belief. A person may believe that the North Sea borders on England and also that this is a fact that does not depend on his beliefs about it. The same person may believe that there is nothing wrong with gay marriage, and also believe that this depends on his own opinion about this subject. This person holds—as far as the example is concerned—two first-order beliefs, one about the relative place of England and the North Sea and the other about the moral standing of gay marriages. He also holds two meta-beliefs, one about beliefs about physical reality and one about moral beliefs. He may even go so far as to assume that the former beliefs are true, while the latter beliefs have no truth value. About the beliefs on which he is a realist, he assumes that he may be wrong, depending on

'propositional attitude'. The reason for this move lies in the step which I will argue in Sect. 1.5.1, namely the replacement of 'belief' by 'position'.

[4]It is also possible to combine the positions, and to be satisfied that there is no connection between a belief being justified as true, and the actual truth of the belief.

[5]The beginning of an argument can be found in Hage (2005, 35–43).

the facts, while about the beliefs about which he is a non-realist he believes that the categories of 'right' and 'wrong' do not really apply.

On this account, 'ontological realism' is not a theory anymore about the relation (or better: the non-relation) between our beliefs and reality. It is a theory about different ways in which we hold our first-order beliefs. About some first-order beliefs we hold realist meta-beliefs, while on others we hold non-realist meta-beliefs. To coin a term by means of which this position can easily be referred to, I propose to call it 'pseudo-realism'.[6] Pseudo-realism then is the view that a belief is taken to be true, if and only if what is believed is taken to be the case in reality.

Pseudo-realism has implications for the justification of our beliefs. If somebody is the only person who believes that the Earth is flat, and this person is a pseudo-realist about this type of first-order belief, then he has reason to question one's belief about the Earth. If everybody holds a different view about a fact which is taken to be about facts which are the same for everybody, this should be evidence that this person's own belief is incorrect. If somebody believes that the paintings by Degas are more beautiful than those by Mondriaan, and also believes that this is a matter of taste, then the fact that everybody else believes that Mondriaan's paintings are more beautiful is not evidence against his own belief. The others merely have a different taste.

As these examples illustrate, much that is attractive in ontological realism can be maintained if one adopts pseudo-realism. In particular it remains possible to stick to the idea that the truth must be the same for everybody, and to the expectation that scientific endeavours will in the end converge upon the truth. Moreover, pseudo-realism can be combined with epistemic internalism, including epistemic coherentism. If the meta-belief is justified that a particular first-order belief is true, and if this first-order belief is justified too, this is a very strong justification for the first-order belief, in particular if the justification of both beliefs consists in the fact that they are elements of the same coherent belief set. Moreover, in this way the truth connection is rescued in the sense that the justification of a first-order belief hangs together with the justification of the meta-belief that this first-order belief is about the 'world outside'.

1.2.3 The Relevance and Nature of Coherence

On the combination of ontological realism and epistemic internalism there is no connection between the truth of a belief and its being justified. No matter which standard for coherence is adopted, the fact that a belief is justified because it belongs to a coherent belief set has no relevance at all for the truth of the belief. That explains at least to some extent why the search for 'the' proper criterion for coherence has remained fruitless.

---

[6] The term 'quasi-realism' has already been taken by Blackburn. See Blackburn (1984, 180).

Coherence has been explained in terms of logical and conceptual relations (Peczenik 2008, Sect. 4.1), explanatory relations (Lehrer 2000, 100–103), constraint satisfaction (Thagard 2000; Araszkiewicz 2010; Amaya 2011), or has been described as a 'seat of the pants feel' (Putnam 1981, 132/3).[7] The search for a criterion for coherence can amongst others be explained by the intuition that although a set of justified beliefs must be logically consistent, mere consistency does not provide a ground for assuming that the beliefs are justified. There must be something 'more' and this 'more' is dubbed coherence. However, from the fact—if it is a fact—that apart from consistency, something more is needed to transform a set of beliefs into a set of justified beliefs, it does not follow that this 'more' is a single thing. Possibly—and in my eyes even probably—there are several criteria which must be met if a set of beliefs is to be justified. Later, I will argue that there is no general answer to the question what these criteria are, but running ahead of that argument I will give some examples which illustrate different ways in which a set of beliefs can be 'coherent'.

One example is that a set of beliefs about physical laws is more coherent if some of the 'lower' level laws can be derived from higher level laws. If, for instance, the laws of the movement of the planets in our solar system can be derived from Newton's law of gravitation,[8] this makes the joint belief in both laws more 'coherent' and therefore more justified.

Another example is that an ethical theory according to which all moral judgements can be based on one (or a few) 'highest' moral principle(s), such as the principle that happiness should be maximized (Bentham 1982, 11/12; MacCormick 2005, 192), is more coherent than a particularist theory according to which every moral judgement stands on its own, without an 'underlying' moral principle (Dancy 2004).[9]

Again another example is that a theory which explains that there is no connection at all between the opening times of the cinema in Lanaken (Belgium) and the timetable of the railroads in Spain is more coherent than a theory which does explain such a connection. If there is reason to assume that two phenomena are disconnected, a theory which explains their connection would not only count as false, but also as incoherent. Falsity translates into incoherence because the reasons why we assume that the theory is false must somehow conflict with the reasons for assuming the connection.

The upshot of these three examples is that there is not one single criterion for coherence which makes that more coherent belief sets are more justified. In fact, there seems to be no single criterion for coherence and it is not obvious at all that a theory which is more coherent according to one such criterion is for that reason more justified.

---

[7] See also the contribution of Bermejo to the present volume.

[8] Cf. http://en.wikipedia.org/wiki/Kepler's_laws_of_planetary_motion#Newton.27s_law_of_gravitation. Downloaded on December 27, 2011.

[9] This example illustrates that the step from being more coherent to being more justified is not an obvious one, at least not in Dancy's eyes.

1.3 Constructive Coherentism

The problems around epistemic coherentism can to a large extent be explained from the fact that coherentism, which is essentially an internalist epistemic doctrine, is linked with ontological realism. These problems should therefore disappear if ontological realism is given up. That may not be a very attractive approach with regard to the physical world, but it is much more plausible with regard to the normative disciplines. Many people do not assume that there exist normative facts 'out there' which merely need to be discovered by sensory perception, or—already more plausibly—by means of reasoning.

1.3.1 Introducing Constructive Coherentism

The alternatives for normative realism are a full-blown non-cognitivism—there is nothing to be known—or some form of constructivism. Constructivism is the view that knowledge in a field depends on the actual or possible arguments which have been, respectively can be, given for a potential piece of knowledge. The conclusions of the best arguments are taken to be true, for the reason that they are the conclusions of the best arguments. Constructivism is only possible on the assumption that there exist standards at the hand of which arguments can be compared. Moreover, these standards themselves should not be based on the assumption that arguments which meet them lead to true conclusions, because that would be circular. Classic examples of such standards in ethics are:

- The utilitarian standard that arguments should point out that a course of action promotes happiness (Bentham 1982, 11/12);
- The Kantian standard that a proposed principle should be shown to be possible as a principle that would guide everybody's behaviour (Kant 1906, 421);
- The Rawlsian standard that a principle would arguably be chosen from behind the veil of ignorance (Rawls 1972, 11–22);
- The coherentist standard that a principle should arguably lead to outcomes that are acceptable in the light of the principle (reflective equilibrium; Rawls 1972, 48–51; Daniels 2011; Sosa 1991b).

With regard to the law Dworkin (1986, 225) has proposed the standard of constructive interpretation, according to which '. . . propositions of law are true if they figure in or follow from the principles of justice, fairness, and procedural due process that provide the best constructive interpretation of the community's legal practice.' As we will see 'best constructive interpretation' has strong links with coherentism.

In this section I will briefly discuss reflective equilibrium and constructive interpretation as examples of coherentism in a constructivist setting. The section will be concluded with some general observations about constructive coherentism.

1.3.2 Reflective Equilibrium

The idea of reflective equilibrium was introduced in ethical theory by Rawls, first in a paper about method in ethics (Rawls 1951) and then later, more influentially, in his *A Theory of Justice*. This version of reflective equilibrium was to become later known as 'narrow reflective equilibrium', to be contrasted with 'wide reflective equilibrium' (Sosa 1991b; Daniels 2011) that will be discussed later in this section.

The basic idea behind narrow reflective equilibrium is that an ethical theory is justified because it leads to practical consequences which fit with one's well-considered intuitive judgements about these cases. That these judgements are well-considered implies, amongst others, that they are considered in the light of the ethical theory that leads to them. An example may clarify this.

Suppose that somebody holds the general view that the capacities of persons in society are a common asset, to the benefits of which not only the individuals who actually possess these capacities are entitled, but society as a whole. These capacities include diligence and the inclination to work. Suppose also, that in practice this view leads to the conclusion that society should adopt a system of progressive taxes which makes it possible to grant a social security benefit to, amongst others, those who lack an income because they do not feel inclined to work for their money. Suppose, moreover, that intuitively one is not in favour of giving money to those who are too lazy to work. Reflective equilibrium requires that this intuitive judgement is reconsidered in the light of one's general view about capacities being a common asset. The result may be that in the end one's intuitive judgement changes and that one comes to see that those who are too lazy to work are still entitled to the benefits created by those who happen to be diligent and willing to work for their money. It is also possible that even in the light of one's theoretical views one is still repelled by the idea that people who are too indolent to work should be rewarded through the money earned by those who did make an effort. In that case, the demand of reflective equilibrium brings along that one modifies one's general theory to ensure that it does not have the repelling consequences anymore.

More in abstract, the following is at stake. Narrow reflective equilibrium is a kind of coherence which exists between more abstract normative principles and more concrete judgements. The more abstract principles support the more concrete judgements, but also the other way round. The connection between the more abstract and the more concrete level is made by logical rules of inference and factual premises. In our example, the factual premises would imply that the principle about capacities being a common asset implies that people who are not willing to work and therefore lack a income should receive a government-provided income, and that the government should raise progressive taxes in order to make this possible.

The important thing to notice in this connection is that the factual premises are excluded from the mutual adaptation process. In narrow reflective equilibrium it is not possible to adapt the (beliefs about the) facts because they do not cohere with other factual beliefs. This limitation of what can be mutually adapted in order to gain an equilibrium is abandoned in wide reflective equilibrium. Then other beliefs, principles and judgements—'positions' from now on, for reasons that will be explained in Sect. 1.5.1—can be included in the process of mutual adaptation, and this may even go so far as to include the inference rules of logic, both deductive and inductive, into the process of reaching equilibrium (Goodman 1979, 63–65; Quine 1986, 100; Sosa 1991b). Narrow reflective equilibrium is then a variant on wide reflective equilibrium, a variant which keeps part of the positions out of the adaptation process. Moreover, wide reflective equilibrium may, depending on how 'coherence' is defined, very well be a version of coherentism.

1.3.3 Constructive Coherence

There are at least two fundamentally different ways to look at the law. On the one view, the law is essentially a social phenomenon, which exists, directly or indirectly, through being accepted by the relevant members of a community. A typical example of this view is the Hartian concept of law (Hart 1994). According to this view, the law consists of a set of rules which derive their status as legal rules from being identified as such at the hand of, in the last instance, a rule that is accepted by the officials of a legal system. Knowledge of the content of the law is on this view knowledge of a part of social reality, and this kind of knowledge would be covered by an epistemic theory such as epistemic foundationalism or epistemic coherentism.

On the other view, the law is the answer to some form of normative question, for instance the question which norms should be enforced by collective means (Hage 2011). The answer to this question is a normative judgement, and it is very well possible to take a constructivist approach to obtaining this answer. One such constructivist approach is the one taken by Dworkin (1986).

The picture that Dworkin sketches of legal justification (in hard cases) is not completely the same as, but nevertheless quite similar to, the above picture of narrow reflective equilibrium. The basic idea is that a set of legal materials, cases and legislation, is used to induce legal principles from. These principles are both brought in harmony (coherence) with the legal materials and a normative theory about law and its relation to politics and ethics. The resulting principles are then used to formulate 'new' rules (which may very well be the old ones) and to solve cases with them. Just like narrow reflective equilibrium, Dworkin's constructive interpretation keeps factual information outside the process of mutual adaptation. Moreover, just like narrow reflective equilibrium may be broadened to make it include other kinds of positions, Dworkin's constructive interpretation may be broadened to make it include other positions. Arguably, if they are both sufficiently broadened, they become both versions of constructive coherentism and they do not even differ from each other anymore.

1.3.4 Conclusions on Constructive Coherentism

A major problem of epistemic coherentism is that the connection between the coherence of a belief set and the truth of the beliefs that are coherently held is unclear. The cause of this problem is the combination of epistemic internalism and ontological realism. It can be overcome by adopting pseudo-realism, but that means effectively giving up ontological realism.

On constructive approaches to a domain, such as ethics or the law, ontological realism has already been abandoned. According to constructivism a domain with respect to which one is a constructivist does not exist independent of arguments about the contents of this domain. To state it less abstractly: what is morally right is not discovered by means of moral arguments, but constructed by means of these arguments (Hage 2012a, b). If a domain about which one takes a constructivist approach is called a 'constructivist domain', it holds that in a constructivist domain, the conclusions of the best arguments are by definition true.

Constructive coherentism is then 'merely' a particular form of constructivism, namely the view that the best argument about a position consists in showing that this position is an element of a coherent set of positions. Because in a constructivist domain the conclusion of the best argument is true, there is no gap anymore between what is coherent and what is true.

Another thing that has emerged from the above discussion of constructive coherentism is that coherentism cannot only be applied to a set of beliefs about reality, but also to values and norms, including norms of logic which govern the issue what can be derived from what else. In particular the step from narrow to wide reflective equilibrium has lifted the coherentist enterprise to a new level, that of integrated coherentism.

1.4 Narrow and Integrated Coherentism

Although coherentism can also be a theory of truth, I will start my exposition of integrated coherentism as a theory of justification. The basic idea is then that a person is definitely justified in accepting a position if and only if this position is an element of the position set held by this person and if this position set is integratedly coherent. This characterisation is full of technicalities which will be explained briefly in this section. I will start with the distinction between narrow and integrated coherentism, because this lies the closest to the discussions of the previous sections.

Narrow reflective equilibrium is characterised by the fact that the sought after equilibrium is established between a limited set of positions. In Rawls' case these positions are normative: abstract principles and concrete well-considered judgements; in a physical science they may be hypotheses and observation statements; in logic they may be logical laws and concrete arguments. In all these cases, the coherentist test is applied only to a subdomain. What coherence amounts to, how it is established, why it is worthwhile, how coherence relates to truth, and, last but not least, all 'background knowledge' which is required to establish coherence or the lack thereof is somehow taken for granted. That is to say: these factors are not taken into account in making the evaluated set coherent.

The total set of positions that are held is divided into two parts:

- One part—the 'coherence set'—that one attempts to make coherent and
- Another part, the 'background set'—which fulfils several functions, including:
  - The provision of background knowledge which is necessary to establish coherence;
  - Defining coherence and providing standards for coherence;
  - Indicating what the relation is between coherence and truth;
  - Making clear why coherence is worthwhile;
  - Indicating how an incoherent set should be modified in order to make it (more) coherent (belief revision).

The step from narrow to wide reflective equilibrium has made it clear that the elements of the second set might just as well be subjected to the test of coherence. It depends on the reason why one wants to have a set of coherent positions which positions are included in the coherence set and which positions are assigned to the background set. It would, for instance, be possible to use values—e.g. the value of coherence—as the background against which beliefs about physical reality are tested, but it would just as well be possible to use beliefs about physical reality as the background knowledge for evaluating a set of values on its coherence.

This raises the question whether the total set of positions should be divided into two parts. Why not join the coherence set and the background set into one all-encompassing coherence set? Then the positions in this set should be used themselves to evaluate the set on 'coherence' or whatever other quality would be considered relevant in the light of this all-encompassing set as a whole. If this step has been taken, wide reflective equilibrium has changed into integrated coherentism.

The word 'coherentism' in this connection does not stand for any particular standard according to which positions might cohere, and not even for the idea of coherence anymore. It only indicates that that no set of positions is granted a privileged position in the sense that it is considered to be 'foundational' or completely immune for revision. *Coherentism is no more than the negation of traditional foundationalism.*

A less traditional form of foundationalism might still emerge in the context of a coherent theory, namely if it fits in a coherent theory that some positions should be considered as foundational or at least have some privileged position in the building of knowledge, etc. The difference with 'traditional foundationalism' is that 'coherentist foundationalism' is the *conclusion* of a coherentist style of thinking, while 'traditional foundationalism' presupposes the foundational nature of some positions.[10]

[10] A splendid example of such coherentist foundationalism is Susan Haack's 'foundherentism' (Haack 2009).

The word 'integrated' is meant to indicate that the standards for a 'good' position set, whether they be traditional coherentist (whatever that may be) or 'coherentist foundationalist' are integrated in the position set that should be integratedly coherent. The position set itself contains the standards which it must satisfy.

Coherentist approaches can now be divided into integrated coherentism and narrow coherentist approaches. The former is characterised by the fact that it works with only one position set, which must satisfy the standards set by itself. The latter are characterised by the fact that they distinguish between a coherence set, which must be made coherent (or which can only justify the positions included in it if it is coherent), and a background set, which contains all the rest.

Depending on how the positions are divided over the two sets, several variants of narrow coherentism can be distinguished, such as epistemic and constructive coherentism. It is also possible to make distinctions within narrow coherentism by means of the standard at the hand of which coherentism is characterised. One such standard might be explanatory coherence (Lehrer 2000, 97–122); another one is coherence as constraint satisfaction (Thagard 2000).

As these two ways of distinguishing within narrow coherentism illustrate, it is the background set that determines which kind of narrow coherentism is at stake. Because integrated coherentism does not separate the background set from the coherence set, it does not allow to distinguish between different variants of integrated coherentism. It all depends on the contents of the coherence set, and this content only allows to distinguish between different coherent sets, but not between different kinds of coherentism.

1.5 Justification

Integrated coherentism is a theory about justification. Its plausibility depends amongst others on what one takes justification to be. In this connection it is important to distinguish between what justification is and the standards by means of which justification is measured. In this section I will briefly deal with the nature of justification, without saying much about the standards that should be used for justification.

1.5.1 Positions

At first sight there are many things that can be justified, such as acts, decisions, policies, rules, beliefs and states of affairs. On closer inspection, everything that can be justified turns out to depend somehow on decision making. For instance, acts can be justified to the extent that they are potentially the outcome of decision making (intentional acts); policies and rules can be adopted and abandoned, respectively abrogated and all of these are the outcomes of decisions. The same counts for beliefs, which can also be adopted and abandoned deliberately. And, finally, states of affairs can be justified to the extent that they are the outcome of decision making, or can be changed intentionally.

The view of justification that I will present here as a presupposition of what follows does not deal with all objects of justification, but is broader than merely a theory about the justification of beliefs. Its topic is the justification of 'positions' in general and it treats a belief as one kind of position. I will use the term 'position' as a catch-all for everything, with the exception of behaviour[11] that is amenable to justification. A position is something that is actually accepted; 'things' that are amenable to position are called 'potential positions'. Potential positions include:

- Beliefs ('London is the capital of the United Kingdom'),
- Practical judgments ('I should review this paper tomorrow'),
- Plans ('I will take the plane to Bologna next Saturday').
- Rules ('One ought to drive on the right hand side of the road'),
- Values ('Truth is valuable'),
- Logical standards ('If $P \rightarrow Q$ and P are both true, Q must be true'), or
- Guidelines for belief revision ('If two positions are incompatible, the one that was more recently acquired should be abandoned').

At first impression one might think that these different objects of justification require different forms of justification, but this impression is only correct in the sense that different standards for justification apply to them. All forms of justification can be reduced to variants on justification of behaviour (including forbearance). This is obvious for actions, and since decisions and verdicts can be brought under the category of actions (*taking* a decision, or *giving* a verdict with this particular content), it should be obvious for decisions and verdicts too. The same counts for using rules.

It is somewhat less obvious for beliefs, but the justification of a belief with a particular content can be interpreted as the justification of *accepting* this belief content. Accepting something can, for justificatory purposes, be treated as a kind of mental action. And just as it is possible to accept belief contents, it is possible to accept goals, values and principles.

It is even possible to continue along this line, by treating the justification of the different forms of actions as the justification of accepting 'that these actions are the ones that should be performed under the circumstances' (Sartor 2005, Chap. 3). In this way, all forms of justification can be treated as the justification of accepting 'something'.

As a catch-all term for things that can be mentally accepted, I will use the already introduced term 'position'. I will use the expression 'position set' for the set of

[11] Legal decisions (e.g. convict the suspect) can both be seen as behaviour, in which case it is not amenable to acceptance and as a judgement about what should be done (the suspect should be convicted), in which case it is a potential position.

all positions accepted by a person.[12] Clearly, the content of a position set may be different from person to person and may change in the course of time.

1.5.2 Local and Global Justification

In the literature on legal justification (e.g. Alexy 1978, 273–278 and MacCormick 1978, Chap. 2), justification has sometimes been pictured as a deductively valid argument. In such an argument the conclusion (what is justified) must be true given the truth of the premises. The idea behind this kind of justification is that the 'justifiedness' of the premises is transferred to the conclusion, analogous to the way in which the truth of the premises is transferred to the conclusion in more traditionally conceived deductive arguments.

It seems to me that this picture is mistaken in at least two ways. First, because it suggests that 'being justified' is a characteristic of positions that is similar to truth, only somewhat 'weaker'.[13] Second, because it overlooks the essentially global nature of justification. In a deductively valid argument, the conclusion must be true if the premises are true. This means that the truth of the conclusion is guaranteed by the truth of the premises, and that nothing else is relevant for this truth.[14] For instance, if the statements 'All thieves are punishable' and 'John is a thief' are both true, the statement 'John is punishable' must be true too. Whatever else may be the case, this cannot influence the truth of the statement 'John is punishable', unless it has the implication that one of the premises is false after all.[15] For instance, the fact that John is only 5 years old either has no impact on John's punishability, because the statement 'All thieves are punishable' is still considered to be true, or—which is more plausible—it has impact, because it makes the statement 'All thieves are punishable' false.

[12]An interesting line of thinking would be to explore what the implications are if one adopts that position sets can also be held by social groups, or for instance by 'physical science' or 'legal doctrine'. I owe this suggestion to Gustavo Arosenema. Popper's work on 'world 3' (Popper 1972, Chaps. 3 and 4) goes in the same direction.

[13]A possible explanation of this use of the term 'justified' is reluctance against the use of 'true' for sentences for the topic of which one uses a constructivist approach. Truth would then be confined to domains for which one adopts realism, and 'justified' for constructivist domains. This usage has the disadvantage that it gives the word 'justified' a double role. Namely to stand for a person being justified in doing something, and as a counterpart for 'true'.

[14]This should be read as 'irrelevant from an argumentation-technical point of view'. The only thing that is really relevant for the truth of a conclusion is whether this conclusion corresponds with the facts. But that has nothing to do with the argument from which the conclusion follows.

[15]This may be interpreted as a reason why justification on the deductive account of it is global too. But then the global nature does not lie in the deductively valid argument itself, but in the justification of the premises.

The general point here is that the truth of the conclusion of a sound justificatory argument (deductively valid with true premises) is not influenced by additional information. If the premises of a deductive justificatory argument are true, its conclusion must be true, and then probably also justified, *whatever else is the case*. Therefore, it is not necessary to consider additional information, because this information cannot change the conclusion anymore. Deductive justification is *local* in the sense that it needs only consider the premises and the conclusion of a deductively valid argument.

The reader who thinks this is unrealistic is probably right. Not because deductively valid justification is not local, but because deductively valid justificatory arguments are seldom offered. They are seldom offered, because they require premises the truth of which cannot be established. Take our example about John, who is a thief and punishable because of the rule that thieves are punishable. A deductively valid argument that leads to the conclusion that John is punishable requires the premise that *all* thieves are punishable. That premise can only be established if it is already known that John is punishable (that would be a necessary condition), or if there is a rule that makes all thieves punishable, without exceptions. The former demand would beg the question, because we need the premise about all thieves to justify a belief about John. The second demand is unrealistic, because rules tend to have exceptions, and these exceptions cannot be enumerated.

Real life justification is normally based on premises that support a conclusion without guaranteeing its truth. If John is a thief, this is a reason to believe that he is punishable, but there may be other reasons which invalidate this conclusion. One such a reason would be that John is only 5 years old. In general a position is justified if the reasons pleading for acceptance outweigh the reasons against accepting it to a sufficient degree. But this means that *all* reasons for or against acceptance must be balanced and that means in turn that justification must be global. A position which is justified in the light of a particular set of other positions need not be justified in the light of an even larger set of other positions, because this larger set may contain additional reasons against adopting it.[16]

In logic there is a technical term for a similar phenomenon: *nonmonotonicity*. A logic is nonmonotonic if a conclusion that follows from a set of premises does not have to follow from a wider set of premises (Ginsberg 1987, 1–2). Analogously we can say that justification is nonmonotonic because a position that is justified in the light of a set of other positions, does not have to be justified in the light of a still wider set of positions (Hage 2005, Chap. 1).

Nonmonotonicity and the global nature of justification go hand in hand. The 'normal' justification of a position is always relative to a position set of limited size. To get rid of this relativity, one needs to idealise and to assume that it is possible

---

[16]In fact, it is even more complicated, because apart from reasons against a position, there may be reasons why the reasons for adoption are in general not reasons after all, or are excluded in this special case. More details on the 'logic of reasons' in Hage (1997, Chap. 4), and in Hage (2005, Chap. 3).

to consider a position in the light of *all* other positions which are actually held. A person would be *definitely justified* in holding a position if and only if he would be justified in holding this position in the light of all (other) positions he holds. In coherentist terminology this would mean that a person is definitely justified in holding a position if and only if the position is an element of an integratedly coherent position set held by this person. Definite justification would therefore be an all-or-nothing matter. A person either is definitely justified in accepting a position, or not. There is no in between, no being more or less definitely justified in accepting a position. Obviously, definite justification and integratedly coherent position sets are unrealistic notions for practical purposes, but they are useful as tools for thinking about the nature of justification.

1.6 Positive and Negative Coherence

1.6.1 Comprehensiveness

The idea behind integrated coherentism is that the standards for evaluating the coherence of a position set are included in the position set itself. A corollary of this starting point is that a position set is taken to be *comprehensive*: all positions a person accepts are assumed to be part of the position set that is judged on its coherence. This means that not only first-order beliefs about the external world would be included but also meta-beliefs, such as the belief that another belief is, or is not, about an independently existing external world, standards for the validity of arguments, guidelines for belief revision in case a position set is (found to be) incoherent, ontological and epistemological views, religious beliefs, values, (other) norms etc.

According to integrated coherentism, such a comprehensive position set should satisfy the standards set by itself. This means that it includes every position that should be accepted in the light of the rest of its content (the counterpart of logical closure), and does not include any position that should be rejected according to the rest of its own content (the counterpart of logical consistency). Notice that the notion of consistency is not used in this characterisation, because both the relevance and the nature of consistency in the traditional sense are to be determined by the position set itself.

Notice also that, for the same reason, logical notions are not mentioned in the characterisation. It is likely that such logical notions will play a role in position sets that are actually held by human beings, but that is not something which is to be included in the characterisation of coherence. That it is not included has everything to do with the fact that integrated coherentism does not single out some positions for being part of the background set in which coherence is defined.

1.6.2 Spontaneous Positions

In Sect. 1.2.2 the objection against epistemic coherence theories was discussed that a coherent position set may be isolated from reality. A set of positions may be coherent while all positions contained in it are false. There are three ways to tackle this objection. One way is to argue that it rests on a misunderstanding of justification. The second focuses on how actual position sets develop in time, while the third focuses on the role of meta-beliefs.

I will be brief about the first refutation of the objection. This holds that the objection confuses truth and justification. That a position is untrue is no objection against a person being justified in accepting this position. For instance, a person may be justified in believing that it is presently raining in a faraway country, because a normally reliable internet site tells her so. That the internet site had a software problem with as a consequence that it reported falsely about the actual weather does not change her being justified in her belief. This would be different if a person knows, or should have known, that a belief is untrue. But then the problem is not the falsity of the belief, but the acceptance of the belief that an accepted position is false, which amounts to inconsistency of the position set.

A second refutation of the criticism that coherence does not really justify acceptance of a position is based on a consideration how a coherency test of justification will operate in practice. One does not come up with a coherent set of positions from scratch. Normally one starts from an already existing set, a 'base' (Raz 1992). The contents of a *real position set*, that is a set that is entertained by some real person, will have two kinds of determinants, rational ones and a-rational ones. The rational determinants make that an existing set should be corrected—new positions should be added and existing ones should be removed—because rationality requires this given the rest of the set.[17] The a-rational determinants cause 'spontaneous' changes to the contents of the set. New positions are added as the effect—notice the causal terminology—of perception, memory, intuition, or any other factors which cause what a person accepts. A person may, for instance, accept something because he mistakenly believes that this is rational in the light of what else he believes. Existing positions are removed, because they are forgotten or abandoned for irrational or a-rational reasons.

These irrational or a-rational influences on a position set are relevant because position sets are biased toward the past. Whether a new position should, from the rational perspective, be added, or an existing one removed, depends on the present contents of the set. To see why, one should notice that a particular position can have one of three statuses in the light of (the rest of) a position set:

[17] Notice that the contents of a position set determine what *should be* added, removed or changed. The position set itself does not lead to the required modifications. Moreover, the definition of integrated coherence does not state anything about the way an integratedly coherent set should be arrived at. It only provides a test on a position set to determine whether it is coherent.

1. It should be adopted (if not already present) because this is rational; the position is *acceptable*;
2. It should be removed (if it is already present) because this is rational; the position is *rejectable*;
3. It is neutral in the sense that it should neither be adopted nor removed; the position is *suspendable*.

As long as a position set is not coherent—that means in practice: always—the judgment whether a particular position should be added or removed should rationally be made on the basis of the full position set, unless there are reasons to assume that some elements are rejectable, because then these elements should not be taken into account. (This runs already ahead of the argument in Sect. 1.7.2 about default reasoning.)

Suspendable positions remain in the set, even if there is no reason to adopt them, and codetermine what is acceptable. So suspendable elements can be justified because they belong to a coherent position set, without being justified by particular reasons in the set. This may, for instance, hold for beliefs caused by perception, or for evaluative judgments caused by 'intuition'. As long as there is no reason to reject them, they will be maintained. Moreover, suspendable elements can also play a role in determining whether other elements can remain in the set and are therefore justified.

Since rational modifications can only take place on the basis of an existing position set, the original elements of any realistic position set must have been spontaneous positions, that is neutral elements. This is one part of the argument why real position sets do not 'hang in the air'. Real sets stem from sets of spontaneous positions, and there is where we should look for the desired 'contact with reality'.

With the view that suspendable positions that are part of a position set should remain there, a position is adopted that is known in the epistemological literature as *negative coherentism* (Pollock and Cruz 1999, 70–71). The demand for coherence is used to weed out positions that do not fit. It is not required that every element in the position set is supported by other elements. If the latter were required, the coherentist view would be positive. The advantage of negative coherentism over positive coherentism is that it can account for positions that are based on perception, (moral) intuition, and memories. In particular the possibility to account for perceptive input makes that the link between the positions in a coherent position set and reality, that is brought about by perception, *can* be maintained. However, whether it *will* be maintained depends on the other position in the set, including beliefs about the relation between the 'external world' and perceptive states. Integrated coherentism allows for an important role for perceptive states, but does not require it.

1.7 Meta-Beliefs

The role of meta-beliefs as a possible way to refute the 'isolation argument' (Pollock and Cruz 1999, 74–75) was already mentioned briefly in Sect. 1.2.2 in the discussion of pseudo-realism. Since this refutation plays an important role in integrated coherentism, that discussion will be elaborated a little here.

1.7.1 Pseudo-Realism

The central question in connection with the 'isolation argument' is how a coherent position set relates to the 'world outside'. To begin with, we believe that there is such a world, and we also believe that through our senses this world influences our spontaneous positions. It should be noted, however, that these beliefs, like all of our other beliefs, belong to our position set, and can be corrected on the basis of the rest of the set. The existence of an external world is like the existence of so-called 'theoretical entities'. Entities like electrons cannot be perceived, but their existence is derived from other things that we can perceive. With the external world it is a little different: we believe that we can perceive it, but its existence is still theoretical in the sense that we postulate its existence on the basis of perceptual impressions. The world is, so to speak, necessary to explain our perceptions of it.

This should not be read as stating that we believe the external world to exist only because that would explain our beliefs about it. Our cognitive apparatus is such that we spontaneously believe that (most of) our perceptive impressions are impressions of the external world. E.g. we do not only spontaneously believe that the sun is shining, but also that the sun is shining in the 'outside' world. In fact, the latter assumption is so natural that we automatically take the first belief to be identical to the second. However, we are able to question this spontaneous belief, and if it is questioned a reason for adopting it (again) is that the external world explains both the existence of our spontaneous beliefs about it, and the convergence of (some of) our beliefs about it with the corresponding beliefs of other persons.

In this connection, agreement plays an important role. If different persons have the same beliefs, this may be taken as a reason to assume that there exists an independent object of belief that causes the unanimity of the beliefs about this object. For instance, the 'objective' existence of a table explains why we all see the table and believe that it is there. Similarly, the existence of some moral disagreements and their resistance against factual information fuels the meta-belief that there is no 'objective' moral reality analogous to the physical reality.

Agreement in beliefs does not have to be explained by an objective external world, however. A second (Kantian) type of explanation would be that agreement on a position is the outflow of the functioning of our cognitive apparatus. Think in this connection of mathematics. Mathematicians tend to agree on many results of their science, but only some of them attribute this agreement to an objectively existing world of mathematical objects, such as for instance natural numbers. Another example would be that our moral intuitions are, at least to some extent, innate (cf. Hauser 2008).

A third possible explanation of agreement is that a position is the result of a procedure that is designed in such a way that it leads to the same outcome for (almost) everybody. A legal example would be that legal arguments based on the same rules and cases and using the same canons of interpretation and argumentation lead in easy cases to the same outcomes for almost everybody.[18]

From the fact that agreement on a particular position may be a sign that this position reflects an outside world that is the same for everybody, it does not follow that where agreement is lacking a position does not reflect the outside world. For instance, we believe that the position 'There is water on the moon' reflects the outside world, but there was (at the moment of writing this paper) no agreement yet amongst scientists whether this position is true. However, because we assume that the position reflects the outside world, we tend to believe that an increase in relevant knowledge should, in the end, lead to agreement.[19] Where we do not even expect that an increase in knowledge would lead to agreement, we apparently do not assume that the position reflects the outside world.

1.7.2 Defeasible Coherentism

For practical purposes, the insight that somebody is justified in accepting a position if this position belongs to the integratedly coherent position set held by this person, is useless. Actual position sets will never be integratedly coherent, if only because they would most likely be infinitely large.[20] If coherentism is to be used as a real test on the justification of positions, a less demanding version should be devised.

One such less demanding version will be described here very briefly. For ease of exposition I will dub it *defeasible coherentism*. The starting point is again the idea that justification should be based on coherence and that the set which is to be made coherent also contains the standards by means of which it is evaluated. What must be dropped is the demand that this set is comprehensive, because a comprehensive set would be unmanageable. Therefore the coherence of the position which is to be justified is not to be with the full comprehensive set, but merely with a 'suitable'

[18] This may even be so by definition, if easy cases are defined as those cases which lead to agreement amongst those who argue by the rules of law. This position was argued in Hage et al. (1994). Presently I am less convinced of this position than I was then.

[19] This comes near to Pierce's circumscription of truth: 'Truth, what can this possibly mean except it be that there is one destined upshot to enquiry with reference to the question in hand.' Quotation taken from Kirkham (1992, 81).

[20] An integratedly coherent position set should contain everything which should be accepted in the light of what else is accepted. Probably this involves the logical closure of the position set, and logical closure under deduction means infinitely large.

subset thereof. This subset should include the position that is to be justified and it should be integratedly coherent.

The crucial extra demand on the subset is that it is 'suitable'. A suitable subset is a subset which does not give a wrong picture of the full set where the position that is to be justified is concerned. Ideally, the subset should only contain this position if the full set would also contain it. Such a small position set is with respect to this position *adequate* for the comprehensive set. Obviously this adequacy cannot be established without having the disposal over the full set, and that is precisely what will not be available.

The solution to this problem can be found in the use of meta-beliefs and the characteristics of negative coherence. Somebody can hold a belief which, *as far as she can see*, fits in the set of all her positions. This means that she believes that her belief fits in her actual comprehensive belief set. She does not know whether this meta-belief about the adequacy of her subset is true, but she nevertheless has it. Moreover, as long as she does not have counter-evidence, she is defeasibly justified in sticking to it.

Not having counter-evidence means in this connection: not being aware of counter-evidence and not having counter-evidence in the same defeasible sense that the subset of her positions of which she is aware contains reasons not to trust it.

An example may make this clearer. A public prosecutor believes that John is a thief and that the rule exists that thieves are punishable. She also uses a rather traditional logic for rule application, including modus ponens style arguments. Given this limited position set, she should adopt the belief that John is punishable. Actually she also believes that minors are not punishable, but she has no reason to assume that John is a minor. Therefore she actually believes that her small position set is adequate for her actual comprehensive set where the belief that John is punishable is concerned. Moreover, as long as she is not aware of counter-evidence (there is no counter-evidence in her subset) she is justified in sticking to this meta-belief. The subset is defeasibly coherent and therefore, this public prosecutor is defeasibly justified in believing that John is punishable.

Defeasible coherentism allows justification to come in degrees. A person can be more or less justified in accepting a particular position (Haack 2009). It even allows the formulation of a standard—not necessarily the only standard—for determining degrees of justification: if a person accepts a position p on the basis of subset S1, he is more justified in doing so than when he accepts position p on the basis of subset S2, if S2 is a proper subset of S1.

1.8 Evaluation

Amaya (2011) has made a brief list of six 'serious problems' which face coherence theories in law, both the constructivist and the epistemic ones. It may be useful to see how integrated coherentism fares with regard to these problems.

1.8.1 *Vagueness*

Coherence theories often leave the notion of coherence undefined, and that is not very helpful if it comes to the justification of legal judgements. Integrated coherentism might be seen as the so-manieth illustration of this criticism, because it leaves the determination of what counts as coherent to the position set that is to be made coherent itself.

And yet, this criticism would not be appropriate. It would be comparable to criticising the word 'good' for being too vague. 'Good' is not vague at all. It is a very general term of recommendation. That is does not specify the grounds on which the recommendation is made does not make its meaning unclear, but merely leaves the conditions for its application unspecified. Analogously, integrated coherentism is clear in the sense that it requires a position set to meet its own conditions for a good position set, without specifying what these conditions are. Requiring that a theory of coherentism specifies the conditions of coherence would be comparable to requiring that a theory about the meaning of 'good' specifies what makes things good.

1.8.2 *Holism*

Coherence theories, at least some of them (Dworkin 1986; Peczenik and Hage 2004), require that legal judgements are justified on the basis of a theory about the whole system of beliefs about law and political morality. A similar requirement exists for epistemic justification. That makes the justification of judgement very difficult and moreover, such a theory is descriptively inadequate.

The accusation of holism applies certainly to integrated coherentism, but in my opinion holism is a strength, rather than a weakness. Admittedly, requiring coherence of a comprehensive position set makes it impossible to apply full-blown integrated coherentism as a tool for justifying legal judgements. But who said that it is a drawback of an analysis of justification that it cannot be applied as a practical tool? This is comparable to criticising a theory about the nature of prime numbers for making it impossible to enumerate all the prime numbers.

An analogous rebuttal applies to the criticism that (integrated) coherentism is descriptively inadequate. Theories about what justification amounts to are not meant to be descriptions of social practices, but abstract analyses of normative standards. Normative, because they specify which standards must be met if a position is to count as justified. Abstract, because the standards are mentioned only in an abstract way. In general, the demand that epistemic theories are descriptively adequate confuses prescription and description.

And finally, as was shown in Sect. 1.7.2, integrated coherentism can be complemented by a theory of defeasible justification which is not holistic, at least not in a way that hampers practical application of integrated coherentism to the process of justifying legal judgments.

1.8.3 Circularity

Coherent theories may be circular, for instance because belief in the occurrence of particular phenomena is justified on the basis of a physical law, while acceptance of the law is justified on the basis of these phenomena.

This objection is a straw man. I have never seen a coherence theory which would allow this simple mistake. Moreover, any feasible criterion for coherence would exclude it.

In integrated coherentism the problem is easily solved. Either such circular arguments are—for as yet unclear reasons—deemed acceptable, and then there is no problem if they are allowed. Or—which is much more likely—such arguments would not be allowed, and then the standards contained in an integratedly coherent theory would not allow them.

1.8.4 Conservatism

Coherence theories have a tendency towards conservatism, because they make the justification of new elements depend on their coherence with a pre-existing structure.

Yes, coherence theories make the justification of new elements depend on their coherence with a pre-existing structure, just as they make the continued existence of the pre-existing structure dependent on its coherence with new positions. Mutual dependence makes the new depend on the old, and the other way round. That is exactly as it should be, and it is unclear why this is mentioned as a problem.

What might have been mentioned is the tendency of conservatism which is attached to negative coherentism. Negative coherentism allows positions to be maintained as long as there are no coherence-based reasons to abandon them. This allows that arbitrary beliefs and moral views to survive, merely because there is as yet no counter-evidence. Integrated coherentism is committed to this negative coherentism, so this 'criticism' would apply to integrated coherentism.

The reason why integrated coherentism is a form of negative coherentism is that this is the best way to allow sensory input and moral 'intuitions' to play a role in the justification of positions. Coherentism is most plausible as a theory about when a position set needs no reconstruction anymore and is in that sense justified. It is not so that any arbitrary set of positions is justified, merely because it satisfies its own standards. It is a person who is justified in holding the position she holds, because her position set has reached a stage in which there is no need any more to modify it because of a lack of coherence.

1.8.5 *It Is Unclear What Coherence-Based Inference Is*

There exists no clear account of the inference-patterns that legal decision makers may use while seeking coherence in law.

This is not an objection against (integrated) coherentism as a theory of justification in itself, but rather a complaint that such a theory does not solve all the problems which a legal decision maker may face. (Integrated) coherentism aims to specify what it means that a person is justified in accepting a set of positions. It does not aim to specify how this set is arrived at. In fact, as far as the justification of the positions in the set is concerned. it does not matter at all how the position set was arrived at. Demanding otherwise risks to confuse heuristics and legitimation.

1.8.6 *It Is Unclear Why Coherence Is Desirable in the Law*

Why should coherence be endorsed with justificatory force in a legal setting, granted that coherence can justify?

For integrated coherentism this question is easy to answer. There is no separate issue of legal justification, but only one general issue of being justified in accepting positions. Some of these position will concern legal issues, but for the purpose of justification they are treated just like other positions. So for integrated coherentism, this question makes little sense.

For narrow coherentism, things may lie differently, because then the issue plays a role which positions are to be included in the coherence set and which ones in the background set. Then it depends on one's theory about the nature of law whether coherentism should play a role in legal justification. Obviously there is much more to be said on this issue, but equally obviously, this is not the place to do so.

In general we can conclude that the problems mentioned by Amaya either are not real problems for coherentism *as a theory about when a person is justified in accepting a position*, or that integrated coherentism does not suffer from the mentioned problem.

1.9 Coherence as Constraint Satisfaction

To give a good impression of integrated coherentism it is useful to contrast it with a modern alternative. In this connection I have selected the work of Amaya again, because it contains a good insight in what is involved in coherentism and applies this insight to the law.[21]

[21] As this volume illustrates, Amaya's work does not exhaust the constraints satisfaction approach to legal reasoning. Earlier examples are Joseph and Prakken (2009) and Araszkiewicz (2010).

Amaya has developed her own coherence theory for law, a theory based on constraint satisfaction. In this paper I will focus on the constraint satisfaction part of Amaya's views, but honesty commands that she recognises three other (?) elements in het model of legal reasoning, which I will only briefly mention. These elements are:

1. *Inference to the best explanation*. 'The claim is that legal decision-makers reach justified beliefs about the law and facts under dispute by first generating a number of alternative interpretive and factual hypotheses and then by selecting one of them as justified.' A brief comment to this element: it contains a description of what legal decision-makers allegedly do. This can only be part of a theory of justification on the assumption that the actual practice has justificatory force, that is on a form of justificatory naturalism. In fact, Amaya adopts such a form of naturalism in a footnote. (Amaya 2011, footnote 1).
2. *Epistemic responsibility*. The basic idea here is that legal reasoners have to fulfil a number of epistemic duties. The duty explicitly discussed is the duty to collect more evidence on propositions that are less than certain on basis of one's evidence.
3. *Context*. As Amaya points out, context is very relevant to the assessment of coherence. Standards of legal justification vary with context.

I will confine myself to a brief discussion of coherence as constraint satisfaction. Amaya has taken this approach from Thagard and Verbeurgt (Thagard and Verbeurgt 1998; Thagard 2000). She describes it as follows (Amaya 2007):

'On this view, coherence maximization is a matter of maximizing the satisfaction of a set of positive and negative constraints among the elements of a given set. The idea is the following one. We start with a set E of elements, which may be propositions or other representations (goals, actions, concepts, etc.). The problem is how we can accept some elements and reject others in a way that maximizes the coherence of E. The claim is that we turn E into as coherent a whole as possible by taking into account the coherence and incoherence relations that hold between pairs of elements of E. These relations put constraints on what can be accepted or rejected. To maximize coherence, we partition E into two disjoint subsets A, which contains the accepted elements, and R, which contains the rejected elements, in a way that takes into account the local coherence and incoherence relations. For example, if a hypothesis h1 explains e1, we want to ensure that if h1 is accepted, so is e1. On the other hand, if h1 is inconsistent with h2, then we will make sure that if h1 is accepted, then h2 is rejected. The coherence problem is thus that of dividing up E into A and R in a way that best satisfies the most constraints.'

A simple example may illustrate the point. Suppose that the set E contains the following elements:

(a) John is a thief.
(b) John is a minor.
(c) John is punishable.
(d) John is not punishable.

There is a positive constraint between the elements a and c, meaning that some positive value is attached to the fact (if it is a fact) that the subset A contains both a and c. Let us assume this value equals 2. There is a negative constraint between the elements b and c, meaning that some positive value is attached to the fact (if it is a fact) that the subset A contains b and subset R contains c, or the other way round. Let us say that this value is 4. Moreover there is a negative constraint between a and d (value 1) and a positive constraint between b and d (value 2). There is a very strong negative constraint between c and d, because they are inconsistent. (If c and d are both accepted, one has to give up bi-valued logic.) Let us assume that the value of this constraint equals 1,000.

Given the value of the last constraint, c and d must be in different subsets. If the one is accepted, the other one must be rejected. If c is accepted, the sum of the values is increased if a is also accepted, and if b is rejected. Id d is accepted the sum is increased if b is accepted and a rejected. The maximum sum (1,007) is achieved by accepting b and d and by rejecting a and c.

This example illustrates how coherence can be given a precise criterion (maximisation of the sum of the constraint values), and how coherence can be a matter gradation (the sum can be higher or lower). Moreover, given a finite set of elements and of constraints, it is possible to compute what the most coherent theory is. These are all advantages for the practical use of a coherentist theory.

However, the example also illustrates some drawbacks of the constraint satisfaction approach. One drawback is that this approach treats constraints as bidirectional. If a supports c, then c supports a (to the same degree). On the one hand this is desirable, because on some occasions we argue from the fact that somebody is a thief to that he is punishable, while on other occasions we hypothesize that somebody might have been a thief, because he is punishable. However, as the wording ('hypothesize', 'might have been') already suggest, the one direction of reasoning is more plausible than the other direction. It is more plausible to conclude that somebody is punishable from that he is a thief, than the other way round. The proposed representation of the constraints does not make it possible to take this into account.

Possibly this drawback can be remedied by introducing more elements and more constraints into the model, but this way to deal with the problem immediately points to a more serious drawback of the approach: it may be necessary to tinker extensively with the constraints and their values in order to obtain the 'right' results. This presupposes that the 'right' results are already given, and that the model is better or worse, depending on how good it is in producing the correct results. Then, however, this approach can only be used in epistemic contexts, where the justification of alleged knowledge is at stake. In the case of constructive coherentism, where the model defines what are the correct elements of a theory, this does not work.

It may be objected that in the constructive context it does not have to work, because any outcome of the model is correct, precisely because it is the outcome of the model. This objection leads us to what is in my opinion the most serious drawback of the constrain satisfaction model, namely that a very substantial part of the information about a domain is stored in the constraints and the values that are attached to them. In a constraint satisfaction model, the coherence of a theory consists in the way in which the ordinary elements of the theory are divided over the accepted-set and the rejected-set. In that way, the information contained in the constraints is not part of the coherent set, although it does play a role in determining what the most coherent set is. The coherence of the set is the coherence of only a part of the available information (Hage 2005, 45–47).

Essentially this criticism amounts to it that coherence as constraint satisfaction is a form of narrow coherentism which places crucial parts of the available information in the background set. But how 'bad' is this? It depends on how one sees the role of coherence in this connection. Coherentism may be seen as the main competitor of foundationalism in the broad field of epistemology. A major attraction of coherentism is then that it lacks the vices of foundationalism. In fact, the way I defined integrated coherentism above (Sect. 1.4) makes it the denial of foundationalism, no more. On this view of coherentism, it is a deadly sin to put crucial parts of the available information in the background set. Constraints should therefore be part of the coherence sets rather than of the background sets.

It is, however, possible to assign coherentism a more modest role in justification, in particular legal justification. Lawyers use a number of tools to justify their views on the proper outcome of legal cases. Many of these tools go under the name of canons of interpretation; others are typical legal styles of reasoning (analogy, e contrario, a fortiori). It is possible to see the strive for coherence as just one amongst these tools. The strive for coherence is on this view comparable to other legal methods and is justified in the same way: this is how lawyers actually work. Coherence as constraint satisfaction would then be justified in the same way: in practice lawyers would strive for coherence by means of constraint satisfaction. Whether practising lawyers such as judges actually strive for coherence in the sense of constraint satisfaction, and whether the invocation of such an actual reasoning practice suffices for the justification of this practice are highly relevant issues on this view, but it is beyond the scope of this paper to discuss these issues in some detail.[22] Personally I doubt whether the strive for coherence as constraint satisfaction plays a substantial role in legal reasoning. Moreover, I do not think that the existence of such a practice—it is exists—would imply that this practice is the right one for legal decision making.

1.10 Conclusions

My purposes with this paper were:

- To argue why coherentism is more attractive as a theory of justification than its main competitor, foundationalism,

[22]My views on legal method are exposed more extensively in Hage (2011).

- To show how coherentism can play a role in moral and legal justification, and finally, on a more negative side
- To argue why coherence as constraint satisfaction, which is coming in vogue now, is less attractive, at least if it is considered as an alternative for foundationalism.

Much of my argument has consisted of making distinctions and by showing how insight of what is at stake in coherentism 'automatically' leads to a particular variant of it, integrated coherentism. As soon as the attractiveness of integrated coherentism has become clear, the main drawback of coherence as constraint satisfaction springs to the eye: it is a variant of narrow coherentism, the coherentist opponent of integrated coherentism.

The best way to draw the conclusions of this paper is to summarise and elaborate the distinctions that were made.

1. Major distinctions that mainly functioned on the background of this paper are those between *justification, explanation and description*. It is possible to describe how, for instance, judges go about when arguing for a particular conclusion, but such a description is not relevant for the question whether the judge was justified in adopting this decision. The exception might be that one adheres to a procedural theory of justification. Neither is it necessary that a theory of justification explains why judges take the decisions they take. A justificatory theory may play such a role, but that would require a kind of rational choice theory to explain legal decision making.
2. Possibly the main distinction in this paper is *between integrated and narrow coherentism*. Narrow coherentism strives for coherence in a limited set of positions, while the other positions held by a person are put into a background set which is either taken for granted, or is evaluated on a different basis than coherence. It is this background set that indicates why coherence is important, and what the criteria for coherence are. Integrated coherentism does not distinguish between two position sets. All positions are lumped together and are jointly evaluated on their coherence. The motivation of and the standards for coherence are part of the single position set themselves.
3. Although it might seem that the *distinction between coherentism and foundationalism* is more basic than that between the two main forms of coherentism, that is not the case from the perspective of integrated coherentism. Foundationalism is from that perspective just a variant of narrow coherentism. A set of positions (e.g. sense-based beliefs, and deductive logic) are set apart in a background set, and form a standard by means of which the positions in the other set are evaluated. This standard will in the case of foundationalism not be a coherentist one, but not even integrated coherentism requires that the positions in a position set are evaluated on the basis of a coherence standard in a narrow sense.
4. If one adopts a form of narrow coherentism, it becomes easy to distinguish between *epistemic and constructive coherentism*. Epistemic coherentism applies the coherence standard to determine whether beliefs about an independently existing reality are true. This is problematic, because there is little reason to assume that coherence of beliefs is relevant for the truth of these beliefs.

This 'isolation problem' is not without reason one of the main problems of coherentism. It is important to notice, however, that it is only problematic on the unlikely combination of epistemic coherentism and ontological realism (about which more soon). Constructive coherentism is the combination of two views. The one, constructivism, is the view that some facts obtain because it is the outcome of the best argument that they obtain. The other one defines the best argument in coherentist terms (e.g. reflective equilibrium, or constructive interpretation). Constructive coherentism presupposes a theory about a domain (e.g. ethics, or the law) which assumes that facts in this domain depend on the best argument. Such domains are called 'constructivist domains'.

5. One way to deal with the isolation problem is to distinguish between *ontological realism and pseudo-realism*. Ontological realism assumes for some domain that the objects and facts in it exist independently of what people accept or believe about it. Pseudo-realism takes existence and truth to be an outflow of a position set, and in particular meta-beliefs. A sentence is on this view considered to be true if its content is accepted (the car is red indeed) and if it is also accepted that the 'world outside' makes it true (there are independently obtaining facts entailing that the car is red).This distinction between ontological realism and pseudo-realism has implications for the relation between the facts and the truth of sentences. Both views can adhere to the correspondence theory of truth; a sentence is true if and only if the fact that it expresses obtains. They give a different reading of the direction of this connection between fact and truth, however. Ontological realism assumes that the facts are already there and that the sentence aims to reflect this fact (word to world direction of fit; Searle 1979, 3–4; Hage 2005, 165). Pseudo-realism, on the contrary, assumes that the fact obtains because the sentence is true (world to word direction of fit). Pseudo-realism sits well together with constructivism, because of the chain: best argument → true sentence → fact.

Integrated coherentism is a very abstract theory about what a person is justified in accepting. Its abstraction has several consequences:

(a) Integrated coherentism in its pure form is not useful as a practical tool to justify or modify beliefs. It is useful, however, to gain insight in what is good in coherentism, and what is not, and to see what is required if one wants to adopt some version of narrow coherentism. It is also useful as an indication how a more practical form of coherentism (defeasible coherentism) can be developed.
(b) Because of its abstraction, integrated coherentism is compatible with adapted versions of foundationalism, constraint satisfaction, and ontological realism. The required adaptation is usually that the other position is embedded in an integratedly coherent position set which explains why that position is worthwhile. For example, the position may be part of a coherent theory that beliefs that are caused by sensory perception take a privileged place in the total position set and cannot be rejected, or can only be rejected for very strong reasons. If this meta-belief about beliefs based on sensory perception is part of

an integratedly coherent position set, the rest of the set functions as an empirical foundationalist set.

(c) Because of this possibility to combine integrated coherentism with many other views which at first sight might seem to conflict with it, it is very difficult to criticize integrated coherentism. The main criticism seems to be that integrated coherentism does not exclude much and is therefore empty. My reply to that criticism would be that mathematics is empty in the same way.

Integrated coherentism is valuable if it is taken for what it is, a very abstract theory about when a person is justified in accepting a particular position and as a demonstration of how and in what sense coherence plays a role in this. It must function as a background against which more specific epistemological theories can be developed, and as a test for the feasibility thereof. It should not be taken as an alternative for these more concrete theories.

References

Albert, H. 1980. *Traktat über kritische Vernunft*, 4th improved edition. Tübingen: Mohr.

Alexy, R. 1978. *Theorie der juristischen Argumentation. Die Theorie des rationalen Diskurses als Theorie der juristischen Begründung*. Frankfurt: Suhrkamp.

Amaya, A. 2007. Formal models of coherence and legal epistemology. *Artificial Intelligence and Law* 15: 429–447.

Amaya, A. 2011. Legal justification by optimal coherence. *Ratio Juris* 24: 304–329.

Araszkiewicz, M. 2010. Balancing of legal principles and constraint satisfaction. In *Legal knowledge and information systems*, ed. R.G.F. Winkels, 7–15. Amsterdam: IOS Press. Proceedings of the Jurix 2010 conference.

Bentham, J. 1982. *An introduction to the principles of morals and legislation*, eds. J.H. Burns and H.L.A. Hart. London: Methuen.

Blackburn, S. 1984. *Spreading the Word. Groundings in the philosophy of language*. Oxford: Clarendon Press.

Bonjour, L. 1985. *The structure of empirical knowledge*. Cambridge: Harvard University Press.

Chisholm, R.M. 1989. *Theory of knowledge*, 3rd ed. Englewood Cliffs: Prentice Hall.

Dancy, J. 2004. *Ethics without principles*. Clarendon Press: Oxford.

Daniels, N. 2011. Reflective equilibrium. In *The stanford encyclopedia of philosophy*, ed. Edward N. Zalta, (Spring 2011 Edition), http://plato.stanford.edu/archives/spr2011/entries/reflective-equilibrium.

Devitt, M. 1991. *Realism and truth*, 2nd ed. Oxford: Blackwell.

Dworkin, R. 1978. *Taking rights seriously*. Duckworth: London.

Dworkin, R. 1986. *Law's empire*. London: Fontana.

Ginsberg, M.L. (ed.). 1987. *Readings in nonmonotonic reasoning*. Los Altos: Morgan Kaufman.

Goodman, N. 1979. *Fact, fiction and forecast*, 3rd ed. Hassocks: The Harvester Press.

Haack, S. 2009. *Evidence and inquiry*, second expanded editionth ed. Amherst: Prometheus Books.

Hage, J.C. 1997. *Reasoning with rules*. Dordrecht: Kluwer.

Hage, J.C. 2005. *Studies in legal logic*. Dordrecht: Springer.

Hage, J.C. 2011. The method of a truly normative legal science. In *Methodologies of legal research*, ed. M. Van Hoecke, 19–44. Oxford: Hart Publishing.

Hage, J.C. 2012a. Legal reasoning and the construction of law. *i-Lex* 7 (2012), 81–105. (http://www.i-lex.it/articles/volume7/issue16/hage.pdf).

Hage, J.C. 2012b. Construction or reconstruction? On the function of argumentation in the law, to appear. In *Legal argumentation theory: Cross-disciplinary perspectives*, eds. Ch. Dahlman and E. Feteris. Dordrecht: Springer.

Hage, J.C., R.E. Leenes, and A. Lodder. 1994. Hard cases: A procedural approach. *Artificial Intelligence and Law* 2: 113–167.

Hart, H.L.A. 1994. *The concept of law*, 2nd ed. Oxford: Clarendon Press.

Hauser, M.D. 2008. *Moral minds: How nature designed our universal sense of right and wrong*. London: Abacus.

Joseph, S. and H. Prakken. 2009. Coherence-driven argumentation to norm consensus. *Proceedings of the 12th international conference on artificial intelligence and law*, 58–77. New York: ACM.

Kant, I. 1906. *Grundlegung zur Metaphysik der Sitten*. Hamburg: Felix Meiner Verlag. First edition 1785. The references use the page numbers of the Akademie Ausgabe.

Kirkham, R.L. 1992. *Theories of truth*. Cambridge: MIT Press.

Kvanvig, J. 2011. Coherentist theories of epistemic justification. In *The stanford encyclopedia of philosophy*, ed. Edward N. Zalta, (Summer 2011 Edition), http://plato.stanford.edu/archives/sum2011/entries/justep-coherence.

Lehrer, K. 1992. Coherentism, lemma. In *A companion to epistemology*, eds. Jonathan Dancy and Ernest Sosa, 67–70. Oxford: Blackwell.

Lehrer, K. 2000. *Theory of knowledge*, 2nd ed. Boulder: Westview Press.

MacCormick, N. 1978. *Legal reasoning and legal theory*. Oxford: University Press.

MacCormick, N. 2005. *Rhetoric and the rule of law*. Oxford: University Press.

Peczenik, A. 2008. *On law and reason*, 2nd ed. Dordrecht: Springer.

Peczenik, A., and J. Hage. 2004. Legal knowledge about what? *Ratio Juris* 13: 326–345.

Pollock, J.L., and J. Cruz. 1999. *Contemporary theories of knowledge*, 2nd ed. Lanham: Rowman and Littlefield.

Popper, K.R. 1972. *Objective knowledge*. Oxford: Clarendon Press.

Putnam, H. 1981. *Reason, truth and history*. Cambridge: Cambridge University Press.

Quine, W.V. 1986. *Philosophy of logic*, 2nd ed. Cambridge: Harvard University Press.

Rawls, J. 1951. Outline of a decision procedure for ethics. *Philosophical Review* 64: 177–197. Also in J. Rawls, *Collected Papers*, edited by Samuel Freeman, Cambridge: Harvard University Press 1999, 1–19.

Rawls, J. 1972. *A theory of justice*. Oxford: Oxford University Press.

Raz, J. 1992. The relevance of coherence. *Boston University Law Review* 72: 273–321. Also in Joseph Raz, *Ethics in the Public Domain*, revised edition, Oxford: Clarendon Press 1995, 277–325.

Rescher, N. 1973. *The coherence theory of truth*. Oxford: Oxford University Press.

Sartor, G. 2005. *Legal reasoning, a cognitive approach to the law*. Dordrecht: Springer.

Searle, J. 1979. *Expression and meaning. Studies in the theory of speech acts*. Cambridge: Cambridge University Press.

Sosa, E. 1991a. The raft and the pyramid: Coherence versus foundations in the theory of knowledge. *Midwest Studies in Philosophy* 5(1980): 3–25. Also in Ernest Sosa, *Knowledge in Perspective. Selected Essays in Epistemology.* Cambridge: Cambridge University Press, 165–191.

Sosa, E. 1991b. Equilibrium in coherence? In *Knowledge in perspective. Selected essays in epistemology*, ed. Ernest Sosa, 257–269. Cambridge: Cambridge University Press.

Thagard, P. 2000. *Coherence in thought and action*. Cambridge: MIT Press.

Thagard, P., and K. Verbeurgt. 1998. Coherence as constraint satisfaction. *Cognitive Science* 22: 1–24.

Young, J.O. 2008. The coherence theory of truth. In *The stanford encyclopedia of philosophy*, ed. Edward N. Zalta, (*Fall 2008 Edition*), http://plato.stanford.edu/archives/fall2008/entries/truth-coherence.

Chapter 2
Coherence and Reliability in Judicial Reasoning

Stefan Schubert and Erik J. Olsson

2.1 Introduction

Suppose that a robbery has taken place and that John has been accused of committing the crime. Imagine sitting on a jury as three witnesses take the stand. The first witness testifies that John was at the crime scene at the time of the crime, the second that John owns a weapon of the type used, and the third that John shortly after the robbery deposited a large sum of money in his bank account. This would be an example of a highly *coherent* set of testimonies, i.e. a set in which the individual elements hang together or are in agreement. The case would have been quite different had the first witness reported that she was having dinner with John at the time of the crime. That would have led to an incoherent set of testimonies.

Empirical research strongly indicates that people, and jurors in particular, are disposed to trust coherent sets of testimonies.[1] According to the influential *story model* of juror decision making (see, e.g., Pennington and Hastie 1993), jurors construct narratives in response to evidence in trials and then choose the one that scores best on Pennington and Hastie's favored criteria or 'certainty principles'—'coverage' and 'coherence'. Jurors then determine the verdict on the basis of their chosen story. Similarly, Lagnado and Harvey (2008) argue that when performing complex reasoning tasks where not all evidence point in the same direction, people group the evidence into different coherent sets as a basis for further consideration.

[1] The following account of psychologists' work on coherence is based on that given in Harris and Hahn (2009).

S. Schubert (✉)
Center for Philosophy of Natural and Social Science, London School of Economics,
Lakatos Building, Houghton Street, London WC2A 2AE, UK
e-mail: s.schubert@lse.ac.uk

E.J. Olsson
Department of Philosophy, Lund University, Kungshuset, Lundagård, 222 22 Lund, Sweden
e-mail: Erik_J.Olsson@fil.lu.se

M. Araszkiewicz and J. Šavelka (eds.), *Coherence: Insights from Philosophy, Jurisprudence and Artificial Intelligence*, Law and Philosophy Library 107,
DOI 10.1007/978-94-007-6110-0_2, © Springer Science+Business Media Dordrecht 2013

In related studies it has been concluded that, if an individual witness delivers inconsistent testimonies, then subjects will assign her a lower degree of credibility; and it has been observed that inconsistency leads to lower rates of conviction (see, e.g., Berman and Cutler 1996; Berman et al. 1995). Finally, Brewer et al. (1999) present evidence supporting the claim that perceived witness credibility is positively affected by consistency between reports from different witnesses, albeit to a lesser extent than intra-witness consistency.

Thus, much speaks in favor of coherence reasoning playing a fundamental role when jury members and judges evaluate evidence as presented before the court. The question, though, is whether this reliance on coherence can be motivated from a normative perspective. Given that *A* is more coherent than *B*, can we conclude that *A* is in some sense more appropriate to believe than *B*? Our first task (subsequent to having introduced the concept of coherence, as that concept is understood in the philosophical literature) will be to review some previous work on our normative question. Thereafter, we present our own preferred account of the normative basis of coherence reasoning, in terms of *reliability conduciveness*, a concept first proposed in (Olsson and Schubert 2007). We add further substance to that account by proving some formal results that reveal the intimate connection between a certain conception of coherence and the probability of reliability. Finally, we draw some parallels between our account and the Evidentiary Value tradition in Scandinavian legal philosophy.[2]

2.2 Coherence and Truth

Epistemologists have generally thought that coherence is an epistemically useful property. But exactly what is it that makes coherence so useful—or, in other words, what positive epistemic qualities do we obtain from a high degree of coherence? The common-sense answer, and the standard view among coherence theorists, is that coherence is related to *truth*. Coherence is, according to this view, evidence of a high probability of truth. In recent years, coherence theorists have spelled out this idea in terms of *truth conduciveness*. Thus we would expect that, if one set *A* is more coherent than another set *B*, then *A* is more likely to be true than *B* (Klein and Warfield 1994). The exact meaning of this claim has been the source of much controversy: both the notion of coherence and the notion of likelihood of truth have been heavily discussed. Let us start with the concept of coherence.

In his 1934 book on idealism, the Cambridge philosopher A. C. Ewing put forward a much cited definition of coherence. In his view, a coherent set is

---

[2]Throughout this article we will rely on the normative correctness of Bayesian reasoning. Even though people do not always live up to Bayesian standards (see, e.g., Fischoff and Lichtenstein 1978; Kahneman et al. 1982; Rapoport and Wallsten 1972; Slovic and Lichtenstein 1971; Tversky and Kahneman 1974) the consensus position among epistemologists is that we should update our beliefs along the lines prescribed by Bayesianism (see, e.g., Howson and Urbach 1989).

characterized partly by consistency and partly by the property that every belief in the set follows logically from the others taken together. On this picture, a set such as $\{p, q, p \wedge q\}$ would, if consistent, be highly coherent, as each element follows by logical deduction from the rest in concert. While Ewing should be credited for having provided a precise definition of an intangible idea, his proposal must be rejected on the grounds that it defines coherence too narrowly. Few sets that occur naturally in everyday life satisfy the second part of his definition, i.e., the requirement that each element follow logically from the rest when combined. Consider, for instance, the set consisting of propositions *A*, *B* and *C*, where

$A =$ 'John was at the crime scene at the time of the robbery'
$B =$ 'John owns a gun of the type used by the robber'
$C =$ 'John deposited a large sum of money in his bank account the next day'

Many of us would consider this set to be coherent, and yet it does not satisfy Ewing's definition. *A*, for instance, does not follow logically from *B* and *C* taken together: that John owns a gun of the relevant type and deposited money in his bank the day after does not logically imply him being at the crime scene at the time of the crime.

From that perspective, C. I. Lewis's (1946) definition of coherence is more promising. According to Lewis, whose proposal can be seen as a refinement of Ewing's basic idea, a set is coherent just in case every element in the set is supported by all the other elements taken together, where 'support' is understood in a weak probabilistic sense: *A* supports *B* if and only if the probability of *B* is raised on the assumption that *A* is true. It is easy to see that Lewis's definition is wider than Ewing's, so that more sets will turn out to be coherent on the former than on the latter. (There are some uninteresting limiting cases for which this is not true. For instance, a set of tautologies will be coherent in Ewing's but not in Lewis's sense.)

To illustrate, let us go back to the example with John. Here one could argue that *A*, while not being logically entailed by *B* and *C*, is nevertheless supported by those propositions taken together. Assuming that John owns the relevant type of gun and deposited a large sum the next day serves to raise the probability that John did it and hence that he was at the crime scene when the robbery took place. Similarly, one could hold that each of *B* and *C* is supported, in the probabilistic sense, by the other elements of the set. If so, this set is not only coherent in an intuitive sense but also coherent according to Lewis's definition.

It is worth noticing that the support the elements of a set obtain from each other need not be very strong for the set to be coherent in Lewis's sense. It suffices that they support each other to some, however miniscule, degree. A second observation is that on Lewis's account whether or not a set is coherent will presumably depend on empirical data that constrain what (conditional) probabilities we are willing to assign. This is not a feature of Ewing's definition, which relies on purely logical notions.[3] Another proposal for how to say something more definite about

[3]Exactly how to interpret probability (in terms of frequencies, betting rates, etc.) is a major topic in itself which is best left out of this overview. See Olsson (2002) for a detailed discussion.

coherence originates from Laurence BonJour (1985), whose account of coherence is considerably more complex than earlier suggestions. While Ewing and Lewis proposed to define coherence in terms of one single concept—logical consequence and probability, respectively—BonJour thinks that coherence is a notion with a multitude of different aspects, corresponding to the following *coherence criteria* (ibid. 97–99):

1. A system of beliefs is coherent only if it is logically consistent.
2. A system of beliefs is coherent in proportion to its degree of probabilistic consistency.
3. The coherence of a system of beliefs is increased by the presence of inferential connections between its component beliefs and increased in proportion to the number and strength of such connections.
4. The coherence of a system of beliefs is diminished to the extent to which it is divided into subsystems of beliefs which are relatively unconnected to each other by inferential connections.
5. The coherence of a system of beliefs is decreased in proportion to the presence of unexplained anomalies in the believed content of the system.

These criteria are formulated in terms of beliefs, but they could just as well be applied to statements made in court. The first criterion, of logical consistency, is nothing new but was employed already by Ewing. The second criterion is somewhat more problematic, mainly due to the fact that Bonjour never clearly states what he means by 'degree of probabilistic consistency'. Nevertheless, the idea seems to be that a system is probabilistically consistent if and only if it contains no belief that *P* such that 'It is highly unlikely that *P*' can be derived from the other beliefs in the system. The criterion then dictates that it is of importance to the degree of coherence to avoid this predicament for as many beliefs as possible.

Both the third and the fourth criterion make use of the idea of an 'inferential connection', which should here be interpreted in a wide sense as including all types of support between beliefs, such as logical or probabilistic support. The suggestion embodied in the third criterion is simply that the degree of coherence is increased in proportion to how much different beliefs support each other. According to the fourth criterion, the degree of coherence is decreased in proportion to the presence of relatively isolated subsystems within the system. As for an extreme case, a person suffering from multiple personality disorder would satisfy the fourth criterion to a very low degree. But there are of course many less spectacular examples of how we sometimes entertain various views without ever connecting them. A child may learn most things worth knowing about cats and dogs without wondering what is common between these two kinds of animal. Eventually, she acquires the concept of a mammal and learns that much of what is true of cats and dogs is true of mammals in general. In science, it often happens that two areas are pursued in isolation until someone discovers that they are but special cases of a more comprehensive theory. In both cases, the unification entails an increase in coherence, as that concept is understood by Bonjour. The last criterion dictates that the presence of anomalies is something that reduces the overall level of coherence. An anomaly is, roughly, an observation that cannot be explained from within the belief system of the person in question.

A difficulty pertaining to theories of coherence that construe coherence as a multifaceted concept is to specify how the different aspects are to be amalgamated into one overall coherence judgment. It could well happen that one system *S* is more coherent than another system *T* in one respect, whereas *T* is more coherent than *S* in another. Perhaps *S* contains more inferential connections than *T*, which in turn has less anomalies than *S*. If so, which system is more coherent in an overall sense? Bonjour's theory remains silent on this important point.

Bonjour's account also serves to illustrate another general difficulty. The third criterion stipulates that the degree of coherence increases with the number of inferential connections between different parts of the system. As a system grows larger the probability that there will be relatively many inferentially connected beliefs is increased. Hence, there will be a positive correlation between system size and the number of inferential connections. Taken literally, Bonjour's third criterion implies, therefore, that there will be a positive correlation between system size and degree of coherence.

The general problem is to specify how the degree of coherence of a system should depend on its size. One possibility is that mere system size should have no impact on the degree of coherence, which should rather only depend on the system's inferential density. Another possibility is that we also need to take into account the number of inferential connections, so that larger systems have a potential to be more coherent for the simple reason that there are more opportunities for inferential connections to arise. This seems to be more congruent with Bonjour's way of looking at things.

Here is another general challenge for those wishing to give a clear-cut account of coherence. Suppose a number of eye witnesses are being questioned separately concerning a robbery that has recently taken place. The first two witnesses, Robert and Mary, give exactly the same detailed description of the robber as a red-headed man in his 40s of normal height wearing a blue leather jacket and green shoes. The next two witnesses, Steve and Karen, also give identical stories but only succeed in giving a very general description of the robber as a man wearing a blue leather jacket. So here we have two cases of exact agreement. In one case, the agreement concerns something very specific and detailed, while in the other case it concerns a more general proposition. This raises the question of which pair of reports is more coherent. Should we say that agreement on something specific gives rise to a higher degree of coherence, perhaps because such agreement seems more 'striking'? Or should we rather maintain that the degree of coherence is the same, regardless of the specificity of the thing agreed upon?

The challenge is to specify how the degree of coherence of an agreeing system should depend on the specificity of the system's informational content. Everything else being equal, should an agreeing system containing very specific, and therefore more informative, propositions be considered more coherent than a system of mainly general, and therefore less specific, propositions?

To illustrate these points about size and specificity consider the following recently proposed coherence measures:

$$C_{Sh}(A_1, \ldots, A_n) = \frac{P(A_1 \wedge \ldots \wedge A_n)}{P(A_1) \times \ldots \times P(A_n)}$$

$$C_{Ol}(A_1, \ldots, A_n) = \frac{P(A_1 \wedge \ldots \wedge A_n)}{P(A_1 \vee \ldots \vee A_n)}$$

Both measures assign a degree of coherence to a set of propositions in probabilistic terms, following Lewis, but they do it in slightly different ways. C_{Sh} was put forward in (Shogenji 1999) and is discussed for instance in (Olsson 2001). C_{Ol} was tentatively proposed in (Olsson 2002) and, independently, in (Glass 2002).

To illustrate the differences, suppose that $A_1, \ldots, A_n$ are equivalent propositions. We first consider the probability of the conjunction which figures in the numerator of both measures. Since $A_1, \ldots, A_n$ are equivalent, $P(A_1 \wedge \ldots \wedge A_n) = P(A_1)$. For the same reason, the denominator in the definition of C_{Sh} equals $P(A_1)^n$. Hence, $C_{Sh}(A_1, \ldots, A_n) = P(A_1)/P(A_1)^n = 1/P(A_1)^{n-1}$. Now as more equivalent propositions are added, i.e., as n grows larger, the denominator will approach zero, making the degree of C_{Sh}-coherence approach infinity. The same is true if the propositions involved are substituted for more specific equivalent propositions or, equivalently, the initial probabilities are reassigned so that the same propositions become less probable. Then, too, the degree of C_{Sh}-coherence will tend towards infinity. Not so for C_{Ol}, which assigns a coherence degree of 1 to every set of equivalent propositions, regardless of size or specificity. On the basis of observations such as these, it has been suggested that these two measures actually measure two different things. While C_{Ol} captures the degree of agreement of the propositions in a set, C_{Sh} is more plausible as a measure of how *striking* the agreement is (Olsson 2002; see also Bovens and Olsson 2000 for a discussion of agreement vs. striking agreement). Since these two proposals were made, a large number of other measures have been suggested, many of which are studied in (Olsson and Schubert 2007).

Given what has been said so far, a case could be made for the special relevance of the Shogenji measure in legal contexts. We recall Pennington and Hastie's observation that jurors deal with trial evidence by constructing narratives, whereby the best explanatory story is the one that conforms most convincingly to the two principles of coverage and (what they call) coherence by accounting, in a coherent manner, for a large subset of the available evidence. An attractive feature of the Shogenji measure, from this perspective, is that it treats 'coverage' (size) as part and parcel of the concept of coherence. Hence we do not need two measures—one measuring coherence, another that measures coverage—but can make do with one. This makes it particularly interesting from the point of view of the story model of juror decision making.

Now that we have a somewhat firmer grasp of the concept of coherence, how should we understand the claim that coherence implies 'likelihood of truth'? Klein and Warfield (1994) claimed, in effect, that the conjunction of the statements in more coherent sets should always have a higher probability of truth (than the corresponding conjunctions of less coherent sets). This proposal was rejected in (Olsson 2001) in favor of an account in terms of the *posterior* probability of truth, i.e., the conditional probability of the statements *given that they have been reported by the witnesses* (see also Cross 1999, referring to Bonjour 1985). This account provided the foundation of much later work in this area (e.g., Olsson 2002, 2005; Bovens and Hartmann 2003).

A further source of controversy concerned the question under what circumstances we can reasonably expect coherence to be truth conducive. Already C. I. Lewis (1946) had observed that coherence does not seem to be interestingly related to truth unless the witnesses delivering the statements are independent, which means that they have not talked to, or otherwise influenced, each other beforehand. Also, Lewis claimed that each witness must be considered to be somewhat reliable for coherence to have confidence-boosting power. Later work has essentially proven Lewis right on both accounts (e.g., Olsson 2002, 2005; Bovens and Hartmann 2003), although there are also dissident voices (Shogenji 2005).

Equipped with precise accounts of coherence as well as likelihood of truth, philosophers and computer scientists set out to show that coherence is truth conducive at least under the conditions of independence and partial reliability. Contrary to the hopes and expectations of most coherence theorists, it was soon shown that coherence is *not* truth conducive (Bovens and Hartmann 2003; Olsson 2005). Importantly, this is so regardless of how coherence is measured.

To get a feel for what these so-called *impossibility results* entail, and the conditions under which they hold, we will review the impossibility theorem in Olsson (2005). This theorem was proved in the context of a so-called *basic Lewis scenario*—a scenario where two independent and partially reliable witnesses give equivalent testimonies. Since the testimonies are equivalent we may suppose that the witnesses in fact utter one and the same proposition. In the following, R_i expresses the proposition that the *i*:th witness is reliable, A is the proposition that the witnesses agree upon, and E_i expresses the proposition that the *i*:th witness asserts that A. Following epistemological tradition (Lewis 1946; BonJour 1985), we will restrict attention to a situation in which each witness is either fully reliable (truth teller) or fully unreliable (randomizer). We will model a basic *Lewis scenario* as a pair $\langle \mathbf{S}, \mathbf{P} \rangle$ where $\mathbf{S} = \{\langle E_1, A \rangle, \langle E_2, A \rangle\}$ and $\mathbf{P}$ is a class of probability distributions satisfying a number of conditions. We will state the conditions first and explain them afterwards. The following should hold (for any i):

(a) $P(E_i|A, R_i) = 1$
(b) $P(E_i|\neg A, R_i) = 0$
(c) $P(E_i|A, \neg R_i) = P(A)$
(d) $P(E_i|\neg A, \neg R_i) = P(A)$
(e) $P(R_i|A) = P(R_i)$
(f) $0 < P(A) < 1$
(g) $0 < P(R_i) < 1$
(h) $P(R_1) = P(R_2)$

The notions of reliability and unreliability are defined by conditions (a)–(d). Condition (a) and (b) state that a reliable witness will give a certain testimony if and only if it is true. Conditions (c) and (d) state firstly that the probability that an unreliable witness will give a certain testimony is independent of whether its content is true and secondly that it equals the prior probability that the content is in fact true. Obviously, these clauses do not hold in general, but they do hold in interesting cases.[4] Under what circumstances would they be realistic? Here is one example: Let A be the proposition 'Forbes committed the crime', and let us imagine that a certain witness, Smith, is presented with a line-up comprising all and only the suspects of the case, Forbes included, among which he has to choose, and that the suspects are equally likely to be the criminal in question. Then the probability that Forbes did it is $1/n$, where n is the number of suspects, and if Smith is completely unreliable, he will pick out Forbes with probability $1/n$, regardless of whether Forbes is actually guilty or not. Condition (e) says that the probability that a given witness is reliable is independent of the truth of the content of the testimonies. Conditions (f) and (g) exclude certain uninteresting limiting cases. Condition (h), finally, expresses that the witnesses have the same prior probability of being reliable. This assumption is included in order to simplify calculations.

Let us by a *coherence measure* mean any function from ordered sets of testimonial contents to real numbers defined solely in terms of the probabilities of the testimonial contents and their Boolean combinations. It follows that a coherence measure, when restricted to a basic Lewis scenario, is a function of the probability of A. Let us furthermore say that a coherence measure C is *informative* in a basic Lewis scenario $\langle \mathbf{S}, \mathbf{P} \rangle$ if and only if there are at least two probability distributions that give rise to different degrees of coherence, i.e., if there are P, $P' \in \mathbf{P}$ such that $C_P(\mathbf{S}) \neq C_{P'}(\mathbf{S})$. We say that a coherence measure is *truth conducive ceteris paribus* in a basic Lewis scenario $\langle \mathbf{S}, \mathbf{P} \rangle$ if and only if: if $C_P(\mathbf{S}) > C_{P'}(\mathbf{S})$, then $P(\mathbf{S}) > P'(\mathbf{S})$ for all P, $P' \in \mathbf{P}$ such that $P(R_i) = P'(R'_i)$, for all i. Using these definitions, Olsson proved the following:

Theorem 1 (Olsson 2005): *There are no informative coherence measures that are truth* conducive ceteris paribus *in a basic Lewis scenario.*[5]

The impossibility results pose a major problem for the coherence theory as an epistemological framework for legal reasoning, shedding doubt, as they do, on the normative correctness of relying on coherence in court. Worried about these seemingly negative consequences of their deductions, coherence theorists have suggested various strategies for how to reconcile the troublesome findings with our reasoning practice.

---

[4] Below, we introduce a version of the witness scenario which uses weaker assumptions than these.

[5] An interestingly different impossibility proof was established by Bovens and Hartmann in their (2003) book.

2.3 Coherence as Conducive to Reliability

Some coherence theorists have argued that the impossibility results are not as consequential as they might seem because, they claim, the results are proved against the background of certain implausible assumptions (e.g., Mejis and Douven 2007; Schupbach 2008). In particular, it has been argued that we need to keep various further factors fixed when measuring the impact of coherence on probability of truth. One of us has argued that these rescue attempts fail: the proposed *ceteris paribus*-clauses do not deliver the goods (i.e., the impossibility theorems hold true anyway) and introducing new *ceteris paribus*-clauses sufficiently strong to save the truth conduciveness thesis would make it trivial (Schubert 2012b).

A second approach is to defend our reliance on coherence reasoning by arguing that coherence has some positive epistemic property other than truth conduciveness. For example, Staffan Angere (2007, 2008) has shown, by means of extensive computer simulations, that while a more coherent set is not always more likely to be true than a less coherent set, there is still a significant correlation between increased coherence and increased likelihood of truth. Thus, to the extent that assessing the coherence of a set is cognitively less demanding than assessing the truth of its content by other means, relying on coherence is a useful heuristic.

According to another proposal in this category due to Olsson and Schubert (2007), coherence can be *reliability conducive* even when it fails to be truth conducive. Roughly, a coherence measure is *reliability conducive* if more coherence implies a higher likelihood that the witnesses delivering the testimonies are reliable. More exactly, a coherence measure is *reliability conducive ceteris paribus* in a basic Lewis scenario $\langle \mathbf{S}, \mathbf{P} \rangle$ if and only if: if $C_P(\mathbf{S}) > C_{P'}(\mathbf{S})$, then $P(R_i|E_i, \ldots, E_n) > P'(R_i|\, E_i, \ldots, E_n)$ for all P, $P' \in \mathbf{P}$ such that $P(R_i|E_i) = P'(R_i|E_i)$, for all i. Olsson and Schubert showed that several measures of coherence are indeed reliability conducive under the same conditions which were used in Olsson's impossibility result. Refinements and extensions of this result have been obtained for more elaborate witness scenarios, including situations with n equivalent testimonies or two non-overlapping testimonies. This research has focused on the Shogenji measure showing this measure to be reliability conducive in these other paradigm cases as well (Schubert 2011, 2012a).

However, it has also been shown that no measure of coherence is reliability conducive in the general case involving n non-equivalent testimonies:

Theorem 2 (Schubert 2012b): *There are no informative coherence measures that are reliability conducive* ceteris paribus *in a scenario of n non-equivalent testimonies.*[6]

---

[6]This theorem was proved against the backdrop of an improved version of the witness scenario that is introduced in the next section.

Let us take a closer look at the more striking and intuitive of the two proofs offered in (Schubert 2012b) of this theorem. This proof compares two sets of testimonies: $S_1 = \{A_1, A_2, A_3\}$, consisting of three pair-wise and jointly independent testimonies, and $S_2 = \{A'_1, A'_2, A'_3\}$, consisting of three jointly inconsistent but pair-wise positively relevant testimonies. If the prior probability of reliability is high, it will go down upon receiving the evidence in S_2 because at most two witnesses can be reliable given the inconsistency of that set. If, by contrast, the prior probability of reliability is low, it will go up when receiving that same evidence, given that it is rather probable that two of the testimonies are true. Because S_1 consists of independent propositions, the posterior probability of reliability of the sources delivering those reports will equal the prior probability of reliability. Hence, for some prior probabilities of reliability, the witnesses giving the information in S_1 will have a higher posterior probability of reliability than the witnesses giving the information in S_2, and for other prior probabilities of reliability, the converse will be true. But reliability conduciveness requires that more coherence implies a higher posterior probability of reliability for *all* prior probabilities of reliability. Hence, no coherence measure is reliability conducive in general.

Notwithstanding the impossibility theorem for reliability conduciveness, it should be remembered that coherence is reliability conducive in many cases in which it fails to be truth conducive. Thus, we have reason to believe that the link between coherence and reliability is stronger than that between coherence and truth. We now move on to uncover some further close ties between coherence and probability of reliability.

2.4 Further Connections Between Coherence and Reliability

Our next result shows that Shogenji coherence and witness reliability are even more closely related than previous work has shown: the probability that a witness is reliable given a set of testimonies is a function of the Shogenji coherence of the set *and its subsets*. After that, we will establish that even if Shogenji coherence falls short of being generally reliability conducive it still is reliability conducive in cases where either all witnesses are reliable or all witnesses are unreliable—i.e., where the witnesses' levels of reliability are (maximally) positively dependent on each other. In the final section we ponder the normative significance of these results for judicial reasoning.

In order to prove the theorems below, we need to introduce the concept of a witness scenario with n witnesses which do not have to give equivalent reports. This version of the witness scenario, which we believe is an improvement in several respects to the earlier ones, was developed and used in (Schubert 2011, 2012a, b). For a discussion of the assumptions of the scenario, see, e.g., (Schubert 2011). In the following, $\boldsymbol{R}_i$, $\boldsymbol{A}_i$ and $\boldsymbol{E}_i$ are propositional variables taking on the values R_i and $\neg R_i$, A_i and $\neg A_i$, and E_i and $\neg E_i$, respectively. R_i and E_i have the same meaning as above, whereas A_i denotes the i:th witness's testimonial content. Now a *general witness scenario* is a pair $\langle \mathbf{S}', \mathbf{P} \rangle$ where $\mathbf{S}' = \{\langle E_1, A_1 \rangle, \ldots, \langle E_n, A_n \rangle\}$ and $\mathbf{P}$ is a class of probability distributions satisfying the following assumptions (for $i, j = 1, \ldots, n$ and $i \neq j$):

(i) $P(A_i | E_i, R_i) = 1$
(ii) $P(A_i | E_i, \neg R_i) = P(A_i | \neg R_i)$
(iii) $\boldsymbol{E}_i \perp \boldsymbol{E}_1, \boldsymbol{R}_1, \boldsymbol{A}_1, \ldots, \boldsymbol{E}_{i-1}, \boldsymbol{R}_{i-1}, \boldsymbol{A}_{i-1}, \boldsymbol{E}_{i+1}, \boldsymbol{R}_{i+1}, \boldsymbol{A}_{i+1}, \ldots, \boldsymbol{E}_n, \boldsymbol{R}_n, \boldsymbol{A}_n | \boldsymbol{R}_i, \boldsymbol{A}_i$
(iv) $\boldsymbol{R}_i \perp \boldsymbol{R}_1, \ldots, \boldsymbol{R}_{i-1}, \boldsymbol{R}_{i+1}, \ldots, \boldsymbol{R}_n, \boldsymbol{A}_1, \ldots, \boldsymbol{A}_n$
(v) $0 < P(A_i) < 1$
(vi) $0 < P(R_i | E_i) < 1$
(vii) $P(R_i | E_i) = P(R_j | E_j)$

In this scenario, the conditions (i) and (ii) define the notions of reliability and unreliability. Condition (i) states that a reliable witness will only report true facts, but it does not state that if a certain fact is true, then a reliable witness will report it (in contrast to the corresponding conditions in the basic Lewis scenario). Condition (ii) says that unreliable testimonies do not affect the probability that the testimonial content is true, but does not, contrary to the basic Lewis scenario, assume that the probability that an unreliable witness will give a certain testimony equals the probability that the content of the testimony is true. Hence these conditions hold true in more real-world cases than the conditions (a)–(d) in the basic Lewis scenario do.

Conditions (iii) and (iv) define the important notion of independence. Condition (iii) states, roughly, that the probability that a witness will report a certain proposition is independent of what other witnesses have reported and of their reliability, conditional on her reliability and the truth value of the reported proposition. By condition (iv), the (un)reliability of one witness is independent of the (un)reliability of the other witnesses, as well as of the truth of the reported propositions. A condition corresponding to condition (v) was already included in the basic Lewis scenario (condition f). Condition (vi) says that the probability that a given witness is reliable conditional on her report is neither zero nor one. Condition (vii), finally, expresses that the probability that one witness is reliable, given her statement, is the same as the probability that another witness is reliable, given her statement. These two last conditions are slight variations of the conditions (g) and (h) in the basic Lewis scenario.

We are now in a position to prove our first new theorem. Let S_k be the sum of the degrees of Shogenji coherence of all subsets of $\{A_1, \ldots, A_n\}$ with k members. (For example, if $n = 3$, then $S_2 = C_{Sh}(A_1, A_2) + C_{Sh}(A_1, A_3) + C_{Sh}(A_2, A_3)$.) Let $S_{A_i k}$ be the sum of the degrees of Shogenji coherence of all subsets of $\{A_1, \ldots, A_n\}$ with k members having A_i as an element. Finally, let

$$x = (1 - P(R | E_i) / P(R | E_i))$$

We can now show that:

Theorem 3:

$$P(R_i \mid E_1, \ldots, E_n) = \frac{S_{A_i n} + xS_{A_i n-1} + \ldots + x^{n-2}S_{A_i 2} + x^{n-1}}{S_n + xS_{n-1} + \ldots + x^{n-2}S_2 + nx^{n-1} + x^n}$$

Proof: See appendix.

This shows that the connection between reliability and coherence, in the sense of the Shogenji measure, is very close indeed. The following two observations bring out the full significance of our theorem.

Observation 1: The posterior probability that a witness i is reliable is a strictly increasing function of the degrees of Shogenji coherence of all sets of testimonial contents that include the content of i's testimony, and a strictly decreasing function of the degrees of Shogenji coherence of all sets of testimonial contents that do not include the content of i's testimony.

Proof: Follows directly from theorem 3.

In other words, given that we hold all other factors fixed, a higher degree of Shogenji coherence of a subset of $\{A_1, \ldots, A_n\}$ which includes A_i implies a higher probability that i is reliable. Conversely, a higher degree of Shogenji coherence of a subset of $\{A_1, \ldots, A_n\}$ which does not include A_i implies a lower probability that i is reliable.

Observation 2: Two factors together determine the posterior probability that a witness i is reliable given a set of testimonies: the probabilities that the individual witnesses are reliable given their respective testimonies, and the degrees of Shogenji coherence of the reported set of propositions and its subsets with at least two members.

Proof: Follows directly from theorem 3.

Observation 2 shows that there is no need for incorporating a third factor, such as (for example) the prior probability that the contents of the testimonies are true, when computing the probability of reliability given the testimonies. The Shogenji coherence of the set of testimonial contents and its subsets, and the probabilities of reliability of the individual witnesses, given their own testimonies, are the only factors needed to determine the probability of reliability given all the testimonies.

As previously mentioned, the Shogenji measure has been shown to be reliability conducive in a number of paradigmatic cases (Schubert 2011, 2012a). We will now extend these results to a further interesting case. In order to set the stage for what is to come we need to make a small digression. Condition (iv) in the definition of the general witness scenario states that for all witnesses, the fact that one witness is reliable (or not) does not directly affect the reliability of the other witnesses. In other words, $\boldsymbol{R_i}$ and $\boldsymbol{R_j}$ are assumed to be independent, for all i, j. But as Bovens and Hartmann (2003, 64) point out in an interesting section, this is often an unrealistic assumption. Sometimes the reliability of one witness positively affects the reliability of another witness, in which case $\boldsymbol{R_i}$ and $\boldsymbol{R_j}$ are positively dependent. For example, if we learn that one member of a group of indigenous people, whom we have very little knowledge of, is reliable, we are inclined to upgrade our beliefs in the reliability of other members of the group. Another important case is of course the case where all testimonies have been given by one and the same witness. In such a case, $\boldsymbol{R_i}$ and $\boldsymbol{R_j}$ should surely be strongly positively dependent.

Bovens and Hartmann construct a model where the witnesses are maximally positively dependent by using a variable $\boldsymbol{R}$ which can take on only two values corresponding to all witnesses being reliable or all witnesses being unreliable. If we replace $\boldsymbol{R_1}, \ldots, \boldsymbol{R_n}$ by $\boldsymbol{R}$ in our definition of a witness scenario, it can be shown that the Shogenji measure is reliability conducive if we use a slightly revised definition of reliability conduciveness where both $P(R|E_i)$ *and* $P(R)$ are kept fixed. In order to see this, let us first define this modified witness scenario formally.

The *witness scenario with a single reliability variable* is a pair $\langle \mathbf{S}^*, \mathbf{P}^* \rangle$ where $\mathbf{S}^* = \{\langle E_1, A_1 \rangle, \ldots, \langle E_n, A_n \rangle\}$ and $\mathbf{P}^*$ a class of probability distributions satisfying the following conditions (for $i, j = 1, \ldots, n$ and $i \neq j$):

(i′.) $P(A_i|E_i, R) = 1$
(ii′.) $P(A_i|E_i, \neg R) = P(A_i|\neg R)$
(iii′.) $\boldsymbol{E}_i \perp \boldsymbol{E}_1, \boldsymbol{A}_1, \ldots, \boldsymbol{E}_{i-1}, \boldsymbol{A}_{i-1}, \boldsymbol{E}_{i+1}, \boldsymbol{A}_{i+1}, \ldots, \boldsymbol{E}_n, \boldsymbol{A}_n | \boldsymbol{R}, \boldsymbol{A}_i$
(iv′.) $\boldsymbol{R} \perp \boldsymbol{A}_1, \ldots, \boldsymbol{A}_n$
(v′.) $0 < P(A_i) < 1$
(vi′.) $0 < P(R|E_i) < 1$
(vii′.) $P(R|E_i) = P(R|E_j)$

We are now in a position to give a precise definition of reliability conduciveness in the case in question:

Definition 1: A coherence measure C is *reliability conducive ceteris paribus* in the witness scenario $\langle \mathbf{S}^*, \mathbf{P}^* \rangle$ with a single reliability variable if and only if: if $C_P(\mathbf{S}^*) > C_{P'}(\mathbf{S}^*)$, then $P(R|E_1, \ldots, E_n) > P'(R'|E'_1, \ldots, E'_n)$ for all P, P' $\in \mathbf{P}^*$ such that $P(R) = P'(R')$ and $P(R|E_i) = P'(R'|E'_i)$, for all i.

Theorem 4: *The Shogenji measure is reliability conducive* ceteris paribus *in the witness scenario with a single reliability variable.*

Proof: In appendix.

Thus, even though the Shogenji measure is not reliability conducive in the witness scenario where the witnesses' degrees of reliability are independent, it is reliability conducive when the witnesses' degrees of reliability are maximally dependent of each other. Theorem 4 shows, together with observations 1 and 2, that there are important further connections between the Shogenji measure of coherence and the posterior probability of reliability.

We will now prove some further observations which make the link between coherence and reliability still stronger. They will also serve to show why theorem

4 holds. We will consider the effect of adding the following two conditions (for $i = 1, \ldots, n$). Together with conditions (i′) and (ii′) above, they correspond to (a)–(d) in the basic Lewis scenario:

(a′) $P(E_i | A_i, R) = 1$
(b′) $P(E_i | A_i, \neg R) = P(A_i) = P(E_i | \neg A_i, \neg R)$

Under these extra assumptions we get a particularly simple formula for calculating the probability that a particular set of testimonies will be given conditional on the fact that all witnesses are reliable.

Observation 3: In a witness scenario with a single reliability variable satisfying (a′) and (b′), $P(E_1, \ldots, E_n | R) = P(A_1, \ldots, A_n)$.

Proof: In appendix.

It should be obvious why this is true. Given that all witnesses know the truth and are willing to share their knowledge, the chance that they will give a certain conjunction of testimonies should equal the probability that the conjunction is true.

Similarly, the probability of the evidence given that all witnesses are unreliable now simplifies to:

Observation 4: In a witness scenario with a single reliability variable satisfying (a′) and (b′), $P(E_1, \ldots, E_n | \neg R) = P(A_1) \times \ldots \times P(A_n)$.

Proof: In appendix.

Thus we get the following elegant corollary:

Observation 5: In a witness scenario satisfying (a′) and (b′), $P(E_1, \ldots, E_n | R) / P(E_1, \ldots, E_n | \neg R) = C_{Sh}(A_1, \ldots, A_n)$.

Proof: Follows directly from Observation 3 and Observation 4 using the definition of the Shogenji measure.

$P(E_1, \ldots, E_n | R) / P(E_1, \ldots, E_n | \neg R)$ is known as the *likelihood ratio.* In general, given evidence E and hypothesis H, the likelihood ratio equals $P(E | H) / P(E | \neg H)$. In this case, the hypothesis is obviously R and the evidence $E_1, \ldots, E_n$. The likelihood ratio is proposed as a measure of the degree to which evidence confirms a hypothesis by various authors (Kemeny and Oppenheim 1952; Good 1983).[7] Thus, in the scenario with a single reliability variable which includes (a′) and (b′), the Shogenji measure of a set of propositions $A_1, \ldots, A_n$ equals the degree to which $E_1, \ldots, E_n$ confirm R, according to the likelihood measure.

[7] They call it the 'likelihood measure'. Often, the ordinally equivalent measure $S_l = \log P(E|H)/P(E|\neg H)$ is used instead. In the confirmation literature, ordinal equivalents are treated as identical, though, for all intents and purposes.

Now using Bayes' theorem, we may note that:

Formula 1:

$$P(R\,|\,E_1,\ldots,E_n) = \frac{P(R) \times P(E_1,\ldots,E_n\,|\,R)\,/\,P(E_1,\ldots,E_n\,|\neg R)}{P(\neg R)+P(R) \times P(E_1,\ldots,E_n\,|\,R)\,/\,P(E_1,\ldots,E_n\,|\neg R)}$$

It follows immediately from observation 5 and formula 1 that the Shogenji measure is reliability conducive in the scenario with a single reliability variable which includes (a′) and (b′).

Let us now consider a scenario where (a′) and (b′) does not hold. Then:

Observation 6:

$$P(E_1,\ldots,E_n\,|\,R) = P(A_1,\ldots,A_n) \times \frac{P(E_1\,|\,R)}{P(A_1)} \times \ldots \times \frac{P(E_n\,|\,R)}{P(A_n)}$$

Observation 7:

$$P(E_1,\ldots,E_n\,|\neg R) = P(E_1\,|\neg R) \times \ldots \times P(E_n\,|\neg R)$$

Proofs: In appendix.

From those observations, the following observation can be made:

Observation 8:

$$C_{Sh}(A_1,\ldots,A_n) = \frac{P(E_1,\ldots,E_n\,|\,R)\,/\,P(E_1,\ldots,E_n\,|\neg R)}{P(E_1\,|\,R)\,/\,P(E_1\,|\neg R) \times \ldots \times P(E_n\,|\,R)\,/\,P(E_n\,|\neg R)}$$

This means that in the general case, the Shogenji measure is rather the ratio between the degree to which $E_1,\ldots,E_n$ *collectively* supports R (as measured by the likelihood measure) and the product of the degrees to which $E_1,\ldots,E_n$ *individually* supports R (as measured by the likelihood measure). Now we may note that:

$$\frac{P(E_i\,|\,R)}{P(E_i\,|\neg R)} = \frac{P(R\,|\,E_i)\,/\,P(R)}{P(\neg R\,|\,E_i)\,/\,P(\neg R)} \text{ for all } i.$$

Hence if $P(R|E_i)$ and $P(R)$ are kept fixed (as demanded by definition 1), the degrees to which $E_1,\ldots,E_n$ individually supports R (as measured by the likelihood measure) will be kept fixed. Hence, it follows from observation 8 and formula 1 that the Shogenji measure is reliability conducive in this case, too.

2.5 Comparison with the Evidentiary Value Model

A model of legal reasoning similar to that outlined above was developed in the 1970s by Swedish philosophers Martin Edman (1973) and Sören Halldén (1973), drawing on ideas from Per Olof Ekelöf, a legal theorist (1963/1982; 1983).[8] The central concept of the Evidentiary Value Model (EVM) is that of an *evidentiary mechanism* (usually denoted by A, B, etc.) linking the hypothesis and the evidence. The *evidentiary value* is correlated with the (probability of) presence or absence of such evidentiary mechanisms. In the terminology of the theory, the *evidentiary theme* (usually denoted H) is the hypothesis to be proved. Various pieces of evidence called *evidentiary facts* (usually denoted by small letters: e, f, etc.) may either confirm or disconfirm the evidentiary theme. The original idea was to interpret such a mechanism as a causal link between an evidentiary theme and an evidentiary fact, although several researchers—among them Edman (1973) and Hansson (1983)—use the notion of an evidentiary mechanism in a more general sense without implying any causal connotations. Sahlin (2011) explains the concept of an evidentiary mechanism as follows:

> One way to think of the evidentiary mechanism is to interpret it as a link between an evidentiary theme and an evidentiary fact which, if present, can be said to 'prove' the theme, given the evidentiary fact. Think of this mechanism (denoted M) as a triple consisting of an evidentiary theme, an evidentiary fact and an event such that, if we know that this event has occurred, and we have received the evidentiary fact, we have a proof of the hypothesis.

The EVM theorists now claim that legal examination of the evidence should focus on $P(A|e)$ rather than on $P(H|e)$. Hence, rather than assessing the probability of the hypothesis given the evidence, we should assess the probability that the evidence proves the hypothesis. Various reasons have been presented for the preoccupation with $P(A|e)$. According to Halldén (1973), it is easier for a judge to assess $P(A|e)$ than $P(H|e)$, whereas Hansson (1983) notes that $P(H|e)$ is not primarily what we are looking for since the evidentiary theme may be very probable for reasons that have nothing to do with the defendant. Thus, to take Hansson's example, even if it is true that 98% of all habitual criminals are in fact found guilty when they are prosecuted for yet another crime, this fact alone is not sufficient for a conviction. This is so even if another defendant is convicted on evidence which indicates guilt with a probability of less than 98%, say 90%, provided that the evidence is directly connected to that person. Sahlin (2011), finally, suggests that what we wish to obtain in court is knowledge and not mere (true) belief and that this is the reason why we should be primarily concerned with assessing the probability of a reliable connection:

> Assume that a judge is in the business of trying to reach an opinion as to whether the evidence gives *knowledge* of the hypothesis under consideration, rather than merely trying

[8]This account of EVM is based on Sahlin (2011). For discussion and further developments of the model, see Sahlin (1986), and Sahlin and Rabinowicz (1997). See also Gärdenfors et al. (1983) for a useful collection of papers on the subject.

> to form a belief as to whether the hypothesis is true. He or she is then trying to ascertain, on the basis of his evidence, the probability of the existence of a reliable link between the hypothesis and the evidentiary fact — trying to ascertain how probable it is that the evidentiary mechanism has worked, given the evidence at hand.

Our emphasis. 'Knowledge' should here be taken in the reliabilist sense of true belief acquired through a reliable process (Ramsey 1931; Goldman 1986).

It is generally assumed by the practitioners of EVM that $P(H|Ae) = 1$. Since H is the evidentiary theme (e.g., whether the suspect did in fact commit the crime), this means that each evidentiary fact is such that, if produced by a working evidentiary mechanism, it suffices to prove the case.[9,10]

The interesting cases, from our perspective, are of course those involving several evidentiary facts that cohere. Suppose that there are two pieces of concurring evidence, e and f, both of which point to the truth of an evidentiary theme, H, via two independent evidentiary mechanisms A (concerning e) and B (concerning f). The EVM theorists now claim that the relevant probability to asses is $P(A \vee B|ef)$, i.e., the probability that at least one of the mechanisms worked. Why is that? Given the assumption that $P(H|Ae) = P(H|Bf) = 1$, it suffices, for the purposes of proving the truth of H, to establish that at least one of A or B worked; it is not necessary that they both did.

---

[9]The consequences of relaxing the assumption that $P(H|Ae) = 1$ are investigated in Sahlin (1986).

[10]In this context, it is worth pointing out that the EVM has salient similarities to several of the most prominent mathematical theories of evidence. Cases in point include the well-known Dempster-Shafer theory of evidence (Dempster 1967, 1969; Shafer 1976) (the similarities between the EVM and the Dempster-Shafer theory are commented upon extensively in several of the papers in Gärdenfors et al. (1983)) and, in particular, J.L. Cohen's theory of evidence, as developed in his (1977). Cohen defines a notion of 'Baconian probability' (as opposed to the standard, 'Pascalian' notion, as Cohen calls it) in terms of 'provability', so that if we do not have any evidence for either P nor $\neg P$, the probability of P, and that of $\neg P$, equals zero, and argues that it is this notion of probability, rather than the standard Pascalian one, that is the relevant one in judicial contexts. Now the EVM theorists differ from Cohen in that they use the Pascalian notion of probability, rather than the Baconian one, but this seems to be a mere terminological difference: they too argue, as we saw, that what is relevant in judicial contexts is not how likely the evidentiary theme is but rather how likely it is that there is a reliable connection between the evidence and the evidentiary theme—i.e., how strong our *proof* is. This focus on the likelihood of the presence of a proof/reliable mechanism helps Cohen and the EVM theorists to avoid a standard objection against mathematical theories of evidence. Mathematical theories of evidence which say that the suspect should be convicted if and only if the posterior (Pascalian) probability is above a certain threshold (say 90%) depend for their success on our ability to assess the *prior* probability that the suspect is guilty. Such assessments are of course fraught with difficulties in any context but particularly so in judicial context: e.g., Rawling (1999) argues that the so-called 'presumption of innocence'—an important tenet of U.S. criminal law—requires us to set the prior probability of the suspect's guilt so low as to de facto make a conviction impossible. As Rawling himself suggests (ibid., pp. 124–125) a way out of this conundrum is to adopt a theory which focuses on the strength of the proof, rather than on the likelihood that the suspect in fact did it. Rawling mentions Cohen's theory, but in view of the above-mentioned similarities between this theory and the EVM, it would seem the latter would do the job as well.

EVM now offers the following attractive formula relating the probability that at least one mechanism worked, given the combined evidentiary facts, to the probability that the first and the second worked, respectively, given their corresponding evidentiary facts:

$$\text{(S) } P(A \vee B|ef) \geq P(A|e) + P(B|f) - P(A|e)\,P(B|f)$$

Halldén (1973) proves (S) using the independence assumption

$$\text{(I) } P(A|e) = P(A|ef\neg B)$$

together with the further principle

$$\text{(P) } P(A|ef) \geq P(A|e),$$

which in the EVM tradition is something of a cornerstone.

The independence assumption states that the evidentiary value of a piece of evidence is not altered by the presence of an evidentiary fact deriving from a malfunctioning evidentiary mechanism. According to (P), a further concurring evidentiary fact increases or leaves equal the probability that the first evidentiary mechanism was working.[11]

As the reader has probably noticed, the principles mentioned above for evidentiary value bear strong resemblance to our principles for reliability. Rather than talking of functioning or malfunctioning evidentiary mechanisms we can talk about reliable or unreliable witnesses. Thus, (P) translates into $P(R_1|E_1, E_2) \geq P(R_1|E_1)$: the probability that a given witness is reliable is not diminished by the appearance of a further witness giving a concurring testimony. The other principles can also be translated into our framework in obvious ways. It can be shown that that the translated versions of (S), (I) and (P) are derivable from our main scenario, the general witness scenario $\langle \mathbf{S}', \mathbf{P} \rangle$.

Observation 9 (corresponding to S):

$$P(R_1 \vee R_2|E_1, E_2) \geq P(R_1|E_1) + P(R_2|E_2) - P(R_1|E_1)\,P(R_2|E_2)$$

Observation 10 (I):

$$P(R_1|E_1) = P(R_1|E_1, E_2, \neg R_2)$$

[11] Edman (1973) derives (S) from a number of assumptions other than Halldén's. Hansson (1983, 83–84) gives an alternative proof of (S) from (P) and $P(AB|ef) = P(A|ef)P(B|ef)$.

Observation 11 (P):

$$P(R_1|E_1, E_2) \geq (R_1|E_1)$$

Proofs: In appendix.

These formal parallels are no coincidence. Rather they reflect similar theoretical interests and goals. This means that the philosophical and legal motivations of the EVM framework carry over to our framework. In particular, we find attractive the view that the quest for reliable knowledge is, in a judicial context, more central than the quest for true belief, making reliability conduciveness a more fundamental property than truth conduciveness. Hence our proofs of close connections between the Shogenji measure and reliability constitute, we believe, an important vindication of coherence reasoning in judicial contexts.

Still, there is a salient difference in focus between our framework and the EVM framework. While our theory is chiefly concerned with assessing the probability that any given witness i is reliable, the EVM theorists were more interested in ascertaining the probability that at least one mechanism worked reliably. This preoccupation on the part of the EVM theorists with (S) (corresponding to our Observation 9) reveals a primary interest in cases in which each evidentiary fact is potentially sufficient for settling the matter under dispute, i.e. the evidentiary theme. A paradigm case would be one in which the fact to be demonstrated by the prosecutor is the guilt of the accused, whereby the evidentiary facts consist in several witnesses reporting, individually, something that, if correct, would be sufficient for convicting the defendant. The relevant probability to be ascertained in such cases is indeed the probability that at least one of these evidentiary mechanisms worked.

Yet, the normal case is surely one in which it is *not* the case that the evidentiary facts, taken by themselves, suffice to prove the evidentiary theme but rather one in which the evidentiary facts are only indirectly related to the evidentiary theme, as the case would be if one witness states that she saw the accused near the crime scene, another that he was told by someone else that the accused did it, and so on. If so, it would not be sufficient for a conviction that only one of the corresponding evidentiary mechanisms worked, making the assessment of the corresponding probability an idle task. Rather, we should be interested in having as many reliably formed testimonies as possible. If this is correct, then the more widely relevant task is to assess—in conformity with our account—the probability that any given witness is reliable.

2.6 Conclusion

We started out by referring to the ubiquity of coherence reasoning in court. When jurors assess the evidence presented before them, they try to construct the most coherent story based on the information at hand, selecting the verdict that they find most appropriate given this story. We then noticed that the impossibility results for coherence shed doubt on the normative correctness of this practice. Our response was to argue, as we have done in previous work, that coherence can still be conducive to reliability in the sense that more coherence implies a higher probability that the witnesses are reliable in several paradigm cases. In further support of this proposal we showed that there are several close connections that have hitherto gone unnoticed between the Shogenji measure of coherence and the degrees of witness reliability. One such observation stated that the probability that a witness is reliable given a set of testimonies is a function of the Shogenji coherence of the set and its (non-singleton) subsets; another that even if Shogenji coherence falls short of being generally reliability conducive, it is reliability conducive in cases where the witnesses' degrees of reliability are maximally dependent on each other—i.e., where either all witnesses are reliable or all witnesses are unreliable. In addition, we proved that, under certain circumstances, the degree of Shogenji coherence of a set equals the degree of support that the testimonies in that set confers on the hypothesis that all witnesses are reliable. In the penultimate section we unraveled the intimate relationships between our framework and that of the Scandinavian School of Evidentiary Value. In particular, we found independent support in the writings of the Evidentiary Value theorists for thinking that assessing the probability that the witnesses are reliable is more fundamental a task than ascertaining the probability that what they are saying is true.[12]

Appendix

Proof of theorem 3:

$$P(R_i \mid E_1, \ldots, E_n) = \frac{S_{A_i n} + xS_{A_i n-1} + \ldots + x^{n-2}S_{A_i 2} + x^{n-1}}{S_n + xS_{n-1} + \ldots + x^{n-2}S_2 + nx^{n-1} + x^n}$$

Let $\boldsymbol{R}_1, \ldots, \boldsymbol{R}_n, \boldsymbol{E}_1, \ldots, \boldsymbol{E}_n, \boldsymbol{A}_1, \ldots, \boldsymbol{A}_n$ be propositional variables. Then:

$$P(\boldsymbol{R}_1, \ldots, \boldsymbol{R}_n, \boldsymbol{E}_1, \ldots, \boldsymbol{E}_n, \boldsymbol{A}_1, \ldots, \boldsymbol{A}_n) =$$

$$P(\boldsymbol{E}_1 \mid \boldsymbol{R}_1, \boldsymbol{A}_1) \times \ldots \times P(\boldsymbol{E}_n \mid \boldsymbol{R}_n, \boldsymbol{A}_n) \times P(\boldsymbol{R}_1, \ldots, \boldsymbol{R}_n, \boldsymbol{A}_1, \ldots, \boldsymbol{A}_n) = \quad \text{(iii)}$$

$$P(\boldsymbol{E}_1, \boldsymbol{R}_1, \boldsymbol{A}_1) \times \ldots \times P(\boldsymbol{E}_n, \boldsymbol{R}_n, \boldsymbol{A}_n) \times \frac{P(\boldsymbol{A}_1, \ldots, \boldsymbol{A}_n)}{P(\boldsymbol{A}_1) \times \ldots \times P(\boldsymbol{A}_n)} = \quad \text{(iv)}$$

$$P(\boldsymbol{A}_1 \mid \boldsymbol{E}_1, \boldsymbol{R}_1) \times \ldots \times P(\boldsymbol{A}_n \mid \boldsymbol{E}_n, \boldsymbol{R}_n) \times \frac{P(\boldsymbol{A}_1, \ldots, \boldsymbol{A}_n)}{P(\boldsymbol{A}_1) \times \ldots \times P(\boldsymbol{A}_n)}$$
$$\times P(\boldsymbol{R}_1 \mid \boldsymbol{E}_1) \times P(\boldsymbol{E}_1) \times \ldots \times P(\boldsymbol{R}_n \mid \boldsymbol{E}_n) \times P(\boldsymbol{E}_n)$$

[12]All new formal results in this paper were proved by Schubert.

Using this derivation, we calculate the probability of $P(R_1 \mid E_1, \ldots, E_n)$, which equals $P(R_i \mid E_1, \ldots, E_n)$, for any i. Let:

$$P(A_i) = a_i$$

$$P\left(A_i, \ldots, A_j\right) = a_{i,\ldots,j}$$

$$P(E_i) = e_i$$

$$P(R_i \mid E_i) = m$$

Then:

$$P(\boldsymbol{R}_1 \mid \boldsymbol{E}_1, \ldots, \boldsymbol{E}_n) = \frac{P(\boldsymbol{R}_1, \boldsymbol{E}_1, \ldots, \boldsymbol{E}_n)}{P(\boldsymbol{E}_1, \ldots, \boldsymbol{E}_n)} =$$

$$= \frac{\sum_{A_1,\ldots,A_n,R_2,\ldots,R_n} P(R_1, R_2 \ldots, R_n, A_1, \ldots, A_n, E_1, \ldots, E_n)}{\sum_{A_1,\ldots,A_n,R_1,\ldots,R_n} P(R_1, \ldots, R_n, A_1, \ldots, A_n, E_1, \ldots, E_n)}$$

$$P(R_1, E_1, \ldots, E_n) = \prod_{k=1}^{n} e_k \times \sum_{k=0}^{n-1} m^{n-k}(1-m)^k b_k \qquad \text{(vii)}$$

where $b_k = \sum_{1<q_2<\ldots<q_r \leq n, r=n-k} \frac{a_{1,q_2,\ldots,q_r}}{a_1, a_{q_2}, \ldots, a_{q_r}}$

$$P(E_1, \ldots, E_n) = \prod_{k=1}^{n} e_k \times \sum_{k=0}^{n} m^{n-k}(1-m)^k c_k \qquad \text{(vii)}$$

where $c_k = \sum_{q_1<,\ldots,<q_r \leq n, r=n-k} \frac{a_{q_1,\ldots,q_r}}{a_{q_1}, \ldots, a_{q_r}}$

Hence:

$$P(R_1 \mid E_1, \ldots, E_n) = \frac{\prod_{k=1}^{n} e_k \times \sum_{k=0}^{n-1} m^{n-k}(1-m)^k b_k}{\prod_{k=1}^{n} e_k \times \sum_{k=0}^{n} m^{n-k}(1-m)^k c_k} =$$

$$= \frac{\sum_{k=0}^{n-1} m^{n-k}(1-m)^k b_k}{\sum_{k=0}^{n} m^{n-k}(1-m)^k c_k}$$

$$= \frac{S_{A_1 n} + x S_{A_1 n-1} + \ldots + x^{n-2} S_{A_1 2} + x^{n-1}}{S_n + x S_{n-1} + \ldots + x^{n-2} S_2 + n x^{n-1} + x^n}$$

Proof of theorem 4: Let $\boldsymbol{R}, \boldsymbol{E}_1, \ldots, \boldsymbol{E}_n, \boldsymbol{A}_1, \ldots, \boldsymbol{A}_n$ be propositional variables. Then:

$$P(\boldsymbol{R}, \boldsymbol{E}_1, \ldots, \boldsymbol{E}_n, \boldsymbol{A}_1, \ldots, \boldsymbol{A}_n) =$$

$$P(\boldsymbol{E}_1 | \boldsymbol{R}, \boldsymbol{A}_1) \times \ldots \times P(\boldsymbol{E}_n | \boldsymbol{R}, \boldsymbol{A}_n) \times P(\boldsymbol{R}, \boldsymbol{A}_1, \ldots, \boldsymbol{A}_n) = \qquad \text{(iii}')$$

$$P(\boldsymbol{E}_1, \boldsymbol{R}, \boldsymbol{A}_1) \times \ldots \times P(\boldsymbol{E}_n, \boldsymbol{R}, \boldsymbol{A}_n) \times$$

$$\frac{P(\boldsymbol{A}_1, \ldots, \boldsymbol{A}_n)}{P(\boldsymbol{A}_1) \times \ldots \times P(\boldsymbol{A}_n)} \times \frac{1}{P(\boldsymbol{R})^{n-1}} = \qquad \text{(iv}')$$

$$P(\boldsymbol{A}_1 | \boldsymbol{E}_1, \boldsymbol{R}) \times \ldots \times P(\boldsymbol{A}_n | \boldsymbol{E}_n, \boldsymbol{R}) \times \frac{P(\boldsymbol{A}_1, \ldots, \boldsymbol{A}_n)}{P(\boldsymbol{A}_1) \times \ldots \times P(\boldsymbol{A}_n)} \times$$

$$\frac{P(\boldsymbol{R} | \boldsymbol{E}_1) \times P(\boldsymbol{E}_1)}{P(\boldsymbol{R})} \times \ldots \times \frac{P(\boldsymbol{R} | \boldsymbol{E}_n) \times P(\boldsymbol{E}_n)}{P(\boldsymbol{R})} \times P(\boldsymbol{R})$$

Then:

$$P(E_1, \ldots, E_n | R) = P(A_1, \ldots, A_n) \times \frac{P(E_1 | R)}{P(A_1)} \times \ldots \times \frac{P(E_n | R)}{P(A_n)} \qquad \text{(i}')$$

$$P(E_1, \ldots, E_n | \neg R) = P(E_1 | \neg R) \times \ldots \times P(E_1 | \neg R) \qquad \text{(ii}')$$

Let:

$$P(R) = r$$

$$P(R | E_i) = m$$

$$\bar{p} = 1 - p, \text{for any variable } p.$$

Then:

$$P(R | E_1, \ldots, E_n) =$$

$$\frac{C_{Sh}(A_1, \ldots, A_n) \times \frac{me_1}{r} \times \ldots \times \frac{me_n}{r} \times r}{C_{Sh}(A_1, \ldots, A_n) \times \frac{me_1}{r} \times \ldots \times \frac{me_n}{r} \times r + \frac{\bar{m}e_1}{\bar{r}} \times \ldots \times \frac{\bar{m}e_n}{\bar{r}} \times \bar{r}}$$

$$= \frac{C_{Sh}(A_1, \ldots, A_n) \times \frac{m}{r} \times \ldots \times \frac{m}{r} \times r}{C_{Sh}(A_1, \ldots, A_n) \times \frac{m}{r} \times \ldots \times \frac{m}{r} \times r + \frac{\bar{m}}{\bar{r}} \times \ldots \times \frac{\bar{m}}{\bar{r}} \times \bar{r}} \qquad \text{(vii}')$$

Thus $P(R|E_1, \ldots, E_n)$ is a strictly increasing function of $C_{Sh}(A_1, \ldots, A_n)$, given the assumptions of the scenario. Hence, the Shogenji measure is reliability conducive, in the present scenario.

Proofs of observation 3 and 4:

$$\boldsymbol{R}, \boldsymbol{E}_1, \ldots, \boldsymbol{E}_n, \boldsymbol{A}_1, \ldots, \boldsymbol{A}_n = P(\boldsymbol{E}_1 | \boldsymbol{R}, \boldsymbol{A}_1) \times \ldots \times P(\boldsymbol{E}_n | \boldsymbol{R}, \boldsymbol{A}_1) \times P(\boldsymbol{R}, \boldsymbol{A}_1, \ldots, \boldsymbol{A}_n)$$

(see proof of theorem 4)

Hence:

$$P(E_1, \ldots, E_n | R) = P(A_1, \ldots, A_n) \quad (a')$$

$$P(E_1, \ldots, E_n | \neg R) = P(A_1) \times \ldots \times P(A_n) \quad (b')$$

Proofs of observation 6 and 7:
See proof of theorem 4.

Proof of observation 9:
Assume for reductio that:

$$P(R_1 \vee R_2 | E_1, E_2) < P(R_1 | E_1) + P(R_2 | E_2) - P(R_1 | E_1)\, P(R_2 | E_2)$$

Let $P(H) = h$. $P(H)$ is the probability of what the witnesses agree upon.

$$\frac{P(R_1 \vee R_2, E_1, E_2)}{P(E_1, E_2)} = \frac{e_1 e_2 m^2 \frac{1}{h} + 2 e_1 e_2 m\,(1-m)}{e_1 e_2 m^2 \frac{1}{h} + 2 e_1 e_2 m\,(1-m) + e_1 e_2 (1-m)^2}$$

(Schubert 2011, 273) together with condition (vii)

$$P(R_1 | E_1) + P(R_2 | E_2) - P(R_1 | E_1)\, P(R_2 | E_2) = 2m - m^2$$

$$\frac{e_1 e_2 m^2 \frac{1}{h} + 2 e_1 e_2 m\,(1-m)}{e_1 e_2 m^2 \frac{1}{h} + 2 e_1 e_2 m\,(1-m) + e_1 e_2 (1-m)^2} < 2m - m^2$$

$$\Leftrightarrow m^2 \frac{1}{h} + 2m\,(1-m) < \left(2m - m^2\right)\left(m^2 \frac{1}{h} + 2m\,(1-m) + (1-m)^2\right)$$

$$\Leftrightarrow (1-m)^2 \left(m^2 \frac{1}{h} + 2m\,(1-m)\right) < \left(2m - m^2\right)(1-m)^2$$

$$\Leftrightarrow 1 < h$$

But this contradicts condition (v), which says that $0 < h < 1$. Hence $P(R_1 \vee R_2 | E_1, E_2) \geq P(R_1 | E_1) + P(R_2 | E_2) - P(R_1 | E_1)\, P(R_2 | E_2)$.

Proof of observation 10:

$$P(R_1\,|E_1, E_2\,, \neg R_2) = \frac{e_1 e_2 m\,(1-m)}{e_1 e_2\,(1-m)\,m + e_1 e_2 (1-m)^2} = m$$

(Schubert 2011, 273) together with condition (vii)

Hence $P(R_1\,|E_1, E_2\,, \neg R_2) = P(R_1\,|E_1\,)$

Proof of observation 11:

$$\frac{P(R_1, E_1, E_2)}{P(E_1, E_2)} = \frac{e_1 e_2 m^2 \frac{1}{h} + e_1 e_2 m\,(1-m)}{e_1 e_2 m^2 \frac{1}{h} + 2 e_1 e_2 m\,(1-m) + e_1 e_2 (1-m)^2}$$

(Schubert 2011, 273) together with condition (vii)

$$= \frac{m^2 \frac{1}{h} + m\,(1-m)}{m^2 \frac{1}{h} + 2m\,(1-m) + (1-m)^2}$$

Assume for reductio that $P(R_1\,|E_1, E_2) < P(R_1\,|E_1)$

$$\frac{m^2 \frac{1}{h} + m\,(1-m)}{m^2 \frac{1}{h} + 2m\,(1-m) + (1-m)^2} < m$$

$$\Leftrightarrow m \frac{1}{h} + (1-m) < m^2 \frac{1}{h} + 2m\,(1-m) + (1-m)^2$$

$$\Leftrightarrow \frac{1}{h} - 1 < m \left(\frac{1}{h} - 1 \right)$$

But, since $1 > m > 0$ and $1 > h > 0$, this cannot hold. Hence $P(R_1\,|E_1, E_2) \geq P(R_1\,|E_1\,)$.

References

Angere, S. 2007. The defeasible nature of coherentist justification. *Synthese* 157: 321–335.
Angere, S. 2008. Coherence as a heuristic. *Mind* 117: 1–26.
Berman, G.L., and B.L. Cutler. 1996. Effects of inconsistencies in eyewitness testimony and mock-juror decision making. *Journal of Applied Psychology* 81: 170–177.
Berman, G.L., D.J. Narby, and B.L. Cutler. 1995. Effects of inconsistent eyewitness statements on mock-juror's evaluations of the eyewitness, perceptions of defendant culpability and verdicts. *Law and Human Behavior* 19: 79–88.
BonJour, L. 1985. *The structure of empirical knowledge*. Cambridge, MA: Harvard University Press.
Bovens, L., and S. Hartmann. 2003. *Bayesian epistemology*. New York/Oxford: Oxford University Press.

Bovens, L., and E.J. Olsson. 2000. Coherentism reliability and Bayesian networks. *Mind* 109(436): 685–719.

Brewer, N., R. Potter, R.P. Fisher, N. Bond, and M.A. Luszcz. 1999. Beliefs and data on the relationship between consistency and accuracy of eyewitness testimony. *Applied Cognitive Psychology* 13: 297–313.

Cohen, L.J. 1977. *The probable and the provable*. Oxford: Clarendon Press.

Cross, C.B. 1999. Coherence and truth conducive justification. *Analysis* 59: 186–193.

Dempster, A.P. 1967. Upper and lower probabilities induced by a multi-valued mapping. *Annals of Mathematical Statistics* 38: 325–339.

Dempster, A.P. 1969. A generalization of Bayesian inference. *Journal of the Royal Statistical Society, Series B* 30: 205–247.

Edman, M. 1973. Adding independent pieces of evidence. In *Modality, morality and other problems of sense and nonsense*, ed. B. Hansson, 180–188. Lund: Gleerup.

Ekelöf, P.-O. 1963-1st ed./1982-5th ed. *Rättegång IV*. Stockholm: Norstedt.

Ekelöf, P.O. 1983. My thoughts on evidentiary value. In *Evidentiary value: Philosophical, judicial and psychological aspects of a theory*, ed. P. Gärdenfors, B. Hansson, and N.E. Sahlin, 9–26. Lund: Library of Theoria.

Ewing, A.C. 1934. *Idealism: A critical survey*. London: Methuen.

Fischoff, B., and S. Lichtenstein. 1978. Don't attribute this to reverend Bayes. *Psychological Bulletin* 85(2): 239–243.

Gärdenfors, P., B. Hansson, and N.E. Sahlin (eds.). 1983. *Evidentiary value: Philosophical, judicial and psychological aspects of a theory*. Lund: Library of Theoria.

Glass, D.H. 2002. Coherence, explanation, and Bayesian networks. In *Proceedings of the Irish conference in AI and cognitive science. Lecture notes in AI*, Vol. 2646, 177–182. New York: Springer.

Goldman, A.I. 1986. *Epistemology and cognition*. Cambridge: Harvard University Press.

Good, I. 1983. *Good thinking: The foundations of probability and its applications*. Minneapolis: University of Minnesota Press.

Halldén, S. 1973. Indiciemekanismer. *Tidskrift for Rettsvitenskap* 86: 55–64.

Hansson, B. 1983. Epistemology and evidence. In *Evidentiary value: Philosophical, judicial and psychological aspects of a theory*, ed. P. Gärdenfors, B. Hansson, and N.E. Sahlin, 75–97. Lund: Library of Theoria.

Harris, A., and U. Hahn. 2009. Bayesian rationality in evaluating multiple testimonies: Incorporating the role of coherence. *Journal of Experimental Psychology: Learning, Memory, and Cognition* 35: 1366–1373.

Howson, C., and P. Urbach. 1989-1st ed./1996-2nd ed. *Scientific reasoning: The Bayesian approach*. Chicago: Open Court.

Kahneman, D., P. Slovic, and A. Tversky (eds.). 1982. *Judgment under uncertainty: Heuristics and biases*. Cambridge: Cambridge University Press.

Kemeny, J., and P. Oppenheim. 1952. Degrees of factual support. *Philosophy of Science* 19: 307–324.

Klein, P., and T.A. Warfield. 1994. What price coherence? *Analysis* 54: 129–132.

Lagnado, D.A., and N. Harvey. 2008. The impact of discredited evidence. *Psychonomic Bulletin & Review* 15(6): 1166–1173.

Lewis, C.I. 1946. *An analysis of knowledge and valuation*. LaSalle: Open Court.

Mejis, W., and I. Douven. 2007. On the alleged impossibility of coherence. *Synthese* 157: 347–360.

Olsson, E.J. 2001. Why coherence is not truth-conducive. *Analysis* 61: 236–241.

Olsson, E.J. 2002. What is the problem of coherence and truth? *The Journal of Philosophy* 99: 246–272.

Olsson, E.J. 2005. *Against coherence: Truth, probability and justification*. Oxford: Oxford University Press.

Olsson, E.J., and S. Schubert. 2007. Reliability conducive measures of coherence. *Synthese* 157: 297–308.

Pennington, N., and R. Hastie. 1993. The story model for juror decision making. In *Inside the juror: The psychology of juror decision making*, ed. R. Hastie, 192–221. Cambridge: Cambridge University Press.
Ramsey, F.P. 1931. Knowledge. In *The foundations of mathematics and other logical essays*, ed. R.B. Braithwaite, 258–259. London: Routledge and Kegan Paul.
Rapoport, A., and T.S. Wallsten. 1972. Individual decision behavior. *Annual Review of Psychology* 23: 131–176.
Rawling, P. 1999. Reasonable doubt and the presumption of innocence: The case of the Bayesian juror. *Topoi* 18: 117–126.
Sahlin, N.-E. 1986. How to be 100% certain 99.5% of the time. *Journal of Philosophy* 83: 91–111.
Sahlin, N.-E. 2011. The evidentiary value model: Too short an introduction. Retrieved 5 June from http://www.nilsericsahlin.se/evm/index.html.
Sahlin, N.-E., and W. Rabinowicz. 1997. The evidentiary value model. In *Handbook of defeasible reasoning and uncertain management systems*, ed. D.M. Gabbay and P. Smets, 247–265. Dordrecht: Kluwer.
Schubert, S. 2011. Coherence and reliability: The case of overlapping testimonies. *Erkenntnis* 74: 263–275.
Schubert, S. 2012a. Coherence reasoning and reliability: A defense of the Shogenji measure. *Synthese* 187: 305–319.
Schubert, S. 2012b. Is coherence reliability conducive? *Synthese* 187: 607–621.
Schupbach, J. 2008. On the alleged impossibility of Bayesian coherentism. *Philosophical Studies* 141: 323–331.
Shafer, G. 1976. *A mathematical theory of evidence*. Princeton: Princeton University Press.
Shogenji, T. 1999. Is coherence truth conducive? *Analysis* 59: 338–345.
Shogenji, T. 2005. Justification by coherence from scratch. *Philosophical Studies* 125(3): 305–325.
Slovic, P., and S. Lichtenstein. 1971. Comparison of Bayesian and regression approaches to the study of human information processing in judgment. *Organizational Behavior and Human Performance* 6: 649–744.
Tversky, A., and D. Kahneman. 1974. Judgment under uncertainty: Heuristics and biases. *Science* 185: 1124–1131.

Chapter 3
Coherence and Probability: A Probabilistic Account of Coherence

William Roche

3.1 Introduction

Is coherence *necessary* for (epistemic) justification, in that one's beliefs are justified only if one's belief system is coherent? Is coherence *sufficient* for justification, in that one's beliefs are justified if one's belief system is coherent?[1] Is coherence truth-conducive, in that coherence implies a *high* probability of truth, or in that coherence implies a *higher* probability of truth, or in that, *ceteris paribus*, *greater* coherence implies a *greater* probability of truth? These questions are important, difficult, and have been widely discussed.[2] It would be helpful in answering such questions, it seems, if we had an account of coherence. It would be especially helpful if we had a *quantitative* account of coherence. I develop an account of that sort (a quantitative account) where coherence is defined (in large part) in terms of *probability*—a quantitative *probabilistic* account of coherence.[3]

---

[1]There are similar questions about justified (or rational) *belief-revision*.

[2]The third question (i.e., the question of whether coherence is truth-conducive), in particular, has been widely discussed of recent. See Angere (2007, 2008), Bovens and Hartmann (2003a, b, 2005, 2006), Bovens and Olsson (2000, 2002), Cross (1999), Huemer (1997, 2007, 2011), Klein and Warfield (1994, 1996), Meijs and Douven (2007), Merricks (1995), Olsson (2001, 2002, 2005a, b), Olsson and Shogenji (2004), Roche (2010, 2012), Schubert and Olsson (2012), Schupbach (2008), Shogenji (1999, 2005, 2007, Shogenji forthcoming), van Cleve (2005, 2011), and Wheeler (2009, 2012).

[3]The account is *not* meant to accurately describe how in fact ordinary people make coherence evaluations. Clarification as to what the account *is* meant to do is given below in Sect. 3.2.1.

W. Roche (✉)
Department of Philosophy, Texas Christian University, 2800 S. University Drive,
Fort Worth, TX 76129, USA
e-mail: w.roche@tcu.edu

M. Araszkiewicz and J. Šavelka (eds.), *Coherence: Insights from Philosophy, Jurisprudence and Artificial Intelligence*, Law and Philosophy Library 107,
DOI 10.1007/978-94-007-6110-0_3, © Springer Science+Business Media Dordrecht 2013

I do not aim to show that the account developed, hereafter "(CR)," is correct (or adequate), or even that it is preferable to all extant alternative accounts of coherence. I aim, rather, to show that *at least in certain respects* (CR) is preferable to (at least some of) the main extant probabilistic accounts of coherence: (i) Igor Douven and Wouter Meijs's account (2007), hereafter "(CDM),"[4] (ii) Branden Fitelson's account (2003, 2004), hereafter "(CF),"[5] (iii) Erik Olsson's account (2002, 2005a), hereafter "(CO),"[6] and (iv) Tomoji Shogenji's account (1999, 2001), hereafter "(CS)." I leave it for further investigation whether (CR) is preferable *all things considered* to (CDM), (CF), (CO), and (CS), whether (CR) is preferable all things considered to all alternative probabilistic accounts of coherence (extant or not) in addition to (CDM), (CF), (CO), and (CS),[7] and whether (CR) is preferable all things considered to all nonprobabilistic accounts of coherence.[8]

The paper is organized as follows. In Sect. 3.2, I set out some desiderata for an adequate account of coherence, and clarify the notion of a "probabilistic" account of coherence. In Sect. 3.3, I explain, in the following order, (CS), (CO), (CDM), (CF), and (CR). Then, in Sect. 3.4, I test the accounts against some cases. I contend that (CR), but not (CS), (CO), (CDM), or (CF), tests well against each case. Next, in Sect. 3.5, I relate (CR) to an important, but little discussed, problem for standard varieties of coherentism, viz., the "Problem of Justified Inconsistent Beliefs." Last, in Sect. 3.6, I conclude.

3.2 Preliminaries

3.2.1 Some Desiderata for an Adequate Account of Coherence

I take there to be *at least* three desiderata for an adequate account of coherence. First, an adequate account of coherence should imply that (a) coherence and incoherence come in degrees, (b) logical consistency is insufficient for coherence, (c) the degree to which a set of claims is coherent or incoherent is independent of the ordering of the claims in the set, and (d) no particular size (greater than 1) is

[4] Douven and Meijs develop three distinct accounts (2007, Sect. 3), and argue that one of them is weakly preferable to the other two (2007, Sect. 4). The account I call "(CDM)" is the account Douven and Meijs argue to be weakly preferable to the other two accounts.

[5] I have in mind the *corrected* version. The initial version is given in Fitelson (2003). Two corrections to that version are given in Fitelson (2004).

[6] Olsson holds, at least, that (CO) has some initial appeal.

[7] See, for example, Bovens and Hartmann (2003a, Chap. 2).

[8] See, for instance, Eliasmith and Thagard (1997), Thagard (1989a, b, 1992, 2000, 2004, 2012), Thagard and Nowak (1988), and Thagard and Verbeurgt (1998). And see Siebel (2005, 356–358, 2011), where it is argued that there can be no adequate probabilistic account of coherence.

needed for a (finite) set of claims to have a degree of coherence or incoherence.[9] Suppose $S_1 = \{p, q, r\}$, $S_2 = \{q, r, s\}$, $S_3 = \{q, p, r\}$, and $S_4 = \{p, q, r, \sim p\}$, where:

p = No ravens are black;
q = This bird is a raven;
r = This bird is black;
s = Some but very few ravens are black.[10]

S_1 is more incoherent (or has a higher degree of incoherence) than S_2; this illustrates (a). S_2 is logically consistent but not coherent (q, r, and s do not "hang together" in the requisite sense); this illustrates (b). S_1 and S_3 differ in the ordering of "p," "q," and "r," and yet S_1 and S_3 have the same degree of incoherence; this illustrates (c). S_2 and S_4 differ in size, and yet each set has a degree of incoherence (S_4's being greater than S_2's); this illustrates (d).

One terminological note is in order. I use the expression "coherence value" so that any degree of coherence is a coherence value, any degree of incoherence is a coherence value, and the neutral point between incoherence and coherence (if there is such a point) is a coherence value.

Second, an adequate account of coherence should be intuitive or plausible (or at least should not be highly counterintuitive or implausible) in what it implies or does not imply with respect to particular cases (artificial or otherwise). Suppose some account implies that S_4 is maximally coherent. This implication is not intuitive, in fact, is highly counterintuitive, and so counts (strongly if not decisively) against the account. Or suppose some account is silent on S_4 in that it has no implication with respect to S_4's coherence value (or even with respect to whether S_4 has a coherence value). The account thus fails to imply what seems obvious, viz., that S_4's coherence value is very (perhaps maximally) low, that S_4's coherence value is less than S_2's coherence value, and so on. This counts against the account.

Third, an adequate account of coherence should be explanatory. Suppose some account implies that S_4 is incoherent, but only because the account has a proviso to the effect that S_4 is incoherent. This counts (though perhaps only weakly) against the account. The account should explain *why*, and not merely imply *that*, S_4 is incoherent.[11]

---

[9] Here and throughout the paper I assume that only *finite* sets of *two or more* claims can have a degree of coherence or incoherence. Cf. Akiba (2000).

[10] This case is adapted from BonJour (1985, 95–96).

[11] Also important, I believe, is the extent to which an account of coherence is *fruitful* in that it leads to results concerning, say, the reliability of witnesses in a witness scenario, the transmission of confirmation, and so on. For relevant discussion, see Dietrich and Moretti (2005) and Schubert (2012). I do not have the space to evaluate (CDM), (CF), (CO), (CR), and (CS) in terms of fruitfulness. Fitelson (2003, 194) gives a desideratum (referred to as "(1)") on which, *inter alia*, an adequate account of coherence should imply that a set $S = \{p_1, \ldots, p_n\}$ is *maximally coherent* if $p_1, \ldots, p_n$ are *logically equivalent* (and S is satisfiable). I would be happy to accept this *part* of the desideratum; (CR), like (CF), implies that a set $S = \{p_1, \ldots, p_n\}$ is maximally coherent if

(CDM), (CF), (CO), (CR), and (CS) all imply (a)–(d) and so all satisfy the first desideratum.[12] But not all of those accounts satisfy the second and third desiderata. Or so I argue in Sect. 3.4.

3.2.2 Probabilistic Accounts of Coherence

Let's say that a "probabilistic" account of coherence is an account on which coherence is defined (at least in large part) in terms of probability.[13] Here is an example. Let $S = \{p_1, \ldots, p_n\}$. Then, on the "joint probability" account, "(CJ)," the degree to which S is coherent, "$C_J(S)$," is given by:

$$C_J(S) = \Pr(p_1 \wedge \ldots \wedge p_n).$$

(CJ) is implausible.[14] But, still, (CJ) serves as an example of a probabilistic account of coherence.

Two additional preliminary points are in order. First, on probabilistic accounts of coherence a set of claims can have different coherence values on different probability distributions, indeed, can be coherent on some probability distributions and incoherent on others.[15] It will help to consider an example. Suppose we have a deck of cards and randomly draw a card from the deck. Let $S = \{p_1, p_2\}$, where:

p_1 = The card selected is a heart;
p_2 = The card selected is red.

Suppose the deck of cards is standard, so that:

p_1	p_2	Pr
T	T	0.25
T	F	0
F	T	0.25
F	F	0.5

$p_1, \ldots, p_n$ are logically equivalent (and S is satisfiable). But I would not be happy to accept the desideratum as a whole. See Sect. 3.4.2.1 below.

[12]It is not trivial that (CDM), (CF), (CO), (CR), and (CS) all imply (a). Not all probabilistic accounts of coherence imply (a). Some probabilistic accounts of coherence are *purely qualitative*. See Douven and Meijs (2007, Sect. 2), where five such accounts are developed and compared. See, also, Lewis (1946, 338); there the term "congruence" is used in place of the term "coherence."

[13]By this standard, which admittedly is somewhat vague, each of (CDM), (CF), (CO), (CR), and (CS) is a probabilistic account of coherence. A more stringent standard could be employed. Perhaps then not all of (CDM), (CF), (CO), (CR), and (CS) would be probabilistic accounts of coherence. But, of course, nothing of importance hinges on how the various accounts are categorized.

[14](CJ) does not do well with some of the cases discussed below in Sect. 3.4, for example, *Tweety* and *Tweety** (3.4.3). See Olsson's discussion of "C_0" (2005a, 98–99).

[15]See Douven and Meijs (2007, 407).

On this probability distribution, $C_J(S) = \Pr(p_1 \wedge p_2) = .25$. Suppose instead the deck of cards is nonstandard in that each of the 26 red cards is a heart, so that:

p_1	p_2	Pr
T	T	0.5
T	F	0
F	T	0
F	F	0.5

On this probability distribution, $C_J(S) = \Pr(p_1 \wedge p_2) = .5$. (CJ) thus implies that S's coherence value is greater on the second probability distribution than on the first.

Second, a probabilistic account of coherence per se is neutral on the *determinants* (other than the axioms of the probability calculus) of the probabilistic facts in a given case. Here Shogenji (speaking in terms of beliefs and not in terms of claims) gives a disclaimer to the effect that his project is to give a characterization of coherence but not to identify what relations are responsible for coherence:

> This paper does not discuss what *makes* beliefs (more) coherent; it characterizes coherence of beliefs without attempting to decide what relations—logical, explanatory, etc.—are responsible for it. Once we separate the characterization of coherence from what is responsible for it, our task is fairly straightforward, but its precise formulation is still helpful in understanding its bearing on truth. (1999, 338, emphasis Shogenji's)

So one can accept a probabilistic account of coherence, and yet allow that the coherence facts in a given case, though *directly* determined by the probabilistic facts in the case, are *indirectly* determined by, say, the explanatory facts in the case—by allowing that at least certain of the probabilistic facts in a given case are determined by (in part) the explanatory facts in the case.[16]

[16]By "explanatory facts" I mean to include facts about the explanatory virtues, for example, simplicity. How can at least certain of the probabilistic facts in a given case be determined by (in part) the explanatory facts in the case? Imagine a case where h_1 and h_2 are scientific hypotheses, and h_1 is preferable to h_2 in terms of *simplicity*. One might hold that $\Pr(h_1) > \Pr(h_2)$, and that this is owing in part to the fact that h_1 is preferable to h_2 in terms of simplicity. Or suppose (adapting a case from Okasha 2000, 702–703) Smith is in some distress, where e describes Smith's symptoms. Suppose h_1 is the claim "Smith has pulled a muscle," and h_2 is the claim "Smith has torn a ligament." Suppose, given background information, e is better explained by h_1 than by h_2 *in that e would be expected if h_1 were true but not if h_2 were true*. Then, the idea goes, $\Pr(e|h_1) > \Pr(e|h_2)$. The issues here, however, are many and difficult, and the relevant literature is vast. See, for starters, Day and Kincaid (1994), Douven (1999, 2011, Sect. 4), Harman (1970), Huemer (2009a, b), Iranzo (2008), Lipton (2001, 2004, Chap. 7), Lombrozo (2007), McGrew (2003), Niiniluoto (1999, 2004), Okasha (2000), Psillos (2004, 2007), Salmon (1970, 1990, 2001a, b), Sober (2002), Swinburne (1973, Chap. 7), Tregear (2004), van Fraassen (1989, Chap. 7, Sect. 4), and Weisberg (2009).

3.3 The Accounts Explained

In Sect. 3.3.1, I set out (CS). In Sect. 3.3.2, I set out (CO). In Sect. 3.3.3, I set out (CDM), (CF), and (CR).

3.3.1 (CS)

Let $S = \{p_1, \ldots, p_n\}$. Then, on (CS) the degree to which S is coherent, "$C_S(S)$," is given by:

$$C_S(S) = \frac{\Pr(p_1 \wedge \ldots \wedge p_n)}{\Pr(p_1) \times \ldots \times \Pr(p_n)}.$$[17]

If $C_S(S) < 1$, S is incoherent. If $C_S(S) = 1$, S is neither coherent nor incoherent. If $C_S(S) > 1$, S is coherent. The minimum value for $C_S(S)$ is 0. There is no maximum value for $C_S(S)$. If some of the claims in S have a probability of 0, $C_S(S)$ is undefined.

Consider a two-member set: $S = \{p_1, p_2\}$. By (CS) the degree to which S is coherent is given by:

$$C_S(S) = \frac{\Pr(p_1 \wedge p_2)}{\Pr(p_1) \times \Pr(p_2)} = \frac{\Pr(p_1) \times \Pr(p_2 \mid p_1)}{\Pr(p_1) \times \Pr(p_2)} = \frac{\Pr(p_2 \mid p_1)}{\Pr(p_2)}.$$

If $\Pr(p_2|p_1) = \Pr(p_2), C_S(S) = 1$. If $\Pr(p_2|p_1) > \Pr(p_2), C_S(S) > 1$. If $\Pr(p_2|p_1) < \Pr(p_2), C_S(S) < 1$. So, whether S is coherent hinges on whether p_1 is positively probabilistically relevant to p_2.

Note that positive (negative) probabilistic relevance is symmetrical. Thus, p_1 is positively (negatively) probabilistically relevant to p_2 just in case p_2 is positively (negatively) probabilistically relevant to p_1. So (CS) implies that whether a two-member set is coherent hinges on whether the claims in question are positively probabilistically relevant to each other.

(CS) is a generalization of the thesis that whether a two-member set of claims is coherent hinges on whether the claims are positively probabilistically relevant to each other. This thesis has some initial plausibility. Thus so too does (CS).[18]

---

[17]Shogenji spells out his account of coherence in terms of sets of *beliefs*, not in terms of sets of *claims*. But nothing of importance, for my purposes, hinges on this difference.

[18]There are alternative generalizations of the thesis that whether a two-member set of claims is coherent hinges on whether the claims are positively probabilistically relevant to each other. One is developed by Jonah Schupbach (2011). I do not have the space to examine this account (or any of the other alternative generalizations). But what I say in Sects. 3.4.1.1, 3.4.1.2, and 3.4.1.3 about (CS) can also be said *mutatis mutandis* about the account developed by Schupbach.

3.3.2 (CO)

Let $S = \{p_1, \ldots, p_n\}$. Then, on (CO) the degree to which S is coherent, "$C_O(S)$," is given by:

$$C_O(S) = \frac{\Pr(p_1 \wedge \ldots \wedge p_n)}{\Pr(p_1 \vee \ldots \vee p_n)}.$$

$C_O(S)$ can take values between 0 and 1 (inclusive). If $C_O(S) = 0$, S is maximally incoherent. If $C_O(S) = 1$, S is maximally coherent. It is unspecified where the neutral point is between incoherence and coherence (or even whether there is a neutral point). If $\Pr(p_1 \vee \ldots \vee p_n) = 0$, $C_O(S)$ is undefined.

Consider a two-member set: $S = \{p_1, p_2\}$. By (CO) the degree to which S is coherent is given by:

$$C_O(S) = \frac{\Pr(p_1 \wedge p_2)}{\Pr(p_1 \vee p_2)}.$$

$C_O(S)$ measures how much of the total probability mass assigned to p_1 and p_2 falls in their overlap (or intersection). If p_1 and p_2 are equivalent to each other so that *all* of the total probability mass assigned to p_1 and p_2 falls in their overlap, then $\Pr(p_1 \wedge p_2) = \Pr(p_1 \vee p_2)$ and $C_O(S) = 1$. If, to take the other extreme, p_1 and p_2 are incompatible with each other so that *none* of the total probability mass assigned to p_1 and p_2 falls in their overlap, then $\Pr(p_1 \wedge p_2) = 0$ and $C_O(S) = 0$ (assuming $\Pr(p_1 \vee p_2) > 0$).

(CO) has some initial plausibility. (CO) is a generalization of the thesis that the degree to which a two-member set of claims is coherent is determined by how much of the total probability mass assigned to the claims falls in their overlap, and this thesis has some initial plausibility.[19]

3.3.3 (CDM), (CF), and (CR)

(CDM), (CF), and (CR) are all instances of a certain schema (adapted from Douven and Meijs 2007; Fitelson 2004). So, before setting out the various accounts I want to set out the schema.

Let $S = \{p_1, \ldots, p_n\}$. Let $S^* = \{S' \mid S'$ is a non-empty subset of $S\}$.[20] Let $S^{**} = \{(S', S'') \mid S'$ and S'' are non-overlapping members

---

[19]Meijs (2006) develops an alternative generalization. And there are yet additional alternative generalizations. I do not, alas, have the space to examine them. What I say in 3.4.1.2 about (CO), though, can also be said *mutatis mutandis* about the account developed by Meijs.

[20]It might be better to define S so that it is an *ordered* set, and to define S^* so that S' is a nonempty *subsequence* of S. See Schubert (2012, 311–312).

of S^{*}}. Let $S^{***} = \{(\wedge S', \wedge S'') \mid (S', S'')$ is a member of $S^{**}\}$.[21] Let m be a measure of confirmation (or evidential support). Let $S^{****} = \{m(\wedge S', \wedge S'') \mid (\wedge S', \wedge S'')$ is a member of $S^{***}\}$. Then, by account "(CX)" the degree to which S is coherent, "$C_X(S)$," is given by:

$$C_X(S) = \text{mean}\left(S^{****}\right).$$

Different measures of confirmation can thus be used to generate different probabilistic accounts of coherence.[22]

It will help to consider a few examples. First, suppose $S = \{p_1, p_2\}$. Then:

$$\begin{aligned}
S^{*} &= \{\{p_1\}, \{p_2\}, \{p_1, p_2\}\};\\
S^{**} &= \{(\{p_1\}, \{p_2\}), (\{p_2\}, \{p_1\})\};\\
S^{***} &= \{(p_1, p_2), (p_2, p_1)\};\\
S^{****} &= \{m(p_1, p_2), m(p_2, p_1)\};\\
C_X(S) &= \text{mean}\left(S^{****}\right) = \frac{m(p_1, p_2) + m(p_2, p_1)}{2}.
\end{aligned}$$

Next, suppose $S = \{p_1, p_2, p_3\}$. Then:

$$\begin{aligned}
S^{*} &= \{\{p_1\}, \{p_2\}, \{p_3\}, \{p_1, p_2\}, \{p_1, p_3\}, \{p_2, p_3\}, \{p_1, p_2, p_3\}\};\\
S^{**} &= \{(\{p_1\}, \{p_2\}), (\{p_1\}, \{p_3\}), (\{p_2\}, \{p_1\}), (\{p_2\}, \{p_3\}), (\{p_3\}, \{p_1\}),\\
&\quad (\{p_3\}, \{p_2\}), (\{p_1\}, \{p_2, p_3\}), (\{p_2\}, \{p_1, p_3\}), (\{p_3\}, \{p_1, p_2\}),\\
&\quad (\{p_1, p_2\}, \{p_3\}), (\{p_1, p_3\}, \{p_2\}), (\{p_2, p_3\}, \{p_1\})\};\\
S^{***} &= \{(p_1, p_2), (p_1, p_3), (p_2, p_1), (p_2, p_3), (p_3, p_1), (p_3, p_2), (p_1, p_2 \wedge p_3),\\
&\quad (p_2, p_1 \wedge p_3), (p_3, p_1 \wedge p_2), (p_1 \wedge p_2, p_3), (p_1 \wedge p_3, p_2), (p_2 \wedge p_3, p_1)\};\\
S^{****} &= \{m(p_1, p_2), m(p_1, p_3), m(p_2, p_1), m(p_2, p_3), m(p_3, p_1),\\
&\quad m(p_3, p_2), m(p_1, p_2 \wedge p_3), m(p_2, p_1 \wedge p_3), m(p_3, p_1 \wedge p_2),\\
&\quad m(p_1 \wedge p_2, p_3), m(p_1 \wedge p_3, p_2), m(p_2 \wedge p_3, p_1)\};
\end{aligned}$$

---

[21]If S' has just one member, then $\wedge S'$ is simply that member. Likewise with respect to S''.

[22]See Eells and Fitelson (2002) for an overview of the main extant measures of confirmation, and for defense of the claim that certain symmetry considerations favor the "difference" measure and (a logarithm-based version of) the "likelihood" measure over their rivals. See also Crupi et al. (2007).

$$C_X(S) = \text{mean}\left(S^{****}\right) = \frac{\begin{array}{c} m\left(p_1, p_2\right) + m\left(p_1, p_3\right) + m\left(p_2, p_1\right) \\ +m\left(p_2, p_3\right) + m\left(p_3, p_1\right) + m\left(p_3, p_2\right) \\ +m\left(p_1, p_2 \wedge p_3\right) + m\left(p_2, p_1 \wedge p_3\right) + m\left(p_3, p_1 \wedge p_2\right) \\ +m\left(p_1 \wedge p_2, p_3\right) + m\left(p_1 \wedge p_3, p_2\right) + m\left(p_2 \wedge p_3, p_1\right) \end{array}}{12}.$$

So, when $n = 2$, $C_X(S)$ is the mean of two confirmation values, and when $n = 3$, $C_X(S)$ is the mean of 12 confirmation values.

It can be shown that, where $S = \{p_1, \ldots, p_n\}$, $C_X(S)$ is the mean of $\sum_{i=1}^{n-1} \binom{n}{i} \left(2^{n-i} - 1\right)$ confirmation values,[23] or, equivalently, of $3^n - 2^{n+1} + 1$ confirmation values.[24] So, when $n = 4$, $C_X(S)$ is the mean of 50 confirmation values, when $n = 5$, $C_X(S)$ is the mean of 180 confirmation values, when $n = 6$, $C_X(S)$ is the mean of 602 confirmation values, and so on.

Instances of the schema thus all agree in the idea that the degree to which a set of claims is coherent is equal to the average degree to which the (claims, or iterated conjunctions thereof, in the) various non-empty and non-overlapping subsets of the set confirm each other.[25] The best possible case is where the various subsets all maximally confirm each other. The worst possible case is where the various subsets all maximally disconfirm each other.

Let's turn now to (CDM), (CF), and (CR). I begin with (CDM).

(CDM) involves the *difference* measure of confirmation:

$$d(h, e) = \Pr(h|e) - \Pr(h).^{26}$$

Suppose $S = \{p_1, p_2\}$. Then, by (CDM) the degree to which S is coherent, "$C_{DM}(S)$," is given by:

$$\begin{aligned} C_{DM}(S) &= \text{mean}\left(\left\{d\left(p_1, p_2\right), d\left(p_2, p_1\right)\right\}\right) \\ &= \frac{\left[\Pr\left(p_1 \,|\, p_2\right) - \Pr\left(p_1\right)\right] + \left[\Pr\left(p_2 \,|\, p_1\right) - \Pr\left(p_2\right)\right]}{2}. \end{aligned}$$

---

[23] That $C_X(S)$ is the mean of $\sum_{i=1}^{n-1} \binom{n}{i} \left(2^{n-i} - 1\right)$ confirmation values follows, ultimately, from the fact that S^{**} has exactly $\sum_{i=1}^{n-1} \binom{n}{i} \left(2^{n-i} - 1\right)$ members. See Douven and Meijs (2007, 412, n. 15).

[24] The result that $C_X(S)$ is the mean of $3^n - 2^{n+1} + 1$ confirmation values is due essentially to Kyle Kloster (to whom I am grateful).

[25] Douven and Meijs (2007, Sects. 2 and 3) give a compelling defense of this idea. This defense, though, can be strengthened a bit. Douven and Meijs fail to prove "Conjecture 2.1" (2007, 408). The thesis in question—viz., that "one-any + partition coherence" does not entail "any-any coherence"—is true, as Douven and Meijs conjecture, and can be proven.

[26] Here "h" and "e" can be iterated conjunctions, e.g., $p_1 \wedge p_2 \wedge p_3$. $d(h, e)$ is defined only if e has a positive probability.

$C_{DM}(S)$ can take values between -1 and 1 (not inclusive).[27] (CDM) is naturally understood so that if $C_{DM}(S) < 0$, S is incoherent, if $C_{DM}(S) = 0$, S is neither coherent nor incoherent, and if $C_{DM}(S) > 0$, S is coherent (though strictly speaking Douven and Meijs never explicitly say this; see Siebel 2005, 348–349). If some of the claims in S have a probability of 0, $C_{DM}(S)$ is undefined.

Note that one can find (CDM) to be attractive even if one does not find the difference measure to be attractive *qua measure of confirmation*. Likewise with respect to the various alternative instances of the schema above and the measures of confirmation involved in them.[28] The crucial question is whether the accounts are intuitive or plausible in what they imply or do not imply with respect to particular cases, and whether the accounts satisfy the various other desiderata for an adequate account of coherence.

(CF) is just like (CDM) except that (CF) involves the following measure of confirmation:

$$\begin{aligned} f(h,e) &= 1 && \text{if } e \vDash h \text{ and } e \nvDash \bot; \\ &= -1 && \text{if } e \vDash \sim h; \\ &= \frac{\Pr(e\,|h) - \Pr(e|\sim h)}{\Pr(e\,|h) + \Pr(e|\sim h)} && \text{if } e \nvDash h \text{ and } e \nvDash \sim h.^{29} \end{aligned}$$

Suppose $S = \{p_1, p_2\}$, and $p_1 \nvDash p_2$, $p_1 \nvDash \sim p_2$, $p_2 \nvDash p_1$, and $p_2 \nvDash \sim p_1$. Then, by (CF) the degree to which S is coherent, "$C_F(S)$," is given by:

$$\begin{aligned} C_F(S) &= \text{mean}\left(\{f(p_1, p_2), f(p_2, p_1)\}\right) \\ &= \frac{\dfrac{\Pr(p_2\,|p_1) - \Pr(p_2|\sim p_1)}{\Pr(p_2\,|p_1) + \Pr(p_2|\sim p_1)} + \dfrac{\Pr(p_1\,|p_2) - \Pr(p_1|\sim p_2)}{\Pr(p_1\,|p_2) + \Pr(p_1|\sim p_2)}}{2}. \end{aligned}$$

$C_F(S)$ can take values between -1 and 1 (inclusive). If $C_F(S) < 0$, S is incoherent. If $C_F(S) = 0$, S is neither coherent nor incoherent. If $C_F(S) > 0$, S is coherent.

---

[27] Why cannot $C_{DM}(S) = 1$? $C_{DM}(S) = 1$ only if *each* of the various confirmation values equals 1. But, *none* of the various confirmation values equals 1. This is because $d(h, e)$ cannot equal 1. Suppose $\Pr(h) = 0$. Then, assuming $\Pr(h \mid e)$ is defined, $\Pr(h \mid e) = 0$, hence $\Pr(h|e) - \Pr(h) = 0$. Suppose, instead, $\Pr(h) > 0$. Then, even if $\Pr(h \mid e) = 1$, it follows that $\Pr(h|e) - \Pr(h) < 1$. Why cannot $C_{DM}(S) = -1$? $C_{DM}(S) = -1$ only if *each* of the various confirmation values equals -1. But, *none* of the various confirmation values equals -1. This is because $d(h, e)$ cannot equal -1. Suppose $\Pr(h) = 1$. Then, assuming $\Pr(h \mid e)$ is defined, $\Pr(h \mid e) = 1$, hence $\Pr(h|e) - \Pr(h) = 0$. Suppose, instead, $\Pr(h) < 1$. Then, even if $\Pr(h \mid e) = 0$, it follows that $\Pr(h|e) - \Pr(h) > -1$.

[28] Douven and Meijs (2007, 411, n. 14) make a point to this effect.

[29] This measure of confirmation is a variant of John Kemeny and Paul Oppenheim's measure (1952).

(CR) is just like (CDM) and (CF) except that the measure of confirmation involved in (CR) is the following:

$$\begin{aligned} a(h, e) &= 1 && \text{if } e \vDash h \text{ and } e \nvDash \bot; \\ &= 0 && \text{if } e \vDash \sim h; \\ &= \Pr(h|e) && \text{if } e \nvDash h \text{ and } e \nvDash \sim h. \end{aligned}$$[30]

Let $S = \{p_1, p_2\}$, and suppose $p_1 \nvDash p_2$, $p_1 \nvDash \sim p_2$, $p_2 \nvDash p_1$, and $p_2 \nvDash \sim p_1$. Then, by (CR) the degree to which S is coherent, "$C_R(S)$," is given by:

$$C_R(S) = \text{mean}(\{a(p_1, p_2), a(p_2, p_1)\}) = \frac{\Pr(p_1|p_2) + \Pr(p_2|p_1)}{2}.$$

$C_R(S)$ can take values between 0 and 1 (inclusive). (CR) is naturally understood so that the neutral point between incoherence and coherence is 0.5.

3.4 The Accounts Tested

In Sect. 3.4.1, I discuss some problem cases for (CS), (CO), and (CDM) (but note that the case discussed in Sect. 3.4.1.1 is a problem case just for (CS) and (CDM)). In 3.4.2, I discuss some problem cases for (CF). In Sect. 3.4.3, I discuss some additional test cases.

3.4.1 Some Problem Cases for (CS), (CO), and (CDM)

3.4.1.1 Sets of Contradictory Claims

Suppose a fair six-sided die was just rolled. Let $S_5 = \{t, \sim t\}$, where:

t = The die came up two.

S_5, it seems, is incoherent, indeed, is highly if not maximally incoherent. Likewise, it seems, with respect to *any* set of contradictory claims.

(CS) and (CDM), though, cannot explain this (why any set of contradictory claims is highly if not maximally incoherent). There are sets of contradictory claims on which (CS) and (CDM) remain silent. Let $S_6 = \{f, \sim f\}$, where:

$$f = 2 + 2 = 4.$$

[30]This measure is best seen as a measure of *absolute*, as opposed to *incremental*, confirmation. Thus the "a" in "$a(h, e)$."

S_6, like S_5, is highly if not maximally incoherent. But consider:

$$C_S(S_6) = \frac{\Pr(f \wedge \sim f)}{\Pr(f) \times \Pr(\sim f)};$$

$$\begin{aligned} C_{DM}(S_6) &= \text{mean}(\{d(f, \sim f), d(\sim f, f)\}) \\ &= \frac{[\Pr(f \mid \sim f) - \Pr(f)] + [\Pr(\sim f \mid f) - \Pr(\sim f)]}{2}. \end{aligned}$$

Given that $\Pr(\sim f) = 0$,[31] it follows that $\Pr(f) \times \Pr(\sim f) = 0$, hence $C_S(S_6)$ is undefined,[32] and it follows that $\Pr(f \mid \sim f)$ is undefined, thus $d(f, \sim f)$ is undefined, thus $C_{DM}(S_6)$ is undefined.[33]

---

[31]I am assuming, here and throughout the paper, that if a claim p is necessarily true, then, on any (admissible) probability function, $\Pr(p) = 1$, and that if a claim p is necessarily false, then, on any (admissible) probability function, $\Pr(p) = 0$. In assuming this I am glossing over some difficult issues in epistemology, philosophy of language, and philosophy of mind. I leave it for further investigation how best to treat these issues and whether the best treatment would require substantive changes to the main points of this paper. For relevant discussion, see Chalmers (2011), Douven and Meijs (2007, Sect. 3.5.1), Garber (1983), and Swinburne (1973, Chap. 4).

[32]This point can be established in two other ways. First, observe that:

$$C_S(S_6) = \frac{\Pr(f \wedge \sim f)}{\Pr(f) \times (\Pr \sim f)} = \frac{\Pr(\sim f) \times \Pr(f \mid \sim f)}{\Pr(f) \times \Pr(\sim f)} = \frac{\Pr(f \mid \sim f)}{\Pr(f)}.$$

Since the numerator in $\frac{\Pr(f \mid \sim f)}{\Pr(f)}$ is undefined, $C_S(S_6)$ is undefined. Second, observe that:

$$C_S(S_6) = \frac{\Pr(f \wedge \sim f)}{\Pr(f) \times \Pr(\sim f)} = \frac{\Pr(f) \times \Pr(\sim f \mid f)}{\Pr(f) \times \Pr(\sim f)} = \frac{\Pr(\sim f \mid f)}{\Pr(\sim f)}.$$

Since the denominator in $\frac{\Pr(\sim f \mid f)}{\Pr(\sim f)}$ equals 0, $C_S(S_6)$ is undefined.

[33]Douven and Meijs (2007, Sect. 3.5.1) raise a problem for (CDM), and for certain other accounts of coherence, and give two proposals for solving the problem. Each proposal has the result that the only sets that should be considered when evaluating (CDM) are sets consisting of *pairwise logically independent* claims. This result entails that, since S_6 is not a set consisting of pairwise logically independent claims, S_6 should not be considered when evaluating (CDM). It seems clear, though, that S_6 has a coherence value, in fact a very low if not maximally low coherence value. Moreover, it seems clear that *many* sets consisting of pairwise logically dependent claims have coherence values. So for the purposes of this paper I shall assume that the two proposals given by Douven and Meijs should be rejected and that the problem raised by Douven and Meijs for (CDM), and for the other accounts in question, can be adequately answered without appeal to those proposals. See Huemer (2011, 46–47) and Schubert (2012, 311–312).

(CO), (CF), and (CR), by contrast, imply that S_6 is maximally incoherent:

$$C_O(S_6) = \frac{\Pr(f \wedge \sim f)}{\Pr(f \vee \sim f)} = \frac{0}{1} = 0;$$

$$C_F(S_6) = \text{mean}(\{f(f, \sim f), f(\sim f, f)\}) = \frac{-1 + -1}{2} = -1;$$

$$C_R(S_6) = \text{mean}(\{a(f, \sim f), a(\sim f, f)\}) = \frac{0+0}{2} = 0.$$

$f(f, \sim f) = -1$ and $a(f, \sim f) = 0$, since $\sim f \vDash \sim f$. $f(\sim f, f) = -1$ and $a(\sim f, f) = 0$, given that $f \vDash \sim \sim f$.

It is clear, of course, *without any appeal to coherence considerations* that one should not believe the claims in S_6. The point remains, however, that S_6 is incoherent and neither (CS) nor (CDM) can explain this.

(CS) could be modified to say that if the members of a set $S = \{p_1, p_2\}$ are contradictory claims, then S is maximally incoherent *even if* $Pr(p_1) \times Pr(p_2) = 0$. Likewise, (CDM) could be modified to say that if the members of a set $S = \{p_1, p_2\}$ are contradictory claims, then S is maximally incoherent *even if* $d(p_1, p_2)$ *or* $d(p_2, p_1)$ *is undefined*. But then (CS) and (CDM) would be unable to explain *why* sets of contradictory claims one member of which is a necessary falsehood are incoherent.

3.4.1.2 Sets of Necessary Falsehoods

Let $S_7 = \{f, s\}$, where:

$$f = 2 + 2 = 5;$$

$$s = 2 + 2 = 6.$$

S_7, it seems, is incoherent, indeed, is highly if not maximally incoherent; $f \vDash \sim s$, and $s \vDash \sim f$. Likewise with respect to *any* set of necessary falsehoods.

(CS), (CO), and (CDM), however, are silent on S_7. Consider:

$$C_S(S_7) = \frac{\Pr(f \wedge s)}{\Pr(f) \times \Pr(s)};$$

$$C_O(S_7) = \frac{\Pr(f \wedge s)}{\Pr(f \vee s)};$$

$$C_{DM}(S_7) = \text{mean}(\{d(f, s), d(s, f)\}) = \frac{[\Pr(f \mid s) - \Pr(f)] + [\Pr(s \mid f) - \Pr(s)]}{2}.$$

Clearly, $C_S(S_7)$ and $C_O(S_7)$ are undefined. $C_{DM}(S_7)$ is undefined because, since both $\Pr(f \mid s)$ and $\Pr(s \mid f)$ are undefined, both $d(f, s)$ and $d(s, f)$ are undefined. The same is true of any alternative set of necessary falsehoods: (CS), (CO), and (CDM) remain silent.

(CF) and (CR), by contrast, do well with S_7:

$$C_F(S_7) = \text{mean}(\{f(f, s), f(s, f)\}) = \frac{-1 + -1}{2} = -1;$$

$$C_R(S_7) = \text{mean}(\{a(f, s), a(s, f)\}) = \frac{0 + 0}{2} = 0.$$

$f(f, s) = -1$ and $a(f, s) = 0$, since $s \vDash \sim f$. $f(s, f) = -1$ and $a(s, f) = 0$, given that $f \vDash \sim s$. Likewise for any alternative set of necessary falsehoods: (CF) and (CR) imply maximal incoherence.

(CS), (CO), and (CDM) could be modified to say, respectively, that any set $S = \{p_1, p_2\}$ consisting of necessary falsehoods is maximally incoherent *even if* $Pr(p_1) \times Pr(p_2) = 0$, that any set $S = \{p_1, p_2\}$ consisting of necessary falsehoods is maximally incoherent *even if* $Pr(p_1 \vee p_2) = 0$,[34] and that any set $S = \{p_1, p_2\}$ consisting of necessary falsehoods is maximally incoherent *even if* $d(p_1, p_2)$ *and* $d(p_2, p_1)$ *are undefined*. But then (CS), (CO), and (CDM) would be unable to explain *why* sets of that sort are maximally incoherent.

3.4.1.3 Sets Involving a Necessary Falsehood

Suppose $S_8 = \{p_1 \ldots, p_n\}$, where $\{p_1 \ldots, p_n\}$ is very large and highly coherent (on any account of coherence). Suppose (adapting a case from Foley 1979, 249) $S_9 = \{p_1, \ldots, p_n, p_{n+1}\}$, where p_{n+1} is the necessary falsehood that 3^8 is greater than 6,562.[35] S_9, it seems, has a lesser coherence value than S_8, but, still, not the minimum coherence value. S_9 has a greater coherence value than, say, the set $\{p, \sim p\}$, where p is the claim that all ravens are black. S_8 is highly coherent and, so, certain of the claims in S_9—viz., $p_1, \ldots, p_n$—hang together in the requisite sense. By contrast, none of the claims in the set $\{p, \sim p\}$ hang together in the requisite sense.

S_9 is problematic for (CO). Consider:

$$C_O(S_9) = \frac{\Pr(p_1 \wedge \ldots \wedge p_n \wedge p_{n+1})}{\Pr(p_1 \vee \ldots \vee p_n \vee p_{n+1})}.$$

Suppose $\Pr(p_1 \vee \ldots \vee p_n \vee p_{n+1}) > 0$. Then, since $\Pr(p_1 \wedge \ldots \wedge p_n \wedge p_{n+1}) = 0$, it follows that $C_O(S_9) = 0$. (CO) thus implies that, even though S_8 is highly coherent

[34] A slight variant of this proposal with respect to (CO) is given in Glass (2005, 384, n. 7).

[35] $3^8 = 6{,}561$.

and S_9 differs from S_8 only in that p_{n+1} (a necessary falsehood) is a member of S_9, S_9 is maximally incoherent.

S_9 is also problematic for (CS) and (CDM). Consider:

$$C_S(S_9) = \frac{\Pr(p_1 \wedge \ldots \wedge p_n \wedge p_{n+1})}{\Pr(p_1) \times \ldots \times \Pr(p_n) \times \Pr(p_{n+1})};$$

$$C_{DM}(S_9) = \text{mean}\left(\{d(p_1, p_2), \ldots d(p_1, p_{n+1}), \ldots\}\right).$$

Since $\Pr(p_{n+1}) = 0$, it follows that $\Pr(p_1) \times \ldots \times \Pr(p_n) \times \Pr(p_{n+1}) = 0$, hence $C_S(S_9)$ is undefined. It also follows that $\Pr(p_1 | p_{n+1})$ is undefined, thus $d(p_1, p_{n+1})$ is undefined, thus $C_{DM}(S_9)$ is undefined. So, (CS) and (CDM) are silent on S_9.[36]

(CF) and (CR), on the other hand, do well with S_9. Suppose $p_2 \vDash p_1$ and $p_2 \nvDash \bot$. Then it follows that:

$$C_F(S_9) = \text{mean}\left(\{f(p_1, p_2), \ldots\}\right) = \text{mean}\left(\{1, \ldots\}\right) > -1;$$

$$C_R(S_9) = \text{mean}\left(\{a(p_1, p_2), \ldots\}\right) = \text{mean}\left(\{1, \ldots\}\right) > 0.$$

Note that $C_F(S) = -1$ only when *each* of the various confirmation values (over which the mean is taken) equals -1, and that $C_R(S) = 0$ only when *each* of the various confirmation values (over which the mean is taken) equals 0.[37]

(CS) could be modified to say that if a claim in a set $S = \{p_1, p_2, \ldots, p_n\}$ has a probability of 0, then, though $\Pr(p_1) \times \Pr(p_2) \times \ldots \times \Pr(p_n) = 0$, S is maximally incoherent. (CDM) could be modified in a similar fashion. But then, for one thing, though (CS) and (CDM) would not be silent on S_9, (CS) and (CDM) would yield the wrong result with respect to S_9.

3.4.2 *Some Problem Cases for (CF)*

(CF), like (CR), does well with sets of contradictory claims, sets of necessary falsehoods, and sets involving a necessary falsehood (at least in that (CF), like (CR),

---

[36] There are variants of the case where (CDM) is silent on the larger set but (CS) is not. Suppose S_{9*} is just like S_8 except that S_{9*} includes *two* additional claims, p_{n+1} and p_{n+2}, where each claim has a nonextreme probability and the one claim entails the falsity of the other claim. (CDM) is silent on S_{9*}; $\Pr(p_{n+1} \wedge p_{n+2}) = 0$, thus $\Pr(p_1 | p_{n+1} \wedge p_{n+2})$ is undefined, thus $d(p_1, p_{n+1} \wedge p_{n+2})$ is undefined, thus $C_{DM}(S_{9*})$ is undefined. (CS), by contrast, is not silent on S_{9*}. $C_S(S_{9*}) = 0$ and so (CS) implies that S_{9*} is maximally incoherent. This, it seems, is the wrong result. S_{9*} has a lesser coherence value than S_8. But, since (by hypothesis) certain of the claims in S_{9*} (namely, $p_1, \ldots, p_n$) hang together in the requisite sense, S_{9*} is not maximally incoherent.

[37] In Sect. 3.5, below, I consider the question of whether $C_R(S_9)$ can have a coherence value greater than 0.5.

implies that sets involving a necessary falsehood can have a coherence value greater than the minimum). I turn now to some test cases with which, arguably, (CF), unlike (CR), does not do well.

3.4.2.1 Pickpocket, Rabbit, and Rabbit*

Mark Siebel argues that (CF) is inadequate in its implications with respect to (at least some) two-member sets of subcontrary claims (2004, 2005).[38] Suppose a murder has been committed. There are ten suspects. Each suspect has a probability of 1/10 of being the murderer, and each suspect has committed at least one crime: two suspects have committed robbery but not pickpocketing; two suspects have committed pickpocketing but not robbery; six suspects have committed robbery and pickpocketing. Let $S_{10} = \{r, p\}$, where:

r = The murderer has committed robbery;
p = The murderer has committed pickpocketing.

Let's call this case "*Pickpocket.*" Each suspect has committed robbery or pickpocketing, so r and p are subcontrary claims (given the background information). Siebel holds that S_{10} is coherent (given the high overlap between the set of robbers and the set of pickpocketers). (CF), though, implies that S_{10} is not coherent:

$$\begin{aligned} C_F(S_{10}) &= \text{mean}(\{f(r,p), f(p,r)\}) \\ &= \frac{\frac{\Pr(p|r)-\Pr(p|\sim r)}{\Pr(p|r)+\Pr(p|\sim r)} + \frac{\Pr(r|p)-\Pr(r|\sim p)}{\Pr(r|p)+\Pr(r|\sim p)}}{2} \\ &= \frac{\frac{.75-1}{.75+1} + \frac{.75-1}{.75+1}}{2} = -.143.^{39} \end{aligned}$$

In fact, (CF) implies that no two-member set of subcontrary claims is coherent. (CR) implies that, as Siebel holds and contra (CF), S_{10} is coherent. Observe that:

$$\begin{aligned} C_R(S_{10}) &= \text{mean}(\{a(r,p), a(p,r)\}) \\ &= \frac{\Pr(r|p)+\Pr(p|r)}{2} = \frac{.75+.75}{2} = .75. \end{aligned}$$

---

[38]Two claims are subcontraries just in case the falsity of the one claim entails the truth of the other.

[39]Here and below at several points I have rounded for convenience. The decision procedure PrSAT developed by Branden Fitelson (in collaboration with Jason Alexander and Ben Blum) provides an extremely efficient means of obtaining or verifying results such as those explained in this subsection (Sect. 3.4.2) and the next (Sect. 3.4.3). See Fitelson (2008) for a description of PrSAT and some applications.

The table below compares the various accounts with respect to *Pickpocket*:

	Pickpocket
$C_S(S_{10})$	0.938
$C_O(S_{10})$	0.6
$C_{DM}(S_{10})$	−0.05
$C_F(S_{10})$	−0.143
$C_R(S_{10})$	0.75

(CS) and (CDM) agree with (CF) that S_{10} is not coherent. (CO) agrees with Siebel and (CR) that S_{10} is coherent.

It might seem that (CR) is incorrect in its implication that S_{10} is coherent. For, it might seem that, at least with respect to two-member sets of claims, *coherence* is a matter of *positive* probabilistic relevance and *incoherence* is a matter of *negative* probabilistic relevance. $\Pr(r|p) = .75 < \Pr(r) = .8$, and $\Pr(p|r) = .75 < \Pr(p) = .8$. So the claims in S_{10} are negatively probabilistically relevant to each other. It might seem, then, that S_{10} is incoherent, hence, contra (CR), is not coherent.

Recall that (CS) implies that whether a two-member set of claims is coherent hinges on whether the claims in the set are positively probabilistically relevant to each other (in that if the claims are positively probabilistically relevant to each other then the set is coherent, if the claims are probabilistically irrelevant to each other then the set is neither coherent nor incoherent, and if the claims are negatively probabilistically relevant to each other then the set is incoherent). It is no surprise then that (CS) agrees with (CF) that S_{10} is not coherent.

The idea that, at least with respect to two-member sets of claims, coherence is a matter of positive probabilistic relevance and incoherence is a matter of negative probabilistic relevance has some initial plausibility. But, it runs counter to another idea with some initial plausibility—the idea that, at least with respect to two-member sets of claims, *maximal coherence* is a matter of *mutual entailment* (where the one claim entails the other claim, and where each claim has a probability greater than 0) and *maximal incoherence* is a matter of *incompatibility* (where the one claim entails the negation of the other claim). Suppose $S = \{p_1, p_2\}$. Suppose p_1 and p_2 are mutually entailing. Suppose $\Pr(p_1) = 1 = \Pr(p_2)$. Then, by the idea that maximal coherence is a matter of mutual entailment and maximal incoherence is a matter of incompatibility, it follows that S is maximally coherent. But, by the idea that coherence is a matter of positive probabilistic relevance and incoherence is a matter of negative probabilistic relevance, it follows that, since $\Pr(p_1|p_2) = \Pr(p_1) = 1$ and $\Pr(p_2|p_1) = \Pr(p_2) = 1$, S is neither coherent nor incoherent, hence is not maximally coherent.[40]

I prefer the idea that, at least with respect to two-member sets of claims, maximal coherence is a matter of mutual entailment and maximal incoherence is a matter of incompatibility.[41] One reason for this preference concerns sets of contradictory

[40]Meijs (2006, 237) gives an argument along these lines.

[41]In fact, I prefer the more general idea that *for any set with two or more members* maximal coherence is a matter of pairwise mutual entailment (where for each pair of claims in the set

claims. Recall $S_6 = \{f, \sim f\}$, where f is the claim that $2 + 2 = 4$. This set, as with any set of contradictory claims, is incoherent, in fact, arguably, is maximally incoherent. But, since $\Pr(f) = 1$ and $\Pr(\sim f) = 0$ and since, thus, it is *not* the case that f and $\sim f$ are negatively probabilistically relevant to each other (for one thing, $\Pr(\sim f \mid f) = 0 = \Pr(\sim f)$), it follows from the idea that coherence is a matter of positive probabilistic relevance and incoherence is a matter of negative probabilistic relevance that it is *not* the case that S_6 is incoherent. By contrast, because f and $\sim f$ are incompatible with each other, it follows from the idea that maximal coherence is a matter of mutual entailment and maximal incoherence is a matter of incompatibility that S_6 *is* incoherent, indeed, is maximally incoherent.[42]

(CF) is initially attractive because, in part, it implies each of the following:

(a) A set $S = \{p_1, p_2\}$ is maximally coherent if p_1 and p_2 are logically equivalent and S is satisfiable;
(b) A set $S = \{p_1, p_2\}$ is maximally incoherent if each of $\{p_1\}$, $\{p_2\}$, and $\{p_1, p_2\}$ is unsatisfiable;
(c) A set $S = \{p_1, p_2\}$ is coherent if S is "positively dependent," where S is positively dependent just in case (a) $f(p_1, p_2) > 0$ and (b) $f(p_2, p_1) > 0$;
(d) A set $S = \{p_1, p_2\}$ is incoherent if S is "negatively dependent," where S is negatively dependent just in case (a) $f(p_1, p_2) < 0$ and (b) $f(p_2, p_1) < 0$.

(a) and (b) capture the idea that maximal coherence is a matter of logical equivalence and maximal incoherence is a matter of unsatisfiability. This idea is similar to the idea that maximal coherence is a matter of mutual entailment and maximal incoherence is a matter of incompatibility. (c) and (d), in turn, capture the idea that coherence is a matter of positive support (or confirmation) and incoherence is a matter of negative support. This idea is similar to the idea that coherence is a

---

the one claim entails the other claim, and each claim has a probability greater than 0) and maximal incoherence is a matter of pairwise incompatibility (where for each pair of claims in the set the one claim entails the negation of the other claim).

[42]There are at least two further reasons for preferring the idea that maximal coherence is a matter of mutual entailment and maximal incoherence is a matter of incompatibility. First, if coherence is a matter of positive probabilistic relevance, it follows that no set of necessary truths is coherent. Hence no set of mathematical necessities is coherent, and no set of philosophical necessities is coherent (for example, no set of logical necessities is coherent), and so on. If, instead, maximal coherence is a matter of mutual entailment and maximal incoherence is a matter of incompatibility, it follows that all sets of necessary truths are coherent, indeed, maximally coherent. Second, if coherence is a matter of positive probabilistic relevance, it follows that there can be sets S and S^* such that the claims in S are mutually entailing, the claims in S^* are mutually entailing, and yet, because the prior probabilities of the claims in S are lower than the prior probabilities of the claims in S^*, S has a greater coherence value than S^*. If, instead, maximal coherence is a matter of mutual entailment and maximal incoherence is a matter of incompatibility, it follows that if the claims in S are mutually entailing and the claims in S^* are mutually entailing, then, regardless of the prior probabilities of the claims in S and S^*, S and S^* have the same coherence value. For helpful discussion of (CF), (CS), (CO), and the issue of "prior-dependence," see Glass (2005). See, also, Fitelson (2003, Sect. 2) and Siebel and Wolff (2008).

matter of positive probabilistic relevance and incoherence is a matter of negative probabilistic relevance. It turns out, though, that because (CF) implies each of (a)–(d) it yields some rather odd results.

This point is due to Meijs (2006). So too are the two remaining cases in this subsection: "*Rabbit*" and "*Rabbit**." First, I shall set out the cases and show what (CF) implies with respect to them. Then I shall show what (CR) implies with respect to them.

Suppose there is a small island somewhere in the Pacific Ocean with a population of 102 rabbits: 100 of the rabbits are grey and have two ears; one of the rabbits is grey and has one ear; one of the rabbits is albino and has two ears. Let this be Situation I. Suppose, instead, 100 of the rabbits are grey and have two ears, and two of the rabbits are albino and have one ear. Let this be Situation II. Let $S_{11} = \{g, e\}$, where:

g = This rabbit is grey;
e = This rabbit has two ears.

This case is *Rabbit*. (CF) implies that in Situation I, where S_{11} is negatively dependent, S_{11} is incoherent:

$$C_F(S_{11}) = \text{mean}(\{f(g,e), f(e,g)\})$$

$$= \frac{\dfrac{\Pr(e|g) - \Pr(e|\sim g)}{\Pr(e|g) + \Pr(e|\sim g)} + \dfrac{\Pr(g|e) - \Pr(g|\sim e)}{\Pr(g|e) + \Pr(g|\sim e)}}{2}$$

$$= \frac{\dfrac{100/101 - 1}{100/101 + 1} + \dfrac{100/101 - 1}{100/101 + 1}}{2} = -.005.$$

Things are quite different with respect to Situation II. (CF) implies that in Situation II, where g and e are logically equivalent (given the background information) and S_{11} is satisfiable, S_{11} is maximally coherent:

$$C_F(S_{11}) = \text{mean}(\{f(g,e), f(e,g)\}) = \frac{1+1}{2} = 1.$$

(CF) thus implies that S_{11} is incoherent in Situation I and is maximally coherent in Situation II, hence has a *very much greater* coherence value in Situation II. This is an odd result, given that the two situations differ hardly at all (in terms of rabbits and their properties). S_{11}, it seems, is coherent in Situation I, and, what is crucial, has just a *slightly* greater coherence value in Situation II.

This result, it turns out, does not depend on the number of two-eared grey rabbits. Suppose there are *ten million* rabbits on the island, where all but two of the rabbits are grey and have two ears, one of the other two rabbits is albino and has two ears, and the one remaining rabbit is grey and has one ear. Let this be Situation I. Suppose instead all but two of the rabbits are grey and have two ears, and the other two rabbits are albino and have one ear. Let this be Situation II. This case is *Rabbit**. In Situation I $C_F(S_{11}) < 0$:

$$C_F(S_{11}) = \text{mean}(\{f(g,e), f(e,g)\})$$

$$= \frac{\frac{\Pr(e|g) - \Pr(e|\sim g)}{\Pr(e|g) + \Pr(e|\sim g)} + \frac{\Pr(g|e) - \Pr(g|\sim e)}{\Pr(g|e) + \Pr(g|\sim e)}}{2}$$

$$= \frac{\frac{9999998/9999999 - 1}{9999998/9999999 + 1} + \frac{9999998/9999999 - 1}{9999998/9999999 + 1}}{2} = -.00000005.$$

In Situation II $C_F(S_{11}) = 1$:

$$C_F(S_{11}) = \text{mean}(\{f(g,e), f(e,g)\}) = \frac{1+1}{2} = 1.$$

So, (CF) yields the odd result that S_{11} is incoherent in Situation I, is maximally coherent in Situation II, and thus has a very much greater coherence value in Situation II.

How does (CR) do with *Rabbit* and *Rabbit**? In *Rabbit* in Situation I:

$$C_R(S_{11}) = \text{mean}(\{a(g,e), a(e,g)\})$$

$$= \frac{\Pr(g|e) + \Pr(e|g)}{2} = \frac{\frac{100}{101} + \frac{100}{101}}{2} = .990.$$

In *Rabbit* in Situation II:

$$C_R(S_{11}) = \text{mean}(\{a(g,e), a(e,g)\}) = \frac{1+1}{2} = 1.$$

In *Rabbit** in Situation I:

$$C_R(S_{11}) = \text{mean}(\{a(g,e), a(e,g)\})$$

$$= \frac{\Pr(g|e) + \Pr(e|g)}{2} = \frac{\frac{9999998}{9999999} + \frac{9999998}{9999999}}{2} = .9999999.$$

In *Rabbit** in Situation II:

$$C_R(S_{11}) = \text{mean}(\{a(g,e), a(e,g)\}) = \frac{1+1}{2} = 1.$$

S_{11} is thus coherent, indeed, highly coherent, in Situation I in *Rabbit*, and is slightly more coherent in Situation II in *Rabbit*. The same is true with respect to *Rabbit**.

The table below compares the various accounts with respect to *Rabbit* and *Rabbit**:

	Rabbit		Rabbit*	
	Situation I	Situation II	Situation I	Situation II
$C_S(S_{11})$	0.9999	1.02	0.99999999999999	1.0000002
$C_O(S_{11})$	0.980	1	0.9999998	1
$C_{DM}(S_{11})$	−0.0001	0.020	−0.00000000000001	0.0000002
$C_F(S_{11})$	−0.005	1	−0.00000005	1
$C_R(S_{11})$	0.990	1	0.9999999	1

(CS), (CO), and (CDM) agree with (CR) in implying that S_{11}'s coherence value is just slightly greater in Situation II in *Rabbit* than in Situation I in *Rabbit*, and is just slightly greater in Situation II in *Rabbit** than in Situation I in *Rabbit**. (CO), but neither (CS) nor (CDM), further agrees with (CR) in implying that S_{11}'s coherence value is high both in Situation I in *Rabbit* and in Situation I in *Rabbit**.

The claims in S_{10} are *negatively* probabilistically relevant to each other. Likewise, the claims in S_{11} both in Situation I in *Rabbit* and in Situation I in *Rabbit** are negatively probabilistically relevant to each other. I turn now to a case, "*Samurai Sword*," where the claims in the set at issue are *positively* probabilistically relevant to each other. I take the case from Douven and Meijs (2007, 414).

3.4.2.2 Samurai Sword

Suppose a murder has been committed on a street in a city with 10,000,000 inhabitants. One thousand fifty of the 10,000,000 inhabitants are Japanese and do not own a Samurai sword, 1,050 of the 10,000,000 inhabitants own a Samurai sword and are not Japanese, and just 9 of the 10,000,000 inhabitants are Japanese and own a Samurai sword. The murderer lives in the city and each person in the city is equally likely to be the murderer. Let this be Situation I. Suppose, instead, the murderer lives on the street on which the body was found, 100 people live on that street, 1 of the 100 people is Japanese and does not own a Samurai sword, 1 of the 100 people owns a Samurai sword and is not Japanese, and 9 of the 100 people are Japanese and own a Samurai sword. Let this be Situation II. Let $S_{12} = \{j, o\}$, where:

j = The murderer is Japanese;
o = The murderer owns a Samurai sword.

Intuitively, S_{12} has a greater coherence value in Situation II than in Situation I, indeed, has a *much* greater coherence value in Situation II than in Situation I. Furthermore, intuitively, S_{12} is *very far* from being maximally coherent in Situation I.

(CF), though, implies that S_{12} has a *just slightly* greater coherence value in Situation II than in Situation I, and that S_{12} is *nearly* maximally coherent in Situation I. In Situation I:

$$C_F(S_{12}) = \text{mean}(\{f(j,o), f(o,j)\})$$
$$= \frac{\frac{\Pr(o|j)-\Pr(o|\sim j)}{\Pr(o|j)+\Pr(o|\sim j)} + \frac{\Pr(j|o)-\Pr(j|\sim o)}{\Pr(j||o)+\Pr(j|\sim o)}}{2}$$
$$= \frac{\frac{9/1059-1050/9998941}{9/1059+1050/9998941} + \frac{9/1059-1050/9998941}{9/1059+1050/9998941}}{2} = .97559.$$

In Situation II:

$$C_F(S_{12}) = \text{mean}(\{f(j,o), f(o,j)\})$$
$$= \frac{\frac{\Pr(o|j)-\Pr(o|\sim j)}{\Pr(o|j)+\Pr(o|\sim j)} + \frac{\Pr(j|o)-\Pr(j|\sim o)}{\Pr(j|o)+\Pr(j|\sim o)}}{2}$$
$$= \frac{\frac{9/10-1/90}{9/10+1/90} + \frac{9/10-1/90}{9/10+1/90}}{2} = .97561.$$

(CR) does well with *Samurai Sword*. In Situation I:

$$C_R(S_{12}) = \text{mean}(\{a(j,o), a(o,j)\})$$
$$= \frac{\Pr(j|o)+\Pr(o|j)}{2} = \frac{9/1059+9/1059}{2} = .008.$$

In Situation II:

$$C_R(S_{12}) = \text{mean}(\{f(j,o), f(o,j)\})$$
$$= \frac{\Pr(j|o)+\Pr(o|j)}{2} = \frac{9/10+9/10}{2} = .9.$$

(CR) thus implies that S_{12} has a much greater coherence value in Situation II than in Situation I, and that S_{12} is very far from being maximally coherent in Situation I.

The table below compares the various accounts with respect to *Samurai Sword*:

	Samurai Sword	
	Situation I	Situation II
$C_S(S_{12})$	80.251	9
$C_O(S_{12})$	0.004	0.818
$C_{DM}(S_{12})$	0.008	0.8
$C_F(S_{12})$	0.97559	0.97561
$C_R(S_{12})$	0.008	0.9

(CO) and (CDM) agree with (CR) in implying that S_{12} has a much greater coherence value in Situation II than in Situation I, and that S_{12} is very far from being maximally coherent in Situation I. (CS), contra (CR) and each of the other accounts, implies that S_{12} has a lesser coherence value in Situation II than in Situation I.

3.4.3 *Some Additional Test Cases*

I now want to consider two additional test cases: "*Tweety*" and "*Tweety**."

Luc Bovens and Stephan Hartmann (2003a, b, 44–45, 50) argue that (CO) is counterintuitive. Let $S_{13} = \{b, g\}$ and $S_{14} = \{b, g, p\}$, where:

b = Tweety is a bird;
g = Tweety is a ground dweller;
p = Tweety is a penguin.

Suppose the probability distribution:

b	g	p	Pr	b	g	p	Pr
T	T	T	0.01	F	T	T	0
T	T	F	0	F	T	F	0.49
T	F	T	0	F	F	T	0
T	F	F	0.49	F	F	F	0.01

This case is *Tweety*. Intuitively, S_{14}'s coherence value is *greater than* S_{13}'s coherence value. (CO), however, implies that S_{14}'s coherence value is *equal to* S_{13}'s coherence value:

$$Co\,(S_{13}) = \frac{\Pr(b \wedge g)}{\Pr(b \vee g)} = \frac{.01}{.99};$$

$$Co\,(S_{14}) = \frac{\Pr(b \wedge g \wedge p)}{\Pr(b \vee g \vee p)} = \frac{.01}{.99}.$$

Douven and Meijs (2007, 416–417) argue that things are even worse for (CO). Suppose a slightly different probability distribution (on which the probability that Tweety is a ground-dwelling bird but not a penguin, for example, an ostrich, is greater than 0 but very small):

b	g	p	Pr	b	g	p	Pr
T	T	T	0.01	F	T	T	0
T	T	F	0.000001	F	T	F	0.49
T	F	T	0	F	F	T	0
T	F	F	0.49	F	F	F	0.009999

This case is *Tweety**. Intuitively, S_{14}'s coherence value is *greater than* S_{13}'s coherence value. But, if (CO) is correct, it follows that S_{14}'s coherence value is *less than* S_{13}'s coherence value:

$$C_{\rm O}(S_{13}) = \frac{\Pr(b \wedge g)}{\Pr(b \vee g)} = \frac{.010001}{.990001};$$

$$C_{\rm O}(S_{14}) = \frac{\Pr(b \wedge g \wedge p)}{\Pr(b \vee g \vee p)} = \frac{.01}{.990001}.$$

(CR) does well with *Tweety* and *Tweety**. In *Tweety*, $C_{\rm R}(S_{13}) < C_{\rm R}(S_{14})$:

$$\begin{aligned} C_{\rm R}(S_{13}) &= \text{mean}(\{a(b,g), a(g,b)\}) \\ &= \frac{\Pr(b\,|g) + \Pr(g \mid b)}{2} = \frac{.02 + .02}{2} = .02; \end{aligned}$$

$$\begin{aligned} C_{\rm R}(S_{14}) = \text{mean}(\{&a(b,g) + a(b,p) + a(g,b) + a(g,p) + a(p,b) \\ &+ a(p,g) + a(b, g \wedge p) + a(g, b \wedge p) + a(p, b \wedge g) + a(b \wedge g, p) \\ &+ a(b \wedge p, g) + a(g \wedge p, b)\}) \end{aligned}$$

$$= \frac{\begin{array}{c}\Pr(b\,|g) + 1 + \Pr(g\,|b) + 1 \\ + \Pr(p\,|b) + \Pr(p\,|g) + 1 + 1 \\ +1+1+\Pr(b \wedge p\,|g) + \Pr(g \wedge p\,|b)\end{array}}{12} = \frac{\begin{array}{c}.02+1+.02+1 \\ +.02+.02+1+1 \\ +1+1+.02+.02\end{array}}{12} = .51.$$

In *Tweety**, $C_{\rm R}(S_{13}) < C_{\rm R}(S_{14})$:

$$\begin{aligned} C_{\rm R}(S_{13}) &= \text{mean}(\{a(b,g), a(g,b)\}) \\ &= \frac{\Pr(b\,|g) + \Pr(g\,|b)}{2} = \frac{.020002 + .020002}{2} = .020002; \end{aligned}$$

$$\begin{aligned} C_{\rm R}(S_{14}) = \text{mean}(\{&a(b,g) + a(b,p) + a(g,b) + a(g,p) + a(p,b) \\ &+ a(p,g) + a(b, g \wedge p) + a(g, b \wedge p) + a(p, b \wedge g) \\ &+ a(b \wedge g, p) + a(b \wedge p, g) + a(g \wedge p, b)\}) \end{aligned}$$

$$= \frac{\begin{array}{c}\Pr(b\,|g) + 1 + \Pr(g\,|b) + 1 \\ + \Pr(p\,|b) + \Pr(p\,|g) + 1 + 1 \\ + \Pr(p|b \wedge g) + 1 + \Pr(b \wedge p|g) + \Pr(g \wedge p|b)\end{array}}{12}$$

$$= \frac{\begin{array}{c}.020002 + 1 + .020002 + 1 \\ + .02 + .02 + 1 + 1 \\ + .9999 + 1 + .02 + .02\end{array}}{12} = .509992.$$

The table below compares the various accounts with respect to *Tweety* and *Tweety**:

	Tweety	Tweety*
$C_S(S_{13})$	0.04	0.040004
$C_S(S_{14})$	4	3.99998
$C_O(S_{13})$	$\frac{.01}{.99}$	$\frac{.010001}{.990001}$
$C_O(S_{14})$	$\frac{.01}{.99}$	$\frac{.01}{.990001}$
$C_{DM}(S_{14})$	−0.48	−0.479999
$C_{DM}(S_{14})$	0.255	0.254991
$C_F(S_{13})$	−0.96	−0.959996
$C_F(S_{14})$	0.4526126	0.4526128
$C_R(S_{13})$	0.02	0.020002
$C_R(S_{14})$	0.51	0.509992

(CS), (CDM), and (CF) all agree with (CR) that S_{14}'s coherence value is greater than S_{13}'s coherence value both in *Tweety* and in *Tweety**.

3.4.4 Summary

In Sect. 3.4.1, I gave some problem cases for (CS), (CO), and (CDM), where each of the cases is unproblematic for (CR). In Sect. 3.4.2, I gave some problem cases for (CF), where each of the cases is unproblematic for (CR). In Sect. 3.4.3, I gave two additional test cases neither of which is problematic for (CR). It does *not* follow, of course, that (CR) is correct or even likely to be correct; more test cases need to be examined. But the results are at least suggestive.[43]

3.5 (CR) and the Problem of Justified Inconsistent Beliefs

I began the paper with the question of whether coherence is *necessary* for (epistemic) justification, in that one's beliefs are justified only if one's belief system is coherent. Standard varieties of coherentism imply that the answer is affirmative. In this section I relate (CR) to an argument for rejecting this answer and, in turn, for rejecting standard varieties of coherentism.

[43]Certain of the accounts, even if inadequate as accounts of coherence, can be useful nonetheless, for example, in contexts of confirmation. See Dietrich and Moretti (2005), for discussion of (CF), (CO), and (CS) and the transmission of confirmation.

3.5.1 Coherentism

Coherentism is distinct from foundationalism, social contextualism, and infinitism in that, *inter alia*, coherentism requires (for justification) a "circular" chain of implication (or evidential support):

> *Circular Chain of Implication* (CCI): *S*'s belief in *p* is justified only if (i) *S*'s belief in *p* is implied (deductively or inductively) by certain of her other beliefs, which themselves are implied by certain of her other beliefs, and so on, and (ii) this chain of evidential support circles back around at some point and does not continue on ad infinitum with new belief after new belief.

(CCI) should be understood so that (ii) does not require that the chain of implication in question literally take the shape of a circle, where, say, *S*'s belief in *p* is implied by her belief in *q*, which is implied by her belief in *r*, which is implied by her belief in *p*. It would be enough if, say, (a) *S*'s belief in *p* were implied by her belief in *q* together with her belief in *r*, (b) *S*'s belief in *q* were implied by her belief in *p* together with her belief in *r*, and (c) *S*'s belief in *r* were implied by her belief in *p* together with her belief in *q*.[44]

Coherentism comes in many varieties. Here is a fairly simple variety:

(C1) *S*'s belief in *p* is justified if and only if (i) *S*'s belief in *p* is implied by certain of her other beliefs, which themselves are implied by certain of her other beliefs, and so on, (ii) this chain of implication circles back around at some point and does not continue on ad infinitum, and (iii) *S*'s belief system is coherent.

(C1) should be understood so that whether *S*'s belief system is coherent is determined by whether the set of claims believed by *S* is coherent, and so that *S*'s belief in *p*, if justified, is justified by (that is, is made justified by) not certain of her other beliefs, but by the fact that (i)–(iii) are satisfied.[45]

The argument set out in the next subsection is spelled out in terms of (C1). But the argument can be generalized so that it applies to other varieties of coherentism. For example, the argument can be generalized so that it applies to varieties of coherentism on which what needs to be coherent is *S*'s system of beliefs *and perceptual experiences*.[46]

[44]For discussion of the "regress problem" and foundationalism, social contextualism, infinitism, and coherentism, and for references, see Cling (2008). It might be best to allow for varieties of coherentism on which some justification is noninferential, and thus on which it is *not* required for justification that (CCI) be satisfied. See Lycan (2012) and Poston (2012).

[45]A circular chain of *implication* should not be confused with a circular chain of *justification*. Coherentists (of the sort I have in mind) deny that justification is transferred between beliefs. Coherentists hold that justification is *holistic*: Beliefs are justified *together* when the requisite conditions are satisfied. For further discussion of this and related issues, see Roche (2012b).

[46]For discussion of varieties of coherentism of this sort, and for references, see Roche (2012b).

3.5.2 The Problem of Justified Inconsistent Beliefs

The Problem of Justified Inconsistent Beliefs (see Foley 1979) can be put as follows. (C1) implies:

(A) *S*'s belief in *p* is justified only if *S*'s belief system is coherent.

It seems obvious that:

(B) *S*'s belief system is coherent only if *S*'s belief system is consistent.[47]

(A) and (B) together imply:

(C) *S*'s belief in *p* is justified only if *S*'s belief system is consistent.

(C) implies that if *S*'s belief system is inconsistent, then *all* of *S*'s beliefs are *unjustified*.[48] But surely this implication is false. Consider, again, $S_8 = \{p_1, \ldots, p_n\}$ and $S_9 = \{p_1, \ldots, p_n, p_{n+1}\}$, where S_8 is very large and highly coherent (on any account of coherence), and where p_{n+1} is the necessary falsehood that 3^8 is greater than 6,562. Suppose Smith believes (all and only) the claims in S_8. Smith is listening to his math professor, who, as it turns out, is quite tired. Smith's math professor utters p_{n+1}. Smith knows his math professor to be highly reliable on matters mathematical, and so comes to believe p_{n+1}. Smith thus comes to believe the claims in S_9. Let's call this case "*Tired Math Professor*." Smith's belief system (when he believes the claims in S_9) is inconsistent, hence by (C) it follows that all of Smith's beliefs are unjustified. And yet, on certain ways of filling in the details, at least some of Smith's beliefs, e.g., at least some of Smith's perceptual beliefs, are justified. So, (C) is false. Therefore, given (B), it follows that (A) is false, hence (C1) is false. Or so the argument goes.[49]

Coherentists, let's suppose, should want to reject (C) and so should want to reject (A) or (B). The question is whether coherentists have a principled means of doing so.

3.5.3 (CR) and Inconsistency

I showed above (Sect. 3.4.1.3) that (CR) allows that S_9 can have a coherence value greater than the minimum value of 0. Perhaps (CR) also allows that S_9 can have a coherence value greater than 0.5. If so, coherentists can reject (B) on the grounds

[47] (B) should be understood so that whether *S*'s belief system is consistent is determined by whether the set of claims believed by *S* is consistent.

[48] (C), like (A), is fully general and so applies to *all* of *S*'s beliefs.

[49] There is a second version of the Problem of Justified Inconsistent Beliefs pertaining to lottery-style cases. See Kvanvig (2012) for an explanation of the problem and an attempted solution. Eric Senseman (2010), a former undergraduate student of mine (at Texas Christian University), considers a variant of (CR) and how that variant relates to the problem.

that (CR) is correct and (CR) implies that (B) is false. Further, coherentists can agree that at least some of Smith's beliefs, e.g., at least some of his perceptual beliefs, are justified. Does (CR) allow that S_9 can have a coherence value greater than 0.5?

The answer, unfortunately for proponents of views such as (C1), is negative. Suppose $C_R(S_8)$ has the maximum value of 1, so each of the confirmation values in S_8**** is equal to 1. Then, since (i) $a\ (\wedge S', \wedge S'') = 0$ for any $a\ (\wedge S', \wedge S'')$ such that (a) $a\ (\wedge S', \wedge S'')$ is a member of S_9**** and (b) $\wedge S'$ or $\wedge S''$ involves p_{n+1},[50] (ii) $C_R(S_9)$ is the mean of $3^{n+1}–2^{n+2} + 1$ confirmation values,[51] (iii) each of the confirmation values in S_9**** but not in S_8**** is equal to 0, and (iv) there are $3^n–2^{n+1} + 1$ remaining confirmation values in S_9**** and each one is equal to 1, it follows that:

$$C_R\,(S_9) = \frac{3^n - 2^{n+1} + 1}{3^{n+1} - 2^{n+2} + 1}.$$

$\frac{3^n-2^{n+1}+1}{3^{n+1}-2^{n+2}+1}$ approaches $\frac{1}{3}$ very quickly as n increases. Let $n = 2$, so $S_8 = \{p_1, p_2\}$ and $S_9 = \{p_1, p_2, p_3\}$. Then:

$$C_R\,(S_9) = \frac{3^2 - 2^3 + 1}{3^3 - 2^4 + 1} = \frac{9 - 8 + 1}{27 - 16 + 1} = \frac{2}{12} \approx .167.$$

This can also be seen by verifying that:

$$\begin{aligned} C_R\,(S_9) &= \text{mean}\,(\{a\,(p_1, p_2) + a\,(p_1, p_3) + a\,(p_2, p_1) + a\,(p_2, p_3) + a\,(p_3, p_1) \\ &\quad + a\,(p_3, p_2) + a\,(p_1, p_2 \wedge p_3) + a\,(p_2, p_1 \wedge p_3) + a\,(p_3, p_1 \wedge p_2) \\ &\quad + a\,(p_1 \wedge p_2, p_3) + a\,(p_1 \wedge p_3, p_2) + a\,(p_2 \wedge p_3, p_1)\}) \\ &= \frac{1+0+1+0+0+0+0+0+0+0+0+0}{12} = \frac{2}{12} \approx .167. \end{aligned}$$

When $n = 3$, $C_R\,(S_9) = \frac{12}{50} = .24$. When $n = 4$, $C_R\,(S_9) = \frac{50}{180} \approx .278$. When $n = 5$, $C_R\,(S_9) = \frac{180}{602} \approx .299$.... When $n = 10$, $C_R\,(S_9) = \frac{57002}{173052} \approx .329$. But, regardless of the size of n (though given the constraint that $2 \leq n < \infty$ where $n \in \mathbb{N}$), $\frac{3^n-2^{n+1}+1}{3^{n+1}-2^{n+2}+1} < \frac{1}{3} < .5$.[52] So, regardless of the size of n, it follows that $C_R(S_9) < 0.5$. Thus, since $C_R(S_9) < 0.5$ in the best case where $C_R(S_8) = 1$, it follows that $C_R(S_9) < 0.5$ in lesser cases where $C_R(S_8) < 1$.

[50]If $\wedge S'$ involves p_{n+1}, $\wedge S'' \vDash \sim \wedge S'$. If $\wedge S''$ involves p_{n+1}, $\wedge S'' \vDash \sim \wedge S'$.

[51]Recall (from Sect. 3.3.3) that where $S = \{p_1, \ldots, p_n\}$, $C_X(S)$ is the mean of $3^n–2^{n+1} + 1$ confirmation values. Thus where $S = \{p_1, \ldots, p_n, p_{n+1}\}$, $C_X(S)$ is the mean of $3^{n+1}–2^{n+2} + 1$ confirmation values.

[52]This follows from the fact that (i) $\frac{3^n-2^{n+1}+1}{3^{n+1}-2^{n+2}+1} < \frac{1}{3}$ when $n = 2$, (ii) $\frac{3^n-2^{n+1}+1}{3^{n+1}-2^{n+2}+1}$ is a strictly increasing function of n (given the constraint that $2 \leq n < \infty$ where $n \in \mathbb{N}$), and (iii) $\lim_{n\to\infty} \frac{3^n-2^{n+1}+1}{3^{n+1}-2^{n+2}+1} = \frac{1}{3}$.

The lesson is that, though (CR) allows that S_9 can have a coherence value greater than the minimum value of 0, (CR) does not allow that S_9 can have a coherence value greater than 0.5. (CR), thus, does not provide coherentists with a principled means of answering the Problem of Justified Inconsistent Beliefs.

I leave it for further inquiry whether one can accept a probabilistic account of coherence and yet avoid (C) by rejecting (B).[53] I want to consider whether coherentists can accept (CR) and, still, avoid (C) by rejecting (A). I aim to show that the answer is affirmative.

3.5.4 Nonglobal Coherentism

Proponents of (C1) are "globalist" coherentists, in that they require that *S*'s belief system *as a whole* be coherent. Coherentists per se, however, need not be globalists. Coherentists can be "nonglobalists" and hold that justification requires not that *S*'s belief system as a whole be coherent, but that a certain perhaps *proper* subset of *S*'s belief system be coherent.[54] Consider the view:

(C2) *S*'s belief in *p* is justified if and only if (i) *S*'s belief in *p* is implied by certain of her other beliefs, which themselves are implied by certain of her other beliefs, and so on, (ii) this chain of implication circles back around at some point and does not continue on ad infinitum, and (iii) the *p*-subset of *S*'s belief system is coherent.

The "*p*-subset" of *S*'s belief system is the subset of his belief system *relevant* to the justification of his belief in *p*. If not all of *S*'s belief system is relevant to the justification of his belief in *p*, then the *p*-subset of *S*'s belief system is a *proper* subset of his belief system, and so (iii) in (C2) can be satisfied even if *S*'s belief system as a whole is not coherent. (C2) thus opens the way for coherentists to reject (C), along with (A), and allow for cases in which *S*'s belief system as a whole is inconsistent, and incoherent, and yet certain of *S*'s beliefs are justified.[55]

Let's return to *Tired Math Professor*. Suppose Smith's belief in p_1 is a perceptual belief. Suppose, as seems plausible, Smith's belief in p_{n+1} is not a member of the p_1-subset of Smith's belief system. Suppose (CR) is correct, and by (CR) the

---

[53] One possibility would be to understand probability so that Pr(*p*) can be greater than 0 even if *p* is a necessary falsehood (and so that Pr(*p*) can be less than 1 even if *p* is a necessary truth). For relevant discussion, see Chalmers (2011), Douven and Meijs (2007, Sect. 5.1), Garber (1983), and Swinburne (1973, Chap. 4). See, also, Kvanvig (2012, Sect. 2) and Lycan (1996, Sect. VII; 2012, Sect. 7).

[54] See Lycan (1996, 2012) and Olsson (1997).

[55] For discussion of an alternative way for coherentists to reject (C), even when (C) is construed not in terms of the notion of *belief* but in terms of the notion of *acceptance*, see Lehrer (1999). Cf. Olsson (1999).

p_1-subset of Smith's belief system is coherent. Suppose, finally, (i) and (ii) in (C2) are satisfied. Then, even though Smith's belief system as a whole is inconsistent, (C2) implies that Smith's belief in p_1 is justified.

A difficult question for proponents of a view such as (C2) is of which of *S*'s beliefs are in the *p*-subset of his belief system. Here I will not try to answer that question.[56] The main point is just that, by accepting a view such as (C2), coherentists can accept (CR) and still allow that in cases such as *Tired Math Professor* certain of the subject's beliefs are justified.

3.6 Conclusion

I have developed a probabilistic account of coherence, (CR), and argued that at least in certain respects it is preferable to Douven and Meijs's account, (CDM), Fitelson's account, (CF), Olsson's account, (CO), and Shogenji's account, (CS). Further, I have argued that (CR) does not provide coherentists with a principled means of answering the Problem of Justified Inconsistent Beliefs, and that nonetheless coherentists can accept (CR) and potentially answer the Problem of Justified Inconsistent Beliefs by rejecting globalist varieties of coherentism such as (C1) in favor of nonglobalist varieties such as (C2).

Acknowledgments I wish to thank Michał Araszkiewicz, Kyle Kloster, Michael Roche, Eric Senseman, and the participants in the Artificial Intelligence, Coherence and Judicial Reasoning Workshop at ICAIL 2011 (the 13th International Conference on Artificial Intelligence and Law) for helpful comments on or discussion of ancestors of this paper. Further, I wish to thank Igor Douven, Kyle Kloster, and Eric Senseman for helpful correspondence on some of the issues discussed in the paper and related issues.

References

Akiba, K. 2000. Shogenji's probabilistic measure of coherence is incoherent. *Analysis* 60: 356–359.
Angere, S. 2007. The defeasible nature of coherentist justification. *Synthese* 157: 321–335.
Angere, S. 2008. Coherence as a heuristic. *Mind* 117: 1–26.
BonJour, L. 1985. *The structure of empirical knowledge*. Cambridge: Harvard University Press.
Bovens, L., and S. Hartmann. 2003a. *Bayesian epistemology*. Oxford: Oxford University Press.
Bovens, L., and S. Hartmann. 2003b. Solving the riddle of coherence. *Mind* 112: 601–633.
Bovens, L., and S. Hartmann. 2005. Why there cannot be a single probabilistic measure of coherence. *Erkenntnis* 63: 361–374.
Bovens, L., and S. Hartmann. 2006. An impossibility result for coherence rankings. *Philosophical Studies* 128: 77–91.
Bovens, L., and E. Olsson. 2000. Coherentism, reliability and Bayesian networks. *Mind* 109: 685–719.

[56] I take up the question elsewhere Roche (2011). See, too, Kvanvig (2012, Sect. 2).

Bovens, L., and E. Olsson. 2002. Believing more, risking less: On coherence, truth and non-trivial extensions. *Erkenntnis* 57: 137–150.

Chalmers, D. 2011. Frege's puzzle and the objects of credence. *Mind* 120: 587–635.

Cling, A. 2008. The epistemic regress problem. *Philosophical Studies* 140: 401–421.

Cross, C. 1999. Coherence and truth conducive justification. *Analysis* 59: 186–193.

Crupi, V., K. Tentori, and M. Gonzalez. 2007. On Bayesian measures of evidential support: Theoretical and empirical issues. *Philosophy of Science* 74: 229–252.

Day, T., and H. Kincaid. 1994. Putting inference to the best explanation in its place. *Synthese* 98: 271–295.

Dietrich, F., and L. Moretti. 2005. On coherent sets and the transmission of confirmation. *Philosophy of Science* 72: 403–424.

Douven, I. 1999. Inference to the best explanation made coherent. *Philosophy of Science* 66: S424–S435. Proceedings.

Douven, I. 2011. Abduction. In *The Stanford encyclopedia of philosophy*, ed. E. Zalta (published March 2011). http://plato.stanford.edu/entries/abduction/. Accessed 1 June 2012.

Douven, I., and W. Meijs. 2007. Measuring coherence. *Synthese* 156: 405–425.

Eells, E., and B. Fitelson. 2002. Symmetries and asymmetries in evidential support. *Philosophical Studies* 107: 129–142.

Eliasmith, C., and P. Thagard. 1997. Waves, particles, and explanatory coherence. *The British Journal for the Philosophy of Science* 48: 1–19.

Fitelson, B. 2003. A probabilistic theory of coherence. *Analysis* 63: 194–199.

Fitelson, B. 2004. Two technical corrections to my coherence measure. fitelson.org/coherence2.pdf.

Fitelson, B. 2008. A decision procedure for probability calculus with applications. *Review of Symbolic Logic* 1: 111–125.

Foley, R. 1979. Justified inconsistent beliefs. *American Philosophical Quarterly* 16: 247–257.

Garber, D. 1983. Old evidence and logical omniscience in Bayesian confirmation theory. *Minnesota Studies in the Philosophy of Science* 10: 99–131.

Glass, D. 2005. Problems with priors in probabilistic measures of coherence. *Erkenntnis* 63: 375–385.

Harman, G. 1970. Induction: A discussion of the relevance of the theory of knowledge to the theory of induction (with a digression to the effect that neither deductive logic nor the probability calculus has anything to do with inference). In *Induction, acceptance, and rational belief*, ed. M. Swain, 83–99. Dordrecht: Reidel.

Huemer, M. 1997. Probability and coherence justification. *Southern Journal of Philosophy* 35: 463–472.

Huemer, M. 2007. Weak Bayesian coherentism. *Synthese* 157: 337–346.

Huemer, M. 2009a. Explanationist aid for the theory of inductive logic. *British Journal for the Philosophy of Science* 60: 345–375.

Huemer, M. 2009b. When is parsimony a virtue? *The Philosophical Quarterly* 59: 216–236.

Huemer, M. 2011. Does probability theory refute coherentism? *Journal of Philosophy* 108: 35–54.

Iranzo, V. 2008. Bayesianism and inference to the best explanation. *Theoria* 61: 89–106.

Kemeny, J., and P. Oppenheim. 1952. Degree of factual support. *Philosophy of Science* 19: 307–324.

Klein, P., and T. Warfield. 1994. What price coherence? *Analysis* 43: 129–132.

Klein, P., and T. Warfield. 1996. No help for the coherentist. *Analysis* 56: 118–121.

Kvanvig, J. 2012. Coherentism and justified inconsistent beliefs: a solution. *Southern Journal of Philosophy* 50: 21–41.

Lehrer, K. 1999. Justification, coherence and knowledge. *Erkenntnis* 50: 243–258.

Lewis, C.I. 1946. *An analysis of knowledge & valuation*. La Salle: Open Court.

Lipton, P. 2001. Is explanation a guide to inference? A reply to Wesley C. Salmon. In *Explanation: Theoretical approaches and applications*, ed. G. Hon and S. Rakover, 93–120. Dordrecht: Kluwer.

Lipton, P. 2004. *Inference to the best explanation*, 2nd ed. London: Routledge.

Lombrozo, T. 2007. Simplicity and probability in causal explanation. *Cognitive Psychology* 55: 232–257.
Lycan, W. 1996. Plantinga and coherentisms. In *Warrant in contemporary epistemology: Essays in honor of Plantinga's theory of knowledge*, ed. J. Kvanvig, 3–23. Lanham: Rowman & Littlefield.
Lycan, W. 2012. Explanationist rebuttals (coherentism defended again). *Southern Journal of Philosophy* 50: 5–20.
McGrew, T. 2003. Confirmation, heuristics, and explanatory reasoning. *British Journal for the Philosophy of Science* 54: 553–567.
Meijs, W. 2006. Coherence as generalized logical equivalence. *Erkenntnis* 64: 231–252.
Meijs, W., and I. Douven. 2007. On the alleged impossibility of coherence. *Synthese* 157: 347–360.
Merricks, T. 1995. On behalf of the coherentist. *Analysis* 55: 306–309.
Niiniluoto, I. 1999. Defending abduction. *Philosophy of Science* 66: S436–S451. Proceedings.
Niiniluoto, I. 2004. Truth-seeking by abduction. In *Induction and deduction in the sciences*, ed. F. Stadler, 57–82. Dordrecht: Kluwer.
Okasha, S. 2000. Van Fraassen's critique of inference to the best explanation. *Studies in History and Philosophy of Science* 31: 691–710.
Olsson, E. 1997. Coherence and the modularity of mind. *Australasian Journal of Philosophy* 75: 404–411.
Olsson, E. 1999. Cohering with. *Erkenntnis* 50: 273–291.
Olsson, E. 2001. Why coherence is not truth-conducive. *Analysis* 61: 236–241.
Olsson, E. 2002. What is the problem of coherence and truth? *Journal of Philosophy* 99: 246–272.
Olsson, E. 2005a. *Against coherence: Truth, probability and justification*. Oxford: Oxford University Press.
Olsson, E. 2005b. The impossibility of coherence. *Erkenntnis* 63: 387–412.
Olsson, E., and T. Shogenji. 2004. Can we trust our memories? C. I. Lewis's coherence argument. *Synthese* 142: 21–41.
Poston, T. 2012. Basic reasons and first philosophy: a coherentist view of reasons. *Southern Journal of Philosophy* 50: 75–93.
Psillos, S. 2004. Inference to the best explanation and Bayesianism. In *Induction and deduction in the sciences*, ed. F. Stadler, 83–91. Dordrecht: Kluwer.
Psillos, S. 2007. The fine structure of inference to the best explanation. *Philosophy and Phenomenological Research* 74: 441–448.
Roche, W. 2010. Coherentism, truth, and witness agreement. *Acta Analytica* 25: 243–257.
Roche, W. 2011. Coherentism and inconsistency. *Southwest Philosophy Review* 27: 185–193.
Roche, W. 2012a. Witness agreement and the truth-conduciveness of coherentist justification. *Southern Journal of Philosophy* 50: 151–169.
Roche, W. 2012b. A reply to Cling's 'the epistemic regress problem'. *Philosophical Studies* 159: 263–276.
Salmon, W. 1970. Bayes's theorem and the history of science. *Minnesota Studies in the Philosophy of Science* 5: 68–86.
Salmon, W. 1990. Rationality and objectivity in science *or* Tom Kuhn meets Tom Bayes. *Minnesota Studies in the Philosophy of Science* 14: 175–204.
Salmon, W. 2001a. Explanation and confirmation: A Bayesian critique of inference to the best explanation. In *Explanation: Theoretical approaches and applications*, ed. G. Hon and S. Rakover, 121–136. Dordrecht: Kluwer.
Salmon, W. 2001b. Reflections of a bashful Bayesian: A reply to Lipton. In *Explanation: Theoretical approaches and applications*, ed. G. Hon and S. Rakover, 61–91. Dordrecht: Kluwer.
Schubert, S. 2012. Coherence reasoning and reliability: A defense of the Shogenji measure. *Synthese* 187: 305–319.
Schubert, S., and E. Olsson. 2012. On the coherence of higher-order beliefs. *Southern Journal of Philosophy* 50: 112–135.

Schupbach, J. 2008. On the alleged impossibility of Bayesian coherentism. *Philosophical Studies* 141: 323–331.
Schupbach, J. 2011. New hope for Shogenji's coherence measure. *The British Journal for the Philosophy of Science* 62: 125–142.
Senseman, E. 2010. The problem of justified inconsistent beliefs: A case for coherentism. Unpublished manuscript.
Shogenji, T. 1999. Is coherence truth conducive? *Analysis* 59: 338–345.
Shogenji, T. 2001. Reply to Akiba on the probabilistic measure of coherence. *Analysis* 61: 147–150.
Shogenji, T. 2005. Justification by coherence from scratch. *Philosophical Studies* 125: 305–325.
Shogenji, T. 2007. Why does coherence appear truth-conducive? *Synthese* 157: 361–372.
Shogenji, T. (Forthcoming). Coherence of the contents and the transmission of probabilistic support. *Synthese*.
Siebel, M. 2004. On Fitelson's measure of coherence. *Analysis* 64: 189–190.
Siebel, M. 2005. Against probabilistic measures of coherence. *Erkenntnis* 63: 335–360.
Siebel, M. 2011. Why explanation and thus coherence cannot be reduced to probability. *Analysis* 71: 264–266.
Siebel, M., and W. Wolff. 2008. Equivalent testimonies as a touchstone of coherence measures. *Synthese* 161: 167–182.
Sober, E. 2002. Bayesianism—Its scope and limits. In *Bayes's theorem*, ed. R. Swinburne, 21–38. Cambridge: Cambridge University Press.
Swinburne, R. 1973. *An introduction to confirmation theory*. London: Methuen.
Thagard, P. 1989a. Explanatory coherence. *The Behavioral and Brain Sciences* 12: 435–467.
Thagard, P. 1989b. Author's response. *The Behavioral and Brain Sciences* 12: 490–499.
Thagard, P. 1992. *Conceptual revolutions*. Princeton: Princeton University Press.
Thagard, P. 2000. *Coherence in thought and action*. Cambridge: MIT Press.
Thagard, P. 2004. Causal inference in legal decision making: explanatory coherence vs. Bayesian networks. *Applied Artificial Intelligence* 18: 231–249.
Thagard, P. 2012. Coherence: the price is right. *Southern Journal of Philosophy* 50: 42–49.
Thagard, P., and G. Nowak. 1988. The explanatory coherence of continental drift. *PSA: Proceedings of the Biennial Meeting of the Philosophy of Science Association* 1988, 118–126.
Thagard, P., and K. Verbeurgt. 1998. Coherence as constraint satisfaction. *Cognitive Science* 22: 1–24.
Tregear, M. 2004. Utilising explanatory factors in induction? *The British Journal for the Philosophy of Science* 55: 505–519.
van Cleve, J. 2005. Why coherence is not enough: A defense of moderate foundationalism. In *Contemporary debates in epistemology*, ed. M. Steup and E. Sosa, 168–180. Malden: Blackwell.
van Cleve, J. 2011. Can coherence generate warrant *ex nihilo*? Probability and the logic of concurring witnesses. *Philosophy and Phenomenological Research* 82: 337–380.
van Fraassen, B. 1989. *Laws and symmetry*. Oxford: Oxford University Press.
Weisberg, J. 2009. Locating IBE in the Bayesian framework. *Synthese* 167: 125–143.
Wheeler, G. 2009. Focused correlation and confirmation. *The British Journal for the Philosophy of Science* 60: 79–100.
Wheeler, G. 2012. Explaining the limits of Olsson's impossibility result. *Southern Journal of Philosophy* 50: 136–150.

Chapter 4
Coherence: An Outline in Six Metaphors and Four Rules

Juan Manuel Pérez Bermejo

From the beginning, the art of the jigsaw looks brief and simple [. . .]: the object at stake . . . is not a list of elements which we should first isolate or analyze; it is an ensemble, one form, one structure: the knowledge of the whole set, of its laws, structure and composition, cannot be deduced from the knowledge of each of its separate pieces. It means that we can stay for days observing one piece of a jigsaw, believing that we know everything about its colour and configuration, and in fact having made no progress: only the fit of this piece with the others matter. There is a resemblance in this description between the art of the jigsaw and the game of go: only the combined pieces have an intelligible sense.

George Perec: *La vie mode d'emploi,* Preambule.

4.1 Introduction

There are nowadays many legal theories relying on 'coherence' as one of the main tests of legal reasoning. We do not need to elaborate any list of coherentist authors in order to confirm this statement; it is enough to recall some explicit and well-known declarations of its truth, such as 'coherence is in vogue' (Raz 1992, 273) or 'we are all coherentists now' (Edmundson 1994, 1).

It is possible to argue that coherence is in vogue among lawyers; if so, it is also certain that they lack a firm and solid idea about its meaning. We still debate whether coherence is a mere synonym of consistency or non-contradiction; any consensus

J.M. Pérez Bermejo (✉)
University of Salamanca, Calle Luis Sala Balust. N34 3E, Salamanca 37006, ES, Spain
e-mail: jbermejo@usal.es

M. Araszkiewicz and J. Šavelka (eds.), *Coherence: Insights from Philosophy, Jurisprudence and Artificial Intelligence*, Law and Philosophy Library 107,
DOI 10.1007/978-94-007-6110-0_4,

on its main demands looks unavailable and, considering this unsafe background, it is understandable that elaborated applications of the concept of coherence to the particular problems of legal philosophy have not been broadly developed.[1]

This situation is also visible in general philosophy. In epistemology, the coherentist theories did not suggest a set of precise rules able to determine when a belief is justified. In some cases, when in need of some clarification, these theories were satisfied with vague images or common places such as 'mutual support', 'explanative power' or 'reciprocal consistency'.[2] In other cases, either because of the complexity of the term, or in order to drive away the standard logic, the project of elucidating the concept is barely ruled out.[3]

However, it is sensible to assume that such a prolific and assorted philosophical literature might obey some common patterns; perhaps these patterns have not been formulated yet in some accurate and satisfying terms, but it does not imply their inexistence. The purpose of this essay is to examine the coherentist philosophical literature, especially the legal one, and shed some light on the implicit demands involved in the value or aspiration of coherence. The final target is to formulate the standards that could distinguish the 'coherent' conclusion of a particular legal reasoning from the others. However, as will be clear throughout the essay, the most we can aspire to is to outline some generic guidelines.

It must be admitted that, despite all the uncertainties expressed above, we already know a relatively clear guide concerning the scope of any reasoning aiming for coherence. This guide is usually designated with the term 'holism'. Coherentist reasoning must be 'holistic' because it requires adopting a global view which encompasses the whole system of reference, the legal system in our domain. If statement x is justified in system S, it is not because of its special connection with a limited subset of elements: it is because x provides a higher state of coherence than its rivals; a state attributed to the whole S. In other words: coherence is a property of the system as a whole, and a statement is justified only if its inclusion brings about a higher degree of coherence than its rivals in the system globally considered. Obviously, to disentangle these ideas would require a separate investigation. We will

[1]In legal theory, the accusation of obscurity is frequent: 'Although Dworkin and Sartorius rely on the concept of coherence, they do not explicate it'. Baum-Levenbook (1984, 355).

[2]The classical coherentists, e.g. Bradley, Bosanquet or Joachim, repeat expressions like *hang together* or *fit well with one another*. Their ambiguity deserved the classical criticism by Ewing (1934, 246). It is also denounced that, although the coherentist authors constantly remark that 'coherence' is more than mere 'consistency', they never explain the meaning of this addition. Bartleborth (1999, 210), Millgram (2000, 82), Bovens and Hartmann (2003, 602).

[3]For Putnam (1982, 133), 'coherence' is not explainable by algorithms: it is something we judge 'by seat of the pants' feel'.

assume that in this essay 'holism' is a right guide of coherence, and, more important, we assume its validity in epistemic,[4] moral[5] and legal[6] coherentist theories.

Notwithstanding, 'holism' is insufficient to elucidate 'coherence'. This is proved by the existence of holistic, but not coherentist theories, some of them in sheer contradiction with important tenets of coherentism, such as the denial of 'canonical' or not revisable elements (Peacocke 1999, 223). We know that any reasoning's conclusion is justified when it positively contributes to the coherence of the system as a whole. However, we still need to decipher upon which this positive contribution depends, and why this conclusion exhibits this title unlike the rest of the candidates. In other words, we need to disclose and formulate the proper demands, guidelines or criteria involved in the concept of coherence.

Unfortunately, this task faces two severe obstacles:

1. The criteria of coherence of a proposition with the other elements of a system depend upon the type of system at stake, especially upon its goal or purpose and its context of development. The set of the pieces of furniture of my house, the different plans for my weekend, my beliefs on climate change, the sentences of a novel or the norms of a legal system obey too different contexts and goals, and it would be difficult to belief that all these systems might obey the same patterns of reasoning. A well contrived novel is normally false, but it does not prevent it from being coherent; we cannot extend this view to my system of epistemic beliefs. To apply the criteria fitting a system to a different one could provoke something similar to the medical rejection proper of an incompatible organ in a foreign body.[7]

   However, this first difficulty is not deterring. It is true that coherence depends upon first-rank criteria that can change in every system. However, it is still possible to search second-rank criteria, 'criteria on criteria' or, as is usual in practical reasoning, values for the organization of other values (McFall 1987, 13). It could be true that any kind of system owns its particular criteria of coherence, but this is compatible with an overarching or unifying view.
2. Coherentist literature is lavish with metaphors: gains in clarity and transparency do not last long, and are soon replaced by new images and comparisons. It is true that, sometimes, the metaphoric resource is an evasive instrument to sidestep demands of accuracy. However, we may think that some of these images are an

[4]Bradley (1914, 223), BonJour (1985, 92), Harman (1973, 160). In the classical Quine's words (1951, 41), 'our statements above the external world face the tribunal of sense-experience not individually, but as a corporate body'.

[5]Brink (2001, 123).

[6]Hoffmaster (1980), MacCormick (1993, 24), Sartorius (1968, 135). 'Legal interpretation is inherently holist, even when the apparent target of interpretation is a single sentence or even a single clause rather than a document'. Dworkin (1996b, 80). I analyzed holistic theories' problems in law in Pérez Bermejo (2007).

[7]Millgram (2000, 85–6). That is why he demands 'sensitivity' towards the internal structure of the analized system, its connections and incompatibilities.

expressive way of condensing rules and patterns of coherence. If this is true, we might turn one of the defects of the coherentist theories into a virtue: a work of philosophical formulation could dip into these metaphors and specify the rules that underlie their images. This is precisely what will be developed in the following sections. From the numerous metaphors we can read in coherentist literature, the next section will select six, which will be introduced and briefly paraphrased; four of these metaphors derive from epistemology, another from political theory, while the remaining one comes from legal theory.[8] The third section will intend to assess these paraphrases and to formulate a minimal code of criteria for any coherentist reasoning. These criteria can only aspire to point to general directions, and cannot be proposed as an accurate formula: this latter goal clearly exceeds the possibilities of this outline.

4.2 The Concept of Coherence in Six Metaphors

4.2.1 The Raft

The first metaphor became a kind of coherentism's logo,[9] and has got a classical formulation due to Neurath: 'we are like sailors who have to rebuild their ship on the open sea, without ever being able to dismantle it in dry dock and reconstruct it from the best components' (Neurath 1959, 203). As it is well known, this formula aimed at Carnap's belief in the existence of some foundational propositions which he named 'protocols'. These propositions were interpreted as direct perceptions such as 'X perceived the f phenomenon in the p place and at a t time'. According to Carnap, they constitute the first link in all our chains of knowledge, and any quest for their justification is meaningless, because that question would necessarily point at something beyond our empirical perception (Neurath 1959, 201–2). The target of Neurath's image is a specific view of science where any particular scientific domain is founded on a set of incorrigible certainties. His well-known criticism states that any new proposition—either a theorem, a corollary or a protocol—is fallible and revisable because it is judged by the tribunal of our whole system of beliefs.[10]

More interesting for us is the image as a description of our knowledge: this is not delivered in harbour as a completely manufactured good, with definite pieces and assembly. Some pieces might be very reliable, but none of them are totally guaranteed for the whole journey. A raft is a device which we have to reform and remodel during the sailing and according to the needs and events of the journey.

[8]We leave aside many others. Dworkin (1996a, 119), e.g., resorts to the geodesic dome: our whole intellectual structure is not a pyramid, but a dome where all the elements support each other.

[9]See 'The Raft and the Pyramid' (Sosa 1980).

[10]'There is no *tabula rasa* . . . The fate of being discarded may befall a protocol statement'. Neurath (1959, 203).

Obviously, this image is successful because it is able to grasp a deep and substantial message. It describes our systems of knowledge, either theoretical or practical, as works in progress nourished by the practice, its aims and the action of any user. Secondly, it denies the existence of canonical or incorrigible elements within any system: there is not any axiom in S; any element could be removed or sacrificed, and, as Neurath remarked, none of them enjoys any kind of noli me tangere (Neurath 1959, 203).

4.2.2 The Net

This image describes the structure and organization of the coherentist systems. Its users sometimes assume the model of neurology in a more or less explicit way. This model describes the working of the human brain as a system of highly interconnected cells or neurons, sustained through the mutual support of all its elements and permanently open to learning by reacting to any external input. Taking the image strictly, any system of knowledge should be organized like a neural artificial system.[11] In the most usual application, the image is not involved in the neurological context, but it retains the ideas of 'interconnection', 'mutual support', 'outward look' and 'complexity'.

We judge the net for the strength or the resilience provided by the joining or the assembly of its nodes. Likewise, a basic aspiration of any coherentist system is the highest degree of interweaving or interconnection of all its elements.[12]

These features of interconnection and mutual support are precisely the rules of admission or rejection in the system for any candidate to join it: the candidate is admitted if it provides a denser or thicker structure of connections and inferences and, unlike its rivals, reduces the risks of isolation or fragmentation. Therefore, the net provides a double and interdependent approach to evaluate any possible conclusion: we search for the conclusion that is inferred or grounded by the largest number of elements and connections, but also the one that provides a better support or a better explanation for all the elements of the system.

The ideal is that everything is related to everything else, so that any element could be called for the justification of any other: the net stresses the idea of solidarity. The problem of justification cannot be solved locally or appealing to some few elements of the system: it is typically a holistic problem, and involves the whole set. Therefore the system is not divided into independent chains or branches of justification. Our knowledge is not like a tree-diagram in which, from a set of foundations, the rest

---

[11]The model of neurology has been successful in some sciences, e.g. robotics and cybernetics. See Carling (1992), Haykin (1999). In epistemology, a defender of this approach is Paul Thagard.

[12]See the image of the net in Spohn (1999, 162), Fritzman (1992, 184). In legal theory, see Alexy and Peczenik (1990, 136).

of the statements are represented as top-down outcomes distributed in hierarchic levels. Explained as a tree-diagram, the system of our knowledge is split into a set of independent chains. They are independent because they only share the first links, the most basic principles of any particular scientific domain. Consequently, any problem concerning a particular chain must be restrictively solved in that chain, because it is assumed that the service which might be payable by any other chain would be meagre. This image contradicts the net's principles of interconnection, mutual support and collective solidarity,[13] where any element can contribute to the justification of the rest. The net may possibly have some priority rules that confer more importance upon some elements; however, the more important elements can also be judged or evaluated from the perspective of the others, and these inferior ones can also contribute to justify the prima facie superiors.[14] Independent justifying chains do not exist in the net. Strictly speaking, all the elements or propositions belong to all the possible chains of justification.[15]

Finally, a net system is open or prone to learning. The system faces the new problems by learning from the environment and increasing its complexity. The system must aspire to be exhaustive and complete in order to give an answer to the problems of its competence and fulfil its functions. It will possibly force the system to include new elements which might not be consistent with its current composition, but bestow a higher interconnection and, therefore, a better working. The admission of new elements will demand a reformulation of the starting formation of the system, which will mean to reorganize its inferences and to dispense with some elements which could become inconsistent. The net is specifically organized to permit these operations,[16] so that the system can be successfully self-corrected.

4.2.3 The Jigsaw

The net was a more appropriate image to explain the morphology of a coherentist system. The jigsaw is mainly a metaphor on the works of judgment and justification we develop when operating within a system, and on the procedures of selection, admission and rejection of new elements.

When we assemble a jigsaw, we analyse the pieces unfolded around the table conforming to some criteria. The first one is mostly included in the idea of coherence, and can be specified as 'local consistency'. Normally, we have already

[13]A coherentist system is 'a interconnected family of theses'. Rescher (1974, 699).

[14]Relationships are always 'symmetrical' or 'reciprocal'. Rescher (1973, 130), Bonjour (1999, 123–4), Dancy (1985, 128).

[15]The chain's resilience is marked by its weakest link; the net's resilience is marked by the strongest one, because it can always be used. Viola (1987, 379).

[16]In neurological slang, the system must 'reorganize its synapses'. Bar-Yar (2003).

achieved some results: we have put together a variable number of pieces, a composition in which we generally trust and that we can call our 'accumulated wisdom'. Our first search looks for a kind of local or peripheral consistency: we focus on the geometric or formal shape of the pieces, what Perec called 'the subtlety of the cutting' (Perec 1978, 14), and we choose the piece more in concordance with the cutting and the drawing of the closest pieces.

However, the local consistency can be very deceptive. The new piece can perfectly fit the local area of our composition, and complete the perfect drawing of a red flower, but where there should not be any flower. Consistency must be comprehensive: the new piece faces a comparison with all our accumulated wisdom, all the pieces already approved. However, the disagreement between the new piece and the accumulated wisdom must not necessarily finish ruling the problematic candidate out. In the example, we hastily said that there should not be any flower in that area of the jigsaw; however, are we sure about that? Considering the perfect match of the pieces forming the flower, might there be a mistake in our accumulated wisdom, in our provisional composition? We have to check and balance both possibilities. Many times, the resilience of our accumulated wisdom will resist any change; however, we have to be open to admit possible past mistakes, and to give up some of the pieces in which we trusted the most.

Finally, a good maker of jigsaws sometimes faces challenges that push him beyond our ideas of consistency. We here assume that a good player chooses a jigsaw which does not disclose in the box the picture with the solution of the game: the jigsaw is a 'puzzle', a riddle, and it is the purpose of the game to unveil it. The system of pieces pursues a specific function: to disclose the hidden figure. During the whole game, the player needs a possible figure in mind which orientates all his movements.[17] It might happen that a perfect match of many pieces could actually be a red herring cunningly planned by the maker of the jigsaw in order to make us pursue a false picture (Perec 1978, 15). In some extreme cases, we would be able to renounce our ideas of consistency, because we have discovered that the solution is not what we had been looking for, and all our accumulated wisdom, including the connections of the pieces, has been revealed to be simply wrong.

[17]Bartelborth (1999, 223). For Rescher (1973, 42), a problem of our epistemic jigsaw is represented by a number of spare or superfluous pieces: the erroneous and contradictory ones. However, Bartelborth seems to remark the opposite: our knowledge depends upon some pieces coming from experience, but also upon 'theories' which are not already included in our box, but must be reconstructed by ourselves. In legal theory, the jigsaw has also been proposed as a metaphor for the judicial reasoning: Alexy and Peczenik (1990, 135). Finally, Aarnio (1997, 42) also remarks that the whole figure must be reconstructed again and again: "In legal reasoning the 'figure' is developing throughout the game, and no one knows in advance which is the entire set of arguments".

4.2.4 *The Crossword*

Suggested by Susan Haack, the crossword is a very close image to the jigsaw, because it attempts to expose approximately the same working method, which means the same rules of justification.[18] In her approach, the justification of a belief or a norm could be described as a process of choice between candidates which resembles the process of solving a crossword or analysing which word should be inserted in every horizontal line and vertical column.

The aim of the game is to find a set of terms matching a list of definitions. The first requirement in use is local consistency: a term is adequate if it correctly answers the definition and, especially, if it fits the attributed number of squares.

However, local consistency can be deceptive because the player must pay attention to the words already crossed, and beware of introducing a term that disrupts the previously approved terms. If the new term is disruptive, it does not necessarily mean that it must be ruled out: we have to think about the already written words, and check again their fit. Sometimes, our conviction referring to a new term could persuade us to change a significant part of our 'accumulated wisdom'. The crossword's main virtue is to make the holistic dimension of coherence clear while highlighting the fragility of the purely local approach.

We cannot forget that the game aims towards a specific end: to rightly answer the list of definitions. It means that local and even global consistency can be misleading. Sometimes, to solve the riddle of five horizontal lines discloses a word hidden in a five letter column. That would be a term justified by mere consistency; however, it can be a mistake: the player must not forget to confirm if this term is the right answer to the respective definition. Any answer matching the definition, but inconsistent with the other answers is not admissible; the answer is not admissible either it fits perfectly with the number of squares and the rest of the words, but is incompatible with the proposed definition (Haack 1993, 116–126).

Finally, the image of the crossword shows vividly that our systems of wisdom aspire to be open, progressively complex and prone to learn. Two terms could match both requirements—definition and number of squares—but we know that there is only one right answer. The search for this answer 'pushes us progressively outward'[19]: we have to carefully examine the nuances of any term and to

---

[18]It must be noticed that S. Haack does not feel comfortable with the label 'coherentism', and sides with a peculiar eclectic theory coined by herself as 'foundherentism'. Her reasons against pure coherentism are its denial of priorities and hierarchies, and the coherentist refusal to accept untouchable beliefs: in her view, it is obvious that our beliefs own a different degree of reliability and value. See Haack (1993, 78ff.). However, I profit from Haack's arguments because, in my view, her departure from coherentism is not substantial: Haack does not either belief in unchangeable hierarchies, and accepts that the pedigree of the most valuable beliefs is revisable. She does not deny that her theory is closer to coherentism than to foundationalism. Haack (1993, 120).

[19]Haack (1993, 123). Haack's intentions are clearly beyond this brief paraphrase. For example, she highlights the importance of definitions, because they represent the superior value she concedes to empirical evidence. Our portrait has underplayed the superior value she assigns to definitions

contrast these nuances with the terms of the definition. Only by increasing our knowledge and the complexity of our system of beliefs can we aspire to solve the problem.

4.2.5 *The Spiral*

If we leave epistemology and resort to other departments, two of the most outstanding coherentist variations are the hermeneutic circle of Gadamer and the reflective equilibrium of Rawls.[20] In both cases, the works of justification conclude when we can present our knowledge in a state of order or balance, and we obtain this balance when all our beliefs form a circle of mutual support. Although clear in many hermeneutic constructions,[21] this image is more thoroughly developed in Rawls' reflective equilibrium. Thus, our comments will focus on Rawls's method, and will be constrained within the province of political philosophy.

The reflective equilibrium is not for John Rawls any metaphor from which we can obtain some analogies on the right procedure of justification: it is the procedure in itself, the formula of justification for his two proposed principles of justice. However, this procedure can be expressively described through another metaphor: the spiral. I attribute this image to Rawls' thought because we find in his reflective equilibrium the typical spiral movement of circles enlarged outward: the first circles capture new elements, and introduce them in a broader circle that reinforces the inner ones. This is the reason why the spiral does not form vicious, but virtuous or fruitful circles, because all the elements reach a state of coherence or equilibrium in which they obtain justification.

It is possible to distinguish an evolution in Rawls' description of his method. However, in spite of its variations, all the versions share some well-known patterns: they reject any foundationalist solution for the problem of justification, and reason the conclusions appealing to relationships of mutual support of many considerations. Rawls excludes reasoning from axioms, 'hard rocks' or self-evident foundations. He admits that our works do not start from any empty moral space, but from some highly reliable judgments obtained by intuition and named by him 'fixed points', such as 'slavery is unjust' or 'freedom is valuable'. Although 'fixed', these judgments are provisional and open to a possible change. According to his words, the investigation proceeds 'going back and forth' (Rawls 1971, 20). It attempts to match some intuitive judgments and the principles of justice which are deduced from the contractual scenario—the 'original position'—constructed upon intuitive

respecting consistence. Nevertheless, we are faithful to her valuation of consistence as a necessary condition for any knowledge, and to the demand of interplay between consistence and respect to definitions.

[20]Reflective equilibrium is not free of unorthodox interpretations. For DePaul (1986, 60ff.), it is an example of foundationalism, the rival theory of coherentism.

[21]See e.g. Osborne (1991).

moral judgments. Sometimes, there will be discrepancies. In this case, the exam must be bi-directional: we 'go forth' to examine the principles, but also 'go back' to check our most intuitive and appreciated judgments. The investigation does not conclude until the entire set of our moral and political propositions is in order, and we have corrected all the discordant ones.

Finally, a brief consideration of the intellectual evolution of this concept in Rawls' work will be instructive. As we know, Rawls' goal was the formulation of a set of principles of justice. In the beginning, the reflective equilibrium which justified these principles consisted in the contrast of two elements: the principles and a set of moral intuitions called by Rawls 'considered judgments'. However, Rawls soon realized that this equilibrium did not achieve a proper justification of principles, and was open to the criticism of being a mere duplication of our moral intuitions.[22] Hence, the circle was enlarged and demanded a comparison between three elements: principles, judgments, and a set of theories or conceptions (a conception of the society and of the citizen).[23] Rawls also prescribed that this equilibrium should be a broad equilibrium. 'Broad' does not mean here that we have to include in the investigation the greatest number of theories and elements; it means that the circle never remains definitely closed: the spiral can always be enlarged and it will actually expand every time we detect any principle or theory never examined before and able to challenge our convictions.

To sum up, the spiral adds an interesting lesson: justification is an open, iterative process in which any coherence previously obtained is progressively corrected (Rott 1999, 404–5). It also means that consistency with the previously accepted moral statements is not a sufficient condition of justification: on the contrary, some inconsistent elements can motivate the correction of the others (Rawls 1971, 48).

4.2.6 The Chain Novel

The Rawlsian 'reflective equilibrium' has influenced many legal philosophers. Despite all the reserves, one of these cases is R. Dworkin's: 'So Rawls recommended that philosophers of justice engage in the interpretive enterprise he called seeking reflective equilibrium [...] We can restate this interpretive exercise as a method for legal philosophers' (Dworkin 2006, 246). Rawlsian spiral's traces are visible in Dworkin's reconstruction of the judicial works. According to Dworkin, when a judge tries to solve a case, he tries to reflect the legal system he serves as a coherent

[22]Rawls (1971, 19–20), Daniels (1996, 60–1).

[23]Rawls (1980). The circle is complex because the theories we are referring to are also selected by some considered intuitive judgments. In order to avoid redundancies, the set of moral judgments which should match the principles and the set of judgments with which we select the theories must be disjoint sets. The complications reach the degree showed by Daniels' diagram in Daniels (1996, 51).

whole or a set in equilibrium. In order to achieve this attractive representation, his research also moves in concentric circles from within outward. He might solve the case 'from within', in the closest normative circle, which means to use the most related rules to the content of the case or, in other words, the rule or the set of rules whose factual description includes the largest number of properties of the particular case. But such a comfortable solution is many times unattainable: perhaps we do not find this kind of rule or, perhaps we do, but its solution might be unsatisfying. The judge must then expand the investigation and move to broader circles such as the domain of constitutional principles or even moral and political theories (Dworkin 1986, 250). As in the Rawlsian equilibrium, the judge reconstructs the correct solution when his sentence reflects the legal system speaking with one voice, when it is presented in its best light and can be identified with a state of order, unity and equilibrium extended to all its elements.

However, law is not exactly justice, but more a complex set of moral and institutional principles. Abridging the issue drastically, we could sustain that legal coherence is qualified by the social and diachronic features exhibited by legal practice. As legal practice is social, the judge cannot solve the case appealing to the coherence of his personal set of values: it is not enough the coherence with oneself; coherence must be attributed to the community as a whole.[24] Therefore, we attribute to the judge a duty of congruence with the most repeated conventions and traditions of the communitarian legal practice: without a minimum of fit with these conventions, it will be impossible to impute any state of order and equilibrium to a legal system. Secondly, coherence must be extended in time, and show a minimum of continuity and balance between past and present practices. Legal coherence must refer to the values of a community, not a generation. Any community is a long-term cooperative enterprise, and this cooperative nature would be threatened if every generation were entitled to do *tabula rasa* with the legal solutions of the past: if that were the case, it could be said that this community lacks any stable and safe legal framework.

Either because of these or other reasons, Dworkin felt the need to suggest a different image and proposed the metaphor of the chain novel as a way of describing the process of judicial justification (Dworkin 1986, 228–238).

The judge's activities can be compared with the works of a writer trying to complete a new chapter for a chain novel. The writer receives a set of completed chapters, and has to write a new one which satisfies two demands: (1) it must be a continuation of the already written chapters; (2) it must form with the rest of the chapters a whole body, a meaningful and likely unity.

To continue the plot of the other chapters will engage the writer with a special attention with the last chapters of the received drafts. However, it does not mean a total subjection to the last scenes. The most important requirement is related to the whole: his contribution must add a value to the novel as a unity, which allows him even to ignore this local consistency.

---

[24]On social and individual coherence, see Sosa (1989, 263ff.).

However, it would be a mistake to represent the works of this writer as a mere continuation of the plot and the profile of the characters as they were designed from the beginning: his work is not mechanical and is not reduced to the discovery of the will's first authors of the chain. The writer can introduce not only substantial changes, but sudden and surprising u-turns in the argument or the characters. However, his possibilities are constrained by a familiar demand: these new turns are only acceptable if they contribute to a more unified and interesting whole. Finally, in order to understand what could make the novel interesting, he will have to meditate about the style, the genre of the novel, and, from these patterns, he will have to draw conclusions about the goals of the novel and the kind of effects it should pursue in the readers. The last message is that consistency is insufficient to encompass all the chain novelist's activities.

4.3 The Coherence in Four Conditions

The previous section displayed the fertile metaphoric skills of the coherentist authors, but also outlined a more important feature: the six images seem to share a common denominator and they appear to be variations of the same motives. This section will try to explain these motives. In this work of formulation, it will not be possible to attribute to these motives the accuracy of an exact counter. However, it is possible instead to show them as approximate standards which could work as a kind of minimal protocol.

These standards will be reduced to four. The first three will be variations of the idea of consistency with the 'accumulated wisdom' or, as we would say in law, the set of legal solutions provided by the tradition and the conventions of the community.[25] The final criterion will push coherence beyond the demands of fit: it genuinely pushes the system outward because it allows its users to learn from the complexities of practice, to integrate new inputs in the system, and to change to a certain degree its structure and composition.

4.3.1 Consistency

Consistency is the most obvious consequence from the previous section's examples. The sailors may fix and refurbish the boat while they are sailing, but they must respect the general structure which keeps it floating. Looking for the greatest

[25]Concepts such as 'legal tradition' or 'inherited legal wisdom' are differently modulated in each community. The Spanish Constitutional Court, e.g., includes not only positive rules (statutes, judicial sentences, etc.) but also 'the extended ideas and convictions generally admitted by lawyers, judges and specialists in law'. STC11/1981, 8th of February.

internal cohesion, the net is continuously open to new inputs; however, it chooses the most adaptable ones, the most compatible with the greatest number of elements. Solving a jigsaw or a crossword basically seems to consist in fitting together a piece or a word with the already assembled pieces or written words. Rawls' reflective equilibrium asks us to adjust the principles of justice and our most rooted moral beliefs or intuitive judgments. A chain novel demands the writer to end his new chapter in a congruent way with the rest of the plot. For Dworkin, consistency or 'fit' is the first of the two necessary conditions to obtain coherence or 'integrity' in law. In his theory, this requirement is morally grounded in the value of fairness: as all the citizens must be placed in fair and equal conditions respecting judges and officials, there are moral reasons to treat the same past and present cases equally, and to repeat in the present cases the solution we adopted for them in the past (Dworkin 1986, 164–6).

However, the holistic nature of the investigation turns this criterion into a complex guide. Using our six metaphors, we will try to analyze the concept, and to separate its meaning into three different demands: concordance, cohesion and unity.

4.3.1.1 Concordance

Concordance is the term we can choose to designate the local consistency. For this criterion, coherence means a special link with a particular sub-set of the system. We presume in this case a concrete, specific or local problem which we can specify in some premises which seem evident and easily available: we need a word with eight letters, a red and oblong jigsaw piece or a legal rule stating if the blind guide dogs are an exception to the rule 'no entrance for dogs' which is valid in the canteen of my University. The most 'concordant' answer is the one that fits better with the premises of the problem. We can say that the solution is justified by the strength of the logical inference linking the solution and the premises. 'Strength' will mean here relevance, a material or substantial adjustment coming from the content or the type of problem at stake.[26] Normally, this strength or substantial adjustment is locally determined. In a legal system, this local context is usually identified with a specific area or department, sometimes even a sub-area o sub-department, whose frontiers are drawn according to the content or the substance of the problems; the conclusion of a legal reasoning is more concordant, consistent and coherent when it fits better with the rules of the area or the department which is more directly concerned with the features of the particular case. If we look outside this particular sub-set of rules included in this area or department, we might observe that the solution keeps a very low number of inferences with the other parts of the legal system; however, if we consider alone the guide of congruence, the intensive strength or relevance of the few links within this sub-set would outweigh any possible reproach of inferential weakness.

[26]On this special link, see BonJour (1985, 95–7), Rescher (1973, 32–35; 75–82).

Concordance is many times a sufficient condition of justification. However, it can occasionally provide an insufficient consistency, and be a source of errors. We might be crossword players needing a word of six letters which means ‘high and eminent’ and starts with ‘gr’, and local consistency will not help us to make a decision between ‘grand’ and ‘great’. We might contrive a plot which is a perfect continuation of the last chapter’s of the chain, but by distorting the general plot of the whole novel. A rule could perfectly match our commercial legislation, but also introduce serious distortions in some foundations of our private or constitutional law. To sum up, consistency must be extended to the proper holistic consistency or consistency attributed to the whole system. This demand can be formulated through two patterns in which we assess not just the strength of the logical inference, but also the number of the logical links with the other elements of the system that any new element could bring about (Bonjour 1985, 98).

4.3.1.2 Cohesion

It is the proper contribution of the net, and it underlies some of the most typical cliches of the coherentist literature, such as ‘solidarity’, ‘mutual support’ or ‘reciprocal consistency’.

According to this guide, the most coherent conclusion is the one which gathers together the highest number of logical inferences with the other elements of the system, increases the links between these elements and provides tighter relationships.[27] The guide disapproves the conclusions which, despite their local relevance or even their strong link with one or few elements of the system, are completely irrelevant to the rest.

This focus on the number of inferences seems to satisfy the yearning for clarity and objectivity, usually missed in the coherentist tradition. It could explain why some legal versions of coherence drastically reduce ‘coherence’ to this pattern (Hoffmaster 1980): in these theories, the challenge of coherence would simply demand from the judge the job of counting logical connections between any candidate to solve the case and the different valid legal norms, especially statutes and precedents. However, coherence cannot be reduced to an elementary account of inferences, and any claim of using ‘cohesion’ as a single standard of coherence faces different obstacles. Firstly, the use of this criterion depends upon an accurate elucidation of the meaning of ‘inference’: it is still a complex problem for logic and legal theory when we really obtain a right or admissible inference between a premise of the system and a conclusion. Secondly, ‘cohesion’ is unable to solve alone many problems of legal coherence. A clear example is revealed when we try to balance two of the most abstract and fundamental principles of the legal system: because of their foundational position, we can presume that they are linked to a

[27]Millgram (2000, 84), Rescher (1973, 173). In legal reasoning, Hoffmaster (1980, 163ff.), Peczenik (1989, 161ff.).

large part of the system, so that we can presume that the counting of links or logical inferences will finish either in an inconclusive couple of figures or in something close to a draw.

4.3.1.3 Unity

This criterion is intimately attached to 'cohesion', and it is also typical of the neural descriptions of any system. It genuinely grasps the holistic dimension of coherence, because endorses the conclusion which increases or intensifies the relationships of order and structure, and warns us against the ones that could cause any fragmentation in the system.[28]

In legal reasoning, it prevents us from importing rules that widen the distance between legal areas or departments, and advocates the rule which shows a common explanation or might be evidence of common principles in different legal areas.[29] The practical applications of this guide cannot be exhaustively formulated here. As an obvious example, this guide solidly supports the work of the unification of jurisprudential doctrine that the highest courts play in many legal systems, a demand which is sometimes represented in the ideal of the 'unique judge' in the legal system (Gascón 1993, 83–4). It can also shed some light onto some controversies still open in the literature regarding judicial evidence. More specifically, cohesion and unity successfully advocate a more appropriate and favourable understanding of the so-called theories of narrative coherence.[30]

---

[28]The conclusion must help us to describe the system as a 'unified structure': BonJour (1999, 6). For DeMarco (1994, 21), the system must be describable as a 'continuum' of principles. Williams (1991, 275) called our last two criteria 'interconnectness' and 'systematicity'.

[29]It means a preference for the conclusion exhibiting a 'systematic import': Hoffmaster (1980, 178ff.). In my view, this criterion matches Peczenik's demands of 'generality' (Peczenik 1989, 172ff.), and the concern for connections 'as tight as possible' in (Aarnio et al. 1981, 268). McFall (1987, 6–7) remarks a link between the moral virtue of integrity and the meaning of coherence as 'non division' in our system of moral beliefs.

[30]These theories have been harshly criticized by the defenders of an 'atomistic' or 'analytical' view of the judicial probatory works. Critics sustain that holism allows the judge to stop the factual investigation as, in his view, he can construct a story which is consistent and able to answer all the debated questions of the case. Possibly, only part of the issues of the case has been corroborated by empirical evidence. However, this part can be sufficient to sustain the consistency of the story and, in this case, coherence allows the judge to safely unveil the rest of the factual issues and circumstances in the same way some secure letters in the crossword allow us to unveil the others. For the critics, this second group of factual issues and circumstances would simply be guessed, but not proven: the only way of proving a story is by dividing or analyzing it into all the relevant issues, and furnishing a separate empirical evidence for any single one (e.g. Taruffo 2008, 187ff., 2010, Chaps. 2 and 3). These accusations of probatory carelessness may be deserved by some radical versions of the so-called theories of narrative coherence. However, when we apply a correctly understood idea of coherence, these accusations become misleading. Coherence theories of evidence do not definitely disregard the scientific requirements of empirical evidence: any reasonable judge knows that they are an important element of the system of knowledge. It is true that the judge may accept new statements without practising new empirical tests, but

4.3.2 Comprehensitivity

Consistency with the past cannot work as a sufficient test of coherence.[31] The net image described the system as a structure arranged for learning, which means the admission of new elements and the resetting of the links connecting all the elements of the system. The jigsaw and the crossword also remark that a new finding might invite us to reconsider all our previous results, and to operate drastic changes on the table or the paper. Reflective equilibrium reminds us that the moral system is open to reconsider any new theory or any new principle, and if we value them highly, we must be ready to correct even our more rooted judgments. Finally, the chain novel allows the writer to contrive sudden twists in the plot, and to sacrifice the consistency with the previous chapters if the literary value of the whole is increased. An element can be inconsistent with the rest, but its inclusion can provide the bonus of coherence unattainable for its rivals. These demands can be formulated in a criterion that works as an ideal: a coherent system aspires to 'comprehensivity'. According to this pattern, the user of any system must permanently open it to the consideration of new elements able to increase the system's coherence, although their admission could be inconsistent with some elements of the whole or could force us to operate some readjustments.[32]

After defining 'consistency' as an essential guide for coherence, this second demand must necessarily be constrained by severe limitations. It must be reminded that the consequence of outweighing 'consistency' by comprehensivity will normally suppose to eliminate all the elements revealed as incompatible with the new ones. Reasons of sufficient weight and importance to justify these changes and corrections must be necessarily provided. More specifically, two important conditions must be demonstrated: (1) the system will achieve its aims better if it counts with the new element; (2) after including the new element and eliminating the incompatible ones, the result is a more cohesive and integrated order.

Dworkin's theory is probably one of the best formulations of this criterion in legal theory. He views legal practice as a search for order or balance in a set of

---

according to some conditions. Firstly, the judge cannot suspect any incompatibility between the new statements and the elementary demands of scientific evidence. Secondly, the new statements must respect to a considerable degree the conditions of cohesion and unity we have described. It means that they must be connected with the rest of the statements—specially the empirically tested ones—by a dense network of logical inferences. This second condition clearly reveals what is problematic in the atomistic theories: it is difficult to understand why we cannot profit from these logical inferences. As we know, a system of beliefs is not anything we can divide into independent or isolated chains or branches, but a network whose elements are deeply interwoven. These connections compose a valuable set of accumulated wisdom, and it is a normal assumption in any investigation that a scientist can profit from it to enlarge the system.

[31] This criterion has been named 'complexity', 'learning', 'soundness', etc. I chose the term 'comprehensivity' following (Aarnio et al. 1981, 268).

[32] BonJour (1985, 100), Bradley (1914, 202), Thagard et al. (2002: Sect. 8, paragraph 'Isolation'), Williams (1991, 275).

moral principles. 'Integrity' or legal coherence aspires to fairness, but also to justice. Sometimes, the most just solution is not the most consistent. However, merely the fact that it is the most just means that the judge has got some prima facie reasons to approve it, even ruling out more consistent solutions.[33]

Thus justice provides a pragmatic standard respecting the legal system's purpose or its prospective end. Every community consults a kind of moral or political agenda with which it is progressively changing its law.[34] This agenda consists in positive and non positive moral principles which constitute the basis of the system, the substratum that nourishes the content of the rules. That is why Dworkin terms 'soundness' this dimension of coherence[35]: this criterion demands to delve more deeply into the moral profile of the system, a work that is analagous to the considerations of 'learning from outside' of the net model, or to the movement in broader and broader circles typical in the spiral or in Rawls' reflective equilibrium.

When one of these principles is implicit or non positive, the interpreter might be in favour of a just solution, although it might be inconsistent with past rules and practices. However, in these cases, the interpreter must keep in mind that the admission of an inconsistent rule would introduce a contradiction in the system that must be corrected by derogating some positive rules or precedents. Hence the reasons of justice can only be considered if they pass a pragmatic test and a logical or inferential test: (1) the gain in justice is superior to the cost of these reforms; (2) the resulting unit is superior in cohesion and unity to the last one, and provides a higher number of logical links. Although it will not be possible to elaborate this conclusion, we may clarify that coherence cannot be explained as a purely inferential ideal, but a combination of inferential and pragmatic demands.

Concordance, cohesion, unity and comprehensivity are prima facie and compulsory rules. They are prima facie because their value cannot be absolute, and they must be balanced. However, they are all compulsory: even in the easiest cases, when we may think that the solution has derived from one single inference of 'concordance' or local consistency, we have actually implied a holistic judgement according to which the solution can be adopted because it satisfies in a reasonable way the other standards. It finally means that we cannot declare 'coherent' any conclusion that is in radical contradiction to any one of these four guides.[36]

---

[33]Dworkin (1986, 219–224). 'People are entitled that the injustice factor in any decision that deprives them of what they are entitled to have be taken into account'. Dworkin (1985, 100–1). The main shortcoming of Sartorius' coherentism is precisely his identification of coherence and consistency, and his complete disregard for the role of justice. Sartorius (1968, 139).

[34]This agenda is called by Dworkin 'pure integrity': Dworkin (1986, 406–7).

[35]Dworkin (1977, 340–1). In 1986, Dworkin renamed this dimension as 'justification', which introduced some confusion: integrity now combines 'fit' and 'justification', as if 'fit' would not play any justifying role. See p.255. In *Justice for Hedgehogs*, when discussing theory of truth, he renames again this addition to fit, and terms it 'conviction' (2011, 120ff.).

[36]This paper reformulates the essay 'Razones de coherencia', printed in *Estudios en homenaje al profesor Gregorio Peces-Barba* (2008, Madrid: Dykinson). I am grateful to my colleagues of Salamanca and Alicante for all their comments and criticisms.

References

Aarnio, A. 1997. *Reason and authority*. Aldershot: Ashgate.
Aarnio, A., R. Alexy, and A. Peczenik. 1981. The foundation of legal reasoning. *Rechtstheorie* 12: 133–158. 257–279, 423–448.
Alexy, R., and A. Peczenik. 1990. The concept of coherence and its significance for discoursive rationality. *Ratio Juris* 3: 130–147.
Bartelborth, T. 1999. Coherence and explanations. *Erkenntnis* 50: 209–224.
Bar-Yar, Y. 2003. *Dynamics of complex systems*. New York: Perseus.
Baum-Levenbook, B. 1984. The role of coherence in legal reasoning. *Law and Philosophy* 3: 355–374.
BonJour, L. 1985. *The structure of empirical knowledge*. Cambridge: Harvard U.P.
BonJour, L. 1999. Foundationalism and coherentism. In *A companion to epistemology*, ed. E. Sosa and J. Dancy. Malden: Blackwell.
Bovens, L., and S. Hartmann. 2003. Solving the ridle of coherence. *Mind* 112: 601–633.
Bradley, F.H. 1914. *Essays on truth and reality*. Oxford: Hart Publishing.
Brink, D.O. 2001. *Moral realism and the foundation of ethics*. Cambridge: Cambridge U.P.
Carling, A. 1992. *Introducing neural network*. Wilmslow: Sigma Press.
Dancy, J. 1985. *An introduction to contemporary epistemology*. Oxford: Blackwell.
Daniels, N. 1996. *Justice and Justification*, Cambridge U.P, Cambridge.
DeMarco, J.B. 1994. *A coherence theory in ethics*. Amsterdam: Rodop.
DePaul, M. 1986. Reflective equilibrium and foundationalism. *American Philosophical Quarterly* 23: 59–69.
Dworkin, R. 1977. *Talking rights seriously*. Cambridge: Harvard U.P.
Dworkin, R. 1985. *A matter of principle*. Cambridge: Harvard U.P.
Dworkin, R. 1986. *Law's empire*. Oxford: Hart Publishing.
Dworkin, R. 1996a. Objectivity and truth: You'd better believe it. *Philosophy and Public Affairs* 25: 87–139.
Dworkin, R. 1996b. *Freedom's law*. Cambridge: Cambridge U.P.
Dworkin, R. 2006. *Justice in robes*. Cambridge: Harvard U.P.
Dworkin, R. 2011. *Justice for hedgehogs*. Cambridge: Harvard U.P.
Edmundson, W. 1994. Comments on "The coherence theory in the philosophy of law". In http://law.gsu.edu/wedmundson/COHERENT.TLK.pdf.
Ewing, A.C. 1934. *Idealism: A critical survey*. London: Methuen.
Fritzman, J.M. 1992. Against coherence. *American Philosophical Journal* 29: 183–191.
Gascón, M. 1993. *La técnica del precedente y la argumentación judicial*. Madrid: Tecnos.
Haack, S. 1993. *Evidence and inquiry*. Oxford: Blackwell.
Harman, G. 1973. *Thought*. Princeton: Princeton U.P.
Haykin, S. 1999. *Neural networks: A comprehensive foundation*. Upper Saddle River: Prentice Hall.
Hoffmaster, B. 1980. A holistic approach to judicial justification. *Erkenntnis* 5: 159–181.
MacCormick, N. 1993. Argumentation and interpretation in Law. *Ratio Juris* 6: 16–29.
McFall, L. 1987. Integrity. *Ethics* 98: 5–20.
Millgram, E. 2000. Coherence: The price of the ticket. *The Journal of Philosophy* 97: 82–93.
Neurath, O. 1959. Protocol sentences. In *Logical positivism*, ed. A.J. Ayer. Chicago: The Free Press of Glencoe.
Osborne, J. 1991. *The hermeneutical spiral*. Downers Grove: InterVarsity Press.
Peacocke, C. 1999. Holism. In *A companion to philosophy of language*, ed. B. Hale and C. Wright, 230–231. Malden: Blackwell.
Peczenik, A. 1989. *On law and reason*. Dordrecht: Kluwer.
Perec, G. 1978. *La vie mode d'emploi*. Paris: Hachette.
Pérez Bermejo, J.M. 2007. Los problemas de las teorías holistas del derecho. *Doxa* 30: 355–382.
Putnam, H. 1982. *Reason, truth and history*. Cambridge: Cambridge U.P.

Quine, W.V.A. 1951. Two dogmas of empiricism. *Philosophical Review* 60: 20–43.
Ralws, J. 1980. Kantian constructivism in moral theory. *The Journal of Philosophy* 77: 515–572.
Rawls, J. 1971. *A theory of justice*. Cambridge: Harvard U.P.
Raz, J. 1992. The relevance of coherence. *Boston University Law Review* 72: 273–321. Also in Joseph Raz, *Ethics in the public domain*, revised edition. Oxford: Clarendon Press 1995, 77–325.
Recher, N. 1974. Foundationalism, coherentism and the idea of cognitive systematization. *The Journal of Philosophy* 71: 695–708.
Rescher, N. 1973. *The coherence theory of truth*. Oxford: Oxford U.P.
Rott, H. 1999. Coherence and conservatism in the dynamics of belief. *Erkenntnis* 50: 387–412.
Sartorius, R. 1968. The justification of judicial decision. *Ethics* 78: 171–187.
Sosa, E. 1980. The raft and the pyramid: Coherence versus foundations in the theory of knowledge. *Midwest Studies of Philosophy* 5: 3–26.
Sosa, E. 1989. Equilibrium in coherence. In *The current state of coherence theory*, ed. J. Bender. Dordrecth: Kluwer.
Spohn, W. 1999. Two coherence principles. *Erkenntis* 50: 155–175.
Taruffo, M. 2008. *La prueba*. Madrid: Marcial Pons.
Taruffo, M. 2010. *Simplemente la verdad*. Madrid: Marcial Pons.
Thagard, P., C. Eliasmith, P. Rusnock, and C. Shelley. 2002. Knowledge and coherence. In (last exam 3 Jan 2012): http://cogsci.uwaterloo.ca/Articles/Pages/epistemic.html.
Viola, F. 1987. *Autoritá e ordine del diritto*. Torino: Giappichelli.
Williams, M. 1991. *Unnatural doubts*. Oxford: Blackwell.

Chapter 5
Legal Interpretation and Coherence

Bartosz Brożek

5.1 Hermeneutics *Modo Analytico*

The key thesis of legal hermeneutics is that one cannot distinguish between understanding, interpretation and the application of law. "As is emphasized by Gadamer, 'the hermeneutical problem' always embraces three inextricably linked moments: understanding (*subtilitas intelligendi*), explanation (*subtilitas explicandi*) and application (*subtilitas applicandi*). For understanding is realized through the act of interpretation, and the essence of interpretation is expressed in its practical application" (Stelmach and Brożek 2006, 190). Moreover, hermeneutics does not aim at constructing a model of understanding, interpretation or the application of law. It is an anti-procedural and anti-formal philosophy: it makes an attempt to describe a certain phenomenon, and is far from encapsulating it within the limits of a more or less formal model (Stelmach and Brożek 2006, 167–205).

On the other hand, however, Gadamer and his followers speak of the structure of understanding, and wherever there is a structure it must be—at least in principle—formally reconstructable: if not in classical logic, then with the use of nonstandard formal techniques. Moreover, I believe that some of the observations of the proponents of hermeneutics are indeed insightful, but it is difficult to appreciate and analyze them as they are usually expressed in vague and awkward language which is characterized by a high level of 'Gads' (Gadamer's students referred to less clear fragments of his works with this phrase) (Grondin 2007, 291).

I posit that is it relatively easy to present a satisfactory—although not the only possible—formalization of the hermeneutic process of understanding, though it requires a non-dogmatic approach to the Gadamerian conceptual scheme. Gadamer

B. Brożek (✉)
Department of Law and Administration, Jagiellonian University,
Bracka 12, Kraków 31-005, Poland
e-mail: bartosz.brozek@uj.edu.pl

M. Araszkiewicz and J. Šavelka (eds.), *Coherence: Insights from Philosophy, Jurisprudence and Artificial Intelligence*, Law and Philosophy Library 107,
DOI 10.1007/978-94-007-6110-0_5, © Springer Science+Business Media Dordrecht 2013

claims that within the process of understanding there takes place "the constitution of sense or meaning (*Sinn*)" (Gadamer 2004, 164). The problem is, what does 'sense' or 'meaning' stand for here, since Gadamer speaks of their 'consistency' or 'coherence', and 'consistency of sense (meaning)' sounds awkward.

This problem may be dealt with when one follows an insightful directive formulated by Karl Popper, who insists on distinguishing subjective, personal and psychological activities and processes, from the

> (more or less successful) outcomes of these activities, from their result: the 'final state' (for the time being) of understanding, the interpretation. (...) [When a subjective] state of understanding [is] finally reached, so a psychological process which leads up to it must be analysed in terms of the third-world objects [i.e., abstract objects] in which it is anchored. In fact, it can be analysed only in these terms (Popper 1972, 163–164).

Popper suggests that—instead of speaking of 'capturing the meaning' or other subjective processes connected with interpretation or understanding—one should rather analyze the outcomes of those processes. Thus, in what follows, I will read what Gadamer says about 'sense' or 'meaning' as if he were speaking of 'propositions' or 'sentences'.

The two key hermeneutic concepts that describe the structure of understanding (interpretation) are: pre-understanding or pre-judgment (*Vorverstandnis, Vorurteil*) and the hermeneutic circle. It is possible, or so I argue, to capture those concepts in a precise way with the use of some formal tools. Of course, it is only a paraphrase of the original conception, but arguably an admissible one.

Gadamer has nowhere defined the concept of pre-understanding and he speaks of pre-judgments as a transcendental condition of understanding. He criticizes the Enlightenment tradition, claiming that by rejecting pre-judgments as not based on the authority of reason, the only admissible authority, it itself embraces a prejudice. One cannot however, Gadamer continues, imagine understanding without a pre-understanding. Gadamerian pre-understanding has at least two dimensions. Firstly, everyone who engages in the interpretation (understanding) of a text is a participant in a certain culture (tradition), and so understanding and interpretation are always relative to a tradition. Secondly, pre-understanding also has an individual 'flavor': one that interprets or 'poses a question to a text', always anticipates an answer, initially ascribes some meaning to the text (Gadamer 2004, 277–304).

These theses are far from clear and dangerously close to nonsense. What does it mean that one 'poses a question to a text'? What is 'the anticipation of meaning'? In what way—apart from the obvious: that context influences interpretation—does tradition play the role of a 'transcendental condition of understanding'? It is tempting to conclude that, while Gadamer may be trying to verbalize something important, the result is vague and imprecise and brings rather more confusion than insight.

However, I believe that it is possible to express the intuitions that stand behind Gadamer's obscure phrase in a more precise way. To do so, I suggest distinguishing between four kinds of pre-understanding. First, the thesis that 'tradition' is a transcendental condition of understanding may be seen as an attempt to say that whoever interprets something must use an interpreted language. Thus, she must have at her disposal a vocabulary, syntactic rules (rules for constructing compound expressions), rules of inference and a function which maps constants to individuals belonging to the domain of language, one-place predicates to sets of such individuals, etc. Second, participation in the same tradition requires a shared set of presuppositions. Usually, it is assumed that a sentence A is a presupposition of a sentence B iff B may be ascribed truth or falsehood only if A is true. Third, two persons participate in the same tradition if they have the same or similar background knowledge, where the term usually refers to all those statements that—within the process of solving a problem—are assumed true or unproblematic. Here, I shall understand background knowledge in a similar way, as consisting of all those sentences that—at least *prima facie*—are taken to be true or justified. Fourth, it seems that the best way to explicate the individual dimension of pre-understanding is to treat pre-judgements as initial hypotheses, i.e. sentences capturing the sense (meaning) of the interpreted text, which one formulates at the beginning of the process of interpretation, and aims at confirming or rejecting them in due course.

The last understanding of pre-understanding is somewhat troubling. What exactly are 'sentences capturing the meaning of the interpreted text'? In other words: what are interpretation hypotheses? To answer this question one needs to analyze a more general problem: what is interpretation? My reply is as follows.

5.2 What Is Interpretation?

It is difficult to define interpretation,[1] but a kind of definition or, at least, elucidation, is needed if we are to talk about it. Fortunately, there is a 'common denominator' among the existing definitions of interpretation: that interpretation is a process leading to the establishment of the meaning of the given text. This is my working characterization of interpretation; I do not consider it to be an absolute one.

This characterization of interpretation does not determine what is meaning. There are many possible explications of meaning, but it is clear that there are two major types of the theories of meaning: representational and procedural.[2] According to the representationalists, the meaning of linguistic expressions is some abstract or mental object (a proposition, an idea, a mental picture) which constitutes the link between linguistic signs and the world. Examples of representational theories include Frege's *Sinn*, Descartes' theory of meaning, Plato's theory of ideas, etc. On this account,

[1]There is a substantive literature on interpretation in general, and legal interpretation in particular (see, e.g., Dickson 2010 and the literature quoted there). However, I decided not to engage in the analysis of various conceptions of legal interpretation in detail, as my goal is to propose a relatively novel account of interpretation in law, one that dispenses with a large part of the received conceptual scheme.

[2]There also exist the so-called referential theories of meaning (e.g., Russell's), but from the point of view of this essay they are too bold idealizations to be considered. Cf. Alston (1964).

the meaning of the term 'bicycle' is an idea of a bicycle, while the meaning of the term 'obligation' is an idea (or some other abstract or mental entity) representing obligation.

The procedural approach, on the other hand, posits that the meaning of linguistic expressions is determined by the rules of use of those expressions. Such a theory was developed by Wittgenstein in *Philosophical Investigations*. According to this view, the meaning of the term 'bicycle' is the set of all rules that govern the application of this term (they identify all the circumstances under which the term 'bicycle' may be properly applied), and so on.

There are two theses I would like to defend which apply to both types of theories of meaning.

1. ***Meaning is underdetermined***. It is typically not the case that when given a text we can determine its meaning on the basis of the text alone (i.e., without taking context into account). The underdetermination of meaning makes interpretation necessary in most cases. In other words, the goal of interpretation as caused by the underdetermination of meaning may be described as the decision of picking out one of the meanings which are *prima facie* (i.e., without considering the context) ascribable to the given text. Let us refer to the set of meanings which can *prima facie* be ascribed to a given expression as the meaning bundle.

   Let us consider the following example. When one interprets the sentence:

   "Vehicles are not allowed into the public park."

it can be—*prima facie*—ascribed different meanings, relative to how one understands such expressions as 'vehicles', 'into' or 'public park'. 'Vehicles' might—but does not have to—include bicycles or scooters; 'into' may—but does not have to—refer to bringing a motorcycle into the park for the annual motorcycle exhibition; 'park', in turn, may—but does not have to—refer only to the green areas which were recognized as parks by some authority.

2. ***Meaning is stable***. Meaning bundles, i.e. the sets of meanings that are *prima facie* ascribable to the given text, are stable. Every competent user of language ascribes—*prima facie*—similar meaning bundles to a given expression. This is not to say that it is always exactly the same set. However, the sets cannot differ substantially, or otherwise linguistic communication would be impossible and language would not serve its purpose, namely the coordination of human behaviour. Usually, even if not always, we are capable of successful communication.

The underdetermination and stability of meaning are closely related to the structural stability of language. Michał Heller notes:

> And ordinary language? How imprecise it is, but at the same time—how efficient! (...) It is probably due to the fact that ordinary language has a special 'mechanism' built into its structure, such that a small disturbance of the meaning of an expression results in equally small disturbance of its understanding. In this way, two language users may efficiently communicate. This feature of language may be deemed its structural stability. If—in an

area of language—there is no structural stability, i.e. the meanings of expressions are too sharply separated, a minimal alternation of meaning may result in major disturbance of understanding and make communication impossible (Heller 2002, 36–37).

Heller points out that the very possibility of communication presupposes that the meanings of linguistic expressions cannot be too sharply defined. In other words, it is due to the fact that there exist meaning bundles and not separate meanings, that language is structurally stable and may serve as means of communication. On the other hand, the structural stability of language presupposes also the stability of meaning. Efficient communication is conditioned by the users ascribing similar meaning bundles to linguistic expressions.

I would like to adopt a convention according to which a method of interpretation consists of procedures of interpretation and criteria of interpretation. Procedures of interpretation are certain actions which enable one to choose one or more meanings of the interpreted expression. The criteria of interpretation, on the other hand, determine which procedures of interpretation are admissible in the given case, and which are not.

It is not easy to define interpretation. What does it consist of? Is it a mental process or should one rather speak of the transcendental conditions of understanding? Does interpretation pertain to (operate on) 'mental images' or rather abstract objects? Irrespective of what the answers to these questions are, they will be controversial as they employ vague notions. Any recourse to mental processes or transcendental structures falls short of the status of the inter-subjectively testable. However, there is a way out of these troubles: one can follow the directive of Karl Popper quoted above, who insists on analysing the processes of understanding and interpretation only in terms of their outcomes, as there is no other inter-subjective aspect thereof. Applied to our problem, this precept requires one to begin with the question of what is the inter-subjective outcome of interpretation. The answer is simple: an inter-subjective result of the interpretation of a certain text is some other text. In connection to this, I claim that there are two procedures of interpretation:

1. **Paraphrase**. Paraphrase consists in translating the given interpreted expression into some other expression. What we obtain is another linguistic expression that is associated with its own meaning bundle. In what way does this help to establish the meaning of the original text? The answer is quite simple. The goal of translation is to limit the meaning bundle of the given text. Thus, the process of paraphrase leads to the claim that the meaning of the interpreted expression lies in the intersection of two meaning bundles: of the interpreted text and of the paraphrase. If one paraphrases the sentence 'Vehicles are not allowed into the public park' by 'Vehicles equipped with petrol engines cannot enter green areas', the intersection of the meaning bundles of both sentences includes such an understanding that cars and motorcycles cannot enter green areas which are not officially proclaimed public parks; it does not include, however, the directive that bicycles cannot enter public parks.
2. **Exemplification**. Exemplification is the process of deciding whether a particular object or class of objects is—or is not—referred to by the interpreted expression.

E.g., if one interprets the sentence 'Vehicles are not allowed into the public park', one can ask whether a given bicycle—or bicycles as such—are allowed into the public park. For interpretation, only negative exemplification is useful, i.e. such exemplification which shows that a certain object or class of objects is not referred to by the interpreted text. Only in this way one can narrow down the meaning bundle of the given text. Positive exemplification leads to reaffirming that a given meaning does indeed belong to the meaning bundle of the given expression and is useless for the purpose of interpretation.

5.3 Coherence in Interpretation

If one accepts the above presented conceptual scheme, it enables the determination of what are interpretation hypotheses or 'sentences capturing the meaning of the interpreted text'. They are either paraphrases of the interpreted text, or else some negative exemplifications. In both cases the goal is to narrow down the meaning bundle of the interpreted text, and so such hypotheses are essential to the process of interpretation.

Given the above, if one is to interpret a text then one is in the following position: she has at her disposal an interpreted language (L), a set or presuppositions (P), background knowledge (K) and a set of initial hypotheses (H), i.e., some paraphrases or negative exemplifications. What does the process of interpretation consist of? Gadamer describes it by recourse to the concept of a hermeneutic circle. He says, for instance:

> But the process of construal is itself already governed by an expectation of meaning that follows from the context of what has gone before. It is of course necessary for this expectation to be adjusted if the text calls for it. This means, then, that the expectation changes and that the text unifies its meaning around another expectation. Thus the movement of understanding is constantly from the whole to the part and back to the whole. Our task is to expand the unity of the understood meaning centrifugally. The harmony of all the details with the whole is the criterion of correct understanding. The failure to achieve this harmony means that understanding has failed (Gadamer 2004, 291).

And elsewhere he adds:

> Every revision of the foreprojection is capable of projecting before itself a new projection of meaning; rival projects can emerge side by side until it becomes clearer what the unity of meaning is; interpretation begins with fore-conceptions that are replaced by more suitable ones. This constant process of new projection constitutes the movement of understanding and interpretation (Gadamer 2004, 263).

According to my interpretation, Gadamer suggests that the structure of interpretation has a non-foundational character. In opposition to the 'linear' character of the classical logic, where from given premises one draws logically valid conclusions, non-foundational reasoning, although it begins with some premises, does not treat them as indefeasible. Michał Heller puts forward the following proposal:

> When one begins to solve a problem, (...), one accepts certain hypotheses (...). It is important to note that these are hypotheses, not certainties (...), and maybe even working hypotheses. By using them one arrives at a solution of a problem (...). The results of the analysis may either strengthen one's initial hypotheses, or lead to their modifications. Such a procedure may be repeated multiple times, resulting in the self-adjustment of the system (Heller 2006, 32).

Heller rightly observes that such an argument cannot be accounted for within classical logic. He urges us therefore to look for a 'non-linear logic', or such a logic that would encapsulate the structure of nonfoundational thinking.[3] Although I cannot offer such a full-blooded logic here, I would like to suggest that non-foundational arguments can be explicated with the use of some non-classical but well-known formal tools and, in particular, the formal theory of coherence.

The idea is simple: with a given language L, presuppositions P and the background knowledge K one puts forward certain hypotheses H aiming at capturing 'the meaning' of the interpreted text. Next, one establishes what are the consistent and relatively maximal subsets of the set $H \cup P \cup K$. These subsets are then compared, and the comparison may take into account in particular the measure of the logical coherence of the respective subsets. The measure in question is determined by taking into account: (a) the level of inferential connections between the members of a subset; and (b) the level of the subset's unification (BonJour 1985). There exist inferential connections between sentences belonging to a given set if they can serve together as premises in logically valid schemes of inference. In turn, a given set of sentences is unified if it cannot be divided into two subsets without a substantial loss of information. It is important to note that the idea of logical coherence is not a binary one, it is rather a matter of degree. The competing subsets of $H \cup P \cup K$ may be coherent to greater or lesser degrees.

I claim that such a formal conception captures the basic insights of the Gadamerian view of understanding (interpretation). Observe that it makes room for pre-understanding: one needs an interpreted language L, embraces some presuppositions P (which may be existential, lexical, etc.), accepts some background knowledge K and formulates her initial interpretation hypotheses H. Moreover, within the above presented formal framework it is possible to work with more than one initial hypothesis (which is in compliance with what Gadamer says: "rival projects can emerge side by side until it becomes clearer what the unity of meaning is"). Still, whether a hypothesis is to be accepted depends crucially on the context, i.e. the background knowledge and presuppositions, which constitute the hermeneutic 'whole' (it is consistent with Gadamer's view that "the movement of understanding is constantly from the whole to the part and back to the whole"). Finally, the chosen hypothesis (or hypotheses) are those which are most coherent with 'what has

[3] The classical relation of logical consequence is a non-linear function. In addition, there exist formal systems called nonlinear logics. However, Heller speaks of something different—a logic of epistemological nounfoundationalism—and hence I used the term 'non-linear logic' in quotation marks.

gone before', i.e. with presuppositions and background knowledge (cf. Gadamer's remark that "the harmony of all the details with the whole is the criterion of correct understanding").

Naturally, coherence does not have to be the only criterion for comparing the relatively maximal consistent subsets of H∪P∪K, although in the context of Gadamer's theory it plays a crucial role. Intuition dictates that one should not be willing to easily reject some of one's presuppositions or the elements of background knowledge. However, it is imaginable that some consistent subset of H∪P∪K which includes all the presuppositions and background knowledge is much less coherent than another subset in which some presuppositions or elements of background knowledge do not appear. In such a case, the latter should be preferred over the former. The rules for choosing from among the consistent subsets of H∪P∪K (logical coherence, 'preferential treatment' of presuppositions and background knowledge) enable one to determine, which of the initial hypotheses (paraphrases and negative exemplifications) are acceptable interpretations of the given text.

The above presented reconstruction of the hermeneutic conception of interpretation gives rise to the following conclusions. First, the process of interpretation consists in putting forward hypotheses which may be accepted, revised or rejected. Second, the hypotheses in question are evaluated by inspecting their logical consequences (more precisely: the logical consequences of H∪P∪K). Third, the hypotheses are evaluated against a certain context (the assumed presuppositions and background knowledge). Fourth, the process of interpretation should lead to making our understanding of the world more coherent: we should choose such interpretations (paraphrases or negative exemplifications) which increase the degree of coherence of our beliefs. Fifth, the formulated interpretation hypotheses are 'weaker', i.e., they are easier to reject, than presuppositions or background knowledge. However, none of the three categories of beliefs is revision-proof. In particular, a very 'successful' hypothesis may lead to the rejection of some elements of the background knowledge or even presuppositions. The last situation may be treated as a partial revision of one's conceptual scheme, as at least some of the assumed presuppositions serve as meaning postulates.

Thus, on the reconstruction proposed here, there are two methods of interpretation (paraphrase and negative exemplification) and one main criterion of interpretation (logical coherence), which may be augmented by some additional criteria (e.g., the 'preferential treatment' of presuppositions and background knowledge). This view may generate the following objection: in traditional legal theory many different conception of legal interpretation are postulated. For instance, the adherents of the Law & Economics movement believe that it is social welfare that should constitute the sole criterion of legal interpretation, while the proponents of some neo-Kantian theories insist that among the interpretation criteria in law there should be moral precepts. There seems to be no room for either position within the conceptual scheme sketched above. This objection is misplaced, or so I argue. My goal was to reconstruct a formal view of interpretation, one that is based on the insights of hermeneutics. I suggest that the formal aspect in question is limited to the two methods and one criterion of interpretation. Moreover, it is easy to incorporate the economic or the neo-Kantian directives into the proposed model: the economic or moral precepts are simply elements of one's background knowledge. If one believes that law should be so interpreted as to promote social welfare (i.e., this precept is included in one's background knowledge), one will choose such paraphrases or negative exemplifications which are welfare-enhancing because they will be more coherent with one's background knowledge than competing interpretation hypotheses.

5.4 Conclusions

The above considerations warrant the following conclusions. Firstly, they enable one to characterize the relationships between understanding, interpretation and application. Interpretation serves to narrow down the meaning bundle of the interpreted expression. The more the meaning bundle has been narrowed, the better one understands the given expression. Thus, understanding is not a binary concept, it should be measured by degree. Application, in turn, is some positive exemplification. When one makes a positive exemplification it does not mean that her understanding was 'final' or 'absolute', but that it was enough to apply the given expression to some object (state of affairs). In other words, when I disagree with the hermeneutic claim that one cannot distinguish between understanding, interpretation and application, I believe there are inextricable links between them.

Secondly, the theory I sketched is not limited to the interpretation of law. It is a theory of interpretation *tout court*. Moreover, it warrants the conclusion that interpretation plays only a secondary or limited role in legal reasoning. This claim is backed by two arguments. On the one hand, what lawyers aim at is positive exemplification. Consider the following legal provision: "Whoever kills a human being shall be imprisoned for the period of at least 8 years." What would it mean to interpret this sentence? One would need a kind of paraphrase or negative exemplification. These would in turn establish what the provision in question does not mean. The ultimate goal of legal reasoning is, however, to say that a concrete person (in the case of judicial reasoning) or an imaginary person or class of persons (in the case of dogmatic reasoning) does fall under the given provision (is in the scope of that provision). In terms of the analytical scheme provided above, the goal of legal reasoning can be described as positive exemplification (concerning a particular object or a class of objects). Naturally, interpretation can serve here as an auxiliary tool. But ultimately, the important legal decision is that some object or state of affairs falls under the scope of a provision. If a lawyer says that *clara non sunt interpretanda*, it does not apply to the process of interpretation as I have portrayed it. It will rarely (if ever) be the case that the process of interpretation has narrowed down the meaning bundle to just one meaning, that all the windows have been closed for the possibility of some other meaning to be ascribed, for some new negative exemplification to be applied etc. However, if a lawyer establishes that the given person—or a class of persons—falls under the interpreted provision, his work is done, even though the process of interpretation may be continued *ad infinitum*.

On the other hand, in what we call the hard cases, interpretation also plays a limited role. Here, we are usually concerned with a conflict of legal norms. If the provision is "No vehicles are allowed into the public park" and the question is, whether an ambulance with a seriously injured person can drive through the park, it is not a problem of interpretation. The provision "No vehicles are allowed into the public park" can under no concrete circumstances be read as saying that vehicles—with the exception of ambulances—are not allowed to enter the park. Rather, what we have here is a conflict between two legal norms: one barring vehicles from entering the park, and the other which urges us to do everything to save human life.

Thirdly, the proposed theory shows that coherence may indeed be a criterion of interpretation. This claim would be contestable if one treated interpretation as a psychological process—in such cases one would need to speak of the coherence of meaning or sense, which is unclear at the best. By proposing the idea of interpretation as narrowing down of the meaning bundle, I believe to have opened the way for discussing interpretation in terms of the relations between sentences, and thus of applying the criterion of coherence. Moreover, my analysis leads to the conclusion that—given the 'hermeneutic insights' pertaining to what is understanding—coherence is the main, if not the sole, criterion of interpretation.

References

Alston, W.P. 1964. *Philosophy of language*. Engelwood Cliffs: Prentice Hall.

BonJour, L. 1985. *The structure of empirical knowledge*. Cambridge: Harvard Unviersity Press.

Dickson, J. 2010. Interpretation and coherence in legal reasoning. In *The stanford encyclopedia of philosophy*, ed. Edward N. Zalta, (Spring 2010 Edition), URL=<http://plato.stanford.edu/archives/spr2010/entries/legal-reas-interpret/>.

Gadamer, H.G. 2004. *Truth and method*. London: Continuum.

Grondin, J. 2007. *Hans-Georg Gadamer. Biografia (Hans-Georg Gadamer. A biography)*. Wrocław: Wydawnictwo Uniwersytetu Wrocławskiego.

Heller, M. 2002. *Początek jest wszędzie (The beginning is everywhere)*. Warszawa: Prószyński.

Heller, M. 2006. Nauki przyrodnicze a filozofia przyrody (The Sciences and the Philosophy of Nature). In *Filozofia i wszechświat (Philosophy and the Universe)*, ed. M. Heller, 28–42. Kraków: Universitas.

Popper, K.R. 1972. *Objective knowledge*. Oxford: Clarendon.

Stelmach, J., and B. Brożek. 2006. *Methods of legal reasoning*. Dordrecht: Springer.

Chapter 6
Normative Inconsistency and Logical Theories: A First Critique of Defeasibilism

Giovanni Battista Ratti

6.1 Foreword

Coherentism in legal theory is often related to defeasibilism in logic. Roughly, coherentist views on law may be said to have stemmed from Dworkin's conception (1978, Chap. 1),[1] where a distinction between defeasible and indefeasible standards was first laid down.[2] Elaborating on such a distinction, coherentist views have lately come to consider that all the standards which belong to, or are applicable in, legal systems are to be considered as inherently defeasible. This turn in legal philosophy was somehow parallel to the elaboration of some defeasible deontic logics, which were designed to provide a better reconstruction and a better handling of normative systems (including legal systems) than standard deontic logic.

More precisely, in recent literature on defeasible logics, there is a tendency to mark the departure from the traditional understanding of the logic of normative and legal reasoning. According to the defenders of defeasible deontic logics, defeasibilist systems provide an explanation of how conflicting norms are processed, which standard deontic logic[3] cannot offer because of its very nature (Loui 1997,

I would like to thank Riccardo Guastini and Andrej Kristan for helpful comments on previous drafts of this article.

[1]A personal anecdote may help: I can recall Jules Coleman lecturing at the Faculty of Law of the University of Toronto and summing up this turn in legal philosophy by means of a catch phrase: "Dworkin is Quine to Hart's Carnap".

[2]See Alchourrón (1993, 67).

[3]For the purposes of this article, I will take as the main sample of standard deontic logic the system proposed in Alchourrón (1969), which is an extension of the system presented by von Wright (1951).

G.B. Ratti (✉)
Department of Legal Sciences, University of Genoa, Via Balbi 30/18, Genova 142160, Italy
e-mail: gbratti@unige.it

M. Araszkiewicz and J. Šavelka (eds.), *Coherence: Insights from Philosophy, Jurisprudence and Artificial Intelligence*, Law and Philosophy Library 107,
DOI 10.1007/978-94-007-6110-0_6,

350–351). This is supposedly so, for standard deontic logic is taken either (*a*) to rule out the very possibility of normative conflicts,[4] or (*b*) not to be able to offer any solution to normative conflicts (Loui 1997, 351).

In what follows, I will try to show that such attacks against standard deontic logic are misfired and that this logical theory may offer a thoroughly successful explanation of normative conflicts but need not offer any operative solution to such conflicts. Furthermore, I will argue that defeasible deontic logics are unclear as for their scope and, depending on the direction of fit that they are assigned, may be liable to several criticisms. Consequently, standard deontic logic is to be regarded as a better logical theory than defeasibile deontic logics. In so doing, I shall therefore demonstrate that, contrary to a widespread view, defeasibilism is no serious ally to any coherentist theory.

6.2 The (Supposed) Impossibility of Explaining Normative Conflicts

The first charge of defeasibilist theories against standard logic is that it is incapable of explaining normative conflicts. What is usually argued is that standard systems of deontic logic validate the sentence "$\sim$(Oa & O $\sim$ a)" and, for this reason, rule out normative inconsistencies. This is so because standard deontic logic is based on the following three axioms:

$$(A-0)\ Pa \equiv \sim O \sim a$$

$$(A-1)\ O\,(a\ \&\ b) \equiv (Oa\ \&\ Ob)$$

$$(A-2)\ Oa\ \supset Pa$$

As a matter of course, the system of theorems which may be developed from this set of axioms seems to have a very restricted scope, since it applies only to those normgivers which have brought about a consistent system of categorical norms, being "$\sim$(Oa & O$\sim$a)" a theorem of such a system (let us call it T-1). We will come back afterwards to the problem of categoricity of normative systems. Let us now consider the consistency problem.

The critique against the standard system of deontic logic according to which it is incapable of explaining normative inconsistencies may seem plausible in so far as it is limited to the prescriptive reading of deontic formulae. However, it must be remembered that, in the most nuanced systems of deontic logic, such sentences receives different treatments according to its interpretation in terms of

[4]See, for instance, Horty (1997, 19), and Ryu (1995).

norms or normative statements (the latter being descriptive propositions bearing upon norms).[5]

In the first interpretation (norms), T-1 is simply taken as a prescription for *optimal* normative systems, whereas in the second interpretation (normative statements upon norms), T-1 is understood as providing a sort of definition of a rational norm-giver, which, of course, can be frustrated in *actual* normative systems (Alchourrón and Bulygin 1984).

It seems clear that the first reading is not meant to rule out inconsistencies: it only determines an *ideal* state of affairs that ought to be satisfied by *ideal* normative systems. By contrast, the second reading is manifestly incapable of doing so and not even meant for it.

So, standard deontic logic, when properly understood in the twofold interpretations which have just been mentioned, seems to be totally capable of accounting for inconsistencies within normative systems.

The systems of logic corresponding to norms and normative propositions only overlap under perfect conditions: that is when the normative system, which is the object of description by means of normative propositions, is complete and consistent. In fact, the logic of normative propositions has two different operators which are intended to describe the permission of a certain state of affairs: the so-called "negative permission", describing the situation where there is no prohibition bearing upon a certain state of affairs which belongs to a certain legal system α (in symbols: $\mathbf{P}_{\alpha}{}^{-}p = O \sim p \notin \alpha$), and the so-called "positive permission", which describes the situation where an expressly authorizing norm belongs to the normative system α ($\mathbf{P}_{\alpha}{}^{+}p = Pp \in \alpha$).

Positive permission and negative permission may only be equated when the system, on which they bear, contains no gaps or conflicts. In fact, in complete normative systems, one may infer expressed authorization from lack of prohibition, and in consistent normative systems, one may infer lack of prohibition from expressed authorization (Rodríguez 2006, 102).

The particular fact that both deontic systems (norms and normative statements) overlap under ideal conditions, may explain why deontic logic is frequently and unduly criticized for not being able to account for normative inconsistency.

By contrast, from our discussion, one may derive that standard deontic logic provides a much richer set of tools for accounting for normative conflicts within legal systems than defeasibilist logical theories, which usually do not deal with (*et pour cause*) normative propositions. Accordingly, the first charge of defeasibilism must be dismissed.

Before turning to the second charge, we must briefly consider another criticism against standard deontic logic, consisting in maintaining that it has some difficulties in explaining conflicts among *conditional* normative sentences. In particular, this criticism is twofold: (1) there are conflicts of conditional norms (broadly understood) which cannot be reconstructed by means of standard deontic logic; (2) there

[5]See Alchourrón (1993), and Rodríguez (2000).

may be normative systems which may contain normative conflicts and, in spite of that, do not need to be revised in order to overcome such a difficulty (what seems to be assumed by common deontic logic, by accepting monotony).[6]

As for the first criticism, the argument is that some conflicts among categorical norms (broadly understood as conditional norms with a tautologous antecedent) and conditional norms are not easily dealt with under a standard logical framework (Horty 1997, 38). This is so because standard deontic logic is committed to augmentation (i.e., strengthening the antecedent), and so it detects a conflict where our ordinary intuition detects none, because, in ordinary reasoning, we constantly take the conditional norm as having priority over the categorical norm. This aspect would require, according to critics, some non-monotonic foundations for deontic logic. In my view, this argument is not convincing. There is no logical reason why a conditional norm should be always given priority over a categorical norm. And, in any case, if we understand that conditional norms should be overriding conflicting categorical norms, we must first recognize that there is a conflict, since it makes no sense to speak of "overriding" between norms which are not conflicting. However, such a conflict can only be spotted by means of augmentation: i.e., only if we admit that from "Oa/T"[7] and "O $\sim$ a/F", it follows that "O(a & $\sim$ a)". So, one cannot hold at once that augmentation should be weakened (at least for some norms) and that nonmonotonic deontic logic provides a better explanation of normative conflicts,[8] since weakening of augmentation would make it impossible to detect normative conflicts.

The second critique seems to conflate different aspects of the problem of normative conflicts (Alchourrón 1991, 424–425). A set of norms may be inconsistent *modulo* certain facts and consistent *modulo* other facts. An eminently inconsistent set is a set inconsistent under the empty set of facts. What the criticism under examination really suggests is that we have an abstractly consistent normative set which proves inconsistent relative to certain facts, because under such circumstances a certain agent is subject to opposite norms. But—as Alchourrón (1991, 425) writes—"From this it does not follow that for another agent or for different facts the set cannot remain practically useful, so we may refuse to apply the system on that occasion and continue to use it without any amendment on other occasions". So, the system can be used when it is consistent *modulo* the facts of the case but cannot be used when it is inconsistent. Accordingly, we need to revise it whenever we want to apply to the circumstances which give rise to the conditional inconsistency, but not in other circumstances. A general derivation from this argument is that the need for revision of a certain normative system is a variable of the scope of normative inconsistencies.

---

[6] See Hilpinen (1987, 37).

[7] "T" is for any tautology.

[8] This is one of the main arguments proposed by Horty (1997).

This holds of course if and only if we accept monotony. As a matter of course, we can detect a contradiction between the conditional norms "O(a/b)" and "O(~a/c)", if the norms "O(a/b & c)" and "O(~a/b & c)" are regarded as logical consequences of the former norms. Defeasibilist logics suggest that they are not. And, by doing so, they hold that the system needs no revision. They should add, however, that it needs no revision, since no conflict between conditional norms can be detected without monotony.

6.3 The (Supposed) Inability of Processing Normative Conflicts

The second charge is that standard deontic logic cannot account for or carry out the *processing* of normative inconsistencies. Defeasible deontic logics (or, more broadly, non-monotonic deontic logics) have supposedly supplied successful ways of dealing with inconsistencies in ordinary and juristic reasoning. Common examples of ordinary reasoning are the Tweety case and the so-called *Nixon Diamond*.

Notoriously, the first example concerns the situation where we commit, at the same time, to the universal sentence "All birds fly" (in symbols: "(x) Bx ⊃ Fx") and to the sentence that, Tweety being a penguin, it does not fly ("(x) Nx ⊃ ~Fx) & Na ⊃ ~Fa").[9] It is clear that our heuristic position is one where we have justified reasons to believe that Tweety both flies and does not fly ("Fa & ~Fa") since it is, at the same time, a bird and a penguin ("Ba & Na"). This complication is usually solved, in theoretical discourses, by the so-called principle of priority of specificity[10]: more specific information defeats more general information.[11]

---

[9]"B" is for "bird", "N" for "penguin", and "F" for "flying".

[10]A sentence with antecedent A is said to be more specific than a sentence with antecedent B, relative to a theory T, if we can derive all of B from A using only the sentences in T, but not vice versa.

[11]It is worth mentioning that, in the discussion of this problem, examples usually introduce other circumstances such as "x has a broken wing", "x has its legs, or wings, tied up", and so on. Now, it seems to me that there is a fundamental difference between the exceptions of penguins and the other mentioned exceptions. In the former case, what lacks is the dispositional property of "being able to fly". This means that a certain individual, which pertains to the subspecies of penguins, cannot possibly be able to fly (they are not able to fly under any circumstances). In the other cases, what lacks is not the dispositional property of being able to fly, which does not characterize any subspecies, but a contingent feature of a possible (viz. not necessary and not impossible) state of affairs (for instance: birds with a broken wing are able to fly if they are cured and they have presumably flown before being injured). The same, with more reason, may be argued as for birds with tied-up wings. So, the revision of the antecedent of the universal referring to penguins ends with the introduction of the exception regarding the fact that penguins cannot fly, whereas the revision of the antecedent of universals regarding "birds with broken wings" or "birds with tied-up

The *Nixon Diamond* problem is famously instantiated by the following state of affairs: Quakers usually are pacifists; Republicans usually are not pacifists. What about Richard Nixon, a Republican Quaker? Monotonic logics suggest we face an insolvable contradiction in such circumstances, precisely because of monotony, while non-monotonic logics do not, for their conclusions hold only in normal circumstances.

Two main approaches have been propounded in the field of non-monotonic logic to handle such conflicting sources of information like the *Nixon Diamond* (Antonelli 2010): the so-called "credulous" one and the "skeptical" one. According to the credulous approach, one should commit to as many defeasible conclusions as possible, subject to a consistency requirement, whereas according to the skeptical approach one should withhold assent from potentially conflicting defeasible conclusions.

The solving of the first antinomy is, upon first consideration, manifestly similar to the application of the *lex specialis derogat generali* principle for legal reasoning: a more specific rule defeats a more general one (this is used when jurists solve what, in the famous terminology of Alf Ross (1958, 128–132), is a "total-partial" inconsistency or antinomy). Indeed, according to some defeasible deontic logics, the more specific antecedent of two conflicting norms ought to dominate over the more general one.[12] As an account of ordinary legal reasoning, however, it is more than doubtful that the principle of specificity has a general scope as a principle of priority among conflicting norms. In many cases, in fact, the criterion *lex specialis* is said to compete with (and is often defeated by) other criteria, such as *lex superior derogat legi inferiori* and *lex posterior derogat legi priori*.[13] Specifically, the relationships among the criteria of solution of normative conflicts are contingent and changing, and no logic can be built in order to capture the "very nature" of conflict-solving in normative reasoning, for the simple reason that such a thing does not exist.[14] In addition to this, there is also a problem of commensurability of the criteria, which we shall discuss later on.

What we can do is to try to shed light on the way the three mentioned criteria actually work in legal reasoning: as has been accounted for, the relationships among the priority criteria are synchronically manifold and diachronically mutable, so that no logic can descriptively capture a stable usage of precedence among such criteria.[15] It can only prescribe, or suggest, a certain stable systematization of them

---

legs" can be endlessly revised due to contingent future facts ("Tweety is cured" or "Tweety's legs have been untied") which can materialize and trigger such a revision.

[12]See Nute (1999, 214–215); cf. also Loui (1997, 350).

[13]On the possible relations among the mentioned criteria, see Bobbio (113 ff.).

[14]Nute (1999, 216) admits that when more than one precedence criterion is taken into account, the relationships which can be envisaged among such criteria, and the defeasible or indefeasible treatment of them, are not easily depicted by a logical model. In this sense, defeasible deontic logics encounter, at a higher level, the same "problems" that classical deontic logic supposedly meet at a lower level.

[15]As Guastini (2010, 363 ff.) has shown, the criterion of speciality is commonly used to give a more specific norm priority over a more general one, but it is also used, sometimes, to give alternative

(this is the second reading of this thesis of the defeasibilist theories, which we will deal with in the following section).

The approaches to the second antinomy (a "partial-partial antinomy" in Ross's terminology) suggested by defeasible logics do not seem to be very promising, for they are either reducible to a deductivist approach or are not able to explain what happens in common, ordinary legal (and especially judicial) reasoning. To hold all the possible (defeasible) conclusions which can be drawn from the same set is viable only under the condition that incompatible results may be considered equally justified. In legal terms, this seems to mean that, when two (or more) incompatible norms may be derived from a certain legal set, the applicator is entitled to deem any of the two (or more) incompatible solutions justified. This is quite a sound idea, even though it runs counter the views of many legal philosophers who hold that, of two conflicting rules, one must necessarily be invalid.[16] At any rate, such an idea does not seem to require any kind of non-monotonic or defeasible reasoning. On the contrary, as we have already seen, the very fact of being able to spot the antinomy is due to the application of deductive, strictly monotonic logic.

In turn, the skeptical approach, consisting in withholding assent from incompatible conclusions, seems to be translatable into a stalemate of legal application, when considered from a jurisprudential standpoint. This of course can be a normal feature for non-evaluative legal science, whose precise task is to expose the possible solutions provided by the law without necessarily choosing one of them. But it cannot be accepted as to the judicial application of law, for no legal decision whatsoever can be taken, if both of two conflicting rules, on the grounds of which the case should be legally decided, are held as inapplicable.

Some further, and more general, qualifications are in order here.

It must be noted that successful logic models, based on "classical" deontic logic, have been propounded in order to explain the repercussions of acts of derogation (or rejection) of norms within inconsistent normative systems.[17] So, one cannot say that standard deontic logic does not have any explanation of how normative

---

priority to one of two rules which connect incompatible solutions to only a subset of the cases which are referred to in their antecedents. The chronological principle is used to cancel *ex nunc* the validity of a norm N1 which has been enacted before norm N2, which has the same hierarchical level as N1 and attaches an incompatible solution to the same set or subset of the cases referred to in the norms' antecedents. Finally, the hierarchical principle is used to solve antinomies between norms of different hierarchical levels, by invalidating *ex tunc* the inferior norm.

[16]As is widely known, this is, among others, Kelsen's as well as Dworkin's view. Cf. Ratti (2008, part I).

[17]The main one is, no doubt, the one elaborated by Alchourrón-Makinson (1981). See also Alchourrón-Bulygin (1981). Perhaps, it is worth recalling that this was one of the main stages to the elaboration of AGM theory (which was already noted on p. 147 of Alchourrón's and Makinson's paper), whose relevance for AI and nonmonotonic reasoning is richly explained in Carnota-Rodríguez (2006, 9 ff.). The analysis provided by Carnota and Rodríguez shows the genesis of Alchourrón's ideas on the topic (from legal theory to beliefs change) and how his works were fundamental in establishing this field of research.

conflicts are dealt with in practical discourse.[18] The criticism at hand, thus, may be understood as suggesting that standard systems of deontic logic do not provide a *solution* for antinomies. But such a criticism is clearly off target, since deductive logic is not meant to provide tools for solving normative conflicts; it is only meant to offer tools to detect them. It must also be observed that logic can be applied only when sentences (in this case, normative provisions) have already been interpreted: consequently, logic can only determine which consequences follow from accepting a certain interpretation of legal sources, but it does not say anything (and it need not say anything) about which interpretation, amongst different possible interpretations, ought to be chosen.

6.4 The Shortcomings of Deontic Logical Defeasibilism

So far, we have sketched logical defeasibilism mainly *via negativa*, by pointing to the theses which are rejected by such a movement. Now, it is time to turn to some features which characterize defeasibilism as theses affirmatively held by its defenders. For the purposes of what follows in this essay, two kinds of defeasibilism must be singled out.

Sometimes, defeasibilism (which we can call "hard defeasibilism") is characterized as being based on the idea that the antecedents of normative conditionals are only contributory (and hence not sufficient) conditions of the normative consequence.

Some other times, defeasibilism ("soft defeasibilism") is characterized as being based on the idea that there are some preference criteria among conflicting norms which may solve or even rule out such conflicts.

As we will see in the following pages, both kinds of defeasibilism are liable to some of the criticisms concerning the defects which they attribute to standard deontic logic. Defeasibilist proposals may indeed be alternatively read as either a descriptive account of how some operators reason within a certain domain or a prescriptive discourse about how they should reason in ideal circumstances. Both readings bring about several doubts, especially when applied to the legal domain.

6.4.1 The Descriptive Reading

If one opts for a descriptive reading of the defeasibilist proposals, one must observe that many systems of hard defeasibilism seem indeed to be incapable of accounting

[18] For this reason, it is very surprising that Royakkers-Dignum (1997, 263) ascribe Alchourrón's and Makinson's model to defeasible reasoning. This misattribution is probably due to a labelling problem: as mentioned in the text, there is a tendency to call "defeasible logics" those which deal with the problem of conflicts of norms.

for normative inconsistencies within normative systems, since they reject modus ponens and augmentation (i.e., monotony). Without the application of such laws, in turn, it is clear that no antinomy may be spotted within normative systems. On the one hand, in fact, it is impossible to derive incompatible solutions for a concrete case, if modus ponens is not admitted. On the other hand, as we have already mentioned, it is also impossible to determine whether two antecedents, which are connected to incompatible solutions, completely or partially overlap, if we do not admit augmentation.

Apart from this, there are also doubts about the explicative powers of soft defeasibilism, especially when applied to the legal domain. In fact, the difficulties of soft defeasibilism in locating the criticism towards standard deontic logic show a bit of conflation of several problems in reconstructing juristic reasoning about or with rules.[19]

Juristic reasoning may be broken down, for theoretical purposes, into three main phases or operations: (1) interpretation; (2) logical development; and (3) ordering.[20] By means of interpretation, jurists move from legal sources to legal norms, thus forming a normative basis. By means of logical development, jurists derive logical consequences from the normative basis, and are so able to detect the possible logical defects, such as gaps and antinomies, which affect the consequences of the normative basis they are handling. It is only with the third operation—i.e., ordering—that jurists deal with gaps and inconsistencies, by bridging the former and solving the latter by means of some priority criteria. It is not clear *where* defenders of defeasible logics locate defeasibility in legal reasoning.

By locating it in phase (2), one may renounce fully developing, from a deductive point of view, a normative basis. But this would make it impossible to spot systemic defects, such as gaps and antinomies. Another understanding, completely different as to its theoretical repercussion, may mean that some of the deductive consequences of the normative basis are held not to be valid, or at least not applicable.[21]

To locate it in phase (3) is tantamount to using the term "logic" in an unusual way, by simply changing the headings under which different juristic operations are accounted for. Development of the logical consequences would be equated with drawing retractable inferences from a certain normative basis, and the "real logical task" would consist in ordering, according to some preferential criteria, inconsistent

---

[19]As a matter of fact, the very "nature" of defeasible logics is controversial. Cf. for instance the following passage from Morado (2004, 324) where many of the typical characterizations of defeasible logic are impugned: "Defeasible reasoning is not necessarily an irrational pattern, nor does it require wrong conclusions or insecure premises. It is an inference which depends on the context and thus may be blocked. Moreover, it does not follow from the fact that rules are revisable (indeed, the majority of scientific rules are such), nor from the fact that it has tacit premises".

[20]See Bulygin (1986). In Ratti (2008), Bulygin's model is refined and eleven different operations usually carried by jurists are singled out and analysed. Here it is important to stress that further action—i.e. application of a general rule to a given case—is typically carried out by judges, but not by commentators.

[21]See Ferrer Beltrán-Ratti (2010).

or incomplete retractable conclusions. Note that such inferences are regarded as retractable because when they bring about gaps and antinomies, they are rejected and changed in favor of other inferences. But, as it is easy to see, this is only a change of lexicon, not of subject matter.

If this is so, the idea of defeasible legal reasoning seems to be capable of being accommodated within a traditional setting of metajuristic inquiry, which accepts the hard kernel of standard deductive logic. One can affirm, thus, that, in systems of defeasible logic, it is not the logic that has changed; it is rather the way of depicting logical tools and locating them in the theoretical reconstruction of jurists' operation that has changed.[22]

The only option left in our threefold model of juristic reasoning is to locate defeasibilism at the level of the interpretation of legal sources. From this perspective, the "defeasibilist turn" in deontic logic and legal theory probably may be read as a suggestion in favor of a wide reconsideration of the study of legal interpretation and its importance in legal reasoning, but has not much to do with logic proper. Such a reconsideration is very much welcome, but does not call for a new logic.

6.4.2 The Prescriptive Readings

As we have seen, standard approaches to law and logic limit themselves to offering the tools for describing the presence of antinomies within the law. Defeasibilist theories do not seem to be content with that, and ask for a more demanding task: to find a way out from normative conflicts. However, there is a basic ambiguity between hard and soft defeasibilist stances, which is worth emphasizing.

"Hard defeasibilism" is interested in implicit exceptions, whereas soft defeasibilism is characterized by its interest in explicit exceptions.

Accordingly, two prescriptive readings of the defeasibilist thesis are available.

In the first, hard, reading, the normative proposal consists in placing on the applier the burden of "closing" the norms antecedents, which are held to be "essentially" open: in other words, the applier ought to decide, mainly on axiological grounds, which is the complete list of operative facts of a certain norm. So, from a legal point of view, "hard defeasibilism" boils down to the prescription on the legal applier to manipulate legal rules in accordance with the demands of justice.[23] But, if justice—as it seems reasonable to believe—is not an objective domain,[24] this would trigger unlimited judiciary discretion.

[22]An analogous idea has been formulated with a catch phrase by Morgan (2000, 347), whose analysis is concerned primarily with ordinary, and not legal, reasoning: "The nonmonotonicity of commonsense reasoning is due to the way we use logic, and not due to the logic that we use".

[23]For discussion, see Tur (2001).

[24]Cf. the seminal Ross (1945).

In the second, soft, reading, the normative proposal consists in completely ordering the criteria of solution of conflicts, which are usually not completely ordered. Some defeasibilist models of processing normative conflicts have been propounded, which are based on the idea of the priority of the specific over the generic. Other theories allow for other priority-giving criteria, such as the principles of *lex superior* and *lex posterior*.[25]

It must be noted that such models are not satisfactory, since they do not take into account that, *qua* elements of a prescriptive theory of decision-making, such criteria are not on the same level. The *lex superior* principle is a criterion of (in)validity of legal rules, whereas the *lex posterior* principle is a criterion of derogation of legal rules. Only the *lex specialis* rule is a genuine criterion of priority, but it is applicable only to cases of inclusion of a norm antecedent into another. We must observe, consequently, that its scope is limited. Probably, these three different criteria need three different theoretical reconstructions, but the logic of such three reconstructions need not be non-monotonic. In any case, it must be born in mind that the task of ordering the criteria has repercussions that go far beyond the simple decision in a concrete case, since—as we have mentioned—the *lex superior* and *lex posterior* principles have derogatory effects, which are absent in the application of the criterion of specificity.

6.5 Concluding Remarks

Normative conflicts are dangerous, since from a contradiction any proposition follows, according to most systems of logic. Defeasibilism is a family of logical systems which run counter this idea. However, to do so, it rejects some of our most intuitive grounds for logical and legal reasoning.[26]

Hard defeasibilism rejects monotony and, by such a move, rules out the very idea of a genuine normative conflict: normative conflicts are only apparent, either because they do not materialize or because they are liable to be solved according to the rules of a certain normative system, by means of a complete revision.[27] So, there is no "all-things-considered" normative conflict. However, the theoretical price to pay is too high: it cancels jurists' intuitions about the possibility of genuine normative irresolvable conflicts and rules out the very conceivability of a theoretical reconstruction of normative conflicts. According to the maxim of minimal mutilation, we should rather be willing of preserving monotony (together with the

[25] See Nute (1999, 216–217).

[26] From a strictly logical point of view, it must reject at least one of the following rules: the rule for introducing the disjunction, the principle of monotony, the disjunctive syllogism, or the rule of cut. This is so because such rules conjunctively imply the *ex falso quodlibet* principle. For discussion, see Alchourrón (2010, 75).

[27] This is Dworkin's view, as I have tried to show in Ratti (2008, 143–173).

possibility of extracting all the interesting consequences from norms) and rejecting the idea that normative standards cannot conflict because they are logically open.

On the other hand, "soft defeasibilism" is either a misrepresentation of what happens in ordinary legal reasoning (by labeling as "logical" operations which are interpretive or axiological) or is the traditional reconstruction under new clothes.

On their prescriptive reading, finally, both versions of defeasibilism are defective. Hard defeasibilism is defective because it suggests that we shift the whole decision-making power on the appliers and, in so doing, undermines one of the main principles of modern democracies: elected representatives make the rules which the citizens ought to obey and the judges ought to apply. In turn, soft defeasibilism is defective for two reasons: (1) first, because it is based on an implicit and wrong comparison of principles which are, conceptually, on different levels of application and which have very different legal consequences; (2) secondly, because, consequently, the scope of its effects on decision-making is limited to a very limited array of cases.

References

Alchourrón, C.E. 1969. Logic of norms and logic of normative propositions. *Logique et Analyse* 47: 242–268.

Alchourrón, C.E. 1991. Conflicts of norms and the revision of normative systems. *Law and Philosophy* 10: 413–425.

Alchourrón, C.E. 1993. Philosophical foundations of deontic logic and the logic of defeasible conditionals. In *Deontic logic in computer science: Normative system specification*, ed. J.-J.Ch Meyer and R.J. Wieringa, 43–84. New York: Wiley.

Alchourrón, C.E. 2010. *Fundamentos para una teoría general de los deberes*. Madrid: Marcial Pons.

Alchourrón, C.E., and E. Bulygin. 1981. The expressive conception of norms. In *New studies in deontic logic*, ed. R. Hilpinen, 95–124. Dordrecht: Kluwer.

Alchourrón, C.E., and E. Bulygin. 1984. Pragmatic foundations for a logic of norms. *Rechtstheorie* 15: 453–464.

Alchourrón, C.E., and D. Makinson. 1981. Hierarchies of regulations and their logic. In *New studies in deontic logic*, ed. R. Hilpinen, 125–148. Dordrecht: Kluwer.

Antonelli, G.A. 2010. Non-monotonic logic. In *Stanford Encyclopedia of Philosophy*, ed. E.N. Zalta. URL=<http://plato.stanford.edu/entries/logic-nonmonotonic/>.

Bobbio, N. 1975. *Studi per una teoria generale del diritto*. Torino: Giappichelli.

Bulygin, E. 1986. Legal dogmatics and systematization of law. In *Vernunft und Erfarhung im Rechtsdenken der Gegenwart*, eds. T. Eckhoff, L.M. Friedman, J. Uusitalo, Rechtstheorie, Beiheft 10, 193–210.

Carnota, R., and R. Rodríguez. 2006. Carlos Alchourrón y la Inteligencia Artificial. *Análisis filosófico* 26: 9–52.

Dworkin, R. 1978. *Taking rights seriously*, 2nd ed. London: Duckworth.

Ferrer Beltrán, J., and G.B. Ratti. 2010. Validity and defeasibility in the legal domain. *Law and Philosophy* 29: 601–626.

Guastini, R. 2010. *Le fonti del diritto. Fondamenti teorici*. Milano: Giuffrè.

Hilpinen, R. 1987. Conflict and change in norm systems. In *The structure of law: Proceedings of the 2nd Benelux-Scandinavian symposium in legal theory*, eds. A. Frändberg, M. Van Hoecke, 37–49. Uppsala: Iustus Farlag.

Horty, J.F. 1997. Nonmonotonic foundations for deontic logic. In *Defeasible deontic logic*, ed. D. Nute, 17–44. Dordrecht: Kluwer.
Loui, R.P. 1997. Alchourrón and von Wright on conflicts among norms. In *Defeasible deontic logic*, ed. D. Nute, 345–351. Dordrecht: Kluwer.
Morado, R. 2004. Problemas filosóficos de la lógica no monotónica. In *Filosofía de la Lógica, Enciclopedia Iberoamericana de Filosofía*, vol. 27, ed. R. Orayen and A. Moretti, 313–344. Madrid: Trotta.
Morgan, C.G. 2000. The nature of nonmonotonic reasoning. *Mind and Machines* 10: 321–360.
Nute, D. 1999. Norms, priorities, and defeasibility. In *Norms, logics and information systems*, ed. P. McNamara and H. Prakken, 201–218. Amsterdam: Ios Press.
Ratti, G.B. 2008. *Sistema giuridico e sistemazione del diritto*. Torino: Giappichelli.
Rodríguez, J.L. 2000. Normative relevance and axiological gaps. *Archiv für Rechts—und Sozial-Philosophie* 86: 151–167.
Rodríguez, J.L. 2006. Naturaleza y lógica de las proposiciones normativas. Contribución en homenaje a G.H. von Wright. *Doxa—Cuadernos de Filosofía del Derecho* 23: 87–108.
Ross, A. 1945. On the logical nature of propositions of value. *Theoria* 11: 172–210.
Ross, A. 1958. *On law and justice*. London: Stevens.
Royakkers, L., and F. Dignum. 1997. Defeasible reasoning with legal rules. In *Defeasible deontic logic*, ed. D. Nute, 263–286. Dordrecht: Kluwer.
Ryu, Y.U. 1995. Conditional deontic logic augmented with defeasible reasoning. *Data & Knowledge Engineering* 16: 73–91.
Tur, R.H.S. 2001. Defeasibilism. *Oxford Journal of Legal Studies* 21: 355–368.
Von Wright, G.H. 1951. Deontic logic. *Mind* 60: 1–15.

Chapter 7
The Third Theory of Legal Objectivity*

Aldo Schiavello

7.1 Objectivity and Coherence: Introductory Remarks

This paper is devoted to a critical analysis of some models of legal objectivity. Considering that this book brings together essays that, with different approaches and perspectives, analyze the notion of coherence, some preliminary observations are required in order to clarify the connections between coherence and objectivity. For this purpose, some general and inevitably approximate considerations on the general notion of coherence and on the role that coherence plays in law and in legal discourse are needed (Schiavello 2001, 233–236).

The topic of coherence occupies an important place in the contemporary philosophical debate. This is due to manifold reasons that only partly converge.

In relationship to theoretical philosophy and epistemology, we have to emphasise the replacement of a model of knowledge of a descriptivist type,[1] typical of the most intransigent neo-positivism, with a holistic model highlighting the systematic

*In 1977, John Leslie Mackie published an essay on Ronald Dworkin, entitled "The Third Theory of Law". In this essay, Mackie presents Dworkin's theory of law's thought as an unsuccessful attempt to indicate a theory of law that was alternative both to legal positivism and to natural law theories. The criticisms that I make here of a conception of aspiring to occupy an intermediary space between strong conceptions and "conventionalist" legal objectivity ones are in line with Mackie's arguments, and this explains the title of this paper.

[1]The term 'descriptivism' refers to the epistemological conception according to which the task of the language of knowledge is to represent the world "as it is." To use a well-known metaphor by Richard Rorty (1980, 12–13), the descriptivists believe that the human mind works like a mirror able "to mirror reality." See also Villa (2004, 141–156).

A. Schiavello (✉)
Dipartimento di scienze giuridiche, della società e dello sport, University of Palermo,
Piazza Bologni 8, Palermo, 90134 Italy
e-mail: aldo.schiavello@unipa.it

M. Araszkiewicz and J. Šavelka (eds.), *Coherence: Insights from Philosophy, Jurisprudence and Artificial Intelligence*, Law and Philosophy Library 107,
DOI 10.1007/978-94-007-6110-0_7,

nature of cognitive activity, meaning it is not possible to predicate the truth or falsehood of the individual utterance but only of the overall system of beliefs and rational convictions.[2] Holism sees knowledge as "the global relationship between a conceptual scheme and a field of experience" (Villa 1993, 203). Joseph Raz points out the existence of a close relationship, not of a logical character,[3] between holism and coherence, as if we were talking about the same theses expressed from different points of view (Raz 1994, 283; see also Bermejo 2007, 51–56). Raz (1994, 278) defines holism as "[. . .] the view that everything depends on everything [. . .]" and, starting from this definition, observes that "if everything depends on everything, how is one to distinguish between truths and falsehoods if not by a test of coherence?"[4]

In relation to practical philosophy, coherence takes on a crucial role in John Rawls' theory of justice. One need only think of Rawls' conception of reflexive equilibrium, according to which our moral intuitions have to be tested out by general principles or even by a complete moral theory. This procedure makes it possible to adapt our intuitions to a coherent moral theory. The latter can in turn undergo some changes, if it proves incapable of justifying some particularly important intuitions. The result of this process is a state of potential equilibrium in which intuitions and moral theory balance one another. Rawls emphasises that this result is not to be considered as a definitive conquest in that, after reaching a position of equilibrium, one passes on to a subsequent stage of instability preluding a further equilibrium, and so on ad infinitum (Rawls 1993, 28, 1999, 15–19; Peczenik 2005, 129–137; Maniaci 2008, 231–326).

Holism and reflexive equilibrium—though often referred to together as basic reasons for interest in coherence in the general philosophical debate—do not necessarily presuppose one another: it is quite possible to take up a conventionalist-holistic position in the epistemological field and, for instance, to adhere to an anti-cognitivist perspective in ethics or to accept reflexive equilibrium starting from a neo-positivistic conception of knowledge. A significant example of the latter possibility is represented by Rawls himself. Rawls, though emphasising that reflexive equilibrium constitutes an argumentative procedure going beyond the sphere of ethics,[5] tends to give major weight to the difference between social sciences and

[2]On holism, see Duhem (1954), Quine (1953a, 20–46, b, 47–64, 1960), Gargani (1985).

[3]In this connection, Andrei Marmor (1992, 79) observes that "holism, however, does not necessarily lead to a coherence theory. It is a negative view in the sense that it provides no answer to the question of a substitute for foundationalism, for which status a coherence theory of knowledge is only one candidate."

[4]There are also weaker conceptions of holism than that presented by Raz. See Iglesias Vila (1999, 215–217), Maniaci (2008, 219–220).

[5]Rawls, for instance, mentions both Nelson Goodman, who uses an argumentative scheme similar to his own to explain inductive and deductive inference, and Joel Feinberg, who compares the argumentative method of philosophical discussion to discussions in courts of justice, where principles and legal precedents are continually adjusted to one another. See Goodman (1973, 64), Feinberg (1973, 34).

natural sciences,[6] and evidently this is not compatible with a constructivist and coherentist conception of knowledge.[7] However, this observation can be put in brackets since it does not invalidate the fact that coherence plays a major role in contemporary philosophical reflection.

Also in the more restricted sphere of law, of legal philosophy and legal science it is possible to identify some main factors that, starting from the last decades of the last century, helped to generate renewed interest in the theme of coherence.[8] Among these factors it is appropriate to mention the burgeoning of theories of legal reasoning, the more and more evident centrality of legal principles—particularly constitutional ones—in judicial and doctrinal reasoning, the passage from theories of law as an "object" (from time to time, norms, judicial decisions and so on) to theories of law as a social practice (Viola and Zaccaria 1999, 21–44; Viola 1990), and the complexity of contemporary legal systems defying traditional theories of the legal system and the sources of law. All this is well summed up by Ronald Dworkin's statement (1986, 13) that "legal practice, unlike many other social phenomena, is *argumentative.*"

It hardly needs specifying that in the past too coherence played a role in the reflections of legal philosophers and jurists, but it was a circumscribed role, linked to the elimination of logical contradictions between the normative materials of a legal system (Bobbio 1993, 201–235).

The preceding observations highlight some of the main links between coherence on one side and truth, correctness and objectivity on the other. Summing up, contemporary theories of truth and objectivity accord increasing space to the requisite of coherence. This space is even ampler in the legal sphere. Aleksander Peczenik (1990, 178), for instance, observes that "coherence is a central element of a fully-fledged concept of justification, rationality and correctness."[9] Nevertheless, broad reflection on the truth and correctness of our claims on law—in other words,

---

[6]After introducing the role that reflective equilibrium plays in moral philosophy, Rawls (1971, 49) writes: "but there is a contrast, say, with physics. To take an extreme case, if we have an accurate account of the motions of the heavenly bodies that we do not find appealing, we cannot alter these motions to conform to a more attractive theory. It is simply good fortune that the principles of celestial mechanics have their intellectual beauty (Hanen 1983)."

[7]I use the expression 'post-analytical constructivism' to refer to the epistemological perspective that derives from Wittgenstein's later reflections. See Hanen (1983). For a full presentation of this philosophical conception see Villa (1993, 187–228).

[8]I here follow Pino (1998, 187–228).

[9]Peczenik (1990, 178) clarifies his statement as follows: "If the norm- or value-system in question is more coherent than any competing system, then it is *prima facie* better justified and more rational than any competing system. If the norm- or value-system in question is more coherent than any competing system, then there exists a *prima facie* reason that it is correct."

reflection on the objectivity of law—makes it possible to set coherence in a general framework. This is the contribution that my paper on the objectivity of law can offer in a debate on coherence and law.

7.2 Objectivity of Law: An Outline

The topic of legal objectivity concerns the determination of the status of the norms that constitute the major premise, the normative premise, of the practical syllogism that represents the formal scheme of justification judicial decisions. The justification of judicial decisions implies the identification of a major normative premise ("if A, then B") and of a minor factual premise consisting in taken as proven that a given individual was engaged in the behaviour A to which the norm indicated in the major premise links sanction B. For instance, if a legal norm establishes that motorists that exceed 50 km per hour in a built-up area must be punished with a fine of £50,000 (major premise) and if it has been proved that a person has exceeded the limit set (minor premise), then it follows that that person must pay a fine of £50,000 (conclusion).

The issue of legal objectivity therefore revolves around the question of whether the existence and, above all, the meaning of the legal norms depends entirely on the opinion of judges and jurists considered individually (subjectivism), or whether it can be affirmed that, at least to some extent, the law is independent of the opinion of judges and jurists considered individually.

A "liberal" conception of law cannot give up the idea that legal norms are objective in some sense. Indeed, one thesis that characterizes liberal legal thought and the very idea of rule of law is the one according to which correct judicial decisions are the result of the subsumption of the specific case under a general and abstract norm promulgated by a democratically elected legislative organ. The judges are called on to decide judicial cases on the basis of reasons furnished by the legislative power. It also needs specifying that this thesis does not imply adhesion to any version of interpretative formalism: saying that legal norms circumscribe the discretion of judges does not mean one has to agree with the Enlightenment idea (taken up by legal positivism in the nineteenth century) that jurisdictional activity is a mechanical activity.

The connection between rule of law and objectivity is already rendered explicit, for instance, by Neil MacCormick in *Legal Reasoning and Legal Theory:* "Judges present themselves as the impartial determiners of disputes between citizen and citizen, or of prosecutions by public authorities of citizens. *They so present themselves at least because within the dominant political tradition that is what they are expected to be. They are appointed to do 'justice according to law', and the watchdogs of the public interest are continually alert to yap at their heels if they appear to do any other thing*" (MacCormick 1994, 17, italics added).

In the most recent writings, this connection leads MacCormick to abandon the legal positivism expounded by Hart and the value-scepticism derived from Hume that were originally in the background of his theory of legal reasoning: "If the Rule of Law means a government of laws and not men, then it is impossible if the judicial infallibility thesis is true. For the governance of laws turns out to be just the governance of the people that do the legal deciding. On the alternative view, the idea of the Rule of Law will acquire a different sense. The idea will be that the persons who do the deciding are charged with upholding and implementing the law rather than making it by their opinions."[10]

If norms do not impose any constraint on judges' behaviour, then, as MacCormick puts it, the Rule of Law turns into the Rule of Men. Precisely this is the principal challenge that normative scepticism throws out to legal normativism: law is nothing but the manifestation of the discretionary and subjective choices of judges, and, therefore, all those theoretical reconstructions of the legal phenomenon that identify a limit to legal discretion in general and abstract norms would be nothing but falsifications of reality.

Here, however, I will not go into this debate in depth. My target is, rather, to analyze critically the conception of the objectivity of law worked out by Jules Coleman and Brian Leiter starting from a legal philosophical background clearly deriving from Hart. The study by Coleman and Leiter is interesting because it is one of the few attempts that contemporary legal positivism has made for the purpose of presenting a philosophically sophisticated conception of the objectivity of law, expressly presented as a confutation of the subjectivism defended by normative scepticism.

Coleman and Leiter reject both objectivity in a strong (or "Platonic") sense, as accepted by the different natural law doctrines, which presupposes metaphysical realism and therefore rules out the possibility that what seems correct to someone can determine what is effectively correct, and minimal objectivity, according to which what seems correct to most members of a community determines what is effectively correct. They therefore defend a "modest" conception of objectivity—halfway between Platonic objectivity and minimal objectivity—according to which what is effectively correct is what seems such to those people who find themselves in the "ideal epistemic conditions."

In the next sections I will show some structural limits connected to the conception of objectivity put forward by Coleman and Leiter. More precisely, the general goal is to show that *modest objectivity* does not succeed in getting over the alternative between objectivity in a strong (or Platonic) sense and objectivity in a weak sense (or conventionalism).

Lastly, I believe that the criticisms made in this essay of the conception of objectivity proposed by Coleman and Leiter identify certain difficulties that, at least to some extent, are shared by all attempts to trace out an intermediary pathway between a "metaphysical" conception of objectivity and a conventionalist conception.

---

[10]MacCormick (2005, 276). For a criticism of the recent developments of MacCormick's theory of legal reasoning, see Schiavello (2011, 139–154).

7.3 Strong Objectivity and Its Limits

Objectivity in a strong sense ("Platonism") implies metaphysical realism.[11] More precisely, this conception of objectivity is characterized by the two following theses: (a) facts are independent of our epistemic access to them; (b) it is possible to know these facts in an objective way.

The main objection that is made to objectivity in a strong sense consists of observing the difficulty of reconciling these two theses: if facts are independent of our epistemic access to them, how can we be certain that our cognitive practices are suited to knowing such facts? That is to say, in relationship to the objectivity of law: "... what reason is there for thinking that conventional adjudicatory practices involve reliable mechanisms for identifying legal facts?" (Coleman and Leiter 1995, 257).

The supporters of this conception of objectivity can follow two pathways in order to reply to this objection.

The first option substantially consists in foregoing thesis b) indicated above. In this way, legitimisation of the authority of law would exclusively depend on the existence of independent legal facts regardless of the concrete judges' skill to identify them. In this way, objectivity and the one right answer thesis would be a sort of regulatory idea in a Kantian sense.[12]

This strategy is not particularly convincing: "The fact that there are right answers would count for very little if judges were invariably to come to the wrong conclusions about them. [...] In order for coercion to be justified it must be employed to enforce answers that are generally correct, not just ones judges happen to reach." (Coleman and Leiter 1995, 257).

In brief, we could call this perspective "metaphysical objectivism": the fact that in the world there exist some objective norms and values does not imply that there are criteria making it possible to establish with certainty what these norms and values are and, accordingly, to settle the controversies. This form of objectivism, however, expresses a philosophical thesis which is of slight interest. As Jeremy Waldron (1992, 173) observes, "...moral disagreement remains a continuing difficulty for realism, even if it doesn't entail its falsity, so long as the realist fails

---

[11]The fundamental thesis of metaphysical realism is that every utterance is made true or untrue by an objective reality whose existence is independent of our knowledge. See, Dummett (1981, 434). Hirst (1967, 77) defines realism as "the view that material objects exist externally to us and independently of our sense experience. Realism is thus opposed to idealism, which holds that no such material objects or external realities exist apart from our knowledge or consciousness of them, the whole universe thus being dependent on the mind or in some sense mental".

[12]This option is accepted by MacCormick (2005, 277) among others: "The kind of reasoning which goes forward in legal decision-making, legal argumentation, and indeed in legal thought in all its forms and levels is, as this book in common with other contemporary authors maintains, a form of practical reasoning. All practical reasoning works on the presuppositions that there may be some matters upon which opinion can be right or wrong. It proceeds under a pretension to correctness, an implicit claim to being correct, not just to being boldly or confidential asserted".

to establish connections between the idea of objective truth and the existence of procedures for resolving disagreement."

The second strategy consists of defending the thesis that interpreters and judges effectively have access to the correct solutions to legal disputes. Upholding this thesis means identifying an epistemology of legal practice that is compatible with metaphysical realism on the subject of legal facts.

An attempt in this direction has for instance been made by Michael S. Moore (1995, 1–29). He defends a "coherentist" position about judicial justification: the justified beliefs in relation to what the law requires in a concrete case are those that show the greatest degree of consistency with one another and with the conception of law endorsed by judges.[13]

This perspective does not face up to the main difficulty; in short, it is not able to explain why the fact that the sum of beliefs of a judge are coherent with one another should be deemed a sufficient reason to think that law is objective in a metaphysical sense and, above all, to think that the decisions of judges mirror law as it effectively is. Apparently, assuming that the world is coherent in turn does not make it possible to overcome this difficulty. Why, in fact, should the coherence of our beliefs correspond to coherence of things in the world?

7.4 Conventionalism and Its Limits

According to minimal objectivity, it is the majority of the members of the reference group that determines what is effectively correct. Therefore it is a conventionalist version of objectivity, which is distinguished from Protagorean subjectivism ("man is the yardstick of all things") only by the fact of shifting the "yardstick" from the single human being to the community as a whole.

Unlike Platonic objectivity, minimal objectivity does not admit the possibility of comprehensive errors: if the truth or correctness of something depends on a conventional accord, then it is logically impossible for everyone to be wrong on the truth or correctness of something (Marmor 1998, 3–31).

> This conception of objectivity is intimately linked to Hart's practice theory of norms. In brief, Hart works out a theory of social rules whose aim is to distinguish social rules from mere habits and regulated behaviours from those that are merely regular. One of the principal criticisms that Hart makes of John Austin's imperativism is precisely not having perceived the importance of this distinction and, as a result, having overlooked the concept of norm.

Social rules, unlike habits, in addition to regularity of convergent behaviours, also present an internal aspect: "what is necessary is a critical reflective attitude to certain patterns of behaviour as a common standard, and that this should

[13]On the role of coherence in law, see Raz (1994, 277–325), Schiavello (2001, 233–243), Pérez Bermejo (2013 in this volume).

display itself in criticism (including self-criticism), demands for conformity and in acknowledgements that such criticism and demands are justified, all of which find their characteristic expression in the normative terminology of 'ought', 'must', and 'should', 'right' and 'wrong'" (Hart 1994, 57).

According to Hart, the rule of recognition, the rule of rules identifying the validity criterion of other legal norms, is a social rule. A rule of recognition exists when it is possible to identify a group of people that accepts this rule from the "internal point of view." The latter does not necessarily imply moral acceptance of a legal system and its fundamental principles, but only a reflective critical attitude that is empirically verifiable. This empirical verification consists both in analysis of the linguistic expressions that go with legal obligations and in observation of the fact that officials, in particular judges, act in accordance with the secondary norms.

A further issue is specifying the group of people whose acceptance is relevant in relation to the existence of a rule of recognition and, consequently, of a legal system as a whole. On this point, Hart's answer is very clear: "the assertion that a legal system exists is therefore a Janus-faced statement looking both towards obedience by ordinary citizens and to the acceptance by officials of secondary rules as critical common standards of official behaviour" (Hart 1994, 117).

The practice theory of norms tells us that a rule of recognition exists when it is accepted (at least) by judges. This ontological thesis on law—that is to say, the thesis that the rule of recognition and, more in general, the law of a community coincides with the attitudes and convergent behaviours of the participants, and of judges in particular—has some implications at a methodological or meta-theoretical level: law is a fact that can be described in a non-evaluative way looking at the attitudes and convergent behaviours of the participants (neutrality thesis).

In general it can be observed that conventionalism seems unable of accounting for that surplus of meaning that prevents us from identifying social practices with the convergent behaviours of participants: "... the practice and the scope of duties to which the practice give rise outruns the scope of convergent behaviour" (Coleman 1995, 65). Nevertheless, when an attempt is made to explain what this "objectivity of practice" consists in or the surplus of meaning in relation to the convergent behaviours, there are such difficulties, and so many of them, as to induce one to "be satisfied" with an explanation of social practices in conventionalist terms. In a sense, a remarkable characteristic of conventionalism (or minimal objectivity) is that of appearing, at least at first sight, as the only reasonable reconstruction of some sectors of human experience and, at the same time, as an artificial way out.

In relation to the specific problem of the objectivity of law, it is possible to make two objections to conventionalism.

In the first place, the fact that the meaning of rules and legal principles is conventionally fixed, and therefore reflects the dominant legal culture, threatens the legitimacy of law as an arbitrator between conflicting interests and conceptions of good. In other words, what we consider objective legal facts would be nothing but the expression of the prejudices of judges who, in most cases, belong to the better-off social classes.

In truth, this objection to conventionalism does not appear insurmountable or even particularly sophisticated. Even a legal realist like Alf Ross, for instance, admits that judges are influenced, in the exercise of their profession, not so much (or, at least, not only) by belonging to a determined social class or, in general, by vested interests, as by awareness of their function, by the "cultural tradition." As Ross (1958, 99) puts it: "[the judge] looks on his activity as a task in the service of the community. He wishes to find a decision that shall not be the fortuitous result of mechanical manipulation of facts and paragraphs, but something which has purpose and meaning, something which is valid."

Secondly, the advocates of a minimal conception of objectivity are in trouble in cases of rational disagreement. According to conventionalism—one thinks precisely of Hart's reflections on social rules—the obligation imposed by the rules is determined by the convergent behaviour of individuals. Consequently, in the absence of a convergent behaviour there is no duty. In most cases, the convergent behaviour under-determines what rule is effectively being followed (for instance: does one always have to stop when the traffic lights are red or, in an emergency, is it possible to go through nonetheless?). However, even in those cases in which there is disagreement with regard to what the law requires, one can still believe, and indeed believes, that the law effectively requires something. This evidently constitutes a problem for minimal objectivity, which affirms, as we have seen, that in the absence of convergent behaviour, there is no rule.[14]

However, this objection too can be countered, at least partially. Coleman (1983, 28–48) himself, in a well-known essay, offers two possible answers.

Firstly, Coleman, taking up some observations by David Lewis (1969, 36–82), clarifies that the obligations imposed by social rules or conventions may not to be identified by mere convergent behaviour but, rather, by the expectations induced by efforts to coordinate the behaviour. Consequently, "vested, warranted expectations may extend beyond the area of convergent practice, in which case the obligations to which a social rule gives rise might cover controversial, as well as uncontroversial, cases" (Coleman 1983, 43).

Secondly, he affirms that when controversies arise on the obligation imposed by a certain rule—Coleman refers particularly to Hart's rule of recognition—it is not necessary to conclude, from a conventionalist perspective, that no obligation exists. In fact, there is (or can be) an obligation that arises from widespread acceptance of the practice of settling such controversies in a certain way, for instance resorting to principles of critical morality.

[14]This objection was presented particularly effectively by Ronald Dworkin (1977, 46–80) in the context of his critical analysis of Hart's theory of obligation. See Hart's replies in Hart, (1994, 254–259). Dworkin refines his criticism of conventionalism in Dworkin (2006, 4 ff.).

7.5 The Third Theory of Legal Objectivity and Its Limits

According to modest objectivity, what is effectively correct is what appears to be so to those people who are in the "epistemic ideal conditions." The latter can be defined, as a first approximation, as the best conditions for reaching reliable knowledge of something.

From this follows that modest objectivity, unlike minimal objectivity, admits the possibility of comprehensive errors. This possibility, however, is not connected, as in the case of objectivity in a strong sense, to any form of realism, but to incapacity to get into the best perspective of observation. To use the words of Coleman and Leiter (1995, 266): "... modest objectivity is not objectivity in the sense of a world whose character is independent of our epistemic tools for gaining access to it; rather, it is objectivity that involves the substantial (but not total) absence of subjectivity. It is an attempt to abstract away from the kinds of subjectivity that might intercede between us and items in the world that we conceive of as possessing some measure of independence from our existing subjective propensities. It is not [...] a kind of objectivity that require abstraction from all aspects of subjective human experience, however."

Coleman and Leiter also specify that they do not necessarily intend to defend modest objectivity as a general conception of objectivity, applicable to every sector of knowledge, but only as that conception of objectivity that makes it possible to explain interpretative practice in the legal sphere in the most appropriate way. In other words, defending a modest conception of objectivity in the case of interpretation of law does not for instance prevent one from upholding the strong conception of objectivity in relation to physical objects of average size.

The main doubts connected with modest objectivity concern the notion of 'ideal epistemic conditions.' Coleman and Leiter clarify this notion by recourse to an example that it is interesting to follow in detail. They consider the quality of colour. According to modest objectivity, something is, for instance, red because it appears to be such to observers in the ideal epistemic conditions. In this specific case, the ideal epistemic conditions require that the observations should not be made at night, that the light should be sufficiently bright, that the observers should not be colour-blind, and so forth.

On what grounds can we affirm that, in the case of colours, the ideal epistemic conditions are precisely these and not others? According to Coleman and Leiter, the ideal epistemic conditions are determined by the shared concept of colour in our linguistic practices. More precisely, to identify the ideal epistemic conditions in this specific case requires "unpacking" our concept of colour, our conception of how the property of colour works in our linguistic practices. Accordingly, modest objectivity presupposes that it is possible to identify a sufficiently uncontroversial notion of the property or field of significant experience.

The operation that we have seen exemplified speaking of the property of colour can also be performed in the case of law, on condition that there exists—which Coleman and Leiter do not doubt—a shared notion of law. In brief, in order to achieve objective knowledge of legal facts, a judge has to be able to identify all the significant sources of law, has to be fully rational (for instance he/she has to respect the rules of logic), has to be free of personal resentment towards either of the parties involved, has to be able to weigh up conflicting interests, and has to be culturally open so as to be able to reason analogically having the ability to distinguish between relevant and irrelevant differences.

This conception of objectivity is in many respects assimilable to the one worked out by Dworkin. Dworkin too, though in a way that is not always linear,[15] seems to go in search of a conception of objectivity that is halfway between objectivity in a strong sense and conventionalism. He maintains that for every legal case a correct answer exists. This answer coincides with that reached by his mythological judge *Hercules*, "[. . .] a lawyer of superhuman skill, learning, patience and acumen [. . .]."[16] In other words, the correct answer is the one offered by a judge that is in the ideal epistemic conditions: "thus, the kind of objectivity involved in the right-answer thesis is not independent of epistemic access to legal facts" (Coleman and Leiter 1995, 275). In conclusion, what Dworkin's reflections on objectivity and those of Coleman and Leiter have in common is above all the attempt to delineate a conception of legal interpretation's objectivity that, though not being independent of interpretative and, in general, linguistic practices, shared by judges, jurists, legal operators and simple citizens, aspires to distinguish itself from mere conventionalism.

The main objection that can be made to this conception of objectivity is that it does not succeed in getting over the alternative between Platonic objectivity and conventionalism.

Coleman and Leiter make the objectivity of legal facts depend on the possibility of identifying a shared notion of law. In other words, they simply shift the problem of objectivity from the legal facts as such to the general notion of law. In this case too, nevertheless, it seems to me that two options remain: either the notion of law has a conventional nature, and then modest objectivity is reduced to a form

[15]Dworkin in some writings develops a "deflationist" attitude to objectivity. He maintains that it is not appropriate to talk of objectivity in relation to interpretation, since the correctness or otherwise of affirmations in this sphere of discourse entirely depends on questions that are internal to the practice in question and not on questions that are in some way to be connected to a reality external to the practice. In other words, in the specific case of interpretative practices he considers 'objectivity' and 'truth' as *redundant words*. Dworkin uses this argument to criticize that form of scepticism that he defines as external or Archimedean. The external sceptic, for instance, thinks that it cannot be affirmed that the utterance 'slavery is unjust' is true since in the universe something like the injustice of the slavery does not exist. According to Dworkin, the mistake of external scepticism is not understanding that "the game being played" does not have among its rules that of correspondence with the reality; it consists, rather, in presenting the best possible arguments in support of one's opinions or beliefs. Therefore, when external scepticism maintains that our convictions are not "real", it affirms a true thing but also an obvious one without any utility. These observations by Dworkin are nevertheless hardly compatible with his criticism of conventionalism and his "one right answer" thesis. See Dworkin (1983, 287–313), Id. (1996, 87–139), Coleman (1995, in particular 48–61), Stavropoulos (1996, in particular 160–162).

[16]Dworkin (1977, 105). See also Greenawalt (1992, 208–212).

of conventionalism, or it has a transcendent nature, and then modest objectivity is nothing but a version of Platonism.

Coleman and Leiter's reply to this objection is not convincing. This reply consists in three arguments that it is interesting to analyze in detail.

In the first place, they affirm that: "there is a difference, however, between saying that the nature of X is determined by what the community believes about X (conventionalism or minimal objectivity) and saying that the nature of X is determined by what people under *appropriate or ideal* conditions would believe about it. Even where what counts as an idealization depends on our 'conventional' practice [. . .], the account of objectivity still obviously differs." (Coleman and Leiter 1995, 270. Authors' italics).

This argument, however, does not make it possible qualitatively to distinguish modest objectivity from conventionalism or from minimal objectivity: we see why by going back to the example of the property of colour.

According to minimal objectivity a rose is (objectively) red if the majority of the members of the reference linguistic community believe that the rose in question is indeed red; according to modest objectivity, instead, a rose is (objectively) red if it appears such to those who are in the ideal epistemic conditions.

There are certainly some differences between these two conceptions of objectivity. The issue, however, is establishing whether such differences are so significant as to allow Coleman and Leiter to qualify modest objectivity as a conception of objectivity that is qualitatively different from conventionalism.

Well, modest objectivity simply shifts to a level of further abstraction the conventionalist aspect connected to the minimal conception of objectivity. Accordingly it is not correct to consider modest objectivity as a conception of objectivity that is radically alternative to conventionalism.

According to the modest conception of objectivity, in order to establish whether an object is for instance red it is necessary to be in the ideal epistemic conditions. Apparently, therefore, according to this conception of objectivity, the possibility of predicating the objectivity of a belief seems not to consider the fact that in a given linguistic community the belief in question is effectively shared by the majority of the participants (for instance: that the rose is red does not depend on this belief being shared by most of the members of the linguistic community, but on its appearing so to those who are in the ideal epistemic conditions).

In effect, however, identification of the ideal epistemic conditions implies that there is a conventional agreement at a conceptual level. In other words, modest objectivity is also a version of conventionalism: the fact that the conventionalist aspect of this conception of objectivity is "screened" or mediated by the introduction of the notion of 'ideal epistemic conditions' is not by itself a sufficient condition for the purpose of considering modest objectivity as a conception of objectivity that is alternative to conventionalism. It is, rather, a version of conventionalism.

An example can perhaps help to clarify this point. In order correctly to identify the grammatical rules of a natural language—of the English language, for instance—it is certainly not advisable to look at the way in which the majority of mother-tongue speakers write and speak. It is advisable, instead, to identify such rules by looking at the way in which the narrow circle of people speak and write who are recognized to have authority in the linguistic sphere (linguists, writers, poets, intellectuals and so forth). Nevertheless, in this case too, the fact that a narrow circle of people is considered an authority in the linguistic sphere presupposes an accord in this sense, of a conventional type, among all the members of the linguistic community in question.[17]

Secondly, Coleman and Leiter believe that the fact that some concepts (or, more exactly, notions) are an integral part of a conventional practice does not mean that such concepts are in turn conventional: "the practices may be conventional, but conventional practices may be committed to practice-transcendent or non-conventional concepts." (Coleman and Leiter 1995, 270).

Well, the claim that conventional practices can involve concepts that transcend practice or are of a non-conventional nature can be understood in two different ways.

In a strong sense, the claim in question resolves into the thesis that there are some concepts that, though applying in conventional practices, nevertheless are not in turn of a conventional nature. For example, defending this position amounts to affirming that the fact that legal practice—that is the set of activities carried out by judges, legislators, lawyers and legal operators in general—is a conventional practice, does not imply that the concept of law cannot be transcendent or, so to speak, cannot be part of the "furniture of the universe." However, this thesis is very difficult to defend, in that it markedly reduces—or even wipes out—the distance that separates modest objectivity from objectivity in a strong or Platonic sense. The fact is that if the ideal epistemic conditions represent the result of the "unpacking" of the notion of law, and if the notion of law has a non-conventional nature, then the ideal epistemic conditions will have also a non-conventional nature.

In a weak sense, the claim by Coleman and Leiter can be linked to the idea that some concepts or some notions would transcend a determined social practice not because they are effectively non-conventional in themselves, but rather because, recurring in different social practices, they would somehow be determined not by a single social practice, but by the interaction between such different social practices. For instance, it is probably possible to identify a unitary notion of law representing the outcome of an effort at harmonization beginning from the notions of law—certainly different from one another, at least in part—that appear in legal knowledge in the common sense, in technical legal knowledge and in scientific legal knowledge respectively. Nevertheless, if this is the meaning of the claim by Coleman and Leiter, then modest objectivity, once again, is nothing but a sophisticated version of conventionalism.

Thirdly and lastly, considering that in order to identify the ideal epistemic conditions it is necessary "to unpack" the reference notion (for instance, the notion of colour or law), it can be said, again according to Coleman and Leiter, that these

[17] A convincing in-depth analysis of this theme can be found for example in Foster Wallace (2006, 66–127).

conditions are not determined through a convention; rather, they are presupposed by a conventional notion.

The latter argument put forward by Coleman and Leiter also lends itself to at least two different interpretations.

On the basis of a first possible interpretation, Coleman and Leiter's thesis would simply consist of stressing the fact that the relationship that connects the ideal epistemic conditions to a convention is a relationship of an indirect type. In brief, the ideal epistemic conditions are not directly identified through a convention; they are determined, rather, by abstracting from a concept (for instance, the concept of colour or law) fixed in a conventional way.

If this is the meaning of the argument put forward by Coleman and Leiter, then what was previously said holds true. The fact that the ideal epistemic conditions are not directly identified through a convention is not a sufficient reason, by itself, for the purpose of being able to affirm that modest objectivity is not a version of conventionalism. The fact is that if, for example, the concept of law has a conventional nature and the ideal epistemic conditions are determined by abstracting from this concept, then the ideal epistemic conditions will necessarily reflect the conventional nature of the concept from which they derive. In other words, the modest conception of objectivity would only be a sophisticated version of conventionalism.

However, Coleman and Leiter's argument can be made more incisive.

It could be said that the fact that the ideal epistemic conditions are derived by abstraction from a conventional concept does not imply that the determination of such conditions must be represented as an activity of a mechanical type. If determination of the ideal epistemic conditions presupposes a certain amount of creativeness and discretion, then it is possible that individuals that share the same concept may nevertheless disagree on what the "correct" ideal epistemic conditions are. In this way one could distinguish modest objectivity from conventionalism in a clear-cut way. Unfortunately, however, this "extensive" interpretation of the argument put forward by Coleman and Leiter inevitably produces an undesired effect of some importance.

In brief, seen in this way, the modest conception of objectivity would in effect only be a form of "disguised subjectivism": if no criteria exist that allow one to determine the ideal epistemic conditions in a univocal way, then it is evident that the minimal conditions are absent for defending any version of objectivity of knowledge. An example can perhaps help to clarify this point: if the ideal epistemic conditions of law derivable from the concept are not the same ones for every judge, then there is no criterion on which to ground a distinction between correct interpretations and incorrect interpretations of law. All that therefore remains is Protagorean subjectivism.

Summing up, the first argument put forward by Coleman and Leiter does not allow one to trace a clear line of demarcation between modest objectivity and conventionalism.

Through the second argument, Coleman and Leiter only succeed in distancing themselves from conventionalism at the cost of complete superimposition of modest objectivity and Platonic objectivity.

In a sense the third argument mirrors the second one: modest objectivity can avoid being considered a version of conventionalism only if one is prepared to recognize that this conception of objectivity is only "disguised subjectivism."

To conclude, it is appropriate at least to mention three further objections that can be made to modest objectivity.

The first one concerns the claim by Coleman and Leiter according to which it is possible to identify a shared notion of law. In reality, this is not to be taken for granted at all. Many authors have emphasised that the notion of law is essentially controversial. Hart (1994, 1), to quote one of the most distinguished, notes for instance that answering the question "what is law?" is a great deal more complicated than answering the question "What is chemistry?" or "What is medicine?". But, if the notion of law is controversial, then we lose one of the fundamental presuppositions for it to be possible to speak of modest objectivity with regard to law.

The second objection is connected to the problem of the relationship between law and morality. Coleman and Leiter are prepared to grant that, as there is not a shared notion of 'morality', moral discourse can be subjective. However, again according to Coleman and Leiter, this does not prevent one from predicating the (modest) objectivity of the law, on condition that one denies that between law and morality there is a necessary connection. In reality, if the separability thesis and the social thesis are interpreted in a weak sense, then it is not at all obvious that the subjectivity of moral discourse has no significant implications, of a conceptual and non-contingent nature, also for law. To this it must be added that even the most informed versions of contemporary legal positivism stress the close connection that exists between law and morality. The existence of some legal norms rather than others is due to the fact that from a moral point of view at least some members of the community prefer (or, at least, say they prefer) the scheme of behaviour identified by such norms as against alternative schemes of behaviour.[18] Maintaining that the existence of a social rule implies that there is someone who deems the behaviour prescribed by a rule preferable to the alternative behaviours obviously does not mean denying the possibility that some people obey this rule out of idleness or hypocrisy, or that others rebel against it. The latter situations, nevertheless, can only be understood by presupposing the existence of a major group that accepts the norms from a moral point of view. All attitudes that can be imagined in relation to the norms are therefore "parasitical" in relation to the attitude of those people who deem the norms adequate from a moral point of view. In other words, while it is possible to conceive the case in which a given norm is approved from a moral

[18]MacCormick (1994, 287–288) for example observes: "That there can be common patterns of criticism of conduct or states of affairs depends upon our conceiving that some patterns are willed as common patterns for all people in given circumstances. We can conceive of that independently of our own will in the matter, but not independently of our beliefs about the will of other members of our social group . . . ". Cf. Duff (1980, 68–73), Id. (1986, 74–98).

viewpoint by everybody, it is instead unthinkable that the behaviour prescribed by a rule is not effectively approved by some from a moral point of view.

The following observations by MacCormick (1994, 233–234) afford a non-banal interpretation of the separability thesis:

> If human beings did not value order in social life, they wouldn't have laws at all, and every legal system embodies not merely a form of social order, but that form of order which is specifically valued by those who have control of the legislative executive or adjudicative process—or at least, it is a patchwork of the rival values favoured by the various groups taking part in such processes. The point of being a positivist is not to deny obvious truths of that sort. The point is rather in the assertion that one does not have in any sense to share in or endorse these values wholly or in part in order to know that the law exists, or what law exists. One does not have to believe that Soviet law or French law or Scots law is good law or the repository of an objectively good form of social order in order to believe that it is law, or to describe or expound or explain it for what it is.

Analogous conclusions are also reached by Joseph Raz, who is convinced of the impossibility of accounting for law and legal interpretation putting in brackets the reasons that induce the participants to consider law morally correct or just: "...while the law may be morally indefensible, it must be understood as a system which many people believe to be morally defensible. While rejecting any explanation of the nature of law or legal interpretation which is true only if the law is morally good, we must also reject any explanation which fails to make it intelligible. This means that to be acceptable an explanation of the law and of legal interpretation must explain how people can believe that their law, the law of their country, is morally good."[19]

The last objection concerns the explicit claim by Coleman and Leiter that it is only possible to predicate the objectivity of legal facts when the law is fully determined, and that is to say in easy cases.[20] If this is true, then their conception of objectivity is effectively not very interesting. In this connection, even if one is not prepared to forego the (troublesome) distinction between easy and hard cases, it is difficult to deny that easy cases are marginal; therefore, a theory of legal objectivity that regards only the latter recognizes that in most cases the interpretation of law is subjective. I really do not believe that this is the best way to reply to normative scepticism.

7.6 Conclusions

In this essay I have not defended any particular conception of legal objectivity or, even less, of objectivity in general. Taking as a paradigmatic case the modest objectivity of Coleman and Leiter, I have identified some objections that can be

---

[19] Raz (1996, 260). See Bertea (2007, 67–81).

[20] "...to the extent that the law is determinate (as it is, for example, in easy cases), the correct answers must be objectively correct". (Coleman and Leiter 1995, 246. Authors' italics).

made to conceptions of legal objectivity that propose to trace out a middle way between objectivity in a strong sense and objectivity in a weak sense. In conclusion, it seems to me that at the end we still remain with two options—strong and minimal objectivity—each of which is flawed by more or less serious problems. If we buy strong objectivity, we should admit that the Rule of law is nothing but a regulative ideal. On the contrary, if we support minimal objectivity we should resign to reduce the distance between the Rule of law and the Rule of men. Nevertheless, to face the problems is always better than pretending they don't exist.

While waiting for a conception of objectivity that really is an alternative to objectivity in a strong sense and objectivity in a weak sense, I believe, nevertheless, that conventionalism, despite the limits previously seen, represents the most promising conception of objectivity for the purpose of convincingly replying to the most radical versions of normative scepticism.

References

Bermejo, J.M.P. 2007. Alcune osservazioni sul valore della coerenza nei sistemi giuridici. *Diritto e Questioni Pubbliche* 7: 43–59. www.dirittoequestionipubbliche.org.

Bermejo, J.M.P. 2013. Coherence: an outline in six metaphors and four rules. In *Coherence: insights from philosophy, jurisprudence and artificial intelligence*, eds. M. Araszkiewicz, J. Šavelka, 93–111. Dordrecht: Springer.

Bertea, S. 2007. A critique of inclusive-positivism. *Archiv für Rechts- und Sozial Philosophie* 93(1): 67–81.

Bobbio, N. 1993. *Teoria generale del diritto*. Torino: Giappichelli.

Coleman, J.L. 1983. Negative and positive positivism. In *Ronald Dworkin and contemporary jurisprudence*, ed. M. Cohen, 28–48. London: Duckworth.

Coleman, J.L. 1995. Truth and objectivity in law. *Legal Theory* 1: 33–68.

Coleman, J.L., and B. Leiter. 1995. Determinacy, objectivity, and authority. In *Law and interpretation. Essays in legal philosophy*, ed. A. Marmor, 203–278. Oxford: Clarendon.

Duff, R.A. 1980. Legal obligation and the moral nature of law. *The Juridical Review* 25: 61–87.

Duff, R.A. 1986. *Trials & punishments*. Cambridge: Cambridge University Press.

Duhem, P. 1954. *The aim and structure of physical theory*. Princeton: Princeton University Press. or. ed. 1914.

Dummett, M. 1981. *The interpretation of Frege's philosophy*. London: Duckworth.

Dworkin, R. 1977. *Taking rights seriously*. Cambridge, MA: Harvard University Press.

Dworkin, R. 1983. My reply to Stanley Fish (and Walter Benn Michaels): Please don't talk about objectivity any more. In *The politics of interpretation*, ed. W.J.T. Mitchell, 287–313. Chicago: The University of Chicago Press.

Dworkin, R. 1986. *Law's empire*. London: Fontana Press.

Dworkin, R. 1996. Objectivity and truth: You'd better believe it. *Philosophy and Public Affairs* 25: 87–139.

Dworkin, R. 2006. *Justice in robes*. Cambridge, MA: The Belknap Press of Harvard University Press.

Feinberg, J. 1973. *Social philosophy*. New York: Englewood Cliffs.

Foster Wallace D. 2006. Authority and American usage. In Id., *Consider the lobster and other essays*, 66–127. New York: Little, Brown and Company.

Gargani, A.G. 1985. *Lo stupore e il caso*. Roma-Bari: Laterza.

Goodman, N. 1973. *Fact, fiction and forecast*. Indianapolis: Bobbs-Merrill.

Greenawalt, K. 1992. *Law and objectivity*. Oxford/New York: Oxford University Press.

Hanen, M. 1983. Justification as coherence. In *Law, morality, and rights*, ed. M.A. Stewart, 67–92. Dordrecht: Reidel.
Hart, H.L.A. 1994. The concept of law. In *with postscript*, 2nd ed, ed. P.A. Bulloch and J. Raz. Oxford: Clarendon Press. 1st ed. 1961.
Hirst, R.J. 1967. Realism. In *The encyclopedia of philosophy*, ed. P. Edwards. New York: Macmillan.
Lewis, D. 1969. *Convention. A philosophical study*. Oxford: Basil Blackwell.
MacCormick, N. 1994. *Legal reasoning and legal theory*, 2nd ed. Oxford: Clarendon. 1st ed. 1978.
MacCormick, N. 2005. *Rhetoric and the rule of law. A theory of legal reasoning*. Oxford: Oxford University Press.
Mackie, J.L. 1977. The third theory of law. *Philosophy and Public Affairs* 1/1: 3–17.
Maniaci, G. 2008. *Razionalità ed equilibrio riflessivo nell'argomentazione giudiziale*. Torino: Giappichelli.
Marmor, A. 1992. *Interpretation and legal theory*. Oxford: Clarendon.
Marmor, A. 1998. An essay on the objectivity of law. In *Analyzing law: New essays in legal theory*, ed. B. Bix. Oxford: Clarendon.
Moore, M.S. 1995. Interpreting interpretation. In *Law and interpretation. Essays in legal philosophy*, ed. A. Marmor, 1–29. Oxford: Clarendon.
Peczenik, A. 1990. *On law and reason*. Dordrecht: Kluwer Academic.
Peczenik, A. 2005. *Scientia juris. Legal doctrine as knowledge of law and as a source of law*. Dordrecht/Berlin/Heidelberg/New York: Springer.
Pino, G. 1998. Coerenza e verità nell'argomentazione giuridica. Alcune riflessioni. *Rivista internazionale di filosofia del diritto*, IV serie, LXXV, 1: 84–126
Quine, W.V.O. 1953a. Two dogmas of empiricism. In Id., *From a logical point of view*, 20–46. Cambridge: Harvard University Press.
Quine, W.V.O. 1953b. The problem of meaning in linguistics. In Id., *From a logical point of view*, 47–64. Cambridge: Harvard University Press.
Quine, W.V.O. 1960. *Word and object*. Cambridge: The M.I.T. Press.
Rawls, J. 1971. *A theory of justice*. Cambridge, Mass: Harvard University Press.
Rawls, J. 1993. *Political liberalism*. New York: Columbia University Press.
Rawls, J. 1999. *A theory of justice. Revised edition*. Oxford: OUP.
Raz, J. 1994. The relevance of coherence. In Id., *Ethics in the public domain. Essays in the morality of law and politics*, 277–325. Oxford: Clarendon Press.
Raz, J. 1996. Intention in interpretation. In *The autonomy of law. Essays on legal positivism*, ed. R.P. George, 249–286. Oxford: Clarendon.
Rorty, R. 1980. *Philosophy and the mirror of nature*. Oxford: Basil Blackwell.
Ross, A. 1958. *On law and justice*. London: Stevens & Sons Limited.
Schiavello, A. 2001. On coherence and law: An analysis of different models. *Ratio Juris* 14: 233–243.
Schiavello, A. 2011. Neil MacCormick's second thoughts on legal reasoning and legal theory. A defence of the original view. *Ratio Juris* 24: 139–154.
Stavropoulos, N. 1996. *Objectivity in law*. Oxford: Clarendon.
Vila, M.I. 1999. *El problema de la discreción judicial. Una aproximación al conocimiento jurídico*. Madrid: Centro de Estudios Políticos y Constitucionales.
Villa, V. 1993. *Conoscenza giuridica e concetto di diritto positivo*. Torino: Giappichelli.
Villa, V. 2004. *Il positivismo giuridico: metodi, teorie e giudizi di valore. Lezioni di filosofia del diritto*. Torino: Giappichelli.
Viola, F. 1990. *Il diritto come pratica sociale*. Milano: Edizioni Universitarie Jaca.
Viola, F., and G. Zaccaria. 1999. *Diritto e interpretazione. Lineamenti di teoria ermeneutica del diritto*. Roma-Bari: Laterza.
Waldron, J. 1992. The irrelevance of moral objectivity. In *Natural law theory. Contemporary essays*, ed. R.P. George, 158–187. Oxford: Oxford University.

Chapter 8
Pattern Languages and Institutional Facts: Functions and Coherences in the Law

Kenneth Ehrenberg

8.1 Introduction

This chapter is a preliminary exploration of the idea of applying two theoretical constructs in an attempt to explain the nature of law and certain norms that govern its development and use, especially the norm of coherence in law. One of these constructs is originally explained using law as an example and was specifically developed in an attempt to understand social institutions. The other construct was developed by an architect, who likely did not have law in mind, but whose construct has already been used outside of the architectural field in computer programming.

I do not intend for this chapter to constitute a complete theory of law or even a complete argument in favor of using these constructs to explain law or to set forth the content of norms that govern its use. However, some elements of law have been under-theorized by previous legal theorists, especially the way in which a legal system is constituted by an interconnected web of legal norms that can sometimes reinforce each other and sometimes interfere with each other, and the artefactual nature of law as a tool for solving social problems.[1] In borrowing these other constructs, I hope to find an easy foundation on which to build out a more developed understanding of certain elements of law and the norms that govern it.

The first theoretical construct I will examine is John Searle's theory of institutional facts,[2] a way of explaining how certain kinds of social facts come into existence and are sustained even without constant attention from those who are sustaining them. This helps to explain how it is possible for certain

[1]This last point has recently received some greater attention. See especially, Shapiro (2011).

[2]Developed primarily in Searle (1995) and expanded upon in Searle (2010).

K. Ehrenberg (✉)
University of Alabama, P.O. Box 870218, Tuscaloosa, AL 35487, USA
e-mail: kmehrenberg@ua.edu

M. Araszkiewicz and J. Šavelka (eds.), *Coherence: Insights from Philosophy, Jurisprudence and Artificial Intelligence*, Law and Philosophy Library 107,
DOI 10.1007/978-94-007-6110-0_8, © Springer Science+Business Media Dordrecht 2013

legal propositions to be true even when they are not the subject of any ongoing enforcement or attention.

One possible issue for any theory of law is to explain how it is possible for there to be valid laws 'on the books' that no one alive is aware of at the moment. If we can say that one who acts in a way prohibited by this unknown law still acts illegally (even if no one would do anything about it since they would not be aware of its illegality), then we are saying that legal validity does not require the ongoing attention of officials or legal subjects. This is true since a claim of illegality is dependent upon the assumption that the law rendering the act illegal is valid. This is more of a challenge for legal positivists than it would be for other theorists. Legal positivists say that the law is nothing more nor less than what its officials and subjects make it, that it is entirely a product of human invention (e.g., Austin 1998; Kelsen 1967; Hart 1994). Other theorists (e.g., Aquinas 2000; Finnis 1980) hold that law is a reflection of an ideal natural, rational, or moral order (or, that it is at least an attempt to reflect that order). If human law is a reflection of such an ideal, then there would be less of a problem explaining how forgotten laws can still be valid since validity is at least partially a matter of how well the law is reflecting the ideal order.[3] However, if we wish to maintain what I take to be the valuable idea that law is the self-conscious creation of human beings and that its validity is a function of the norms articulated within the wider, but still created, jurisdictional system of which any law is a part, then we are faced with the problem of explaining how validity can come apart from human awareness.

It might appear that validity is merely a question of what officials are paying attention to at the moment, and the way they apply the system's norms. Searle's theory is helpful in understanding the way in which the uses to which we put law, its functions, are assigned to the legal norms, offices, roles, and institutions we use the law to create. It provides for the possibility of an institutional reality that is entirely (and mostly self-consciously) created by human beings while explaining how that reality lives on beyond the particular individuals who created the institution.

In a way, it is this that magnifies, if not creates, the problem of coherence in the law. It is the fact that the law lives on (in time or jurisdictional space) beyond its creators and the current officials who interpret and enforce the law that gives rise to the possibility that legal norms will conflict with one another. In its simplest understanding, coherence is the meta-norm that such conflicts should be minimized.[4] The norm is holistic in the sense that every other element of the legal

---

[3]For more on this dispute, in the context of questions about the objectivity of decisions about legal validity, see Aldo Schiavello's paper "The Third Theory of Legal Objectivity," at p. 134 in this volume.

[4]This presentation focuses on normative coherence as distinguished from factual coherence. See in this volume Amalia Amaya's paper "Ten Ideas about Coherence" at p. 226.

system is potentially relevant to a judgment of whether a given proposition of law coheres well with the rest of the system.[5] It is a meta-norm in the sense that it is a norm that governs the interpretation and application of other legal norms.

Nevertheless, coherence is still only one norm among many that determine the success of a legal system. I would caution against jumping to the conclusion that talking about coherence in law makes one a "coherentist," who believes that there are no foundational legal propositions, or that legal validity is a web of mutually supporting norms.[6] It is perfectly consistent to see legal coherence as an important norm for a legal system to meet for it to be successful and also to hold a belief in unwritten fundamental validity rules or core legal propositions that are not open to modification in their application or interpretation. That a given legal interpretation or proposed alteration coheres well with others already articulated within the legal system is, on its own, actually quite a weak recommendation for it. Perfectly coherent systems can be morally pernicious or completely dysfunctional.

The second construct I will examine is the concept of design patterns, as developed by the architect Christopher Alexander (1977), and further applied in the area of object oriented computer programming (Gabriel 1996; Gamma 1995). The idea of analogizing law and the principles of its design to architecture is not new. Lon Fuller began discussing the idea in the early 50s (2001, 64–5, 285ff.). Here I will simply be developing this analogy within a particular architectural theory. There are several reasons for choosing this particular architectural theory, which I will go into in greater detail when presenting the theory.[7] In support of analogizing the law to architecture, consider the fact that there are a variety of ways to fulfill the functions we have for buildings and other structures, but they also have significant constraints in terms of their construction that must be met for the structures to operate at all.[8] Similarly for law, there are a variety of specific ways to guide and coordinate behavior in pursuit of specific and general societal goals, and allowing for individual ones. But there are also significant constraints in the formulation of legal rules for them to perform those functions. As we will see, one desideratum for both systems is a certain notion of coherence that straddles the line between

[5]See in this volume, Juan Manuel Pérez Bermejo, "Coherence: an Outline in Six Metaphors and Four Rules" at pp. 92–93, and Jaap Hage, "Three Kinds of Coherentism" at p. 20, on the relation between coherence and holism.

[6]See in this volume William Roche, "Coherence and Probability: A Probabilistic Account of Coherence" at p. 82. On reasons in favor of coherentism in its different forms, see in this volume Hage, *passim*.

[7]The use of an architectural metaphor also reinforces my earlier claim that talking about coherence does not make one a coherentist. In the epistemological literature, coherentists characteristically reject the foundationalist metaphor of the building in favor of the metaphors discussed by Bermejo in this volume at pp 94–100.

[8]On the relation of coherence to constraint satisfaction, see in this volume Michał Araszkiewicz, "Limits of Constraint Satisfaction Theory of Coherence as a Theory of (Legal) Reasoning," at pp 204–06, Amaya, pp 225–27, and Hage, pp 22–25.

a minimum standard for the structure(s) or system of rules even to be capable of fulfilling their functions, and a more aspirational aesthetic notion that contributes to some sense of excellence in that fulfillment.[9]

In laying the theoretical groundwork, I will be primarily concerned with linking sub-concepts within the idea of design patterns with concepts in general jurisprudence. As such, I will not here articulate a complete theory of design patterns for legal systems. Rather, I hope to suggest a blueprint from which one can be developed. Furthermore, since I am interested in Alexander's theory only insofar as it is applicable to an understanding of the law, I will reject or ignore some elements of his work that I deem unhelpful to my project. A fair worry will be whether the rejection of those elements undermines the theory to such an extent that the analogy to law becomes weak and artificial. But I do not think I am leaving out anything essential. Alexander's theory will be most useful in pinpointing a conception of coherence that is easily applied to the law as a genre norm that governs the relation of individual legal norms to the wider systems of which they are a part (what I called a "meta-norm" above). That is, as one can already guess from the focus on coherence, it is a norm that applies to law as a genre of human activity by governing how well specific laws fit with the jurisdictional system of which they are a part.

Methodologically speaking, there are both normative and explanatory elements to this discussion. I will begin with a brief discussion of Searle's theory and what it says about the assignment of function in legal institutions. That part is primarily explanatory as it is simply a framework for understanding what law is and what we do with it. Understanding law's functions allows us to make judgments about its efficacy (both in terms of individual legal enactments and law as a general means for accomplishing social change). However, this part of the paper is not intended to deploy or suggest any particular normative judgment about law generally or particular legal enactments. In the second part I will apply Alexander's theory to the law. That part more explicitly mixes normative and explanatory elements in that it offers a framework for understanding the interrelated nature of law, and also suggests norms by which to judge how well given legal designs are performing (especially with regard to the norm of coherence in legal systems).

Since the notion of functions will figure heavily in this discussion, one additional note about their nature and role is important before we begin in earnest. While I believe that understanding the social functions that law performs in and for society is necessary for a complete picture of the nature of law, I do not believe that this means law is defined functionally or constitutes a functional kind. A functional definition sets forth the necessary and sufficient conditions for membership in the class of things being defined. Hence, were we to define something functionally, then defective exemplars would not be members of the class, which I take to be an unpalatable result. (Broken chairs are still chairs.) Functional kinds are entities that are understood sufficiently in terms of their function (leaders, as

[9] See Fuller (1969, 5–9), explaining this as the morality of duty and of aspiration.

opposed to presidents[10]). This is not a good characterization for law as there are other activities and institutions that perform many of the same functions as law (etiquette, religion, morality, education, etc.), so law's functions cannot be sufficient conditions for identifying it. Instead I believe that law, like other artifacts and institutions, is to be explained by the function that it is centrally to perform (as well as by the means by which it performs that function). But since we are dealing with an explanation rather than a definition, defective legal systems or laws are still examples of the kinds since the relationship between explanandum and explanans is not one of strict necessity and sufficiency.[11]

8.2 Institutional Facts and the Assignment of Function

Searle begins by distinguishing between brute facts and social facts. Brute facts are facts that do not depend on an observer to be true and are true independent of any understanding of them (Searle 1995, 27, 2010, 10). Social facts depend in some way on human (or perhaps animal) collective intentionality (Searle 1995, 26; Smith and Searle 2003, 304).[12] An institutional fact is a certain kind of social fact, one in which a status function[13] is assigned by constitutive rule via collective intention to an object, practice, event, or other social phenomenon (Searle 1995, 23–26, 40–45). More recently, Searle has equated institutional facts with the status functions themselves, where those status functions carry deontic powers that can provide desire-independent reasons for action (Searle 2010, 23). In other words, we collectively assign a special status to an object, event, or person, by declaring it has that status using some kind of constituting formula. These are important facets of the theory for seeing its application to law. The institution is constituted by the assignment of a function that is a power to affect people's reasons for action (Searle 2010, 99). Specifically, it conveys the ability to create desire-independent reasons for oneself and others, i.e., the ability to impose duties and obligations (Searle 2010, 85). The status function usually (but not always) can be reduced to the form "X counts as Y in context C" (Searle 1995, 28, 2010, 19–22; Smith and Searle 2003, 301). For example, "The person who wins the Electoral College vote counts as the President of the United States in all legal and governmental contexts after taking the Oath of Office." This constitutive rule—which depends in turn on

---

[10]This example comes from Green (1998, 119).

[11]For a more complete discussion my views on this, see Ehrenberg (2009). For an overview of the use of functions in general jurisprudence, see Ehrenberg (2013).

[12]For a fuller explanation of his notion of collective intentionality see Searle (1995, 23–26, 2010, 8, 43–50).

[13]For Searle, a function is simply the use to which an object is intentionally put (1995, 20, distinguishing "imposed," "agentive" functions from "discovered," "non-agentive" functions). *See also* Fotion (2000, 179–80); Searle (2010, 43–44, 58–60).

other rules setting forth what is needed to win an Electoral College vote, the duties of the President, and the text and circumstances of the Oath of Office—does not regulate the President or other officials' relations to the President. The assignment of function constitutes the office itself, and there is a societal collective intention that the object performs the function imposed upon it (or him), which is the power to affect others' reasons for actions by issuing verbal orders (for example in his role as Commander in Chief), signing legislation (in his Constitutionally-specified role as executor of the law), and by signing executive orders (in his role as head of the executive branch of government). When the status is conveyed to an object or event, coming into some relation with the object (such as possession), or somehow participating in the event, will be what changes the rights and duties of those in relation to the object or participating in the event.

To be an institutional fact, the imposition of function must be collectively intended in a specially empowered context. Generally, to be an institutional fact, the imposition of function must be conferred on a *type* of object, person, or practice rather than only on a particular *token*. That is, what lends it its institutional character is the possibility of iteration, applications of that function can be repeated at different times, on different objects or people, and possibly in different places. Imposing the function on a *type* of object, person, or practice allows for this repetition. This happens where the assignment of function in the constitutive rule is itself institutionalized by codification (a general and perhaps metaphorical term, of which legal codification is but one kind). "Codification specifies the features a token must have in order to be an instance of the type . . . " (Searle 1995, 53). When the function is imposed only on tokens, we may speak of them as institutions, but their institutional character is less formal and more metaphorical. So we can speak of "informal institutions," which have all of the hallmarks of an institution but are not codified (Searle 2010, 91). The advantage of codification is that it allows the status function with its attendant deontic powers to attach to a type of entity (e.g., Presidents, dollar bills, spouses, etc.).

Law is the institution *par excellence* for institutionalizing other social facts. That is to say, it is itself an institution that is used to create other institutions by providing a mechanism for official codification. In constitutional legal systems, we can understand a historical and nested process by which an entire legal system comes into being. A group of individuals gather as a constitutional convention. This might be informal if not authorized by previous official action. If informal, they confer on their gathering an informal institutional status by simply collectively assigning themselves the status of a constitutional convention (and hence their status applies only to their one token gathering until they create an official process). They draft a constitution and devise a process for its ratification. That process counts as an institution when they "officially" adopt it, assigning it the function of ratifying the constitution. The constitution is then adopted when it is ratified according to this process and we have moved explicitly into formal institutions. The constitution is then the foundational document for all other legal institutions in that jurisdiction (itself a stipulation of that document), setting forth the processes for legislation, interpretation, and application. It now sets the contexts under which other official actions are to be deemed legally valid and the implications of that validity for other officials and institutions like courts, administrative bodies, law enforcement officials, etc. We can imagine similar stories being told in non-constitutional systems or systems with unwritten constitutions.

We can understand each step in this process as another instance of the collective assignment of a function to set deontic powers via a constitutive rule. The specific gathering of people counts as a constitutional convention when it resolves to make that its purpose. The processes they devise count as the official ratification for the documents they draft when they resolve to adopt those processes by their official processes. The document they draft counts as the constitution for their legal system (defined and delimited within the document itself) when it has passed the ratification process. The document itself has many provisions that can themselves be understood as instances of the assignment of status function "X counts as Y in context C," including a description of the offices of chief executive, legislator, high court interpreter, as well as details about what shall count as valid law and the implications of those laws. Laws passed under the constitution can then assign further status functions on objects, practices, people, or institutions, such as detailing what counts as legal tender, what processes must be followed for people to enter into marriage (and what constitutes the legal aspects of that institution), what actions constitute infractions and what punishments can be given in response. Those laws in turn provide for their own multiplication as well as the creation of sub-institutions such as administrative rule-making bodies, provisions for economic governance, and the creation of petty officials tasked with mundane governmental functions. The law is therefore the institution-creating institution, an institution whose function is the creation of other institutions, the imposing of other functions. Institutions are social artifacts collectively intended to solve social problems and conflicts, or to pursue social goals. So we have one institution whose special job is to be the catch-all means of generating solutions through the imposition of functions on other objects, events, people, actions, and institutions.

The advantage of Searle's analysis for our purposes is that it allows for reducing the essential elements and processes of law to a simple formula for the assignment of function that is then iterated across the legal system (and even between systems). It is a means by which we can highlight law's functions and how precisely these explanans relate to their explananda. It makes no mention yet of suitability to purpose, whether law is the best means for solving certain kinds of social problems. (It is clearly not the best means for solving some issues—but which issues it is ill-suited for are likely to differ between societies.) For us, it will also simplify the application of the notion of pattern languages to the law and to see why coherence is a normative constraint on many institutional systems. Given that primary reason to create an institution is to allow people to convey and alter deontic powers, changing the relationship among them, we can begin to see the importance of coherence. The more internally inconsistent those deontic powers and their resultant norms become, the less useful the institutional system will be.

8.3 Pattern Languages and Coherence

Christopher Alexander developed the notion of pattern languages in order to facilitate the accessibility of architectural design and planning (1964, 1979; Alexander et al. 1977), in an attempt to make it accessible even to people without formal training (1979, 218–19). In using his notion, I make no comment on its success in architecture,[14] although it has been adapted for use in object-oriented programming (Gabriel 1996; Gamma 1995). The term "pattern" is used here in the same sense as a sewing pattern, a kind of template to be followed, rather than as in a tessellation. In this it is a kind of rule to be followed in making certain design decisions (Alexander 1979, 179, 182, 247, explaining patterns as rules). As a "language" it is a network of interrelated patterns, each also understood as a three-part rule relating a context, a problem and a solution-type serving as a model for other design decisions. The context is the aspects of the situation that are relevant to the kind of problem and how it calls for the solution-type.

Alexander develops a set of design principles of various degrees of specificity at a wide range of scales (from the size of crown moldings in certain rooms to the distances between cities and towns). Each design choice is an attempt to solve a particular design problem given a set goal such as how to build a window into a wall without the wall collapsing, how to locate a garden so that it is sheltered but still has easy access, etc. Some of the constraints that govern these choices are physical, some are aesthetic, while some are practical given human needs and goals.

The amount of individual choice and flexibility within each pattern is determined by the constraints of the problem, but the choices are further constrained by other choices made regarding related design problems and their patterns. Some choices are failures (also called "mistakes") in that they do not solve the problem presented; some are misfits in that they respond to the problem but multiply or cause other problems in ways that argue against adopting that particular choice as a solution (Alexander 1979, 233–34).

When a set of choices along these design parameters exhibits a kind of harmony among solutions such that all the "forces" are in balance and new demands upon the system are straightforwardly accommodated, Alexander says the set exhibits the "quality without a name" (1979, 135–36). This is clearly a norm of internal coherence among elements in the system and is a regulating principle for the wider system itself. So the theory has an explanatory element in that the patterns are already present in the types of contexts and problems that arise. But a more explicit recognition of these patterns can streamline and harmonize the design process, minimizing misfits and failures, generating the quality without a name.

Since a pattern is a solution-type in a context-type, the legal analog using the Searlean analysis would be to treat the constitutive rule form ("X counts as

---

[14]Some projects built on the theory are considered failures, Kaplan et al. (1987); Dovey (1990). *But see* Montgomery (1970, 56), discussing successes in classroom, multi-service center, and Peruvian low income housing designs.

Y in C") as a kind of master pattern and general ways of filling in the constitutive rule constitute the patterns themselves. These are then further specified through legislation, court decision, and administrative application.

Take an example of a social problem in pre-legal societies: conflicts over property or other goods the use of which excludes use by others. A common solution to this problem is to invest some decision-making body with authority to determine which party's interest in the property trumps that of the other party. The recognition of that authoritative determination is intended to settle the conflict and preclude further dispute over the issue. The pattern then counsels the creation of such a body using the constitutive rule: The decisions rendered by a defined official count as authoritative solutions to conflicts over property when such conflicts are brought before her.

The pattern language for legal systems will contain a host of general patterns that are then further specified by the particular circumstances of each society, as well as choices made in the fleshing out of each legal system, narrowing the choices available for other solutions as governed by the values exemplified by the choices already made. So we can try to articulate very general patterns that are present in all legal systems based on certain reasonable assumptions of what is universally taken to be valuable such as protection of life, the minimization of disputes, etc. Some plausible examples are "Serious punishment for unjustified killings;" "Formal recordings for high-value commitments;" "Supreme interpretive authority;" "Regulation of highly risky yet commonly practiced activities." (Alexander tends to title his patterns with one-line descriptions like "One inch trim," and "Teen-ager cottage.") These patterns will then be fleshed out with further specificity as the legal system is filled in. For example, what constitutes an unjustified killing will be limited by the standards of justifications as articulated elsewhere in law.

The way in which those other specifications limit the range of options inherent in the generally worded patterns will be governed by a principle of coherence as the legal analog of Alexander's "quality without a name." Part of that limitation process will also involve the interpretation of legal norms in application to particular cases and examples, as well as in determining how to execute policy. So the limiting normativity of coherence operates at all levels of legal action: development, execution, and interpretation.

Coherence can therefore be understood as an internal harmony among norms in the legal system when those norms are maximally satisfied while the system is still responding well to the social problems that arise within its jurisdiction. Some of those norms are inherent in the way law operates, governing its fitness for purpose. This is exemplified by Fuller's eight internal legal norms: generality of legal rules, publication, clarity, minimal retroactivity, non-contradiction, not requiring the impossible, relative stability, and convergence between the rules as written and as executed and interpreted (Fuller 1969, 39).

While it might be tempting to identify coherence simply with the notion of non-contradiction (understood as both counseling against directly conflicting directives and directives that conflict only in application or interpretation), the idea of fitness to purpose helps us to see that coherence is a wider notion. Once we understand law in terms of its function to guide behavior in pursuit of solving social problems, coordinating behavior, pursuing social goals, etc., then coherence becomes a norm that regulates legal systems in their performance of those general functions. Elements of the system that are not well adapted to purpose by falling short on one of the eight desiderata are not cohering well with the wider project represented by legal governance of behavior.

Recall that Alexander articulated two different kinds of design failures: misfits and mistakes or failures. The "quality without a name," which we are analogizing as coherence in applying the pattern language construct to law, obtains for the designed system when it avoids misfits and failures and allows for easy accommodation and the solution of new problems as they arise. It seems that, given the notion of fitness for purpose that is represented by Fuller's eight desiderata, it is most correct to understand failures in those eight areas as akin to Alexander's mistakes or failures. They are instances where the law is structurally unable to do its job, akin to an architectural element not performing the task for which it was designed. But there is then another element we should expect to see in the norm of legal coherence, corresponding to a lack of misfits. This is found in that aspect of coherence that theorists attribute to a unity among the values expressed by and within a legal system. As Joseph Raz puts it: "The more unified the set of principles expressed within the law, the more coherent it is" (1992, 286).[15]

The notion of coherence as a minimization of misfits, along with its aspect as representing Fuller's eight desiderata, underscores the fact that it is a norm that cannot be perfectly upheld in any realistic legal system. For one, as Fuller notes, members of the eight desiderata are themselves already in tension (Fuller 1969, 41–43, 93). Generality and clarity are naturally in some tension, as are non-retroactivity and convergence between the written and the applied (in that any application of a rule in a hard case will be retroactive in the first instance since the interpretation is necessarily novel). Similarly, given that one function of law is to settle disputes, it can never truly be univocal in its expression of value. Since disputes frequently arise in cases of competing values, and it is likely that the law will need to strike a balance among those competing values, it is exceedingly difficult to imagine a legal system that articulates a perfectly consistent set of values. Rather, what is called for is minimizing tensions with expressed systemic values. For example, where a system emphasizes equality before the law, structural elements that necessarily favor the wealthy (where higher quality representation is available to those who can afford it) are exhibiting a lack of coherence with stated principles.

This is the way in which the pattern language construct offers both an explanatory and normative approach to jurisprudence. It is explanatory in the sense that it offers a model for capturing the ways in which legal problem-solving is adapted

[15]As mentioned above, by sketching an account of the nature of coherence and its regulative role in the design and development of legal systems, I do not mean to imply that I adopt a coherentist theory of law, reducing the law itself to the set of principles that makes the most coherent sense of legal enactments. *See* Raz (1992, 286).

to its purpose, offering a way of understanding how the design process works. It is normative in that its templates provide, in the first instance, a means for a judgment of ground-level suitability to purpose. Beyond that, it helps to flesh out and generate a notion of coherence that can then be used for judgments about given laws, legal systems themselves, and as grounds for legal reform.

8.4 Conclusion

As indicated, this was only intended as a preliminary exploration of the possibility of using two theoretical constructs in an attempt to articulate the role of functions in understanding the law and how it operates and for developing an account of coherence as a regulating norm for law. If this appears successful, several further projects could be developed on its basis. For one, the pattern language notion and Searlean constitutive rules offer a natural way to reduce many legal norms to algorithms that can then be assessed computationally. That is, if it proves possible to translate legal systems into sets of data, it might also prove possible to compute the extent to which a set of that data is internally consistent. While I can't hold out hope that normative values can be computationally teased out of that data for use in determining, e.g., the unity of a given legal system with regard to its stated principles, I can imagine that Fuller's eight desiderata and existing understandings of social values that are meant to be pursued by law can be reduced to some kind of test for that data. I can imagine that computers could then calculate the degree of coherence within a legal system, perhaps pointing out elements that do not cohere well and helping to predict likely future conflicts. This could then be used by human framers to alter the system to add to its coherence or even allow the computers themselves to suggest alterations along those lines. More broadly, however, the hope has been to focus the attention of legal theorists upon a more precise notion of coherence that can be used (among other norms) to evaluate the role of individual actual or proposed laws within a given legal system, and legal systems themselves more widely.

References

Alexander, C. 1964. *Notes on the synthesis of form*. Cambridge: Harvard University Press.
Alexander, C. 1979. *The timeless way of building*. New York: Oxford University Press.
Alexander, C., S. Ishikawa, and M. Silverstein. 1977. *A pattern language: Towns, buildings, construction*. New York: Oxford University Press.
Aquinas, T. 2000. *Treatise on law*. Translated by Richard J. Regan. Indianapolis: Hackett Pub. Co. Original edition, 13th c
Austin, J. 1998. *The province of jurisprudence determined and the uses of the study of jurisprudence*, Edited by H.L.A. Hart. Indianapolis: Hackett Pub. Original edition 1832.
Dovey, K. 1990. The pattern language and its enemies. *Design Studies* 11: 3–9.

Ehrenberg, K. 2009. Defending the possibility of a neutral functional theory of law. *Oxford Journal of Legal Studies* 29: 91–113. doi:10.1093/ojls/gqp001.
Ehrenberg, K. 2013. Functions in jurisprudential methodology. *Philosophy Compass* 8: forthcoming.
Finnis, J. 1980. *Natural law and natural rights, Clarendon law series*. Oxford/New York: Clarendon/Oxford University Press.
Fotion, N. 2000. *John Searle*. Princeton: Princeton University Press.
Fuller, L.L. 1969. *The morality of law*. Rev. ed. New Haven: Yale University Press. Original edition, 1964.
Fuller, L.L. 2001. *The principles of social order: Selected essays of Lon L. Fuller*. Edited by Kenneth I. Winston. Rev. ed. Oxford/Portland: Hart Pub. Original edition, 1981.
Gabriel, R.P. 1996. *Patterns of software: Tales from the software community*. New York: Oxford University Press.
Gamma, E. 1995. *Design patterns: Elements of reusable object-oriented software*. Reading: Addison-Wesley.
Green, L. 1998. The functions of law. *Cogito* 12: 117–124.
Hart, H.L.A. 1994. *The concept of law*, 2nd ed. Edited by Penelope A. Bulloch and Joseph Raz. Oxford: Clarendon Press. Original edition, 1961.
Kaplan, S., F.D. Dale, and R. Kaplan. 1987. Patterns as Hypotheses: An empirical test. In *Public Environments, Proceedings of 18th Meeting of the Environmental Design Research Assn., May 29–June 2, Ottawa*. Edited by J. Harvey and D. Henning, 55–60. Washington, DC: Environmental Design Research Assn.
Kelsen, H. 1967. *Pure theory of law*. Berkeley: University of California Press. Original edition, 1934.
Montgomery, R. 1970. Pattern language. *Architectural Forum* 132: 52–59.
Raz, J. 1992. The relevance of coherence. *Boston University Law Review* 72: 273–321.
Searle, J.R. 1995. *The construction of social reality*. New York: Free Press.
Searle, J.R. 2010. *Making the social world: The structure of human civilization*. Oxford: Oxford University Press.
Shapiro, S.J. 2011. *Legality*. Cambridge, MA: Harvard University Press.
Smith, B., and J. Searle. 2003. The construction of social reality: An exchange. *American Journal of Economics and Sociology* 62: 283–309.

Chapter 9
Consistency and Coherence in the "Hypertext" of Law: A Textological Approach

Wojciech Cyrul

9.1 Introduction

In 1982, R. Dworkin in his article "*Law as Interpretation*" presented the law as a particular kind of novel (Dworkin 1982, 527–550).[1] Using instruments of the literary theory, he defended this idea stating that in hard cases, judges play a role similar to novelists who write fragments of the same work one after the other. The mere fact that a work is common is supposed to necessitate that each subsequent author become familiar with the text already created before commencing their work. Otherwise, the text would not be consistent, so the next part of the text could not be part of the same novel. Therefore, each new co-author, in order to maintain a continuum of legal text, must first understand not only what his predecessors have written separately, but what they have created together (Dworkin 2000, 542).

The metaphor of the novel used by Dworkin is certainly elegant, and its attractiveness has made some law researchers promote the idea of law as a "chain novel". However, unfortunately neither Dworkin nor his followers managed to adequately explain a number of important theoretical and practical issues associated with writing the text of the law by the courts (Balkin 1987, 403 ff.). First of all, the question was not unequivocally answered of where the duty of collaborative writing, which integrates all the work and makes it consistent, actually comes from. This is a crucial issue because empirical research indicates that "*the growth of precedent in an area does not appear to restrict judicial discretion; if anything, the development of the law may increase such discretion*" (Lindquist and Cross 2005, 1206). Moreover,

[1]This idea was further developed in his book, *A Matter of Principle,* Dworkin (2000, 146 ff.).

W. Cyrul (✉)
Department of Law and Administration, Jagiellonian University, Bracka 12, 31-005 Kraków, Małopolskie, Poland
e-mail: cyrulwojciech@hotmail.com

M. Araszkiewicz and J. Šavelka (eds.), *Coherence: Insights from Philosophy, Jurisprudence and Artificial Intelligence*, Law and Philosophy Library 107,
DOI 10.1007/978-94-007-6110-0_9, © Springer Science+Business Media Dordrecht 2013

it is not completely clear what the consistency in question is, especially if we notice that the novel created by the courts does not meet the requirement of subjective and objective unity. It is hard to deny the obvious facts that different precedent settlements may have a different sender and a different recipient, and may refer to completely different problems. A doubt also arises about the argument that the text of the law created by courts serves one overriding communication objective, which, for legislative discourse, is regulation. After all, whether the ruling will be considered a binding precedent depends not only on the authority which has formulated it, but also on the courts that in further practice will invoke the binding nature of ratio *decidendi* formulated therein. The last objection, which refers to the use of a novel metaphor in the text of the law, is that the novel, like any classic linear text forms a sequentially organised whole. Taking into account that precedents may be divided between binding and persuasive precedents, and that precedents may be overruled by the rulings of higher courts, questions arise about the possibility of establishing a stable, linear structure of such a text. The analysis above shows that in the text of the law, as Dworkin understands this concept, it is not possible to directly apply traditional cohesion mechanisms distinguished by the linguistics of text, among others for the genre, which is novel.

In addition to theoretical objections, arguments of a practical and legal nature may also be posed against Dworkin's thesis. Namely, taking into account the linear and clearly sequential construction of the text of law established by Dworkin, it is difficult to understand how in this context to include the simultaneity of actions of the different courts in various precedent cases, which after all cannot be excluded a priori. In addition, the metaphor of the novel written by the courts does not only take into account the significant differences between the texts of judgments and literary texts, but it also fails to fulfil the role which in judicial discourse, even in difficult cases, is fulfilled by statutory regulations. Dworkin, in speaking of the legal text as a novel, arbitrarily excludes positive law from its "framework", and excludes formal lawmakers from being among the co-authors. In other words, the text of law in his theory is created solely by the courts. Leaving aside the question of the arbitrariness of such an operation, it should be noted that in the continental tradition, the notion of text of law is typically combined primarily with the texts of positive law.[2] Not ruling at this point on the dispute over the scope of the text of the law, it should be noted that Dworkin's concept is unable to explain either the specifics of the language of legal texts or their specific modal and illocutionary characteristics, both in case of texts of precedential decisions and the texts of legal acts.

[2]On the controversies with the concept of positive law see more in Opałek (1999, 153–167).

As can be seen then, the concept of the text of the law is not clear.[3] It is not clear either who the author (sender) is or who it is addressed to, or what is its subject, purpose and structure (van Hoecke 2002, 80 ff.). It should therefore be assumed that what the text of the law, is determined by legal culture and the norms of specific legal systems. Although for a lawyer, this remark is not problematic, from the viewpoint of the theory of text it constitutes a serious challenge. The fact that the text of the law may consist of either articles of statutory law or judicial texts or both, or possibly even other texts, is the reason that an adequate theory of text of law must be able to take into account the very different types of text. With that in mind, and initially for the purposes of further discussion, the text of law is defined as a system of texts of legal acts, binding in a specified time, in a defined territory. At the same time, to simplify the discussion the term legal act is hereinafter construed as a communication of the establishment of legal provisions, fixed, structured, adopted and promulgated according to the rules of the lawmaking procedure.

Classical textological analyses focus mostly on studies of specific types of texts, treating particular legal texts simply as examples of the official language. The problem of text of law, as a whole, however, remains outside the current interest of textology. Whilst the characteristics of legal texts make them subject to analysis in the traditional conceptual grid of textology, the text of law defies the traditional categories.[4] Thus, it is sufficient to notice that the texts of legislation have a clear beginning and end with a specific topic, given to them by a subject of regulation or agreement, and they have at least formally defined an author and receiver and have a clear foundation of a linear structure, characteristic to sequential texts. In this way, with some modifications they can be successfully analysed in terms of traditional categories of literary theory. An attempt at describing the text of the entire law is much more complex. In analysing the various systems of sources of law it is easy to see that the text of law can be produced simultaneously in discourses that are significantly different from each other. In contemporary legal theoretical discussion there is a distinction between at least a few main types of discourse functionally and structurally related to the different ways of lawmaking, i.e. regulation, contract,

[3]In reality, the notion of text itself is also ambiguous. Cf. Rosengren (1980, 275 ff.); Agricola (1969, 88); Dobrzańska (1993, 8); Isenberg (1968, 4); Wilkoń (2002, 43 ff.); de Beaugrande and Dressler claims that sentences or statements together form the text, if the relationships between them satisfy the condition of consistency, coherence, informative function, intertextuality, intentionality, acceptability and situationality (de Beaugrande and Dressler (1981)). The last two conditions, however, became the subject of numerous controversies and including them in the criteria of textuality has received criticism in the literature (see Renkema (1993, 34 ff.); Gansel and Jürgens (2007, 31 and quotes ibidem)).

[4]Analysis of texts of legal acts shows that they have some paradigmatic syntactic qualities. In particular, we may mention here their impersonal nature, and hence the lack of expression in the first or second person, not normally found in other discourses the length of sentences, a statistically significant number of noun verbs, wealth of complex prepositional forms, etc. More in Bhatia (1994, 140 ff.); ibidem (1984, 90 ff.).

judicial precedent and common law (Wronkowska 2005, 115).[5] Bearing in mind that these discourses most often operate in parallel with each other and co-create at different levels the legal order of a given political community, in building a model of text of law one should reject in advance any linear and sequential approach characteristic of traditional forms of feeding the text. The text of the law, whether in Dworkin's terms, or in the terms proposed in this paper, does not have either formally or conventionally extracted beginning or end. It is a multi-thematic and multidimensional text that remains in a state of constant change. Unlike the texts of specific legislative acts, it does not even have the foundations of linear structure that could determine its reading. This is a spatial, dynamic and multi-threaded text without a clear framework, open to many ways of parallel reading. Consequently, the text of law remains formally closed by the borders of the texts of lawmaking acts, and it goes beyond each of them separately at the same time without being reduced to their simple sum.

The above characteristic allows two questions to be posed, first whether one can speak of the text of law at all, and second, assuming an affirmative answer to the previous question, what text is the text of law. The answer to both questions is important in that every theory of the text presupposes a theory of writing and interpreting a work and thus the criteria of its consistency and coherence.

9.2 Consistency, Coherence and Forms of Feeding the Text

Difficulties with the use of the conceptual grid of classical linguistic theory for the analysis of cohesion and coherence of legal text lead to the conclusion that the text of the law assumes a particular form of feeding the text, which is significantly different from traditional forms, i.e. monologue and dialogue. This claim is significant because the form of feeding determines text-generating measures and mechanisms that affect the consistency and coherence of the text. However, the issue here is not only with the grammatical and logical cohesion of sentences,[6] but also with cohesion construed as structural dependence, in which hyper-sentence text structures remain, making the text appears meaningful as a whole and thus coherent (de Beaugrande and Dressler 1981, 3 ff.; Gansel and Jürgens 2007, 26 ff.). It should be noted nethertheless that even a high degree of grammatical and logical consistency of individual sentences cannot guarantee coherence of the text as a

[5] To this list one could add discourse of learned lawyers whose opinions take effect, known to Roman law and the law of Islam.

[6] Also at this level one can detect fundamental differences between the texts of speech in monologues and dialogues. This is due to practical limitations to the ability to construct complex sentences in the dialogue. Significant differences also arise from the contextual binding of expression in the dialogue, which sometimes is the reason that outside the context of their creation, significant differences occur at the semantic and pragmatic level of their meaning. For more on the concept of cohesion see Halliday and Hassan (1976, 28 ff.).

whole.[7] Moreover, the coherence of the text is a quality determined not only by the same text-generating categories, but also by the knowledge and experience assumed by the author to be necessary for its proper understanding. This, it is sufficient to notice that the monologue form, which provides continuity and uni-directionality of expression, not only helps to maintain the broader semantic consistency of speech, but also gives an author the ability to control the consistency of theme throughout the text.[8] Ultimately, it allows the author to unilaterally organise text into certain hierarchical and horizontal structures using different means. One can for example mention the segmentation of text, and thus structural elements of starting and closing a text, such as title, introduction or conclusion, the extensive expansions and summaries of previous statements, etc. Moreover, with a written form the author of monologue is also given a series of graphical measures for determining text coherence, which in the spoken texts do not exist or are of marginal importance, such as tables of contents, indexes, references, detailed definitions, etc. All of this gives the monologue texts continuity, closure and a linear nature. No restriction of communication typical of the dialogue also results in the expressions in monologues being significantly longer than the operating statements in the dialogue, and they are essentially linguistically homogeneous.[9] As a result, monologue texts are either structurally or semantically independent of the context of the functioning of the audience (undirected monologues) or directly include the context of their reception (directed monologues) in their structure and content. As can be seen, both types of monologues implement the requirements of coherence of text in a substantially different way.

Maintaining semantic and thematic coherence in dialogic text is much more difficult than in the monologue, since as long as the text is a record of an actual conversation it must include idiolects of both interlocutors. In contrast to the monologue, a form of dialogue involves interactive structuring in the text. This feature of dialogic texts makes them a substantially different form of feeding text from the monologue. Texts of dialogues are usually not only structurally open and discontinuous but also incomplete and linguistically heterogeneous. In addition, dialogic text has the features of both the existence of specific relationships between sequences of responses and semantic dependence on the situation in which the dialogue is conducted. Together, these elements determine whether the text of the dialogue breaks down into stand-alone pieces, or appears to be a consistent, coherent and integral whole. Thanks to them, seemingly autonomous and interpretatively

---

[7] For more about the distinction between consistency and coherence see Wintgens (2012, 238 ff.).

[8] On ways of creating thematic unity see Wilkoń (2002, 74 ff.).

[9] It should be noted that the linguistic homogeneity of individual expressions is not sufficient to ensure that their collection makes meaningful text. In other words, the semantic comprehension of individual sentences or statements does not guarantee the correct understanding of the text, which has been created by individual sentences or statements as an interconnected whole. Not only understanding, but even the existence of text as a certain conventionally isolated whole requires the determination of certain relationships between different sentences or statements that form the composition.

independent expressions can create a larger, coherent complex, remaining within the inner, interpretative dependence.[10] As can be seen, the dialogue as a form of text feeding involves a specific meaning of consistency and coherence of text. The simultaneous co-creation of text requires a particular organisation of its structure and language. At both levels, the dialogue enables interlocutors to use instruments that generate the effect of harmonisation, so that both the one currently speaking, and the one who listens at the time can interact with each other, in an effort to make their utterances fit together. The speaker does so most often through the introduction of statements concerning the course of the dialogue, correcting his earlier statements or asking for repetition or clarification of the interlocutor's statements. The recipient does so by commenting on or completing the predecessor's statements, or by trying to take over the voice. Each subsequent statement must therefore take account of the earlier one and also at least to some extent determine the next. Consequently, we can say that coherence of the text of dialogue is the result of intertextual and functional relations between the participants' utterances. Every response may in fact create a kind of metatext, in the context of which the current dialogue text or its fragments are each time subject to harmonisation.

A new form of the text feeding is hypertextual form.[11] In textology, the concept of hypertext is understood most often as texts of non-sequential or non-linear structure (Janangelo 1998, 24). However, the essence of the difference between the hypertextual form of text feeding and traditional forms is the manner of presentation and dissemination of the information, enabling the reader through its dynamic ordering. Thus, we must remember the difference between so-called simple hypertexts, where we deal only with a collection of linked and marked up documents (Cyrul et al. 2010) and adaptive hypertexts (Kay and Kummerfeld 1997), in which such a "simple" hypertext is enhanced by intelligent information management systems that support user actions. Such advanced hypertexts become a mixture of texts written in natural language, marked up languages and a computer system that allows interactive management of the accessible information, and this is regardless of its form.[12]

Given that the above hypertext is distinguished from the classic forms of feeding the text not so much by the quantity and quality of information available in it as the manner of recording, results in the possibility of its aggregation, multidimensional analysis, and various forms of presentation. A characteristic feature of hypertexts is their dynamic nature, due to their interactive structure. Electronic media allows grouping and dynamic display of information in a way unavailable to traditional texts, in particular, they allow the use of independent or automated management of information sets stored in the database. User-directed navigation enables browsing

[10]For more information see Thomas et al. (1982, 141–155).

[11]For more on hypertextuality see Landow (1992); idem (2006); Bolter (2001); Vandendorpe (2009); Cyrul (2009).

[12]Hypertext may contain multimedia messages as well as text. See Bieber and Kimbrough (1992, 77 ff.).

and viewing the nodes of the hyperdocument and automatic search, viewing, and even generating the desired information. Most often it is also possible to create in an imperceptible way, for example a new or modified way, and delete the old documents and links and/ or their properties. Hypertext also enables meta information about the text such as properties of links and documents to be entered or displayed, and the hypertext management electronic system can provide users with support tailored to their individual needs and capabilities. For example, it can display explanations of the options available and give advice or indicate the recommended course of action. For more complex hyperdocuments, hypertexts can be equipped with navigation maps or indexes. The former provide the user with information about the specific area or a general overview of the structure of hyperdocument, the latter facilitate searches of the hypertext for specific terms or phrases. Navigation maps can also be multi-level, i.e. the selected items on the main map can contain linked and more detailed maps. In this way, they facilitate the use of hyperdocuments and improve access to its individual parts. It is worth noting that building a navigation map determines the system and number of relationships in which individual nodes will operate and will be interpreted. All of these solutions can affect readers' strategies and therefore influence the role of coherence in hypertext (Foltz 1996, 128).

The above, necessarily brief presentation of the various forms of text feeding supports the argument that the hypertextual form involves a number of changes in the meaning of cohesion and coherence of a text. The first change is due to differences in the consistency requirements that underlie the creation and reading of linear texts, and which underlie the functioning of hypertexts. In particular, the consistency of the hypertext, differently than with linear text, need not be a constant. In linear text it can be obtained by maintaining syntactic—semantic coherence of individual sentences or logical consistency of larger parts. In the case of hypertext, even the fact of cohesion within the fragments contained in different documents is not proof of its consistency. Individual documents may contain inconsistent content, which will not however be displayed simultaneously or will not be shown to the same recipients. Moreover, in the case of hypertext, the problem of assessing its consistency and coherence is strongly associated with the problem of its stability and integrity. It should be remembered that, unlike the printed texts, texts in electronic form can still be physically altered and combined in a way not only invisible to the reader, but also in a way that would prevent them from comparing the version being read with the previous versions. In other words, if the user is not provided with information about the version of the text being read, then the text displayed on a computer screen will be perceived as the only version. What's more, the opportunity for a third party to intervene in the content of the text can make the reader unable to distinguish between text that is in a shape given to it by its author, and the text modified by unauthorised persons. As can be seen then, the consistency and coherence of hypertext require that it is provided with at least relative stability and integrity, which is understood as the inability for unauthorised persons to modify the text. Thus, from the perspective of the author, hypertext can be consistent and coherent only on condition that (a) they predicted all the ways of reading it, (b) have provided stability during the reading of the text and there is a lack of contradictions and inconsistencies between the connected parts, and (c), they have assured the integrity of the text being read, meaning that the hypertext only contains content given to it by its author.

Consistency and coherence in hypertext can also be viewed from the perspective of its user (Slatin 1990, 877). For readers, coherence in the hypertext is a function of the objective that guides them, and which determines their decisions as to the type of information displayed and the sequence of reading. Thus, although the hypertext as a whole may contain inconsistent information, the information displayed on the user's screen can still be coherent when one is reading hypertext passages. Whether the reader will be given access to incoherent information in the hypertext depends on the effectiveness of the management system that can filter inconsistent content. In the absence of such a system, it should be considered that the construction and operation of hypertext means that it is not possible to talk about its sequential or logical consistency. However, the lack of consistency in the hypertext does not necessarily prevent reading strategies employed by concrete individuals from maintaining the coherence of the interpreted texts. Furthermore, if there is a system for managing the information available to the user, the structure of the hyperdocument or algorithms of information management system can significantly reduce the combination of different contents or documents, and thus noticeably reduce inconsistencies in the text being read (Foltz 1996, 122 ff.). Moreover, such a system can physically create specific relationships between the elements of hypertext and reduces the risk of the user missing certain parts that the author had intended the reader to read together.

Consideration of the integrity of the hypertext in the context of discussing its consistency and coherence is also important because the hypertextual form of feeding text allows the simultaneous co-creation of the text by multiple authors. While traditional forms of text feeding assumed such a possibility, they still dictated a number of obvious limitations to the process, mainly related to the number of contributors, with maintaining the formal unity of the text and the possibility of taking into account the actions of different people in different places at the same time taking part in its creation. That is why comparing the law to the novel written by many authors, should be considered as a rather inaccurate metaphor (Dworkin 1982, 540 ff.). The process of creating the text of the law is more accurately illustrated by the analogy of hypertext, as only hypertext can enable both simultaneous work on the same basic text for many people and the physical connection of texts by various authors with one another within a single information system. At the same time, the manner of recording the text allows the use of tools to guarantee both quality control of the text creation process itself and its effect. This is evident considering the fact that not every user must be authorised to add new information to the hypertext and that not every new piece of information produced by the co-authors of the hypertext must be automatically and permanently incorporated. What is more, information deleted from hypertext does not necessarily leave visible traces after its removal, because the actions of the participants do not need to be permanently overwritten in the text in the original database, but can only work on a copy of the specified user on the computer until a decision is made about their inclusion. In other words, adding information to the hypertext may require either authorisation of the authorised agent or consent of the other contributors.

Another problem with the consistency of hypertext, at least in the classical concept of text coherence, results from the above-mentioned dynamic nature of hypertexts. Hypertext *ex definitione* is aimed at interaction with a recipient. This dynamic nature combined with the immanent features of the electronic medium makes hypertext never appear to the user (and impossible to perceive) as a whole. Since hypertext has neither a formally distinguished beginning nor end, the user, by necessity, reads only some fragments that are displayed on the screen. As a result, from the reader's point of view consistency, in the above sense, can be discussed either at the level of individual nodes, which are designed for it, as some internally coherent, linearly ordered whole, or at the level of available information, which the user reads in a given time.[13] As previously indicated, however, hypertextuality is not expressed at the level of individual nodes, but in the relationships between them or their fragments. Similarly, the coherence of the law is not reducible to the internal cohesion of the various texts of legal acts and requires consideration of their mutual relationship.

The foregoing observations suggest the idea that the hypertextual form of text feeding also provides for a special role of text coherence. As mentioned above, in the case of linear text, limited and fixed, coherence of the text is a structural relationship in which hyper-sentence text structures remain, and through which the text is seen as a meaningful whole. Since coherence of the text is to be perceived as a meaningful whole, this coherence is a function of the reader's knowledge, assumed by the author and real reader's knowledge about the assumptions adopted by the author. Hypertext however alters the traditional relationship between author and addressee and blurs the distinction between the role of the reader and author (Patterson 2000, 76). Electronic medium allows the reader a real participation in the creation of the text that appears on the screen, so it is difficult to determine in this case the function of coherence.

The traditional printed form of the text stresses the difference between the interpretation made in the process of creating a text by the author and the creation of the text as a result of the interpretation made by the recipient (Dworkin 1982, 541). In hypertext, this distinction loses its importance. As a result, if the requirement of coherence of the texts available to readers in the traditional way forces the author to exercise the fullest possible verbalisation of communication and to provide the highest degree of semantic self-sufficiency, it is possible to achieve this effect in the hypertext in at least two other ways. The first is based on control by the author of the mechanisms that link the information contained in the system and gradually make it available to the recipient according to its purpose. The second way is based on enhancing hypertext with an information management system, determines the

[13]In the case of modern legal information systems, such wholes are nodes containing for example texts of formal sources of law in the system, which exactly duplicate the structure of the printed originals.

range of possible operations on the text and indicates the information considered by the author to be relevant from the point of view of a specific user question. Thus, the coherence of a higher level than in the individual documents may be the result of matching the disclosed text on the screen to the needs and expectations of a particular type of recipient. In the ideal situation, both the whole hypertext and each of its documents would be coherent. However, if the information in the hypertext is not combined by the author in a manner that provides for all the possible ways of reading it, or if the system does not match the contents of the displayed information to the needs and capabilities of a particular user, then the hypertext may appear as inherently incoherent. In such a case, the coherence of the read text depends exclusively on the readers' needs and reading strategies.

Based on the foregoing discussion, it should be concluded that coherence in hypertext can be defined only in functional terms, as its ability to facilitate familiarisation with the texts that form the context of a specific document, which at the moment is subject to the user's interpretation. Information technology systems can help in obtaining additional information and simultaneously allows a better understanding of the main information. In other words, if the user can decide in which constellations the information will be disclosed and in what sequence he will use it, then coherence in hypertext can be defined as its ability to raise the level of comprehension by the recipient of primary information by giving them access to additional information.

9.3 Consistency and Coherence in the Legal Text

The foregoing observations allow the thesis that the text of law is a sort of hypertext. Respectively, it can also be difficult to speak both about its structural consistency, (called cohesion) in the case of legal text, and its semantic coherence (i.e., coherence), in the traditional sense. Coherence of the text requires not only that it does not contain any logically contradictory statements, but also that it consists of statements linked together by means of specific text-generating mechanisms, such as subjective or objective unity, the overall objective, and temporary or cause and effect relationships, which in legal text generally do not occur. In other words, the coherence of text in the traditional sense depends on whether the sentences included in it together form a specific meaning. Given the fact that the text of law as opposed to linear texts does not create the structured whole, the question arises as to what it means for the text of law to be consistent. The problem is important in that the analyses of various texts of legal acts show a lack of even a legal text-specific thematic field (Gizbert-Studnicki 2004, 44). One can only determine the thematic fields of individual legal texts, which are usually determined by their subject matter of regulation or possibly the thematic fields of so-called branches of law. As a result, adopting the traditional network of concepts of literary theory would lead to the conclusion that the text of law is inconsistent, and thus is not a text at all. However, if the text of law is not a text, how can the legislative practice and process of its interpretation and application be explained? So it seems a more accurate view that the legal text is a text, but the theory of narrative coherence of text underlying the traditional theories of text is not adequate to explain the specific criteria for coherence of non-sequential texts, such as the text of the law. A specific feature of non-sequential texts is that the lack of one thematic field and the possible inconsistency between their elements does not make them immediately senseless and does not automatically reduce their communicativeness. Therefore, in this case it is more reasonable to speak about levels of coherence than about the coherence as the principle of textuality.[14] Remember that in the case of non-sequential texts and hypertexts, the text shape is usually not the result of the actions and properties of individual, historical individuals but is the result of collective action and complex communication processes involving a large number of unspecified entities. Therefore, it is the texts of the law, which are the result of actions and properties of legislative bodies, which are not concrete historical entities but agents or structures in legal discourse. As a result, the subjective unity characteristic of linear texts in legal texts is replaced by the communication processes of a certain structure. In this sense, the consistency and coherence of the text of law should be seen rather in terms of its compliance with the requirements of communication processes, of which it is the product, for example with the rules of legislative procedure, rules of legislative technique or the rule of interpretation of the law.

With this in mind, it is important to consider not so much whether the legal text is consistent and coherent, but how it is consistent and coherent. In Polish literature, an attempt to create textological coherence criteria of legal texts was made by R. Sarkowicz (2004). Referring to his levelled concept of interpretation (Sarkowicz 1995), he proposed an examination of the consistency of legal text at a descriptive level, directive level and at the level of presuppositions of the text. The descriptive level concerns the vision of a world expressed directly in legal language, the directive level includes a collection of directives contained in the legal texts, and the level of presupposition includes all the information presupposed by the legal text about the world, society, man and broadly understood culture (Sarkowicz 2004, 55 ff.). Without going into polemics regarding the isolation of such levels of text and their mutual relationships, from the viewpoint of further considerations, it is important to note that the level concept of coherence in legal texts still refers to the theory of narrative coherence,[15] which is not a convincing solution, taking into account the non-sequential construction of legal text.[16]

---

[14] For example Wintgens distinguishes between four different levels of coherence, i.e. level of coherence$_0$ (internal or synchronic coherence), level of coherence$_2$ (diachronic or rule coherence), level of coherence$_3$ (compossibility or system coherence) and level of coherence$_4$ (environment coherence) (Wintgens 2012, 242 ff.).

[15] For more about narrative coherence in law see Jackson (1988).

[16] It would be fair to say that R. Sarkowicz himself is aware of the limited usefulness of the theory of narrative coherence in legal texts analysis.

The specificity of the main objective of legal texts, which is the legally binding regulation of social interactions, and the fact that they encompass provisions that refer to each other or refer to texts outside the text of law, justify distinguishing the concept of consistency of the text of law from the concept of its coherence. The text of law is consistent if it is free from logical contradiction. However, in order to be coherent the text of law must present a picture of the world that corresponds with the reality that it creates or the existence of which it presupposes. Moreover, the image of the world that functions in the text of law must also correspond with the picture of the world that operates in the texts, to which it formally refers or which form the context determining the effectiveness of its communication.

Taking the above into account, a theory of coherence of the text of law must take into account the specific structure and purpose of law. As a result, at least three layers of the coherence of the text of law can be distinguished, i.e. semantic, syntactic (intertextual) and pragmatic layers. With this approach, the consistency of text on the law is fuzzy and depends both on the coherence of each of its layers and on the degree of the coherence between them.

The degree of coherence in the semantic layer of legal text depends on the degree of its semantic and axiological integrity. The text of law is semantically coherent if it is logically consistent, i.e. if it does not contain analytically contradictory provisions and if the same concepts are expressed using the same words, and different concepts are expressed by different words. The text of law is coherent in an axiological sense if it is based on a set of core values which it protects and expresses. In particular, the text of law is axiologically coherent if it is integral i.e. if it treats similar cases in a similar way.

The text of law is syntactically (structurally) coherent if each of its elements is consistent with its internal rules of correctness and shall remain in certain pre-defined relationships with other elements formally separated in its structure.

At a practical level, the text of law is coherent insofar as it is capable of being understood and used by its recipients in sufficient detail to enable both the achievement of its own objectives and/or the purposes of lawgivers. This means in particular that it does not contain instrumentally or communicatively ineffective rules.

9.4 Consistency, Coherence and Intertextuality of a Legal Text

The concept of intertextuality, introduced to textology by Julia Kristeva in her seminal work *Desire in Language: A Semiotic Approach to Literature and Art* (Kristeva 1980, 37) has become one of main ideas of literary theory (Marko 2009; Allen 2000; Worton and Still 1991). Though originally intertextuality meant that "*all discourse depends upon, builds upon, modifies, and/or react to prior discourse and prior use of words, concept and ideas*" (Ciampa 2008, 41), soon the concept became abused, as rightly observed by Posner, and nowadays it has a very different meaning than intertexuality in legal theory (Posner 2009, 285) However, Posner's definition of intertextuality, which reduces it to the context dependency of meaning of words or sentences, is too narrow to explain the role of intertextuality in legal texts. This is so because the intertextuality of legal text explains the relationships between individual provisions within a text of law, with relationships between particular texts of legislative acts and the relationships between the text of law and other texts that constitutes its metatextual frame. In fact, one of the central problems of legal theory is the relationship between rules, standards and polices within the legal system and the relationships that exist within and between texts of different legal acts and between the text of law and different normative orders. As a result, from the textological perspective the distinction between the system of law and the system of legal sources can be defined in terms of the distinction between the potential text and the real text of law. The real text of the law is created in the legislative process by the formal lawgiver and so is the one established, published, and operating in a legal discourse as an integral and authentic source of the law. In contrast to the real text of the law, the legal system is a potential text, and thus a mental text. From this perspective, the legal system is subject to reconstruction in the process of the actualisation and concretisation of meaning of real text of law in the process of its interpretation and application. As a result, and as rightly observed by M. Wojak, formal intertextuality of real legal text can be contrasted with communicatively realised intertextuality in the text of its interpretation (Wojak 2004, 137 ff.). Respectively, the problem of consistency and coherence of real text of law shall be discussed separately form the problem of consistency and coherence of a legal system. The real text of the law does not consist merely of standards or rules, as is the case of the potential text of law i.e. legal system, but also contains additional information. In legal texts, one can find information about their titles, dates and sometimes about the author. Contemporary legal texts usually have a formally distinguished header, different editorial units, drawings, designs etc. and often are supplemented with preambles, stamps and signatures.

The differences between the real text of law and potential legal text (legal system) are such that in the case of the latter, dynamic (formal) and the static (substantial) relationships between legal norms are of crucial significance. Although the potential legal text consists not only of the norms clearly expressed in real text, but also of the norms forming their "logical" consequence, nevertheless the potential text of law may not contain inconsistent norms. In this way, potential text of law becomes dependent in a very particular way upon the requirements of legal interpretation, which determine its communication effectiveness. The potential text is thus a product of the interpreter or interpretative tradition. It comes into existence in the process of interpretation, when legal norms are reconstructed on the basis of the real text of law. Thus, potential text of law is a kind of ideal epistemic structure. Although it reflects the hierarchical, temporal and content relationships existing in the real text of law it aims toward the ideal consistency.

The influence of the structure of real text on the shape of a potential text gives fundamental importance to both the issue of intratextual relationships, in which the former operates and the intertextual relationships that exist within it. These relationships presuppose the possibility of assessing their consistency and coherence, and thus determine the manner and scope of their coherence in the process of legal interpretation.

Analysing the issue of the effect of intertextual relationships on consistency and coherence in the text of law, one should take into account its particular structure. Construction of the real text of law makes the status and function of the intertextuality it plays in this case different from the status and function it plays in classical sequential texts. In the latter case, intertextuality can be defined as the relationship in which the text functions with other texts. Its primary role is to provide coherence of text and reduce information redundancy, which would lead to repetition of the same content in different parts. Intertextuality for sequential texts substantially weakens the semantic autonomy of the text making it dependent on the context of the texts to which it explicitly or implicitly refers. In the case of non-sequential texts, particularly hypertexts, the situation is different because in this case, intertextuality is a condition of semantic autonomy of the text and its existence as a real and functionally distinct whole. For example, within the text of law, intertextuality not only reduces ambiguity but also increases the intelligibility of texts of legal acts, because in limits the need to make them full self-sufficient and semantically univocal. Furthermore, formal internal relationships also make text of law distinguishable from other texts. This claim, at least to some extent corresponds with Hart's thesis that the essence of law is a union of primary and secondary rules (Hart 1994, 81 ff.). In the words of Hart, only due to the existence of secondary rules, such as rules of recognition, change, and rule of adjudication is it possible to avoid the disadvantages arising from the uncertain, static and ineffective character of primary rules (Hart 1994, 94 ff.). But the concept of intertextuality underlying Hart's theory of law has been overly simplified. The special construction of the text of law and the specificity of its making and application makes an adequate theory of intertextuality of law to cover both the intertextual relationships within the text of the law, as well as external intertextual relationships in which the text of the law functions in relation to other texts. Within the first group, one should also distinguish intratextual relationships, occurring within a legal provision,[17] intertextual relationships that occur between concrete legal provisions or their groups formally distinguished within a text of a legal act,[18] and the transtextual relationships that occur between the provisions of texts of various legal acts or their sets or between texts of different legal acts and their sets.[19] Within this second group, i.e. the group of external references, one must distinguish references from other texts of law, as is the case for example with private international law, and references to the texts belonging to the broader legal culture in which the text of the law functions.

[17] E.g. art. 812 § 9 sentence 1 of Polish Civil Code (Dz.U. 1964.16. 93).

[18] E.g. art. 812 § 9 sentence 2 of Polish Civil Code.

[19] E.g. art.775 of Polish Civil Code.

The distinction within the text of law of the above-mentioned internal and external intertextual relationships clearly implies not only an opportunity for the distinctions between the various texts of the law, but also a distinction between law texts and other texts (e.g., literary texts). Moreover, this also implies the possibility of distinguishing the text of law from the texts of particular legal acts and from individual legal provisions. This assumption allows us to analyse the types of text-generating relationships occurring at the level of individual legal provisions, at the level of their formally distinguished sets, and at the level of relationships between the text of legal acts and at the level of relationships between the text of law and other texts, such as the texts of jurisprudence and texts of legal dogmatic. Furthermore, it enables us to observe the impact of these relationships on the problem of consistency and coherence of text of law.

The specificity of intertextual relationships of legal text justifies, in analysing the concept of coherence of legal text, taking into account their synchronous (static) and diachronic (dynamic) dimension. The static approach focuses on forms and conceptual systems operating in the legal texts of different countries or different legal cultures and on studying semantic and syntactic relationships that exist within the texts of law in a given time. As a result of synchronic analyses, it is possible to distinguish between at least three basic types of relationships in which the text of law remains, determining its coherence. First, the relationship between the text of the law and broadly understood legal culture; second, the relationship between the various texts of law and third, relationships that occur within a specified time between elements within a given text of the law. The first two types of references hereafter shall be referred to as the extrasystemic references, and relationships belonging to the third type as the intrasystemic references.

Among the intrasystemic references, there are internal references, i.e. references within the rules belonging to a single legislative text, and external references, with which we deal when the provisions of one act refer to the text of any other act. References of this type can be either specific or general, simple or complex. With specific references, a reference provision refers to a specific provision. With general references, the referring provision refers to a group of provisions isolated in a more or less formal way in another part of the same text or in the text of other act. Simple references are discussed when the reference provisions contain behaviour patterns which define the rights and obligations of legal subjects. Complex or cascaded references are discussed when the provision to which one refer does not itself contain a behaviour pattern, but refers again to another provision which specifies this pattern.

In addition, internal references may be horizontal or vertical in nature. We deal with the vertical references if the provision refers to the legal text of higher or lower rank in the hierarchy of sources of law, and a horizontal reference is when references occur between the provisions of legal acts belonging to the same rank.[20] On should

[20]E.g. § 4 of the Polish Regulation on Principles of Legislative Technique (Dz.U.2002.100.908) provides that within an act one can refer to the provisions of the same or another act. It is also

notice that any incoherence between formally linked provisions or gaps resulting from the lack of the provisions to which other provisions refer to does undermine the coherence of the whole text of law, but does not need to simultaneously undermine its logical and semantic consistency.

In contrast to intrasystemic references forming part of the internal context of the operation of legal provisions, extrasystemic references open up text of law to the external social and historical context within which the text of law functions as a formally separate entity. Extrasystemic references may take the form of explicit and implicit references. In the case of explicit references, the provision of law contains a reference clause directly to other normative texts such as the texts of foreign laws or texts of deontological codes produced in specific professional practice or the social and moral rules, such as rules of social conduct, the principles of justice, local customs, etc.[21] The implicit references usually occur in the case that a provision contains a vague term or statement requiring reference to external practices, discourses or values when deciding a case (Zieliński 1988, 55 ff; Leszczyński 2000, 17, 23 ff.).[22]

Synchronic analyses that assume the static nature of the intertextual relationships of legal text do not allow for inclusion of the role of a series of dynamic changes taking place between the elements of text of the law over time. The specific nature of the text of law requires the enrichment of synchronous analysis with diachronic analyses. The latter allows us to study the mutual influences of various legal texts and to observe the impact of the legal and social culture on the change of the legal text and thus on its coherence.[23] Furthermore, the diachronic approach allows us to distinguish the static references from dynamic references. In the case of static references, a referring provision refers to a specific content of reference provision, such as was in force at a given time, regardless of its current wording.[24] In the case of dynamic references, a provision always refers to the currently existing content of provisions. Dynamic references may take the form of validation references and information references. The function of validation references is to change text of the law in force and they take on the form of amending, derogatory or modifying provisions. The function of information references is to reduce the communication inefficiency of the text relating to its dynamic nature. References of this type most often take the form of transitional and introductory provisions. A special intermediate case of provisions are blanket provisions, which we deal with when the

---

possible to make references to provisions of the international agreements ratified by the Polish Republic. In some cases, it is also permitted to refer to the provisions of normative acts established by international organisations or international bodies.

[21]E.g. art 354 §1 of Polish Civil Code.

[22]E.g. Article 3.1. UN Convention on the Rights of the Child of 20 November 1989.

[23]Note that legal systems are momentary normative systems. This means that each time a provision is added to or derogated from the text of law by a competent authority, simultaneously a new legal system appears. See Moreso and Navarro (1998, 277).

[24]See § 160 of Polish Regulation on Principles of Legislative Technique (Dz.U.2002.100.908).

text of a provision does not contain the pattern of behaviour, but merely indicates which authority is responsible for determining such a pattern in the future.

The existence of formally separate internal and external intertextual relationships of the text of law explicitly specifies the elements of legal text, which must be consistent in the logical sense and coherent in sufficient detail to enable their understanding and application. It is worth noting that the existence of formal references in the text of law semantically organises the entire text as it extracts information from the whole text, which the author intends to operate in closer semantic or functional relationships. Of course the fact that formally connected provisions or their groups, identified by the legislature, create a consistent and coherent whole does not guarantee that these provisions are also consistent with all other laws for the time being belonging to the text of the law. However, as is the case with hypertext, finding analytically inconsistent provisions within the text of law contained in the legislation not linked by explicit references, and all the while principally governing other issues, requires a very particular reading strategy. More common is the lack of coherence within the text of law resulting from legislative errors associated with the use of so-called tacit derogation (Moreso and Navarro 1998, 281).[25] This results in the text user having doubts about the relationships between the provisions governing a similar range of social relationships and forces them to make validation or interpretation decisions. It must be remembered however that the process of interpreting the real text of the law, which aims to remove contradictions or gaps discovered in it by the interpreter, is the process of creating a new text, which meets the requirements of a potential legal text, and so the entirely coherent and complete text.

9.5 Conclusions

In summing up the above considerations, it should be stated that one of main characteristics of the text of law is the relationship of its cohesion and coherence with intertextual relationships in which its various parts function, or in which it functions as a whole. The fact that these relationships are usually of an explicit character, and are formally imposed by the same provisions of law allows for the extraction of horizontal, vertical and temporal relationships between the various texts of legal acts and between the various provisions of law. What is more, the specificity of intertextual relationship justifies the conclusion that the text of the law is a peculiar form of feeding the text, which is significantly distinguishable from linear texts and similar to hypertexts. The existence of this relationship allows it to be classified into the group of non-sequential texts, not only allowing for a number of different ways of reading it, but also assuming specific mechanisms for the effective management of the information contained therein. It should be emphasised

[25] See Moreso and Navarro (1998, 281).

that these mechanisms build relationships between the provisions contained in the text of the law, which may result in additional information that cannot be inferred from each of the provisions themselves, and which often determines the consistency and coherence of the whole text or fragment thereof. Thus, the concept of text of law, and the impact of intertextual relationships on the amount and importance of the information contained in it explains at least to some extent the dispute between Hart and Dworkin about the scope of the legal system. Perceiving the law not only in terms of rules or principles, but also through the prism of texts containing them allows us to see the impact of complex relationships in which information functions in the legal text, and which determine both the consistency and coherence in the real text of law and the consistency and coherence in texts produced in the process of its interpretation. This claim, to some extent supports the thesis by Dworkin that the law does not consist only of the clearly articulated legal rules. Through the intertextual relationships, the text of law also refers to information generated and functioning in the texts of legal and political discourses that constitute its textual frame, thereby largely determining its coherence and communicative effectiveness.

References

Agricola, E. 1969. *Semantische Beziehungen im Text und im System*. Halle: VEB Max Niemeyer.

Allen, G. 2000. *Intertextuality*. London: Routledge.

Balkin J.M. 1987. *Taking ideology seriously: Ronald Dworkin and the CLS critique, faculty scholarship series. Paper 293*. 392–433. http://digitalcommons.law.yale.edu/fss_papers/293.

Bhatia, V. 1984. Systematic discontinuity in legislative writing and its implication for academic legal purposes. In *Reading for professional purposes—Studies and practices in native and foreign languages*, ed. A.K. Pugh and J.M. Ulijn. London: Heinemann.

Bhatia, V. 1994. Cognitive structuring in legislative provisions. In *Language and the law*, ed. J. Gibbons, 136–155. London/New York: Longman.

Bieber, M.P., and S.O. Kimbrough. 1992. On generalizing the concept of hypertext. *MIS Quarterly* 16(1): 77–93.

Bolter, J.D. 2001. *Writing Space: Computers, Hypertext and the Remediation of Print*. Mahwach: Lawrence Erlbaum Associates.

Ciampa, R.E. 2008. Scriptural language and ideas. In *As it is written: Studying Paul's use of scripture*, ed. S.E. Porter and Ch D. Stanley, 41–57. Atlanta: Society of Biblical Literature.

Cyrul, W. 2009. Lawmaking: From text to hypertext. In *Law and legal cultures in the 21st century: Diversity and unity*, ed. M. Pieniążek, 9–23. Kraków: Oficyna.

Cyrul, W., J. Duda, J. Opiła, and T. Pełech-Pilichowski. 2010. Zarządzanie informacją prawną w tekstach prawnych przy użyciu języków znaczników (Management of legal information in legal texts by utilisation of mark-up languages). In *Aspekty inżynierii produkcji*, ed. P. Łebkowski, 65–95. Kraków: Wydawnictwa AGH.

de Beaugrande, R.A., and W.U. Dressler. 1981. *Einführung in die Textlinguistik*. Tübingen: Niemeyer.

Dobrzańska, T. 1993. *Tekst próba syntezy (Text: Atttempt at synthesis)*. Warszawa: Instytut Badań Literackich.

Dworkin, R. 1982. Law as interpretation. *Texas Law Review* 60(60): 527–550.

Dworkin, R. 2000. *A matter of principle*. Cambridge, MA: Harvard University Press.

Foltz, P.W. 1996. Comprehension, coherence and strategies in hypertext and in linear text. In *Hypertext and cognition*, ed. J.-F. Rouet, H.J. Levonen, A. Dillon, and R.J. Spiro, 109–138. Mahwah: Lawrence Erlbaum Associates.

Gansel, Ch, and F. Jürgens. 2007. *Textlinguistik*. Gottingen: Vandenhoeck & Ruprecht Gmbh & Co KG.

Gizbert-Studnicki, T. 2004. Sytuacyjne uwarunkowanie językowych właściwości tekstów prawnych (Situational conditioning of the legal texts linguistic characteristic). In *Język—Prawo—Społeczeństwo (Language—Law—Society)*, ed. E. Malinowska, 37–48. Opole: Wydawnictwo Uniwersytetu Opolskiego.

Halliday, M., and R. Hassan. 1976. *Cohesion in English*. London: Longman.

Hart, H.L.A. 1994. *The concept of law*. Oxford: Oxford University Press.

Isenberg, H. 1968. Überlegungen zur Texttheorie. In *ASG-bericht nr.2*. Berlin.

Jackson, B.S. 1988. *Law, fact and narrative coherence*. Merseyside: Deborah Charles Publications.

Janangelo, J. 1998. Joseph Cornell and the artistry of composing persuasive hypertexts. *College Composition and Communication* 49(1): 24–44.

Kay, J., and B. Kummerfeld. 1997. User models for customized hypertext. In *Intelligent hypertext: Advanced techniques for the world wide web*, ed. Ch Nicholas and J. Mayfield, 47–69. Berlin: Springer.

Kristeva, J. 1980. *Desire in language: A semiotic approach to literature and art*. New York: Columbia University Press.

Landow, G.P. 1992. *Hypertext: The convergence of contemporary critical theory and technology*. Baltimore: Johns Hopkins University Press.

Landow, G.P. 2006. *Hypertext 3.0: Critical theory and new media in an era of globalization*. Baltimore: The Johns Hopkins University Press.

Leszczyński, L. 2000. *Tworzenie generalnych klauzul odsyłających (Creation of general reference clause)*. Lublin: Wydawnictwo UMCS.

Lindquist, S.A., and F.B. Cross. 2005. Empirically testing Dworkin's chain novel theory: Studying the path of precedent. *New York University Law Review* 80(4): 1156–1206.

Marko, J. 2009. *History and poetics of intertextuality*. West Lafayette: Purdue University Press.

Moreso, J.J., and P.E. Navarro. 1998. The reception of norms, and the open legal system. In *Normativity and norms: Critical perspectives on Kelsenian themes*, ed. S.L. Paulson and Paulson B. Litschewski, 271–291. New York: Oxford University Press.

Opałek, K. 1999. The concept of positive law. In *Kzimierz Opałek selected papers in legal philosophy*, ed. J. Woleński, 153–167. Dordrecht/Boston/London: Kluwer Academic.

Patterson, N.G. 2000. Hypertext and the changing role of readers. *English Journal* 90(2): 74–80. Technology and the English Class.

Posner, R. 2009. *Law and literature*. Cambridge, MA: Harvard University Press.

Renkema, J. 1993. *Discourse studies: An introductory textbook*. Amsterdam: John Benjamins.

Rosengren, I. 1980. Texttheorie. In *Lexikon der germanistischen Linguistik*, ed. P. Althaus, H. Henne, and H.-E. Wiegand, 275–286. Tübingen: Max Niemeyer Verlag.

Sarkowicz, R. 1995. Levels of interpretation of a legal text. *Ratio Juris* 8(1): 104–112.

Sarkowicz, R. 2004. Koherencja tekstu prawnego świetle koncepcji poziomowej interpretacji tekstu prawnego (Coherence of a legal text in light of the concept of leveled interpretation of legal text). In *Język—Prawo—Społeczeństwo (Language—Law—Society)*, ed. E. Malinowska, 49–60. Opole: Wydawnictwo Uniwersytetu Opolskiego.

Slatin, J.M. 1990. Reading hypertext: Order and coherence in a new medium. *College English* 52(8): 870–883.

Thomas, A., P. Bull, and D. Roger. 1982. Conversational exchange analysis. *Journal of Language and Social Psychology* 1(2): 141–155.

van Hoecke, Mark. 2002. *Law as communication*. Oxford: Hart Publishing.

Vandendorpe, Ch. 2009. *From papyrus to hypertext: Toward the universal digital library*. Urbana: University of Illinois Press.

Wilkoń, A. 2002. *Spójność i struktura tekstu (Text cohesion and structure)*. Krakow: Universitas.

Wintgens, L. 2012. *Legisprudence: Practical reason in legislation*. Farnham/Burlington: Ashgate.

Wojak, M. 2004. Gatunki urzędowe na tle innych typów piśmiennictwa użytkowego—Zakres problematyki (Official genres compared to other types of utility writing—The scope of issues). In *Język—Prawo—Społeczeństwo (Language—Law—Society)*, ed. E. Malinowska, 131–142. Opole: Wydawnictwo Uniwersytetu Opolskiego.

Worton, M., and J. Still (eds.). 1991. *Intertextuality: Theories and practice*. Manchester: Manchester University Press.

Wronkowska, S. 2005. O źródłach prawa i aktach normatywnych raz jeszcze (On sources of laws and normative acts once more). In *Prawo prywatne czasu przemian. Księga pamiątkowa dedykowana prof. Stanisławowi Sołtysińskiemu* (*Private law of the time of transformations. The book of remembrance dedicated to prof. Stanisław Sołtysiński*). Poznań: Wydawnictwo UAM.

Zieliński, T. 1988. *Klauzule generalne w prawie pracy (General clause in the labor law)*. Warszawa: PWN.

Chapter 10
Case Classification, Similarities, Spaces of Reasons, and Coherences

Marcello Guarini

10.1 Introduction

How do we understand the kind of similarity at work in analogical reasoning in ethical or legal discourses? State space models of similarity have been around for some time, and a defense (Guarini forthcoming) against some criticisms of state space approaches (Laakso and Cottrell 2006; Markman and Gentner 2005) has been taken up elsewhere. Here, I will present an artificial neural network (ANN) model that classifies cases, and then undertake an analysis of the similarity state space constructed by the trained network. I will argue that the state space is usefully understood in terms of contributory standards, as engaged in the moral philosophy literature on particularism and generalism. A new tool for visualizing high dimensional spaces will be introduced in the process of analyzing the ANN's behavior. The final portions of the paper contain a discussion of similarity and coherence. A role for local forms of procedural and substantive coherence will be defended.

10.2 Background

10.2.1 Types of Substantive Principles

For the purposes of this paper, the expressions "principle," "rule," and "standard" will be used interchangeably. In the literature on moral philosophy, there are a number of different conceptions of moral standards (Dancy 2000, 2004; McKeever

M. Guarini (✉)
Department of Philosophy, University of Windsor, 401 Sunset Avenue, Windsor, ON N9B 3P4, Canada
e-mail: mguarini@uwindsor.ca

M. Araszkiewicz and J. Šavelka (eds.), *Coherence: Insights from Philosophy, Jurisprudence and Artificial Intelligence*, Law and Philosophy Library 107,
DOI 10.1007/978-94-007-6110-0_10,

and Ridge 2006). What has come to be referred to as the contributory or pro tanto standard in that literature has much in common with what Kevin Ashley (1990) has referred to as factors. A contributory standard is not the sort of normative standard that, when combined with a statement of fact, licenses a monotonic deduction about some particular case. To a first approximation, a contributory standard asserts that some feature (monadic or relational) makes a contribution towards permissibility (or impermissibility), but the contribution it makes may be outweighed by other features contributing in a different way.

Particularists such as Jonathan Dancy (2000, 2004) reject all kinds of general standards, including the contributory. When challenged (Jackson et al. 2000) as to whether a particularist understanding of reasons would allow us to understand how we learn the difference between right and wrong, permissible or impermissible, or the like, Dancy (1999) gestured in the direction of Artificial Neural Networks (ANNs). The hypothesis was that such systems might be able to (a) generalize to new cases based on cases already learned, and (b) do the preceding without making use of general rules, principles, or standards of any kind.

10.2.2 Training the Moral Case Classifier

Some work has already been done with respect to testing and critically assessing this hypothesis (Guarini 2006, 2010, 2011, forthcoming). Building on this work we will examine a simple recurrent network designed to classify moral situations into two categories: permissible (output = 1) and impermissible (output = −1). The output layer of this ANN has one unit; the input layer has eight units, and the hidden layer has 24 units. There is a context layer with 24 units connected one-to-one with the hidden units. Vectors representing phrases are presented to the network sequentially. Every case presented to the network consists of one of two individuals, Jack or Jill, either killing or allowing someone to die. See (Table 10.1) for a list of sample training or testing cases. All the cases have the following form, where the parentheses indicate an optional component:

Agent, Action, Agent, (Motive (s)), (Consequence (s))

Sometimes the cases have multiple motives, sometimes multiple consequences, sometimes just motives and no consequences, and sometimes just consequences and

Table 10.1 Sample cases

Input	Output
Jill kills Jack to make money	−1
Jack allows to die Jill out of revenge	−1
Jill kills Jack in self defense, to defend the innocent; the lives of many innocents are saved	1

no motives. Sometimes there is just a single motive or single consequence. All cases in the training set included at least one motive or one consequence. Some of the testing cases had no motives or consequences at all. Since the initial training and testing was done on moral situations, I have referred to the ANN in question as the Moral Case Classifier (or MCC). However, there is nothing that prevents this sort of architecture from classifying legal cases since all that is required is a vectorized description as input and a classification goal for output.

10.3 Looking Inside the "Black Box"

In the early days of computational neural modeling, there was some concern that neural networks were black boxes: they might be able to do pattern classification, but it was not clear how they did what they did. Many techniques have been developed for understanding the internal workings of an ANN. In this section, we will consider (a) a sample classification task and (b) a visualization technique that will allow us to see what is going on in the network. Let us consider an example.

Imagine you are kidnapped, knocked unconscious, and when you wake up, you find yourself connected to another individual. You are informed by the hospital staff that the society of music lovers did this to you to keep their beloved violinist (to whom you are connected) alive. You are free to disconnect yourself and walk away, but this will result in the certain death of the violinist. In discussing the ethics of abortion, Judith Thomson (1971) used this example for a number of reasons. At one point she suggested that the violinist case is similar to the case of pregnancy resulting from rape. The idea appears to be that in both cases, one life has been made dependent on another through force. (Thomson grants that the fetus becomes a person not long after conception, and she argues in the aforementioned paper for the moral permissibility of some abortions even if the fetus is a person). Some have claimed that in the case of the violinist, unplugging yourself and walking away amounts to allowing the violinist to die, and in cases of abortion, killing is taking place. Thomson claims that there is sufficient similarity between the case of the violinist and the case of rape induced pregnancy that, if it is morally permissible to "walk away" from the violinist (or allow the violinist to die), then it is permissible to have an abortion (or kill the fetus). The moral case classifier (MCC) was trained and tested on cases that are designed to mimic how some see the violinist and rape induced pregnancy cases. Before seeing how the MCC handles these cases, let us consider a new way of visualizing a network's hidden unit activation vector state space.

We can understand what the MCC is doing during training as building up an internal or hidden unit level representation of every case that is being presented to it. The context units are being used as a kind of working memory that allows a representation for the entire case to be built up at the level of hidden units. If we plot the value of every hidden unit on an axis, we get a 24 dimensional moral state space for the network. It is a straightforward matter to plot three dimensions on a two dimensional surface, but three dimensions does not allow us to see very much of what is going on in a 24 dimensional space. Consider the following strategy: instead of representing each 24 dimensional vector for each case with a point, let us represent each case with a cone in three dimensional space. The center of the base of the cone in this space gives us three dimensions of information. The width of the base gives us a fourth dimension; the height of the cone gives us a fifth dimension; the location where the vertex of the cone is pointing gives us another three dimensions; the color of the shell of the cone if coded using RGB color coding gives us another three dimensions, and the color of the base of the cone (again with RGB coding) gives us another three dimensions. In this way we can represent 14 dimensions of information. Using cones in three dimensional space, we can project the first 14 principal components of the vectors (or moral cases) from the original 24 dimensional space. This improves our ability to visualize what is going on in this space, and it will come in handy, shortly. Each of the cones in the three figures in this article presents 14 dimensions of information (most of which will go unexplored for the purpose of this short piece).

The MCC was trained so that cases of the form

x allows to die y, freedom from imposed burden results

were classified as morally acceptable—think of these as violinist type cases. Cases of the form

x kills y, freedom from imposed burden results

were classified as impermissible—think of abortion in cases of rape induced pregnancy. Some who hold positions of this sort have been persuaded by the similarity between the violinist and rape induced pregnancy to change their views. In other words, in spite of the fact that they initially, say at time t_0, classified the cases in different ways, they saw a similarity (of some sort) between the cases when questioned at t_1, and that lead to a change in classification at t_2. How do we understand the nature of this similarity? How can it turn out that cases classified in different ways at t_0 can be seen as, in some sense, similar? Is there an incoherence involved in the preceding? The remainder of the paper explores these questions.

Each of the 326 cones in (Fig. 10.1) represents one of the training or testing cases for the MCC. The first principal component is plotted on the x-axis. It turns out that cases to the right of zero on the x-axis are impermissible, and those to the left of zero are permissible. Say we take impermissible cases and plot them on their own (Fig. 10.2), and permissible cases and plot them on their own (Fig. 10.3). Actually, (Fig. 10.2) contains one permissible case; more on that soon enough. In (Figs. 10.2 and 10.3), the x-axis is the Mahalonobis distance from the mean of the cluster being plotted. Mahalonobis distance is a non-Euclidean, statistical distance measure that can be used to check the distance/similarity of a case from/to a cluster of cases. The remaining dimensions of information plot the first 13 principal components. The highlighted cone in (Figs. 10.2 and 10.3) represents the following case.

C:Jill kills Jack to obtain freedom from imposed burden; freedom from being bedridden for 9 months results; freedom from invasion of privacy results.

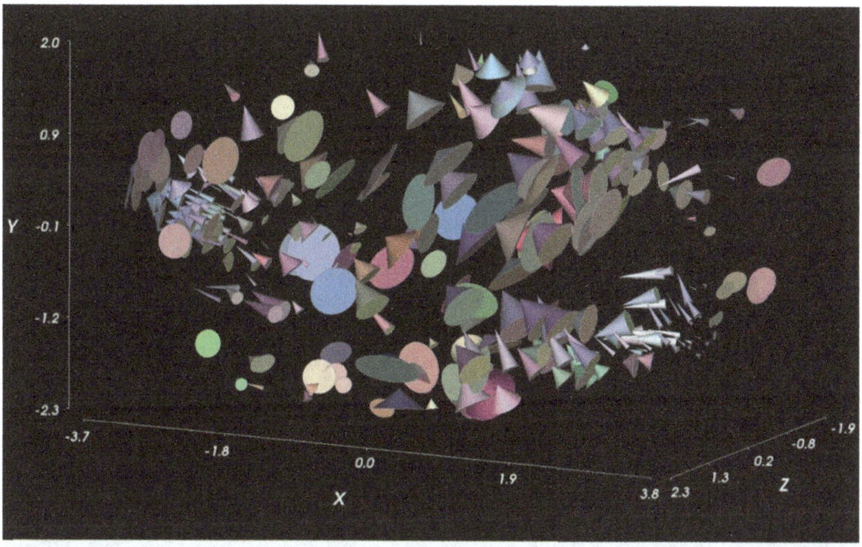

Fig. 10.1 Each cone represents one of 326 cases. (Labels for the cases are omitted). The *x-axis* represents the first principal component of the distribution of cases from the MCC's 24 dimension hidden unit state space. All cases to the right of zero on the x-axis are impermissible; all cases to the left of zero are permissible

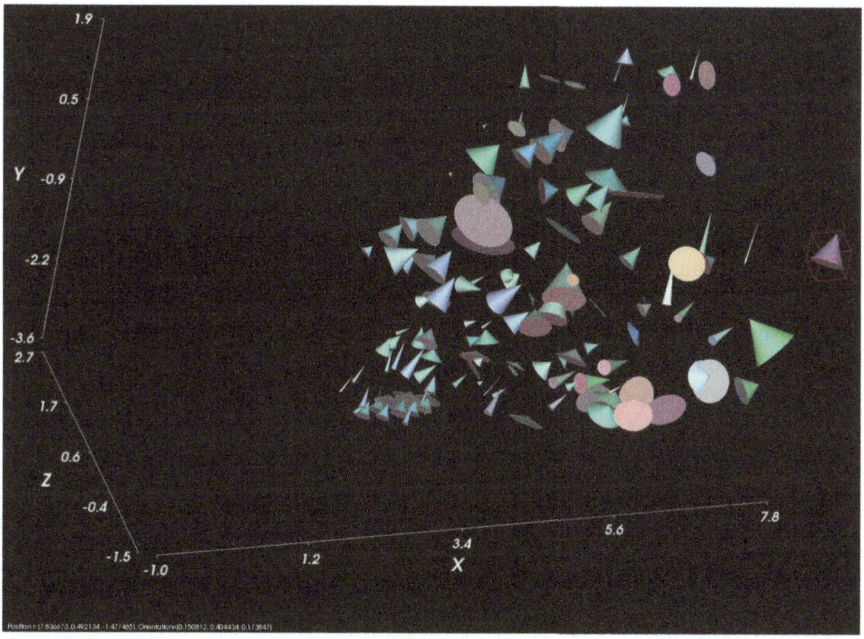

Fig. 10.2 The cases represented here are all classified as impermissible. The *x-axis* represents the Mahalonobis distance from the mean of impermissible cases. The case highlighted with a *red cube* (*far right of x-axis*) is case C discussed in the text. Compare its location here with its location in (Fig. 10.3)

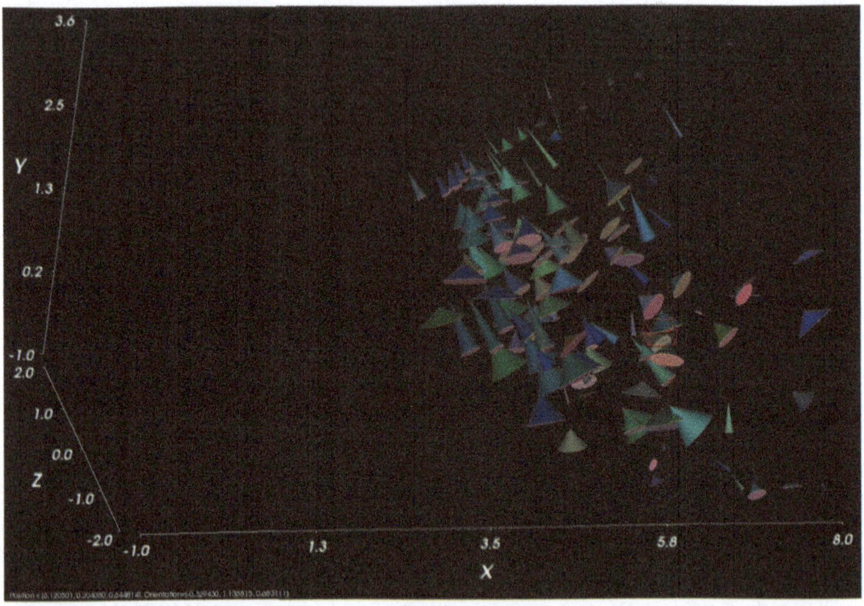

Fig. 10.3 The cases represented here are all classified as permissible, except for case C, highlighted with a *red cube* (*near six on the x-axis*). The x-axis represents the Mahalonobis distance from the mean of permissible cases. Case C is closer to permissible than to impermissible cases

This case could be thought of as an instance of the abortion of a very difficult pregnancy resulting from rape. ("Jack" is the fetus). The network was trained to classify this case as impermissible, and it did so, and it showed up in the impermissibility subspace of (Fig. 10.1). C is the only impermissible case included in (Fig. 10.2). When we check the Mahalonobis distance of C (see the cone with red cube highlighting in (Fig. 10.2)) from the mean of the impermissibility subset and compare it to the Mahalonobis distance of C from the mean of the permissibility subset (see the cone with the red cube highlighting in (Fig. 10.3)), it turns out that C is closer to or more like the permissibility cases than the impermissibility cases (in spite of the fact that it was classified as impermissible). This happened because the network was trained on many cases involving "freedom from invasion of privacy results" and "freedom from being bedridden for 9 months results" and "to obtain freedom from imposed burden." Moreover, many of those cases were classified as permissible. These other features appear to be contributing to permissibility, but for purposes of the final output classification, in case C, killing appeared to outweigh these other considerations. However, those other considerations appear to still "carry weight" in the sense that they have an effect on the location of the case in similarity space. The location of the case in similarity space depends on the first set of synaptic weights between the input layer and the hidden layer. There is still a second set of synaptic weights, between the hidden layer and the output layer, that contributes to the final classification. Even if the features in question have a particular weighting in the similarity space, the output or final classification makes use of another set of synaptic weights that further modifies the contributions of specific features. See Guarini (forthcoming) for further details.

10.4 Spaces of Reasons

The MCC only performs a low-level classification task. It does not do any high-level reasoning or reflection. However, it is conceivable that hidden unit representations of the MCC could be fed into another process that does high-level tasks. The properties of the low-level representations would then be available to the high-level processes. Contributions made by specific features or relations would be among these properties since the information is implicit in the representations. Something else that might become available to the high-level process(es) is information about how one case is related to clusters. It may turn out that one case that is classified as impermissible, but is closer to the permissible cases (using Mahalonobis distance, or perhaps some other metric), may play an important role in understanding which sorts of agents are more open to changing their minds on certain kinds of cases, or at what point in the process of argumentation they may become open to changing their minds.

We can speak of two spaces of reasons. One space of reasons operates at the subreflective level. Let us call this a space of implicit reasons. The MCC is a crude, simplistic, toy-like approximation of how different contributory considerations can be at work for the purpose of unreflective, fast classification of situations. In the space of explicit or reflective reasons, we represent, articulate, and argue about considerations that make normative differences. Getting clear on the relationship between these two spaces is no easy matter. One of the interesting features of that relationship is that genuine surprise or discovery is possible: in attempting to articulate or make explicit what we take to be contributory considerations that are implicitly at work in classification, we can be presented with examples that show us that our reflective understanding of implicit space is not as well developed as we thought it was. The fact that some who treat abortion as impermissible in cases of rape are genuinely surprised by the force of the violinist argument (or its variants) is just one of many examples of that phenomenon. The working hypothesis for the rest of this paper is that understanding the interplay of these different spaces of reasons can contribute to our understanding of coherence.

10.5 A Role for Procedural Coherence

Elsewhere (Guarini 2007) I argued against the usefulness of a specific type of coherence model of reasoning, the multiconstraint model of coherence understood as operating in a global manner. My concern in that paper was (a) that we could not consciously compute the required coherence values without aids, and (b) to rely on external aids or unconscious computation does not capture much of what we think is important about normative, reflective reasoning. The coherence being argued against there was a kind of global substantive coherence (applying to all beliefs, goals, actions and the like). It does not follow from any of the arguments in that paper that there is no role for coherence or incoherence to play. Schiavello (this volume) also expresses concerns about global or large scale forms of coherence. It is completely consistent to express certain kinds of skepticism about global coherence and take seriously local forms of coherence. Let us examine this possibility further.

If we say that two or more things cohere, we are suggesting that they, in some sense, "fit together" or "go together" or some such. If two or more things incohere, the reverse is true. Consistency is one contributor to coherence, but pretty much everyone agrees it is not the only one. If we take similarity to be another contributor to coherence, cases that are similar and treated in the same way cohere, but cases that are similar and treated in different ways without an explanation of the different treatments are said to incohere. Note well: there is no inconsistency in saying that we should classify the violinist case (V) in one way and the case of abortion in pregnancy resulting from rape (R) in another way. If you take V and R to be sufficiently similar, then you may feel or claim there to be an incoherence in doing so (but none of this commits you to anything of the form p and not p). Arguments from analogy often turn on making use of an incoherence present in one or more interlocutors. If individuals acknowledge that V and R are normatively similar (without any significant dissimilarities), then they should not classify them in different ways. Sometimes, the argument is not so much from the analogy as it is to the analogy. Individuals may simply not see any similarity at all between V and R, and the burden would then be to try to get them to see the similarity, which leads to their different initial classifications for V and R being incoherent, which may then force a revision. For reasons of space, I will focus on the former scenario, the argument from the analogy.

Imagine that someone is opposed to abortion in cases of pregnancy resulting from rape, and this individual is presented with the violinist argument. He sees the similarity between V and R, concedes the incoherence of admitting similarity but classifying differently, and revises his view. On the state space account developed herein, what happened is something like this. An initial classification of cases lead to R being classified as impermissible even though R was more like V with respect to the balance of permissibility- and impermissibility-making considerations, so much so that R is more like the permissible cases (in terms of Mahalanobis distance) than the impermissible cases. If something like this were going on in a person, we should in no way suggest that the individual in question would have conscious access to all the contributory considerations and how they structure the distribution of cases such that R is closer to one subset of cases rather than another. What the individual has is an intuition that R is similar to V; that intuition may be the result of processing at the subreflective or unconscious level. At the conscious or reflective level, there is a recognition that it would be incoherent to concede that (a) R and V are normatively similar and (b) that they are treated differently, without (c) citing some normative difference-making considerations. We do try to avoid that kind of incoherence, but the reflective and articulated avoidance of that kind of incoherence is a local affair. We never consciously consider all the cases in our normative state space or even a significant subset in any given argument. Moreover, the incoherence in question pertains to asserting that two or more cases are normatively similar while treating them differently and not being able to distinguish the cases; the corresponding form of coherence requires that when we assert that cases are normatively similar, we treat them in the same way, and if we do not, then we recognize an obligation to cite differences that warrant different treatments of the cases (normative similarities notwithstanding). This is a kind of procedural coherence. One person (or system) could take one view on a given case and claim that it is analogous with a given precedent, and a different person (or system) might admit that there are normatively weighty similarities, but argue that these are outweighed by even more weighty dissimilarities. Both would be procedurally coherent.

Our willingness to say, our intuition if you will, that a pair of cases is normatively similar (or dissimilar) may well be informed by much that is going on at the subreflective level, but at the reflective level we can only ever deal with a small number of cases. Even if (for the sake of argument) we assume that computational processes going on at the subreflective level are coherence promoting in some global sense, it does not follow that at the reflective level what makes analogies normatively appropriate is the maximization of global coherence. Reflectively, we consider things like cases, principles, and similarity statements (which sometimes cite principles); we do not appear to do anything like evaluate global coherence, nor is it clear that we could even if we wanted to. To see this, imagine that we have 100 cases. Consider three-wise similarity comparisons of this form, where X_i are cases:

$$X_1 \text{ is more similar to } X_2 \text{ than it is to } X_3.$$

Given 100 cases, there are 100^3 (or 1,000,000) possible three-wise similarity comparisons. Imagine the conjunction of all those similarity statements; assuming bivalence, checking that conjunction for consistency (which would be a contributor to global coherence) would require $2^{1{,}000{,}000}$ steps using an exhaustive truth table method. Even if we checked only 2^{100} similarity statements for consistency, it would be more than we could consciously reflect over in a lifetime. (To put this in perspective, 2^{100} is approximately 10^{30}. Assuming the universe is about 15 billion years old, the total number of seconds in the history of the universe is on the order of 10^{17}). So even if some sort of computational process could help us to usefully approximate global coherence at the subreflective level, it does not follow, without further argument, that this plays an important role at the reflective level. The same point can be made for a probably approximate correct—PAC—account of global coherence or other accounts that might be inspired by the machine learning literature. Even if they play a role at the subreflective level in approximating coherence, it does not follow, without further argument, that such global coherence approximations would play a role at the normative, reflective level.

10.6 A Role for Surveyable, Substantive Coherence

In the previous section, we have only considered the coherence or incoherence of cases and their classifications. Normative principles of different sorts, goals of different sorts, and beliefs about empirical matters could also factor into more broadly conceived types of coherence—there is no room to explore all of that here. (Indeed, other papers in this collection are considering types of coherence not considered in this paper, and the arguments herein need not and should not be interpreted as applying to all imaginable types of coherences). It might be argued, though, that with respect to the coherence of cases, the remarks of the previous section are too pessimistic. Perhaps, it might be suggested, we could design a system that could compute coherence better than we could. I have said a few things about that line of thought elsewhere (Guarini 2007). For now, let us imagine that there is a disputed case X, and we provide it as input to a system that considers two possible verdicts on the case. When we take X, assign it a specific verdict, and add it to a system's case base B_0 (the set of cases for which it already has verdicts) we get set B_1. When we add X with the opposite verdict to B_0, we get set B_2. If the system returned the result that B_1 is more coherent than B_2 and nothing else, I doubt we would find this helpful in normative matters. If the system returned the result that a given case should be treated in a certain way because it bares important similarities to some other case (or several other cases), and the apparent differences are explained away, then this would be quite useful from a normative, reflective perspective. However, it is not clear what simply adding, "B_1 is more globally coherent than B_2," would add from a normative perspective (even if we included numerical descriptions of the coherence levels).

It does not follow from anything said thus far that a coherence engine that seeks after or approximates some sort of substantive coherence would have no role to play. Perhaps it could inform the search for relevant cases to use in analogical reasoning or argument. If that sort of usefulness obtains, it does not follow that what makes the analogy a good or bad one has to do with global coherence. Being able to evaluate the analogy would appear to have more to do with (1) showing that specific similarities are to be afforded normative weight (or not), and (2) showing that specific similarities outweigh specific differences (or vice versa). Objection: but the considerations involved in doing the preceding could come from anywhere, so that means everything has to hang together, so global coherence is required in the end. Reply: perhaps considerations pertaining to (1) and (2) could come from almost anywhere if we are considering the matter in general, but that does not mean that they come from everywhere when we are examining a specific problem Substantive, global, coherence about cases is computationally exacerbating because all cases (in some sense) are used in the computation. There may be no way to specify in advance of any given dispute which sorts of considerations (including which cases may be appealed to) may become relevant for carrying out (1) or (2). It does not follow that we need to make reference to global coherence in carrying out normative or reflective tasks focused on a specific problem. For example, consider two lawyers arguing about some target case T. Lawyer one appeals to precedent P_1, and lawyer two appeals to P_2, and each makes a strong argument because, for the sake of argument, T is similar to both P_1 and P_2, and the P_i cases were decided in different ways by different courts in the past. This stalemate may be broken if one of the lawyers comes up with an argument that can show that her way of deciding the case fits better with the past practice of the courts in a range of cases. That said, it must be possible to survey this range of cases in an argument in order for the appeal to fit with prior cases to have normative force. This appears to allow a substantive role for coherence because an appeal to better fit is playing a substantive normative role: it may contribute to one argument being better than another in virtue of the fit or coherence between the cases. Still, this is a local form of coherence. It may be true that, to a first approximation, all cases decided in the past and even hypothetical cases are "fair game" with respect to which cases we could potentially appeal to in such coherence arguments, but it does not follow that all cases are or need to be (or could be—think of all the logically possible hypothetical cases!) appealed to in such arguments. Once again, to put it roughly, just because considerations could come from anywhere, it does not follow that they come from everywhere. This is especially so at the level of conscious, reflective reasoning.

So far we have considered local forms of coherence—which are restricted to what can be consciously reflected over—and global forms of coherence. A global form of coherence with respect to cases and verdicts would have to consider all cases and their verdicts. A global form of coherence without any qualifiers would consider everything that could factor into coherence (principles, goals, beliefs about empirical matters . . .). To all this, we could add the idea of a non-local form of coherence. A non-local form of coherence with respect to cases and verdicts would encompass more cases than we could ever hope to individually, consciously reflect over for purposes of considering coherence, but would fall short of considering all cases and verdicts. The term "global" is pretty strong, even if we qualify it by saying it refers only to the role of cases and verdicts and their contributions to coherence. The consideration of all cases would include even hypothetical cases. Someone might want to restrict the cases involved in coherence calculations to those which and individual has encountered in his or her lifetime. This is clearly something less than global coherence, but the calculations involved in the coherence assessment would still be more than we could expect someone to do in a lifetime—hence the expression non-local coherence. As we saw above, computing coherence over 100 cases is not manageable at the reflective level, and as a general rule people will encounter more than 100 cases that they will be expected to classify in a lifetime. There may be subreflective processes that could examine more than we could examine consciously, but even if those processes are of a coherence promoting nature, two things need to be kept in mind. First, given the computational complexity involved, there are likely limits even here with respect to the number of cases that can be examined feasibly. Even if we abandon globality and opt for some sort of non-local coherence, a high level of complexity is still in play. Second, even if we subreflectively implement procedures that usefully approximate non-local coherence, it does not automatically follow that that non-local coherence considerations are normatively or reflectively helpful. That point still would have to be defended.

10.7 Some Methodological Reflections

A computational model was discussed above, and others in this volume discuss such models as well, so some methodological reflections on their use are in order. There are different kinds of criticisms that are aimed at simple or "toy" computational models. One type of critique wonders of what possible relevance descriptive considerations could be for prescriptive or normative theorizing. The response to this is to point out that if in some sense or other we can say that ought implies can, that before claiming someone is obligated to reason in a given way it should (as a matter of fact) be possible for them to reason in that way, then empirical and computational considerations are relevant to normative theorizing. Indeed, some of my own arguments about the computational complexity of certain kinds of coherence are an attempt to use empirical and computational considerations in an attempt to constrain normative theorizing about what kinds of reasoning may be appropriate. A second type of critique starts by pointing out that since existing models tend to be very simple, there is not much point to them either descriptively or prescriptively. Descriptively, they are known to be too simple (even by those who propose them), and if they are descriptively incomplete, then (it is claimed) they could not possibly inform prescriptive or normative theorizing. What is the point of using a descriptively incomplete model to constrain or otherwise inform theorizing about coherence (or reasoning more generally)?

That is a good question. I will start my answer by borrowing a metaphor from Wilfred Sellars (1963), who proposed that our manifest and scientific images of ourselves and our world needed to be fused, and he compared this to the way our two eyes bring together two different and overlapping images of the world. Instead of discussing our manifest and scientific images, I will speak of our prescriptive and descriptive images. If we can say that ought implies can, then there is an area of overlap between these images, since what we ought to do is constrained by what we can do. But that is not the only overlap: what we take to be the case regarding descriptive matters is informed by what we take to be appropriate or inappropriate forms of reasoning or gathering evidence. Consider the example of the multi-site, double blind, clinical trial. Over the years, empirical research turned up results about placebo effects, about bias in individual researchers, and about variations in research cultures in different institutions. These empirical findings were used to develop new methods of gathering evidence, new methods for arriving at conclusions about how we ought to reason about the prospects of using newly developed medicines or treatments. These new methods have lead to the overturning of some past empirical results and to more reliable ways of discovering effective treatments. It is almost surely the case that we have not uncovered all the potential ways in which bias and culture can skew experimental results, but it does not follow that we stop experimenting. Research continues on various psychological and sociological factors that can affect the results of research, and, no doubt, new methods will be developed to control for those effects. No one would suggest that we stop doing research until we are done acquiring all the empirical information about how the aforementioned factors can skew research.

In fusing our descriptive and prescriptive images, I want to suggest that neither is prior to the other. The metaphor of the images being side-by-side (one for each eye as it were) is useful since neither is taken as more basic than the other. If descriptive considerations are relevant to and can inform prescriptive claims, then it is difficult to argue that the prescriptive is prior to or more basic than the descriptive. If, on the other hand, the prescriptive can inform and constrain how we acquire descriptive information, then the descriptive is not basic either. We start where we are, modifying each image using the other. If this is right, then there is no point in saying that we have to be "done" with descriptive work before we can do the prescriptive work; nor does it help to say that we have to be "done" with our prescriptive theory before we can do empirical work. Each image informs the evolution of the other in an on-going manner. If the idea of equally basic images is on the right track, then we can begin to see how even simple descriptive models can be helpful. A descriptive model does not have to be done or complete before it is useful. Our descriptive models of how research is done in various fields are not complete, but they have already usefully informed prescriptive claims about how research should be done. We now need to return to models of coherence and show how the fusing of two images is relevant.

One virtue of models, even simple ones known to be incomplete, is that they may make predictions, which can lead to new research, including the need to further refine the model. Thinking about coherence in terms of computational models may lead to new insights about what coherence may or may not be. The main idea behind coherence theories is that, in some sense, the way propositions (or other "things") "hang together" or "fit together" contributes to their justification, warrant, or some other sort of reasonable or normatively appropriate status. Left at that, we have an intolerably vague position. Adding that consistency and explanation are contributors to coherence might help, but it is still pretty vague. Exactly how are ideas supposed to fit together in a way that contributes to positive normative status? It is difficult to specify what it means for things to "fit together" in the relevant respects. Both here and elsewhere, I have expressed some skepticism about what can be accomplished with certain kinds of coherence models. It is a virtue, though, of computational models that they are clear enough to allow for specific criticisms. Assuming some type(s) of coherence play a role in human reasoning, constructing computational models of coherence(s) is a useful way to develop clarity and rigour with respect to what coherence may or may not be. Better descriptive models (which have to start somewhere) could lead to a better understanding of how we can reason, which could be used to place constraints on how we (normatively) expect people to reason. Of course, since coherence is supposed to increase positive normative status, our views on what is normatively appropriate in reasoning will be informing any attempt to build a computational model of coherence. So, our normative views about reasoning inform attempts to build computational models, and the descriptive work of building the model has the potential to feed back on our normative views by showing us that they are too vague, incompletely specified, or otherwise flawed to allow for rigourous modeling, which would force us to revise our normative views. This would lead to better attempts at model development, which will surely run into further problems, and the cycle continues.... The normative and descriptive images inform one another.

To all this it might be replied that many models of coherence are really, really simple, so how could they be useful at this stage in their development? Well, judging by the number of different things the authors in this collection are saying about coherence(s) (and what so many authors have said elsewhere) it may well be that our understanding of coherence(s) is really, really inadequate. If that is right, then it may well be that even working with simple models could lead to important clarifications, more rigour, and new insights for testing and development. It is not just something descriptive that will be tested; it is also something normative. For if the computational model fails to work or is demonstrably incapable of scaling up when we have implemented our best insights on what amounts to normatively appropriate reasoning (coherence-based or otherwise), then maybe our best insights about such reasoning are not good enough.

10.8 Conclusions

The preceding has implications for computational modeling, whether we are interested in moving toward a model of how humans reason, or whether we are interested in constructing a system that can aid humans even though it may not work in the way humans work. For example, coherence as constraint satisfaction may have a role to play at the level of reflective or explicit reasoning, but the cases or other considerations being appealed to would have to be surveyable in the course of an argument. There might be a role for coherence to play at the level of subreflective considerations (i.e. considerations that would not be explicitly articulated and offered for normative consideration), but even here we need to be wary of computational complexity, though the constraints operative at this level need not be identical to the constraints operative at the reflective level. Also, we should not assume that machines designed to do reasoning will be subject to human constraints. The access a machine has to a subreflective state space of the kind considered in section four may be different from the kind of access a human has. That said, if some sort of computational system is to interact with humans and be able to provide persuasive reasons to humans about how to classify cases, the constraints on the human cognitive architecture will have to guide the sorts of reasons any such system would communicate to us if they are to be useful in helping us understand why a given case should be treated in some prescribed or suggested manner.

Acknowledgments I thank the Shared Hierarchical Academic Research Computing Network (SHARCNet) for a digital humanities fellowship that made this research possible. The fellowship included funding for course releases and programming support. Special thanks go to SHARCNet programmer Weiguang Guan for coding the visualization software used to render (Figs. 10.1, 10.2 and 10.3). For comments and suggestions, thanks also go out to Michał Araszkiewicz and Jaromir Šavelka, organizers of the ICAIL 2011 workshop on Coherence, as well as Kevin Ashley, Thorne McCarty, and other workshop participants for their comments and suggestions.

References

Ashley, K.D. 1990. *Modeling legal argument: Reasoning with cases and hypotheticals*. Cambridge, MA: MIT Press.

Dancy, J. 1999. Can a particularist learn the difference between right and wrong? In *Proceedings from the 20th world congress of philosophy*, Ethics, vol. 1, ed. K. Brinkmann. Bowling Green: Philosophy Documentation Center.

Dancy, J. 2000. The particularist's progress. In *Moral particularism*, ed. B. Hooker and M. Little, 130–156. Oxford: Clarendon-Oxford press.

Dancy, J. 2004. *Ethics without principles*. Oxford: Oxford University Press.

Guarini, M. 2006. Particularism and the classification and reclassification of moral cases. *IEEE Intelligent Systems Magazine* 21: 22–28.

Guarini, M. 2007. Computation, coherence, and ethical reasoning. *Minds and Machines* 17: 27–46.

Guarini, M. 2010. Particularism, analogy, and moral cognition. *Minds and Machines* 20: 385–422.

Guarini, M. 2011. Computational neural modeling and the philosophy of ethics. In *Machine ethics*, ed. M. Anderson and S. Anderson, 316–334. Cambridge, UK: Cambridge University Press.

Guarini, M. (forthcoming). Moral case classification and the nonlocality of reasons. *Topoi*. http://link.springer.com/article/10.1007%2Fs11245-012-9130-2

Jackson, F., P. Petit, and M. Smith. 2000. Ethical particularism and patterns. In *Moral particularism*, ed. B. Hooker and M. Little, 79–99. Oxford: Clarendon-Oxford press.

Laakso, A., and G. Cottrell. 2006. Churchland on connectionism. In *Paul Churchland*, ed. B.L. Keeley, 113–153. Cambridge, UK: Cambridge University Press.

Markman, A.B., and D. Gentner. 2005. Nonintentional similarity processing. In *The new unconscious*, eds. T. Hassin, J. Bargh, and J. Uleman, 107–137. New York: Oxford University Press.

McKeever, S., and M. Ridge. 2006. *Principled ethics: Generalism as a regulative ideal*. Oxford: Oxford University Press.

Sellars, W. 1963. Philosophy and the scientific image of man. In *Science, perception, and reality*, ed. W. Sellars, 1–40. Atascadero: Ridgeview Publishing Company.

Thomson, J. 1971. A defense of abortion. *Philosophy and Public Affairs* 1(1): 47–66.

Chapter 11
Coherence as Constraint Satisfaction: Judicial Reasoning Support Mechanism

Jaromír Šavelka

11.1 Introduction

Legal profession has always been in its core a problem solving business. It may be true that a task of an attorney advising her client (struggling to find the best possible solution on the pragmatic level), a task of a judge deciding a case (struggling to find the most righteous solution while still taking into account necessary pragmatics of the situation) and a task of a legal theoretician to grasp the meaning of selected legal concept (struggling to find the most accurate and sound solution) differ greatly at first sight. However, on an abstract level no difference remains. They are all problems defined by a set of available information[1] waiting to be processed in such a way an adequate solution is reached. And as surprising as it may sound it can be easily concluded that legal problems essentially do not differ from any other problem we may encounter, even in our everyday lives. And adhering to the Wiener's definition of living entities the efforts put in solving legal problems are consistent with a natural tendency and ability of living beings to make adjustments on their environment.

> Information is a name for the content of what is exchanged with the outer world as we adjust to it, and make our adjustment felt upon it. The process of receiving and of using information is the process of our adjusting to the contingencies of the outer environment, and of our living effectively within that environment. [C]ommunication and control belong to the essence of man's inner life, even as they belong to his life in society (Wiener 1989, 17–18).

---

[1]For the sake of simplicity I do not make any difference between data and information. It would not help in any way to struggle with their definitions in the pursuit of the intended aim and would unnecessarily complicate the message the chapter communicates.

J. Šavelka (✉)
Faculty of Law, Masaryk University, Vevefi 70, Brno 611-80, Czech Republic
e-mail: jaromir.savelka@law.muni.cz

M. Araszkiewicz and J. Šavelka (eds.), *Coherence: Insights from Philosophy, Jurisprudence and Artificial Intelligence*, Law and Philosophy Library 107,
DOI 10.1007/978-94-007-6110-0_11,

Thus, it seems that any legal problem, as well as any other problem, can be solved if and only if an adequate collection of information is acquired and processed to the form of a solution. At this point one can hardly avoid the obvious parallel to the very well established concept of algorithm that is usually used within the computer science.

To understand the procedure of legal problem solving within the framework of algorithms and computer science one must at first be able to recognize the information that are—to put it in legal terminology—relevant to the given problem. These information can be considered an input to the process. In case of algorithms we usually speak of 'some value, or set of values' [5] that is an input of an algorithm. Secondly, it is necessary to characterize the information that is to be regarded as an output of the legal problem solving process. Since in case of algorithms we once again speak of 'some value, or set of values' in case of legal problem solving procedures we can settle with the statement that the output of the process is the information relevant to the solution of the problem. In this sense, both algorithm and legal problem solving procedure can be understood as a 'sequence of [. . .] steps that transform the input into the output'. However, the algorithm is usually characterized in a more concrete way as a 'sequence of computational steps'. And this is the exact moment when the parallel ends. The AI and Law community members have worked hard for more than 40 years to allow the parallel go further. However, despite enormous successes in certain areas such as the field of legal information retrieval a large portion of legal problem solving resists to be computerized. Judicial reasoning can be considered a member of the portion. At any time in history in any country in the world no computerized formalism for judicial reasoning has ever been employed on a large scale in everyday practice.

Why it is so difficult to formalize legal reasoning[2] and transform it to a computable problem is a question that can be answered in a rather informal manner. Consider a task of a judge and the way in which she has to proceed in order to solve a legal problem, i.e., to decide a case. At first she receives information from a party asking a court to start the decision making process. These information have to be processed in such a way to decide if the grounds for the process do actually exist. It is done by assessing the information within the context of existing law. If the process is eventually started a rather extensive collection of information is usually created. Since both opposing parties are involved in the process quite intensively it is often the case that individual information contravene and a judge has to decide which one to prefer over the other. The situation is even more complicated by the fact that it is not only expected that a judge would apply the relevant legal rules to the relevant facts of the case. As law tends to be intentionally vague at certain points leaving some space for judicial discretion it is expected that a judge would apply her

[2]By no means, I do assert that no progress has been done in the field—quite opposite is true. However, it remains undisputed that an actual implementation of the outcomes of the research in the field of formalization of judicial reasoning to everyday legal practice is virtually non-existent.

common sense, social experience, sense for equity and occasionally benevolence and kindness in order to reach a righteous decision.

Furthermore, it is worth drawing the attention to Dworkin's elaboration on 'hard cases' (Dworkin 1977, 81–130). In his opinion certain cases exist that cannot be decided upon existing legal rules, yet the rights of the parties exists and a judge must employ his best capacities to discover them. Dworkin asserts that the judicial reasoning in these kind of cases can hardly be formalized since as he puts it:

> [No] mechanical procedure exists for demonstrating what the rights of parties are in hard cases. (Dworkin 1977, 81).

Dworkin probably does not say that formal techniques cannot be employed in decision processes of hard cases in such a way to make certain part of the procedure computable. He rather seems to suggest that different opinions regarding a procedure of assessing rights in these cases may exist. In such a view the employment of formal techniques would not be excluded within the domain of hard cases.[3] It would simply remain doubtful which technique should be preferred and how exactly should it be implemented. Yet the same applies for the hard cases if decided in absence of formal techniques—different opinions regarding the solution may legitimately exist as well (Dworkin 1977, 81–130).

All this has to be taken into account when designing a formal technique for judicial reasoning which is the main issue of this paper. Furthermore, all the above mentioned aspects would have to be quantified and measured in some way to make judicial reasoning computable—as Garey and Johnson provide a definition of computable problem as follows:

> [A] problem will be a general question to be answered, usually possessing several parameters, or free variables, whose values are left unspecified. A problem is described by giving: (1) a general description of all its parameters, and (2) a statement of what properties the answer, or solution, is required to satisfy. An instance of a problem is obtained by specifying particular values for all the problem parameters (Garey and Johnson 1979, 4).

Thus, not surprisingly in order to employ formal methods in judicial reasoning it has to be done in such a way that the implementation would allow an instantiation of a problem using parameters and assigning values to individual variables. Though, this may seem as the main reason for not employing any formalism that would allow computation of judicial reasoning in everyday practice other causes have contributed to the situation significantly as well.

In this paper I follow in the steps of the work of Thagard (2000), Bench-Capon and Sartor (2001), Amaya (2007), and Araszkiewicz (2010) to propose computation of coherence as constraint satisfaction as a promising formalism that would provide a solid basis for making implementation of computing methods to the process of judicial reasoning feasible. First, I introduce and briefly describe the proposed formalism. Secondly, known objections towards application of the method

---

[3]It is worth noting that the domain itself is characterized by rather vague borders and it is not always possible to conclusively denominate a particular dispute as a hard case.

within the process of judicial reasoning are summarized from the point of view of both legal and computer science. Certain parallels considering the difficulties of applying coherence as constraint satisfaction to judicial reasoning are identified between the assessed points of view. The parallels clearly show that computer science does not lack the doctrinal foundations and methods to enter into general debates led in the fields of legal theory and philosophy regarding the suitability of employing computation to the process of judicial reasoning. Upon the objections—raised from both fields (the set seems to be surprisingly compatible)—a list of requirements for any formalism to be employed within the process of legal reasoning is formulated. The coherence as constraint satisfaction formalism is then examined if the requirements are met.

11.2 Computing Coherence as Constraint Satisfaction

To approach coherence as a problem of constraint satisfaction is a method proposed by Thagard and Verbeurgt (1997) to formalize coherence in such a way to provide a solid grounds for its computation. The key idea is to define a coherence problem as a unification of a finite set E of elements $\{e_1, e_2, \ldots e_n\}$ and finite set C of constraints among the elements. The constraints may be either positive or negative with values assigned respectively.

The output of the procedure is a partition of the set E into sets of A of accepted elements and set R of rejected elements. The partition must be realized in such a way that a total value W of constraints among the elements included in the set A is maximized. Only the value of such constraint that exist between elements that are both included in the set A is added to W. The values of constraints existing within the set R and the values of constraints in situations in which one element is included in the set A and second in the set R have no impact on W. Elements that have no impact on W have to be included in the set R.

Thagard and Verbeurgt provide more formal definition as follows:

> Let E be a finite set of elements $\{e_i\}$ and C be a set of constraints on E understood as a set $\{(e_i, e_j)\}$ of pairs of elements of E. C divides into C+, the positive constraints on E, and C-, the negative constraints on E. With each constraint is associated a number w, which is the weight (strength) of the constraint. The problem is to partition E into two sets, A and R, in a way that maximizes compliance with the following two coherence conditions:
>
> 1. If (e_i, e_j) is in C+, then e_i is in A if and only if e_j is in A.
> 2. If (e_i, e_j) is in C-, then e_i is in A if and only if e_j is in R.
>
> Let W be the weight of the partition, that is, the sum of the weights of the satisfied constraints. The coherence problem is then to partition E into A and R in a way that maximizes W.

Thus, on its surface—i.e., as regards the input and the output—the procedure is rather straightforward. On the other hand, its actual execution considering larger set E is much more complicated. The purpose of this paper does not require to go into these details.[4]

11.3 The Grand Issue of Complexity: Perspective of Law

There are countless explanations on the grounds of which it is possible to understand why does the everyday practice of judicial reasoning resist the employment of formalisms and AI methods. One of them is very simple—the methods are beyond comprehension of common people. Even judges would most likely not be able to employ these methods and would have to educate themselves extensively in fields very different from Law. However, imagine an ordinary layperson losing a case in front of the court alongside with a lump sum of 200,000 USD she has been ordered to pay as a result of the dispute. Would not such a person be deprived of her fundamental right for a fair trial if she would receive the order in a form of a collection of logical formulas and mathematical equations, she would be completely unable to understand?

However, it should be noted that the argument is rather prejudicial and does not take into account opinions advocating the formal methods stating that they should be employed in such a way to reach the exact opposite, i.e., to make judicial decisions more comprehensible to an ordinary layperson.[5] This goal can indeed be achieved by means of pictures, graphs and schemes.[6] Another aspect the argument does not take into account is a current phenomenon caused by an extensive use of ICT technology—as a result of the use people tend to think in more formalized and mathematical way. Thus, in the future the situation may shift completely and the decision containing a limited number of logical formulas and mathematical equations may be appreciated for its preciseness and the decision formulated in plain language criticized for its incomprehensibility.[7]

Legal reasoning in general may appear to be a set of inferences performed over the base of facts and rules. This makes the field extremely attractive for experts in logical programming which is itself based on checking the validity of goals (can be understood as questions or tasks) within a given set of facts and rules. However, such a view has been argued to be erroneous. As Leith puts it:

---

[4]For more details see Thagard (2000), Thagard and Verbeurgt (1997).

[5]One of the advocates is e.g., Bengez, R.Z. The opinion has been expressed on many occassions, e.g., at the QAJF Conference held at Fiesole on February 25–26, 2011.

[6]See e.g., Boehme-Nessler (2011).

[7]This statement is surely nothing more but a speculation. However, I felt an urge to make the note since I believe it adds different perspective to the opinions expressed above.

> Proponents of legal expert systems have picked up on the ideology of law as unchanging and missed the observable facts that law is ever changing and constantly being interpreted. I do not mean that law changes gradually over time—it certainly does that—but it also depends largely upon the context in which it is used and how it is used to produce a narrative from the interpreted facts of a situation (Leith 2010).

Thus, another objection of lawyers towards the formal methods and AI employment in judicial reasoning may rise out of the past failures of technicians with no legal education attempting to transform law into a set of simple if-then-else rules. Such attempts may have very well made lawyers to adapt a defensive approach against those techniques in understandable effort to prevent an obvious 'degradation' of law.

A different line of argumentation stresses out the absence of an actual demand for an employment of formal methods and AI techniques in judicial reasoning.[8] Judges would obviously not appreciate a computerized tool that would be able to perform all the tasks they usually perform. Leaving aside the pragmatics of the situation—no one wants to lose her job and be replaced by a machine—there exists a strong believe that personal and moral qualities of a judge are essential in the process of judicial decision making and these can never be replicated by any form of AI. These qualities do not only have an impact on the decision itself but they also give a legitimacy to it. Thus, not only judges but virtually any reasonable person would not be in favor of AI techniques employment in the process. This kind of reservation springs out of the fear of excluding a human element from a judicial decision making process.

Very similar objection aims at the potential of formalization to unnecessarily constrain a judge. It may be vividly illustrated on the example kindly provided by Schäfer[9] regarding his personal experience with student essays assessment after the formalization of the process at his home University of Edinburgh. The difference between an informal assessment and the assessment using a prescribed form with given criteria was not only that the distribution of marks changed slightly but more importantly the overall average seemed to drop by 10%. In this context it is quite interesting to note that the new form of assessment was actually advocated by the students representative body of the University. However, the observation can be nicely generalized in a way Schäfer puts it—'the formal methods of assessment have deprived him of 10% of kindness'. The very same may apply to the area of law which should be appreciated for a certain degree of vagueness leaving space for a judicial discretion and perhaps 'kindness' of individual judges. Thus, a fear of losing this appreciated quality of law due to the employment of formal methods seems legitimate.

[8] One of the most prominent proponents of the opinion is according to my knowledge Philip Leith.

[9] QAJF Conference held at Fiesole on February 25–26, 2011.

11.4 The Grand Issue of Complexity: Perspective of Computer Science

A number of reasons to consider judicial reasoning to be an extremely delicate and complicated activity has been provided. In context of computer science I believe it is not too daring to categorize judicial reasoning as an activity that can be informally characterized as AI-complete, i.e., it would require to create an AI entity matching the full capabilities of human mind in order to be able to carry out judicial reasoning in a fully computerized way. To provide some context for the statement the whole scope of natural language processing (ranging from operation with phonemes to linguistic pragmatics) is sometimes referred to be AI-complete as well.

However, there is much more elaborated classification of computational problems as regards their complexity. And as we were able to establish at least a limited parallel between legal problems solving procedures and algorithms it is very interesting to extend the parallel to the area of complexity as well. The problem of complexity is traditionally defined within the notion of time required to carry out the algorithm. As different computers with different computing powers would not require the same amount of time for the procedure Garey and Johnson provide a following definition that allows to abstract from the individual machines:

> The time used in the computation of a deterministic Turing machine program M on an input x is the number of steps occurring in that computation up until a halt state is entered (Garey and Johnson 1979, 26).

Consequently there is a complete hierarchy of individual problems time complexity starting with constant, linear, quadratic and going towards exponential and beyond. On the extremely informal level it is possible to say that these terms are used to explain the relationship between the size of the input and the time needed to transform the input into the output. Thus, if the algorithm exists that is able to carry out the procedure with the input of the length n in time that does not asymptotically exceed n^2 (for all the possible inputs) we can refer to the problem as being of quadratic complexity. This division has extremely practical utilization since problems characterized by high computational complexity are often referred to as intractable which means that for certain inputs the time required for the computation makes the algorithm actually unusable.

As regards the aim of this paper it is much more suitable to recognize the following classes of the complexity—P problems, NP problems and NP-complete problems (Garey and Johnson 1979, 7). In order for a problem to qualify as P an algorithm must exist to 'solve' the problem in polynomial time, i.e., in time that does not asymptotically exceed n$ˆk$ steps of the deterministic Turing machine (both n and k are natural numbers). It is worth noting that only P problems are considered to be tractable. NP problems can be simply characterized as all the problems that are not P problems which also means that they are to be considered as intractable.

Another notion necessary to grasp at least informally in order to proceed is NP-completeness. Obviously it is not always easy to recognize if a particular problem belongs to class of P or NP problems. Thus, the issue has been traditionally dealt with in such a way that if it has been possible to transform a problem to a problem that has already been proven to be NP the problem has been considered NP as well. A rather large set of problems have been traditionally referred to as being NP-complete. The important characteristic of these problems, besides being 'believed' to be NP, is that they can be transformed one to the other. If an algorithm that would solve any NP-complete problem in polynomial time would be discovered it would simply mean that all NP-complete problems are in fact P. However, it is widely believed (although not conclusively proven) that this will never happen.

It is quite interesting that computing coherence as constraint satisfaction that is examined in this paper whether it should be regarded a suitable technique for judicial reasoning support has been proven to be NP-complete (Thagard and Verbeurgt 1997). Thus, it basically means that this particular formalism assigns judicial reasoning a status of NP-complete problem. In this context computer science seems to approve what has been written above regarding the impossibility of employing AI in judicial reasoning—judicial decision making should be regarded as computationally intractable.

As a concluding remark to this part of the paper it is worth mentioning that NP-problems have not been defined under the notion of deterministic Turing machine (Garey and Johnson 1979, 23–27) in computer science. Instead, they have been traditionally defined under the notion of nondeterministic Turing machine (Garey and Johnson 1979, 30–32). The important underlying idea of the nondeterministic Turing machine is a presence of a guessing module which is a part of the procedure capable of correctly guessing the next step leading to the solution. The nondeterministic Turing machine is capable of solving the NP-complete problems in polynomial time. It should be also noted that once the solution has been found it is possible to prove its correctness in polynomial time using the deterministic Turing machine.

Thus, a theory of algorithms seems to suggest that judicial decision making procedure-if represented in a form of computing coherence as constraint satisfaction-cannot be entangled into a set of deterministic steps, i.e., it cannot be computed. The AI tool designed to support judicial reasoning process would have to be equipped with the guessing module which can be easily understood within the notion of human intuition. It can be concluded that from this point of view a theory of NP-completeness can be used as yet another objection to the employment of AI techniques to the judicial reasoning.

11.5 Judicial Reasoning and Computing Coherence as Constraint Satisfaction

Above a number of obstacles and objections have been introduced as regards potential employment of AI techniques to the process of judicial reasoning on a large scale, i.e., to everyday practice. If any formalism should be regarded as possible candidate for introduction to everyday practice it has to address all the issues and demonstrate that it is capable of coping with them. These issues include but are definitely not limited to:

1. The formalism should not be applicable solely in the domain of law but should rather be a general problem solving procedure (at least in its essence).
2. The formalism should be simple and easily comprehensible—not only to a lawyer but to a layperson as well.
3. The formalism should not constrain legal reasoning in any way, i.e., it must be descriptive, not prescriptive.
4. There must be an actual demand for the employment of the formalism from practicing lawyers.
5. The formalism should not exclude human element from the judicial reasoning process.
6. The formalism should preserve space for judicial discretion (and 10% of kindness).
7. The formalism should be computable.
8. The formalism should allow validation of its output (solution).

The following text examines the individual obstacles to the employment of AI in the everyday legal practice from the point of view of computing coherence as constraint satisfaction. I do not assert that the method is the best and only way to formalize judicial reasoning, nor that it should be regarded as superior to other methods. Thus, the aim of the following text is to simply demonstrate that coherence as constraint satisfaction formalism is capable to address the raised objections in quite a decent way.

Computing coherence as constraint satisfaction has been developed by Thagard and Verbeurgt as a general method to compute coherence (Thagard and Verbeurgt 1997). Thagard himself demonstrated the technique using his ECHO computer program (Thagard 1992) to solve issues from various fields including the 'Vincennes' incident (a decision of USS Vincennes captain to shoot down Iranian aircraft), (Thagard 1992, 138–141) the deception in the Normandy Invasion, (Thagard 1992, 141–143) various theories of the dinosaurs extinction causes (Thagard 1991) and the debate concerning the nature of light that took place in eighteenth and nineteenth century (Eliasmith and Thagard 1997). The results of the application have been equally satisfying no matter the issue they have been applied to. I believe it would be possible to apply the method to support judicial reasoning almost as it is, i.e., in the genuine form as has been proposed by Thagard. I base this assumption on the fact that he has already used the ECHO computer program to analyze several legal cases (Thagard 2003). Although, it may be beneficial to adjust the model to suit judicial reasoning even more[10] it has been demonstrated that the method can be considered a general problem solving procedure that is not specific to a legal domain (1).

[10]As has been advised e.g., in Hoadley et al. (1994) or Araszkiewicz (2010).

Despite a vast theory behind coherence and its computation as constraint satisfaction the idea is rather simple on its surface. A set of available information—propositions—is divided into a subset of those that are accepted and those that are rejected. Furthermore, it reflects rather adequately what a judge actually does during the judicial reasoning process. With no regards to what does the proposition actually encompass—a fact, legal rule, legal principle, moral principle, law of nature, potential outcome of a case[11]—a judge has to decide whether it is relevant to the case and can form a coherent whole. And in case it can it is a possible candidate for a decision—for what else can a judicial decision actually be regarded at an abstract level but a ruling and a set of information it is based upon (reasons). Besides, it is possible to agree with Thagard that:

> A computational approach to coherence has the potential to provide both a powerful theory of important cognitive mechanisms and a non-foundational solution to philosophical problems about justification (Thagard 2000, 13).

Thus, a method represents a state-of-the-art description of actual workings of human mind. Based on these facts, it is in my opinion possible to consider computing coherence as constraint satisfaction as intuitive method for both lawyers and laypersons in a sense that its underlying principles are easily comprehensible and seemingly natural (2).

To demonstrate persuasively that the method does not constrain judge in carrying out the judicial reasoning process is a task of such difficulty that it goes far beyond the scope of this paper. However, I believe that it is still possible to show that the method does not impose any restrictions concerning the process that would not have been already present even without the employment of the method. As has been already mentioned above, the method does not impose any restrictions regarding propositions to be included in a set upon which a computation is expected to be performed. Thus, the actual input is limited solely by a judge's capability of coping with the mass of information—which is a limit that exists independently on the employment of the method. Besides, computing coherence as constraint satisfaction is a highly scalable process. It can be performed at a completely abstract level—considering only the fundamental features of the case—or at a level of high granularity—considering the tiniest details of the case. Furthermore, the problem can be represented as a whole and computed in a one step or it can be divided to smaller problems. In that case it would be possible to deal with minor issues separately and make the whole process more transparent and easier to comprehend. The only restriction the model in fact imposes is the necessity to divide a set of propositions to those that are accepted and those that are rejected eventually. However, this restriction seems to correlate with the judge's duty to actually decide

[11]In a sense I believe that anything can be introduced to the process as the proposition. The computation of coherence as constraint satisfaction is immune towards the introduction of completely irrelevant propositions. Since no positive or negative constraints would exist between relevant and irrelevant propositions. However, certain moderation has to be applied in order to prevent explosion of the sets to unmanageable sizes.

the case even if it seems undecidable at first sight.[12] Thus, computing coherence as constraint satisfaction is very far from reducing law to a set of if-then-else rules and in my opinion does not constrain judge within the process of judicial reasoning (3).

The issue of actual demand for the employment of the method from practicing lawyers, in this cases judges,[13] may be regarded to be the most serious obstacle. Although, it may be often beneficial to examine the formalism theoretically with no intention to introduce it in everyday practice it should be regarded as a serious detrimental if no practical applications can be foreseen. Court decisions, especially those issued at the lower instances, often contain a rather high number of conflicting statements. Often, it is not easy to find out what are the actual reasons the ruling is based upon. Thus, space for improvement of consistency and coherence of the judicial reasoning exists while the goal is at the same time desirable to achieve. This is the exact place in everyday practice in which computation of coherence as constraint satisfaction may fit in. First of all it can be used as a tool for argumentation analysis capable of identifying inconsistency and incoherence in the argumentation as well as weak spots—helping to successfully attack or fortify a particular scheme of argumentation at these spots (retrospective use). Secondly, it can be employed within the process of building up the argumentation from scratch as a tool ensuring its consistency and coherence (prospective use). On the other hand, it is virtually impossible to imagine employment of the formalism in the everyday practice as it is. With no doubt it would have to be implemented within an easy-to-use straightforward tool that would modify the process of court decision preparation in such a way that the computation of coherence as constraint satisfaction would be a natural, inherent and seamless part of the whole process. Achieving this seems impossible in absence of the integration of the formalism within a larger framework of document assembly and information management. It should be concluded that employment of the method into everyday practice cannot be discarded as impossible (4).

As regards the process of computing coherence as constraint satisfaction in the form proposed by Thagard the role of AI is fairly limited. The process merely accepts a set of propositions and positive and negative constraints and attempts to find the subset of the propositions with the maximum level of the constraint satisfaction. Thus, it remains a task of a judge and respective parties to the case to define the set. It also remains within a discretion of a judge to process the output. She may decide to modify the results and opt for a suboptimal solution (for whatever reason) or she may, based upon the result, decide to redefine the initial set and run the process once again. Ultimately, it remains solely at the disposal of the judge to transform the set of accepted propositions to the decision itself. Thus, it is fairly conclusive that implementation of computing coherence as constraint satisfaction to the judicial reasoning does not exclude human element from the process (5).

---

[12]In order to prevent *denegatio iustitiae*.

[13]Other lawyers should not be excluded from the group of possible users—at least for the purpose of court decisions analysis.

As regards the issue of preserving adequate space for judicial discretion (and not forcing judge to lose the 10% of kindness) it is possible to point out at the conclusion that the method does not constrain a judge within a process of judicial reasoning. It may seem that certain space for vagueness in law (Endicott 2000)-that should be definitely considered as valuable-is lost due to the implementation of the method. At the same time the vagueness can be considered as one of the basis for a judicial discretion. Thus, it would seem that the space for judicial discretion would be reduced by employment of the computation of coherence as constraint satisfaction. However, in my opinion the method only decrease-to a certain degree-a vagueness in reasoning (by establishing a stronger link between the propositions and the actual decision, i.e., between the ruling and the reasoning) while the vagueness of law remains intact (6).

The issue of computability seems to disfavor coherence as constraint satisfaction formalism since, as has been mentioned above, the problem is computationally intractable. Thagard and Verbeurgt themselves paid considerable attention to the issue and suggested five algorithms to compute coherence as constraint satisfaction—exhaustive, incremental, connectionist, greedy and semidefinite programming. The first two as they put it are useless while the others do not guarantee that the procedure would eventually generate the optimal solution. Thagard and Verbeurgt have mostly experimented with the connectionist—neural network-like model—and the results they have presented can be considered as rather promising (Thagard and Verbeurgt 1997, 7–12). They also point out to the fact that coherence as constraint satisfaction problem may be transformed into the MAX CUT problem (Thagard and Verbeurgt 1997, 12 and appendix) for which Goemans and Williamson have found an algorithm that guarantees the result would be at least 0.878 of the optimum (Goemans and Williamson 1995). Thus, it is theoretically possible to guarantee that the set A generated by the procedure would be characterized by the value of W no lower than 0.878 of the possible optimum. Intuitive comparison to the proximity of the results of judicial reasoning deployed in absence of the formalism to the optimal results suggests that the intractability of the problem should not be fatal to it (7).

An important part of judicial reasoning and eventual decision making is its openness to be studied, assessed and validated. As regards judicial reasoning that encompasses computation of coherence as constraint satisfaction it should be stressed out that the expected result of the whole process is a court decision expressed in a standard form. Thus, from legal point of view the possibility to validate the decision is preserved. From computational point of view the outcome of the algorithm can be validated in polynomial time—thus, a formalized procedure to validate a decision may be designed (8).

11.6 Conclusions

In this chapter I have summarized what have been widely believed to be the main causes for as Leith puts it fall of legal expert system (Leith 2010) and what can be also held as a basis of explanation why there is currently no computable model to support judicial reasoning deployed in everyday legal practice. By suggesting to approach a limited part of judicial reasoning as a problem of computing coherence as constrain satisfaction I was able to expose judicial reasoning to the issue of computational tractability and especially to the theory of NP-completeness. Interesting—though purely speculative—parallels have been consequently drawn between the issues perceived as controversial from the point of view of law and computer science, e.g., the parallel between a human intuition and a guessing module of nondeterministic Turing machine which serves as the basis for the NP-problems definition. This exposition allowed to draft a list of requisites any formalism must meet in order to be considered a possible candidate for the implementation in the judicial reasoning process. Eventually, the list provided a rather detailed means to assess coherence as constraint satisfaction formalism from the point of view of its suitability to be employed in support of judicial reasoning. As the outcome of the assessment a computation of coherence as constraint satisfaction is suggested as an interesting candidate for a judicial reasoning support. It is worthwhile exploring the method on experimental bases—firstly in the analysis of court decisions (retrospective) and secondly in the modeling of court decisions (prospective). The outcome of the analysis can provide a solid base for deciding if a coherence-based tool that should actually assist judges in preparing court decisions on everyday basis would be worth trying to design.

References

Amaya, A. 2007. Formal models of coherence and legal epistemology. *Artificial Intelligence and Law* 15: 429–447.

Araszkiewicz, M. 2010. Balancing of legal principles and constraint satisfaction. In *Legal knowledge and information systems: JURIX 2010 conference proceedings*, ed. R.G.F. Winkels, 7–15. Amsterdam: IOS Press.

Bench-Capon, T., and G. Sartor. 2001. Theory-based explanation of case law domains. In *Proceedings of the eight international conference on AI and Law*, 12–21. St. Louis: ACM Press

Boehme-Nessler, V. 2011. *Pictorial law: Modern law and the power of pictures*. Heidelberg: Springer.

Dworkin, R. 1977. *Taking rights seriously*. Cambridge, MA: Harvard University Press.

Eliasmith, C., and P. Thagard. 1997. Waves, particles, and explanatory coherence. *British Journal for the Philosophy of Science* 48: 1–19.

Endicott, T.A.O. 2000. *Vagueness in law*. Oxford: Oxford University Press.

Garey, R., and D.S. Johnson. 1979. *Computers and intractability: A guide to the theory of NP-completeness*. San Francisco: W.H. Freeman.

Goemans, M.X., and D.P. Williamson. 1995. Improved approximation algorithms for maximum cut and satisfiability problems using semidefinite programming. *Journal of the Association for Computing Machinery* 42: 1115–1145.

Hoadley, C. M., Ranney, M., Schank, P. 1994. WanderECHO: A connectionist simulation of limited coherence. In *Proceedings of the sixteenth annual conference of the cognitive science society*, 421–426. Hillsdale

Leith, P. 2010. The rise and fall of the legal expert system. *European Journal of Law and Technology* 1: 179–201.

Thagard, P. 1991. The dinossaur debate: Explanatory coherence and the problem of competing hypothesis. In *Philosophy and AI: Essays at the interface*, ed. J. Pollock and R. Cummins, 279–300. Cambridge, MA: MIT Press/Bradford Books.
Thagard, P. 1992. Adversial problem solving: Modelling an opponent using explanatory coherence. *Cognitive Science* 16: 136–137.
Thagard, P. 2000. *Coherence in thought and action*. Cambridge, MA: MIT Press.
Thagard, P. 2003. Why wasn't O.J. convicted? Emotional coherence in legal inference. *Cognition and Emotion* 17: 361–383.
Thagard, P., and K. Verbeurgt. 1997. *Coherence as constraint satisfaction*. Waterloo: University of Waterloo.
Wiener, N. 1989. *The human use of human beings*. London: Free Association Books. First published in 1950.

Chapter 12
Limits of Constraint Satisfaction Theory of Coherence as a Theory of (Legal) Reasoning

Michał Araszkiewicz

12.1 Introduction

The theory of coherence as constraint satisfaction (CaCS, Thagard and Verbeurgt 1998; Thagard 2000) recently has become the object of interest of legal theoreticians interested in formal representation of legal reasoning[1] CaCS has several interesting features: (1) it offers a precise, formal definition of the concept of coherence and a definition of this concept must be a basis of any coherence-based theory of legal reasoning; (2) this theory is abstract and therefore in principle applicable to different domains of reasoning in general and legal reasoning in particular; (3) it offers a possibility of implementation, due to the existence of connectionist algorithms and working computer programs, such as ECHO, applied by Thagard and his collaborators to multiple instantiations of reasoning (Thagard 2000). CaCS is also an object of criticism for authors who are adherents of coherentist position in legal philosophy.[2] It is not my aim here to discuss all possible objections against CaCS as a theory of legal justification. These objections can be classified on the five levels of generality:

Michał Araszkiewicz thanks the participants of the "Artificial Intelligence, Coherence and Judicial Reasoning" workshop (ICAIL 2011, Pittsburgh, USA, June 10) for their comments concerning argument of this paper. Special thanks are due to Jaap Hage for numerous discussions related to coherence (also as constraint satisfaction) in general and to this paper in particular. I am also grateful to Stefano Bertea for his comments on this paper.

[1] Amaya (2007, 2011), Araszkiewicz (2010), see also Amaya and Šavelka in this volume.

[2] Cf. Hage (2005) and Hage in this volume.

M. Araszkiewicz (✉)
Department of Legal Theory, Faculty of Law and Administration, Jagiellonian University, Bracka 12, Kraków 31-005, Poland
e-mail: michal.araszkiewicz@uj.edu.pl

M. Araszkiewicz and J. Šavelka (eds.), *Coherence: Insights from Philosophy, Jurisprudence and Artificial Intelligence*, Law and Philosophy Library 107,
DOI 10.1007/978-94-007-6110-0_12, © Springer Science+Business Media Dordrecht 2013

1. The general philosophical level. On this level, the acceptance of CaCS for the purposes of modelling of legal reasoning may be contested because of general rejection of coherentism as sound theory of human cognition.[3] If coherentism is seen as essentially flawed on this most general level, then it does not make sense to discuss its applications to the field of legal reasoning. This level of generality is beyond the scope of the present contribution.
2. The legal-philosophical level. Even if one either accepts coherentism as a proper theory of justification, or remains agnostic in regards to general philosophical controversies, he or she may still be reluctant to acknowledge the relevance of the concept of coherence in the field of jurisprudence and theory of legal reasoning in particular (cf. the sceptical view of Raz 1992). In this paper we accept the thesis that coherence is crucial to the understanding of legal reasoning, the perspective being adopted by legal scholars like MacCormick (1978), Peczenik (2008) and Hage (2005).
3. The level of (legal) coherentism. CaCS may be criticized also by scholars who are generally supportive of coherentism, either as a general theory of human cognition, or focusing only on the usefulness of the concept of coherence for the account of legal reasoning. Because two contributions in this volume deal explicitly with this problem (a supportive view of Amaya and a critical one of Hage), we will not enter this discussion here thoroughly, although we will indicate some attractive features of application of CaCS to legal reasoning.
4. The discussion concerning instantiation of CaCS. On this level not CaCS as such, but the concrete manner in which it is applied to the problems of legal reasoning, may be discussed and contested. Due to the high level of generality of CaCS it may be structured in many different manners. Let us note that a convincing concretization of CaCS may also serve as an argument on level (3), to support the usefulness of application of this theory to the problems of legal reasoning. This paper's argument and discussion is situated mainly on level (4), in connection with level (3).
5. The discussion of concrete implementations. On this level, concrete (computational) implementations of CaCS models are discussed; representation of concrete problems are analyzed. This very technical level is left beyond the scope of this paper, because successful implementation of the CaCS models of legal reasoning depends on overcoming difficulties on level (4), leading in consequence to strengthening of the position of CaCS on level (3).

The structure of the paper is as follows. In the next section the basic features of CaCS are recalled and briefly commented on. We concentrate on such features which are relevant for the development of models of legal reasoning based on coherence and explain the methodological status of such models. Then in Sect. 12.3 we present some objections against CaCS concerning the problems of representation

[3] Such theories may have different methodological characteristics, namely they can aim at description or justification as regards human cognition (I am grateful to Hage for this remark). However, this very general level can be seen as encompassing all these different types of theories.

of argumentation and relation between arguments—which are the problems relevant mainly to level (4) described above. In Sect. 12.4, these objections are discussed in the context of a possible model of legal justification based on CaCS. Finally, we formulate conclusions from the discussion and important perspectives for further research.

12.2 Coherence as Constraint Satisfaction as a Basis for a Model of Judicial Reasoning

In any contribution related to the conception of coherence as constraint satisfaction it is necessary to recall the basic features of the theory. However, due to the fact that the theory is already well known and, in particular, it has been presented to legal-philosophical community on several different occasions,[4] a concise outline will be sufficient.[5]

According to CaCS, coherence should be understood as maximal satisfaction of multiple constraints. Let us consider a set of elements E (these elements can, for instance, be propositions) and let C be a set of constraints on pairs of elements $<e_i, e_j>$, where $e_i, e_j \in E$. A pair of elements $<e_i, e_j>$ belongs to C+, the set of positive constraints, if and only if these two elements cohere with each other. If two of the elements incohere with each other, there is a negative constraint (C−) between them. Each constraint between two elements e_i, e_j is accompanied by a number w_{ij}—the weight of this constraint. The weight of positive constraints is larger than 0 and the weight of negative constraints is below 0.

The solution of a coherence problem consists in partitioning of the set E into two disjoint subsets—the set of accepted elements (A) and the set of rejected elements (R) in such a way which maximizes the satisfaction of the two following conditions:

1. If $<e_i, e_j> \in C+$ then $e_i \in A$ if and only if $e_j \in A$.
2. If $<e_i, e_j> \in C-$ then $e_i \in A$ if and only if $e_j \in R$.

The solution should result in finding such partition which maximizes W—the weight of all satisfied constraints. The number W is the degree of coherence of the obtained partition of the initial set of elements E.

The conception presented above is very abstract—neither the elements nor the relations between them are structured. This high degree of abstraction enables the theory to be applicable to numerous different fields of reasoning. The author of the theory (Thagard 2000) applies it, *inter alia*, to explanation in epistemic justification and ethical reasoning. In the discussed examples he identifies the

---

[4]Hage (2005), Amaya (2007), Araszkiewicz (2010); also Amaya, Hage and Šavelka in this volume.

[5]The presentation here is based mainly on the authoritative exposition in Thagard (2000).

elements which form the set E and the types of constraints which relate the elements to each other. According to Thagard, the following types of (in)coherence relations: explanatory, analogical, deductive, visual, conceptual and deliberative constraints, are sufficient "to cover the main kinds of inference that people perform" (Thagard 2000, 66). Various types of constraints are informally characterized by sets of principles; the characterization of explanatory coherence relations plays the role of a prototype. It is possible to employ different kinds of constraints in one set of elements.[6] The constraints between elements are bidirectional relations and should not be confused with deductive entailment in the standard sense even in the case of the so-called 'deductive constraints' (Thagard 2000, 53).

Not all instances of human cognition and reasoning may be represented as coherence problems. For instance, creative reasoning which consists in inventing new elements (and new types of constraints) is generally outside of the scope of this theory. Yet, it is obvious that a great amount of human cognitive activities, if not a significant majority of them, may be accounted for as instances of creation of coherence (understood for instance as constraint satisfaction).

Let us now present some arguments for accepting the theory presented above as a basis of a model of legal (judicial) argumentation.

It is intuitively appealing to see judicial legal reasoning as a kind of a coherence problem. The judge starts reasoning with the material presented before him by parties to a legal dispute and typically, this material will be highly incoherent. The parties provide the court with inconsistent factual statements and present evidence to support their claims.[7] The parties invoke different legal provisions to support their claims and they advocate different interpretations of these provisions. Depending on the rules of a given procedure, the judge is entitled to modify this initial set of elements, for instance by eliminating some obviously irrelevant elements and by introducing new elements and constraints. After the initial set of elements is specified, the role of the judge seems to align very closely to the conception of CaCS as defended by Thagard[8]: the judge should reject some of the elements presented before him to obtain the most coherent (the most justified, the most defensible) subset of accepted elements. Let us note that the judge is not free in determining the outcome of his reasoning: his activities are constrained by the rules of procedure and the wording and purpose of the applicable statutes or case law; moreover, he or she should take into account the possibility of appeal from the judgment by the losing party and the anticipated decision of the higher court. All these observations seem to support the conclusion that reasoning related to judicial decision-making can be modeled as a coherence problem as introduced by Thagard. A problematic

---

[6]Thagard's analysis of Paul Bernardo's case in the domain of ethics is a good example, cf. Thagard (2000, 143).

[7]Our example is based on continental legal procedures and not on common law legal procedures, which include trial before the jury.

[8]But, presumably, not earlier. Let us not that CaCS, as defined above is not constructive; it does not specify a procedure of adding new elements to the initial set E.

feature of this thesis is that in the absence of a structured, coherence-based model of judicial reasoning, the relation between actual judicial argumentation and CaCS remains vague.[9]

One of the most important questions which should be asked at this point concerns the purpose of representation of legal reasoning by means of CaCS. The functions the model should be able to perform (or at least aim to perform) should be discussed. In principle, such a model could perform the following functions:

1. Descriptive function—the model could provide a faithful representation of actual legal reasoning before the court.
2. Analytical function—it could systematize actual judicial argumentation and provide a unified structure to it, enabling the performance of the analysis and assessment of legal decisions.
3. Explanatory and predictive function—the model could provide answers to 'why-questions' concerning the outcome of legal decision-making in the cases in which the judge does not explain the rationale for his decision thoroughly and it could present predictions concerning the judicial decisions in future cases, relevantly similar to the cases already analyzed by the model.
4. Normative function—the model could present the possible rational argumentation which could be helpful for the judge in his actual decision-making, and useful for the parties dissatisfied with the actual decision in the case.

These functions are connected in various ways and it would be too demanding to comment on character of these relations in this place. In this paper, we will focus mainly on the second function, namely, on the problem of imposition of a unified structure to judicial reasoning and representation of legal arguments in constraint satisfaction framework.

Intuitive similarity to actual judicial reasoning and the possibility of performance of multifarious functions are not the only reasons for adopting CaCS as a basis for a model of legal reasoning. It should also be emphasized that the very abstract formulation of CaCS makes it possible to account for legal reasoning in different domains and in different legal systems. Moreover, the existence of connectionist algorithms for computation of coherence makes it possible to test the developed model empirically, by conducting experiments and comparing the obtained results to the expected ones. Importantly, CaCS seems to be very adequate to account for the well-known phenomenon of defeasibility of reasoning.[10] Obviously, the relations of coherence (and incoherence) in constraint satisfaction networks, taken in isolation, do not provide conclusive reasons for acceptance (resp. rejection) of a given conclusion. The only ground for acceptance of a conclusion stems from the fact that it belongs to the set of accepted elements in coherence-maximizing partition

---

[9]The link between coherent legal theories and persuasive legal arguments was emphasized by L. Thorne McCarty (1997, 221), who also acknowledged difficulties in accounting for the concept of coherence in the field of legal reasoning.

[10]Cf. for instance Pollock (1995, Chap. 3), Prakken (1997), Hage (2003), Sartor (2005, Chap. 2).

of the set E. Further modifications of the set E may alter the outcome and lead to the acceptance of another conclusion. Due to the fact that addition of new information may lead to retraction of previously accepted conclusion, CaCS may be deemed suitable to represent defeasible reasoning. This is also a pro-reason for adopting it as a basis for a model of legal argumentation, which is largely nonmonotonic in structure—providing of new evidence and interpretative argumentation may alter the conclusion which was previously accepted; this phenomenon is particularly obvious in the case of control of the judgment performed by the higher instance court.

However, the project of constructing a CaCS-based model of legal reasoning is not uncontroversial. In spite of its abstract character and other attractive features, CaCS seems to be limited in certain ways which lead to formulation of objections against the application of this theory to legal reasoning. The next section is devoted to the discussion of chosen objections against it, situated on level 3 and 4 as defined in the Introduction above.

12.3 Limits of Constraint Satisfaction Theory of Coherence

In this Section we present some shortcomings of CaCS concerning its expressive power as regards arguments and the relations between arguments. We will focus on the following issues: (1) the argumentation within CaCS is not structured, which results in difficulties of assessing examples that could verify/falsify the theory (the Structure Problem); (2) in consequence, it is difficult to indicate criteria according to which two given elements are related to each other with a given type of constraint (the Constraint Definition Problem); (3) CaCS assumes that all elements in the initial set are more or less relevant to the coherence problem at hand and this theory does not provide for criteria of elimination of obviously irrelevant elements, and on the other hand, it is not clear how the theory should work in the case we do not have all relevant elements (the Relevance Problem); (4) although the assignment of weights to constraints seems to be decisive to any inference performed on the basis of the theory, the very procedure of assignment of weights is—obviously—placed outside the procedure of computation of coherence. In consequence, the latter procedure may in some settings yield quite trivial results (because all important decisions are contained in the procedure of weights assignment) (the Weight Assignment Problem); (5) because the constraints are defined as binary relations between elements, it seems difficult (if not impossible) to represent reasoning *about* constraints in the framework of CaCS (the Meta-Argumentation Problem), cf. (Hage 2005, 47 ff.).[11] In particular, it seems difficult to account for undercutting argumentation within this framework.[12]

[11]This reference will be discussed more broadly below.

[12]The definition of undercutting will be given below with an example.

Let us now consider the following simple example which will enable us to discuss more thoroughly the problems indicated above. Let us assume that Ted (guitarist and leader of the band), Brian (bass player) and Jacob (drummer) form a jazz trio. The band has a scheduled concert on September 20 and this concert is the last one in the series. The concert is so successful that it is perfectly possible to arrange another one for the next day. However, Jacob refuses to play, claiming that he had promised his family to return home on September 21. Ted and Brian try to persuade Jacob to stay for another day and he is determined to return home. It is possible to hire a local drummer for one concert, but Ted and Brian are unhappy about the situation: the concert would be so much more successful with Jacob on drums. Eventually, Jacob goes home without discussing the issue with his colleagues and the band plays with a substitute drummer.

Now, Ted is considering whether he should fire Jacob from the band or not. This immediately leads to generation of two mutually incompatible elements in the initial set E:

e1 [Ted fires Jacob from the band]
e2 [Ted does not fire Jacob from the band].

Obviously, these two elements cannot be accepted together and there are different considerations which support or demote these potential conclusions. For instance, it could be stated that by leaving his band-mates and refusing to discuss with them, Jacob infringed the principle of loyalty towards his colleagues. In consequence, this principle would in this case support the conclusion e1. On the other hand, one could state that Jacob had important reasons to go home, because he had promised to do so and because spending time with family is a good thing. These circumstances would support conclusion e2, because musicians should not be fired from bands even if their behavior is disruptive to some career opportunities, when such behavior is motivated by very important reasons. Let us then formulate the two additional elements:

e3 [disloyal band members should be fired from the band]
e4 [band members should not be fired from the band when they have important reasons not to cooperate with the band temporarily]

The elements defined below create some kinds of ethical principles and presumably there would be a deductive constraint between pairs (e1, e3) and (e2, e4) respectively (Thagard 2000, 133).[13] It is also possible to add some other considerations, related to prospective, deliberative reasoning. For instance, firing Jacob from the band will mean hiring a new drummer instead of him and it will be a time consuming endeavor for him to play the band's music as well as Jacob. On the other hand, the further presence of Jacob in the band causes a risk of disrupted

[13]Note that the order of elements is not important because the (in)coherence relations are symmetric in CaCS.

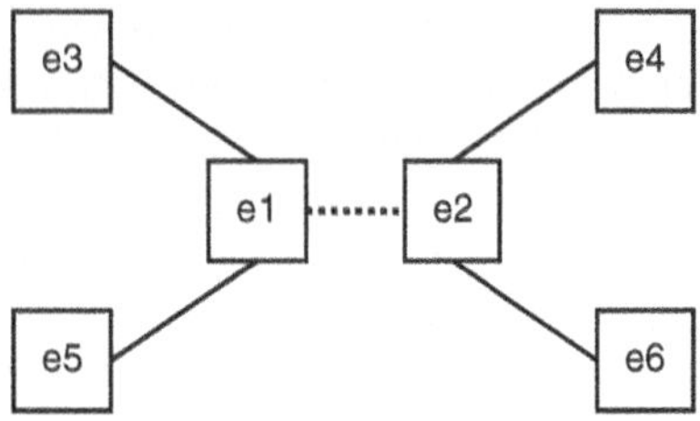

Fig. 12.1 Constraint network for the Jazz Band case

career opportunities (because Jacob will insist on spending time with his family). Let us now add the two following elements to the net of Ted's beliefs:

e5 [band members should be flexible]
e6 [practicing with new band members is time-consuming]

Intuitively, e5 will be positively constrained with e1 and e6 is positively constrained with e2. Consequently, we obtain the following network of elements where the positive constraints are indicated with solid lines and negative constraints—with dotted line (Fig. 12.1).

The network presented above is simplified, because there is only one negative constraint (between two incompatible conclusions); however, it is sufficient for the purposes of the paper's argument.[14] The question is, which of the conclusions (e1 or e2) is better justified in the light of the existing information. Because the network is very simple, the answer to this question is reducible to comparison of weight of satisfied constraints in a partition is which e1, e3 and e5 are accepted together and in a partition in which e2, e4 and e6 are accepted together. Of course, the answer to this question does not stem from the network itself, but it is the only one problem out of many which could be discussed here. Starting from the example, we will now discuss briefly all the problems indicated at the beginning of this Section.

12.3.1 The Structure Problem

Obviously, the elements in the Jazz Band example are not structured. They are taken from natural language. They are sentences in English, but three of them (e3–e6) make use of the verb 'should' which makes them norm-propositions. CaCS, as presented by Thagard, is an abstract theory of argumentation and in this respect it is parallel to Dung's Abstract Argumentation Frameworks.[15] However, CaCS

[14]The issue of bipolarity of CaCS (that is, the problem of whether positive constraints and negative constraints are reducible to each other, are they mutually definable and so on) is largely unexplored. For a general account of bipolarity cf. Dubois and Prade (2006) and for an extensive discussion of bipolarity in the context of abstract argumentation frameworks—Amgoud et al. (2008).

[15]AAF; most famously, Dung (1995).

is not only concerned with abstract relations on mathematical structures but is also strongly inclined to deal with concrete examples.[16] In consequence, CaCS in its original formulation has a more experimental than logical flavor. It is rather designed to test and predict justification based on expressions formulated in natural language than on logical formulas. Obviously, this can lead to difficulties concerning the assessment of these experiments, because one natural language formulation of elements may suggest one answer and another formulation may suggest another one. In consequence, one could state that the results yielded by CaCS computation of coherence are relative to the formulation of elements (in other words, that they are element-formulation sensitive). However, it does not seem very problematic to introduce structure to CaCS elements due to the presence of multiple logical languages.[17]

12.3.2 The Constraint Definition Problem

Paul Thagard introduces six types of (in) coherence relations: explanatory, analogical, deductive, visual, conceptual and deliberative. Thagard claims that no other types of coherence are needed to represent the main kinds of inference people perform (Thagard 2000, 66). Each of these constraints is characterized by a set of what Thagard refers to as principles. Let us examine, for instance, a list of principles for deductive coherence:

Principle D1. Symmetry. Deductive coherence is a symmetric relation between propositions, unlike deductive entailment.

Principle D2. Deduction. (a) An axiom or other proposition coheres with propositions which are deducible from it. (b) Propositions that together are used to deduce some other proposition cohere with each other.(c) The more hypotheses it takes to deduce something, the less the degree of coherence.

Principle D3. Intuitive Priority. Propositions that are intuitively obvious have a degree of acceptability on their own. Propositions that are obviously false have a degree of rejectability on their own.

Principle D4. Contradiction. Contradictory propositions are incoherent with each other.

Principle D5. Acceptance. The acceptability of a proposition in a system of propositions depends on its coherence with them. (Thagard 2000, 53).

Obviously, the principles presented above, as they aim to regulate the relation between unstructured elements, are somewhat vague. The key principles are D1 and

[16]Cf. many examples in Thagard (2000).

[17]By 'introducing structure' I mean here imposition of rigours of certain logical language on elements and constraints in CaCS framework.

D2. D1 may seem perplexing for logically oriented scholars, especially when one reads it in connection with D2. On the one hand, deductive coherence is a symmetric relation and is juxtaposed against deductive entailment. On the other hand (D2) it is claimed that a proposition cohereres with other propositions which are 'deducible from it' (D2), where by 'deducible from' we should understand the standard relation of logical entailment. However, the analysis of Thagard's examples for deductive coherence reveals that elements related to each other by a deductive constraint are not bound by the relation of logical consequence and that much information has to be added to obtain the latter relation. Let us now return to the elements e1 and e3 from Jazz Band example (the relation between these two elements is similar to Thagard's examples for deductive coherence in ethical reasoning, cf. Thagard 2000, 133).

e1 [Ted fires Jacob from the band]
e3 [disloyal band members should be fired from the band]

How should the two elements be adjusted in order to obtain deductive inference? First of all, the 'natural direction' of this inference is from e3 to e1 and not the other way round.[18] Let us then reformulate e3 to obtain a more precise proposition (1) here below. I also introduce the rest of necessary propositions.[19]

1. For any x, y, IF x is a disloyal band member and y is the leader of the band, THEN y should fire x from the band.
2. Jacob is a disloyal band member.
3. Ted is the leader of the band.
4. For any x,y, IF y should fire x from the band, THEN y fires x from the band.
5. Ted fires Jacob from the band.

Obviously, it was necessary to introduce two empirical premises ((2) and (3)) and one of them (that is, (2)) is highly debatable: many people could argue whether Jacob's behavior was disloyal after all. However, the most important thing we would like to indicate is that if the relation of 'deducibility' of one proposition from another is satisfied each time and it is possible obtain a relation of logical entailment given that some premises are added, then this relation becomes problematic because it is always possible to establish a deductive link between two propositions if a sufficient number of properly formed premises is added. In particular, it would be possible to establish such a link from the proposition (5)–(1). However, the added premises would have different form and content than in the link from (1)–(5).[20] Of course, this line of criticism is not sympathetic to the main idea of Thagard's proposal, but the criticism is sound. In consequence, in the context of general CaCS we remain with to the large extent intuitive account of deductive constraints (and of constraints

[18]Cf. insightful comments on this subject by Hage in this volume.

[19]I do not introduce formalism to make the argument more readable.

[20]And let us emphasize that the propositions e1 and e3 (that is (1) and (5)) should be symmetrically deductively constrained.

in general). The examples provided by the author should serve as prototypical relations and the sets of principles should be helpful in determining of the character of relations between two types of elements. Of course, this feature of the theory is not sufficiently clear from the point of view of precision of representation.

12.3.3 The Relevance Problem

How can we know, in the framework of CaCS, whether our initial set of elements (1) contains all relevant elements and (2) does not contain any completely irrelevant elements? It should be emphasized that what we have in mind here is not what could be referred to as 'ultimate relevance' of elements in accepted set, but a feature of these elements which makes them at least minimally important for the process of reasoning in question. Obviously, the whole research on defeasible reasoning was built around the phenomenon of incomplete information and of changing the status of previously accepted beliefs when new information is available. Thagard states explicitly that not all human cognition can be represented by means of CaCS and that generative mechanisms are not covered by this theory (Thagard 2000, 67–68). He admits that sometimes generation of new information may be stimulated by the impossibility of obtaining a coherent result out of a given piece of information, but this contention does not alter the conclusion that the generation of new, potentially relevant elements is not represented in CaCS.[21] Similarly, sometimes in initial sets there will be some totally irrelevant elements which should not have any influence on computation of coherence. However, CaCS does not offer any mechanism for filtering such elements out before the process of computation starts. It could be argued that such elements would not be connected to the rest of elements (relevant ones) by any intelligible coherence relation. This point is interesting, but it moves the focus back to the problem of definitions of constraints, as Thagard himself acknowledges, 'for coherence to be assessed, constraints among elements need to have been generated' (Thagard 2000, 67).

For instance, in the Jazz Band case, one could argue that e3 is not relevant for the assessment of the case either because it is not applicable to the case (Jacob's disloyalty being contested) or because this 'principle' is too general and has to be revised to become relevant. Once could also argue that so much relevant information is missing (concerning, for instance, the existing relations between band members, the situation of Jacob's family and so on) that it would not be prudent to engage in computation of coherence basing on the six given elements only. In fact, these considerations are not represented well in CaCS and should be assessed intuitively before the computation of coherence is begun. However, one could claim that this

[21] It is worth noting that generative power of coherence was emphasized by Hage, cf. Hage (2005, 54), and the example discussed on preceding pages when Hage shows how filling in the 'missing links' makes a theory of a case more and more coherent.

objection is overly demanding. CaCS is a theory designed to assess coherence once the set of initial elements is established. Although it is not possible to ignore irrelevant elements at the outset, they would be probably rejected as a result of any plausible partition of the initial set of elements.

12.3.4 The Weight Assignment Problem

Let us recall that the degree of coherence of a set of accepted elements in CaCS is equal to the number W, that is, the weight of all satisfied constraints. Each constraint is assigned with a number representing weight of this constraint. In consequence, obviously, the weights assigned to different types of constraints play a decisive role in computation of coherence. However, the procedure of assignment of these weights is not encompassed in constraint networks: it must be at least to some extent predetermined (at least, the algorithm of assigning weights must be known before the process of computation of coherence starts). This problem is convincingly addressed elsewhere in this volume (Hage) so I will comment on it only briefly. Let us assume that in Jazz Band case the issue of loyalty of band members is seen approximately twice as important as good family relations. *Ceteris paribus*, the set of elements e1, e3 and e5 should be accepted. But what justifies such assignment of weights to the elements? Obviously, a meta-proposition concerning this issue is not encompassed by the constraint network. In fact, the answers to questions concerning justification in CaCS are relative to the predetermined assignment of weights to different types of constraints.[22]

12.3.5 The Meta-argumentation Problem

As is clear from the discussion so far and from representation of an exemplary case, CaCS is able to represent the support relations between different types of elements as well as conflicts between incompatible arguments. For instance, in the representation of Jazz Band case the key problem is whether the arguments based on (allegedly breached) loyalty and on fostering career opportunities will outweigh the considerations based on family values and avoiding of time-consuming training of a new musician (or vice versa). However, CaCS seems to be not able to adequately account for meta-argumentation, that is, in this context, argumentation about constraints. It is a well known phenomenon that in the process of argumentation some propositions may attack not only other propositions, but also links between other propositions. As regards the discussion of CaCS in literature, this issue was assessed by Jaap Hage in his *Studies in Legal Logic*. Hage presents his argument

[22] And to an adopted algorithm for the computation of coherence. Cf. Thagard (2000, 25 ff.).

in the context of a case study concerning judicial proof. The following facts of the case are relevant for this argument: Lord Hard was found in his room, murdered by means of knife. The butler was seen entering Lord Hard's room. The butler had a motive to murder Lord Hard, because the latter seduced butler's daughter Harriet (Hage 2005, 45). Now, let us quote a passage where Hage indicates a limitation of expressive power of CaCS as regards meta-argumentation:

> (...) consider the relation between the belief that the butler was seen entering Lord Hard's room and the belief that the butler murdered Lord Hard. At first sight there is a positive constraint between these two beliefs. But what to think of the case in which one also believes that Harriet saw Lord Hard alive and well after her father, the butler, left his room? If Harriet saw Lord Hard after her father left the Lord's room, the link between the belief that the butler was seen entering Lord Hard's room and the belief that the butler murdered Lord Hard loses its force. So the presence of this link is negatively connected to the belief that Harriet saw Lord Hard alive after her father left his room. This connection between the belief that Harriet saw the Lord and the constraint between the beliefs about the butler entering the room and murdering the Lord, should be part of the theory. More theoretically this means that one would like positive and negative constraints to be treated as elements of the theory. Moreover, it should be possible to have positive and negative constraints, not only between beliefs mutually, but also between beliefs and constraints (Hage 2005, 47).

Hage rightly observes that albeit a pair of elements may be (positively or negatively) constrained when analyzed in isolation, addition of a new element may change the situation so that these two elements are no longer constrained. Importantly, the relevance of elements is not contested here, but the link between two elements disappears when a new elements is introduced. It is easy to construct similar extensions of our Jazz Band case. Assume that before the concert on September 20 took place, Jacob explained his private situation to his fellow musicians and that he asked them to agree that this concert will definitely be the last one in this season, and that Ted and Brian agreed to it. The introduction of this new information attacks the link between elements e3 and e1.

This phenomenon may be easily generalized. There may be links not only between elements and constraints, but also between constraints and constraints, between constraints and 'constraints about constraints' and so on. Let us refer to as 'objects' to any CaCS structure which is either (1) an element or (2) a constraint understood as a pair of objects (where objects can be elements, constraints understood as pairs of elements, constraints between elements and constraints understood as pairs of elements, and so on). This definition of objects is obviously recursive. Following this definition it could be postulated that CaCS should be able to account for any relation between any objects.

In this connection, an important technical (but also epistemological) problem arises for CaCS. Let us assume that an introduction of a given element e_k breaks a positive link between elements e_i and e_j, but of course in isolation, the two elements e_i, e_j are positively constrained. How should we account for this situation if e_k is ultimately rejected for the reasons of its incoherence with some other elements? Should the constraint e_i, e_j be given its full force but only in the set of accepted elements? It seems that the weights of all constraints should be determined before the computation of coherence starts (and e_k is of course present in the initial set of elements and it seems to decisively destroy the link between e_i and e_j). This problem could be solved by privileging e_k (being for instance a well-established factual information, such as 'Harriet saw Lord Hard alive after her father left his room') so that it must be accepted in any acceptable partition of the initial set E into the subsets of Accepted and Rejected elements. However, this solution seems to possess rather *ad hoc* character. Dealing with this shortcoming would involve a serious extension of CaCS which will be discussed below.

Examples discussed here are modeled in a way which suggests that the introduction of a new element (or more generally, objects) lead to a definite attack on link between other elements (objects). In particular, the knowledge about the past arrangements between Jacob and his fellow musicians is a reason for not firing him from the band in the existing circumstances. However, it may also be the case that such object does not interfere with a link between the two objects and automatically support the opposite conclusion, but only weakens the link between objects so that it cannot count as a support relation anymore. This phenomenon is referred to as undercutting; the concept was introduced by John Pollock (Pollock 1995, 41). Let us recall Pollock's original example; assume that we have two propositions: P1 "I see a red object" and P2 "This object is red". Typically, there will be a positive relation between these two elements, but the situation changes if we introduce the third element P3: "this object is illuminated by red light". For the reasons similar to the reasons discussed in the context of previous examples, undercutting attack may not be modeled adequately by basic CaCS because undercutting is a relation between and element (object) and the relation between other elements (objects). This is a drawback, given the significance of undercutting attacks in defeasible reasoning (Sartor 2005, 65).

The discussion in this section revealed some problematic features of the basic version of CaCS. However, these drawbacks are in my opinion not fatal to the enterprise of construction of a model of legal reasoning on the basis of CaCS. In the next section, the prerequisites for construction of such model are presented and discussed.

12.4 Prerequisites for a Model of Legal Reasoning Based on Constraint Satisfaction Conception of Coherence

The aim of this section is to formulate the proposals for dealing with the shortcomings of CaCS theory in order to make it more suitable for modeling of judicial legal reasoning. Such a model was partially elaborated and outlined in Araszkiewicz 2010. However, my aim in this paper is not to present an operative model (this would exceed the scope of the paper) but to indicate how the limits of CaCS discussed in the previous Section may be overcome to make a full-blown model plausible. Satisfactory solutions to these problems should be seen as prerequisites for a CaCS-based model of legal reasoning. Let us begin with five introductory points.

First, it should be emphasized that the prerequisites for the model discussed here below pertain to a model of legal normative reasoning, not to reasoning about facts. Keeping in mind that these two layers of legal reasoning are strictly interconnected[23] we limit the scope of our investigations to the domain of legal reasoning about norms.[24]

Second, from methodological point of view, the aim is to construct an analytical model of legal reasoning. Such a model should not only be purely descriptive, but it should reveal the structure of legal justificatory reasoning and therefore enable the researcher to assess the reasoning of the judge. In consequence, the model should be able to perform the optimizing function: to show the weak points in judicial reasoning and to indicate how the reasoning could be adjusted to meet certain criteria of correctness.[25]

Third, in spite of general intuitive appeal of coherentism, this general epistemological stance seems to be particularly plausible candidate for an adequate theory of legal justification about norms. In the world of reasoning about legal rules and principles there is apparently no 'solid ground' except maybe for very obvious empirical contentions like 'In the version x of a statute y it is written that (the content of the provision)'. However, such contentions are just the point of departure for legal reasoning about norms. Presumably, this is the reason for such big interest of legal philosophers in coherentist epistemology (Aarnio et al. 1998; Alexy and Peczenik 1990; Amaya 2007, 2011; Hage 2001, 2005; MacCormick 1978, 2005; Peczenik 2008; Joseph and Prakken 2009; and all papers in this volume). It is not our aim to discuss this general issue more thoroughly, because it belongs to level (2) as presented in the Introduction to this paper. However, once we admit the plausibility of coherentism for modeling of normative legal reasoning, CaCS becomes a natural candidate for a basis of an operative model of legal reasoning, even if it can be criticized on more general philosophical level (cf. Hage in this volume).

Fourth, CaCS, in spite of its drawbacks, has also several important features which make it attractive, in particular in the light of realization of analytical and optimizing methodological goals emphasized above. Some of these features were outlined by Šavelka in this volume, namely: generality, simplicity (on the most basic level), descriptive power, appeal to lawyers' community, margin for a human element in reasoning, room for judicial discretion, computability and validation of a solution. Let us note that the generality of CaCS makes it in principle able to account for both Rule Based Reasoning and Case Based Reasoning as regards legal issues concerning questions of norm. The list of attractive features is lengthened by flexibility of the CaCS framework (it can be

[23]For instance, recently, Bex and Verheij (2011).

[24]More about the necessity of accounting for these two layers of legal reasoning may be found in Amaya in this volume.

[25]At this point we can mean either the criteria accepted by the court but violated by it or some higher criteria than actually applied ones.

easily adjusted to different normative systems and to changes in legal systems). Moreover, the basic mechanism of CaCS is analogous to judicial legal reasoning in many respects. The judge typically begins with a set of incoherent elements, including incompatible legal grounds for claims of the parties, mutually exclusive interpretations of statutes, and the body of case law which will often contain decisions supporting one or another party to the legal dispute. Moreover, the judge typically has to take into account that his or her decision may be appealed, and in consequence, it is necessary for the judge to foresee the possible objections to his or her argumentation and the probable decision of the higher court. These phenomena are naturally accounted for as constraint satisfaction problems.

Fifth, although the discussion of different examples of application of CaCS leads to multiple questions with no easy answers (like in our analysis of Jazz Band case here above), it may be claimed that legal reasoning about norms has some specific features as a domain of reasoning which make overcoming of these difficulties presumably more feasible than in many other domains. These possibilities are indicated in the following subsections.

12.4.1 Structure of Elements

For the sake of the preciseness of modeling of legal reasoning in a CaCS-based model, the elements of reasoning ought to be given structure. In the domain of legal reasoning about norms, the plausible structure of elements should resemble the expressions which can be found in the statutes and legal decisions. In AI and Law literature and in the literature concerning logical analysis of law, there are numerous proposals concerning the representation of elements of legal reasoning about norms and the interconnections between these elements and it would be neither useful nor possible to indicate the evolution of this research here. However, I would like to point out an important jurisprudential distinction concerning the basic elements of legal system, namely, the distinction between rules and principles. According to this theory rules can be abided by or breached, *tertium non datur*, while principles can be realized to different degrees (Dworkin 1967 and Alexy 2002). Although this distinction is often seen as an oversimplification, it is still to some extent influential in AI and Law literature (Sartor 2010, 177 ff. on action norms and goal norms; cf. also Hage 2001). In Araszkiewicz 2010 I have developed a very simple account of reasoning with rules and principles in constraint satisfaction framework.

In consequence, the distinction between rules and principles could play a role at the point of departure of constructing a CaCS based model of legal reasoning. In the framework of CaCS it is natural to think about rule-elements as defeasible rules. If in a given case a fact-element of this case would be subsumed under the rule's antecedent, a positive constraint between this rule and its antecedent-element would appear. Defeasibility of such reasoning is apparent, because ultimately the antecedent-element could be rejected if this is demanded by maximization of the degree of coherence. On the other hand, principles can be modeled as expressions demanding realization of a certain value to the greatest degree possible (Optimization Command, cf. Alexy 2002). Such elements would be positively constrained to other elements if and only if the latter elements are positively assessed from the point of view of realization of value which is prescribed by a given principle.[26] In consequence it can be claimed that the basic elements can be modeled as formulae of defeasible logic. There is no necessity to model the elements of the model of legal argumentation is such manner, but this option seems plausible due to the inherently defeasible character of reasoning in the framework of CaCS.

A model of legal reasoning should account for a special type of elements, namely, legal conclusions, that is, answers to legal questions in consideration. Here, legal reasoning possesses an important feature which helps in providing structure to its elements: the space of possible answers to legal cases will be typically limited by the nature of the parties' claims and the background of the procedure before the court. Indeed, the scope of types of the courts' decisions will be typically strictly described by the provisions of law. Hence, it seems straightforward to model possible legal conclusions as atom propositions (for instance: [is entitled to damages](x)). Let us note that in typical cases there will be at least two possible and mutually contradictory legal conclusions (cf. Araszkiewicz 2010).

Bringing a claim before the court usually involves invoking a legal ground for this claim. In the framework of CaCS based model of legal reasoning, legal grounds can be represented as rules which have possible legal conclusions as their consequences (of course this is the most basic account of legal ground which can be also accounted for, and often will be, as a complicated configuration of elements).

So far, we have indicated three possible types of elements which play an important role in legal reasoning: legal conclusions, rules (some of which may have the characteristics of legal grounds) and principles. Obviously, this list of element types is not exhaustive[27], but optimally the full catalogue of element types should not be very long for it would affect the model's simplicity. The structuring of elements appears not very problematic due to the possibility of basing the existing research on defeasible logics. Let us note that in the framework of CaCS the only mechanism which is responsible for the selection of a conclusion is computation of coherence, so the application of a given formalism aims rather at attaining syntactical rigor to the model than at introducing an a competitive inference mechanism to it.[28]

---

[26]The possible structure of these constraints will be dealt with in the next subsection.

[27]Cf. Araszkiewicz (2010, 14–15), for introduction of another element type related to factor-based reasoning.

[28]Introducing syntactical rigor could be helpful as regards the verification of whether there is a relation of (in)coherence between two elements or not.

12.4.2 Types of Constraints

After introducing the basic types of elements relevant to legal reasoning concerning norms, let us focus on the types of relations which can be defined by them, that is, positive and negative constraints. In my opinion, in order to preserve resemblance of the representation of the model to actual legal reasoning, it seems plausible to define the types of constraints on the basis of the catalogue of typical rule-based arguments employed by lawyers while interpreting statutes. The catalogue of such elements is very similar in any legal system in which interpretation of statutes is important (MacCormick and Summers 1991). For instance, a rule may be applicable to the facts of the case if these facts may be adequately described by the wording of antecedent of this rule, according to an existing linguistic convention. This contention makes it possible, for instance, to define the so called linguistic constraint between a legal rule and a legal conclusion, like in Araszkiewicz 2010 (terminology slightly modified):

Definition 1: Positive Linguistic Constraint There is a positive linguistic constraint between a Legal Rule and a Legal Conclusion in a case C ($L_{C+<LR,\,LC>}$) if and only if, according to well-established linguistic conventions, the facts of the case C may be subsumed under the circumstances mentioned in the antecedent of a given Legal Rule.

Definition 2: Negative Linguistic Constraint There is a negative linguistic constraint between a Legal Rule and a Legal Conclusion in a case C ($L_{C-<LR,\,LC>}$) if and only if, according to well-established linguistic conventions, the facts of the case C must not be subsumed under the circumstances mentioned in the antecedent of a given DC.

Of course, such definitions of constraints may be criticized due to the fact that the element warranting the satisfaction of this constraint is not represented in the constraint network (cf. the criticism of Hage in this volume). The representation of such element would involve some extensions of the basic CaCS, however, the possibility of which will be discussed in the remainder of this paper.

12.4.3 Relevance

The introduction of the notion of element types and constraint types makes it possible to deal with the problem of relevance of element and constraint tokens. Generally, the list of element and constraint types should be (at least provisionally) exhaustive in the model and elements and constraint tokens which do not fit in the schemes provided by the relevant element and constraint types. Although this proposal may be criticized from coherentist point of view (the list of element and constraint types functions similarly to a set of axioms), it must be emphasized that it represents well the necessary locality of legal reasoning. Some assumptions concerning for instance the sources of law and methods of legal interpretation are so deeply rooted in legal cultures that it would be hardly possible to question them in the proceedings before the court. These deep convictions shared by the community of lawyers may be referred to as 'legal paradigm' (Peczenik 1990, 287–290). Although legal paradigms may change over time[29] and although they may be contested in exceptional cases, they remain generally stable. What is more, in the context of legal reasoning, although it may remain unclear which legal argument is ultimately the most acceptable, often it is very clear which arguments are definitely fallacious and should be rejected immediately. This observation supports the plausibility of making use of list of element and constraint types. At the same time, this list may be amended if the model, as a result of the presence of this list, is not able to account for important parts of legal reasoning.

12.4.4 Assignment of Weights to the Constraints

The characteristic feature of CaCS concerning each constraint being accompanied with weight can be possibly represented in a model of legal reasoning on two layers, namely, on the layer of constraint types and constraint tokens. In some legal cultures, for instance, linguistic arguments in statutory interpretation are typically seen as more important than other types of arguments; which can justify adding slightly greater value to the former ones as types of constraints. Yet, in given cases, the degree of confidence of satisfaction of a given constraint token may be so big that eventually it will be assigned greater weight than another constraint token, even if the latter constraint token belongs to a constraint type which is assigned slightly greater weight in abstraction. We should be, however, aware of the fact that the application of such rules concerning assignment of weights to constraints may have significant impact on the process of coherence computation and therefore such rules should be applied with a great degree of caution. In consequence, such 'unequal treatment' is not well-established and commonly accepted in the legal culture which is to be represented by the model. Due to this fact, in the analysis in Araszkiewicz 2010 we postulated assigning equal weight to each constraint which made it possible to compute the coherence of the partitions on the basis of the number of elements only. However, it seems that in actual legal reasoning slight differences in weights assigned to different types of legal arguments are visible, in particular in the cases in which judicial discretion is allowed by the law. It should be noted that if, in certain settings, the abstract privileged character of an element is necessary, it can be represented by adding some initial weight to a given element, for instance on the basis of its source.[30]

[29]For instance due to political processes like European integration, cf. Hesselink (2001).

[30]On the different types of priority between the rules cf. Sartor (2005, Chap. 7).

12.4.5 Meta-argumentation

Although the specific features of legal reasoning provide (arguably plausible) solutions to the problems discussed above, the problem of representing meta-argumentation remains a serious challenge for CaCS. At the point of departure let us note that the seminal theory of argumentation developed by Dung in its original formulation (Dung 1995) had the same problem which resulted in many important extensions of the original proposal (Modgil and Bench-Capon 2009 (Metalevel Argumentation Frameworks)). A problematic feature of CaCS is that it is not structured mathematically like Dung's AAF and until it is structured, each possible 'extension' of CaCS to encompass meta-level argumentation remains debatable and subject to intuitive assessment and not to rigorous mathematical verification. Yet, at the present state of the development of the theory, it is possible to discuss the potential solutions of the problem which can in consequence foster mathematical formalization and extension of the theory. Let us discuss the four possible approaches to the problem of representing meta-argumentation in the framework of CaCS.

1. The simplest possible approach is based on the following reasoning. The only mechanism which is responsible for generating answers in CaCS is the coherence-maximizing partitioning of the initial set of elements. The process of partitioning cannot be started before all constraints are defined on this set of elements. What is more, these constraints have to be defined on the whole set of elements that is at ones disposal; in consequence, it is not relevant to consider the relations between the pairs of elements in isolation and some types of constraints may be defined relatively to the presence of some types of elements in the set. Let us assume that we have a pair of elements $<e_i, e_j>$ and when considered in isolation, there would be a positive constraint between the two. However, the definition of this constraint type may contain an 'unless' clause, which can have for instance the following structure: "unless in the initial set of elements there is an element of the type UD", where the element UD would play a role of undercutting defeater for the link between e_i and e_j. These considerations concerning undercutting defeat can be generalized to encompass other types of meta-argumentation. This solution, although possible, has several disadvantages. It seems to excessively enlarge the initial set of constraints types. It does not offer a clear question how the relation between e_i and e_j should be treated if UD element is eventually rejected. In consequence, this solution can be seen as a provisional only and is suitable for rather *ad hoc* representations of relatively small problem domains.
2. The second technique concerning the representation of meta-argumentation in general and undercutting argumentation in particular would involve an extension from the basic CaCS in which all the constraints are defined pairwise to an extended CaCS in which the constraints are defined on sets of elements. In consequence, constraints between pairs of elements would be only a specific

case of constraints between sets of elements.[31] Obviously, it is not possible to introduce such an extension in the scope of this paper. However, it seems possible to signalize the possibility of such representation of argumentation with a simple example. Let us assume that we have a positive constraint between and element e_i and a pair of elements e_j, e_w–$<e_i, (e_j, e_w)>$ where e_w represents a general rule according to which e_i and e_j should be accepted together. In such situation, a negative constraint $<e_v, e_w>$ can work as an undercutting defeater—if e_v is accepted, the according to the conditions of coherence concerning the partitioning of an initial set of elements, e_w should be rejected. However, once e_w is rejected, the positive relation between e_i and e_j is no longer warranted.[32] The solution discussed here seems to be more advantageous than the first one as regards the representation of actual argumentation. On the other hand, it involves a considerable extension of original CaCS theory. In consequence, it should be seen as an open problem.

3. The third option does not involve any intervention of the general level of CaCS theory, but much work on the layer of representation of the structure of the domain knowledge on the basis of definitions of types of constraints. The idea of this option is to define types of elements and of constraints in such manner that meta-argumentation is not necessary for representation of a given part of reasoning (because all meta-argumentation is encompassed by these definitions). Although such solution seems not to be plausible on abstract level, it seems that in the domain of legal reasoning concerning norms it is possible to formulate such definitions of elements and constraints for which only rebuttal attacks (that is, attacks against a given conclusion and not concerning the links between conclusions and supporting elements) are necessary. A simple model presented in Araszkiewicz 2010 is an example of such representation: only rebutting attacks are considered there. Obviously, this solution is automatically subordinate to an objection that it puts too much information in the definitional section of theory (cf. Hage in this volume). However, it has the advantage of computational simplicity. What is more, this kind of model would have a feature of precise indication of legal problems in a given case. Only the problematic feature would be the subject of computation of coherence while the rest of reasoning would be encoded in the set of definitions. The main drawback of this solution is that it would presumably involve very huge sets of element and constraint types. However, if our aim is to use a relatively simple inference engine, which is applied in basic CaCS, it is often necessary to put much information in the meta-theoretical level. In AI and Law literature the connection between using relatively simple inference engine (in the context discussed there: first-order

[31] Similar extensions have been recently formulated in the context of Abstract Argumentation Frameworks. Cf. Nielsen and Parsons (2007).

[32] A similar representation of undercutting argumentation, albeit in different formal setting, is discussed by Thomas Gordon and Douglas Walton is their seminal paper on Carneades argumentation system, cf. Gordon and Walton (2006, 202).

classical logic) and the importance of exact description of meta-knowledge, had been emphasized by Yoshino (for instance, Yoshino 1995).

4. The fourth technique involves a very deep extension of the basic CaCS and is based on the idea of defining 'objects' in CaCS, developed in this paper above. Let us define 'object' recursively in the following way:

Definition 3: Object For any element $e_i \in E$ (the initial set of elements), e_i is an object.

For any objects o_i, o_j, if $<o_i, o_j> \in C+$ or $C-$, then $<o_i, o_j>$ is an object.

This definition makes it possible to talk not only about constraints between elements of the initial set E, but also about the constraints between elements and constraints, constraints between constraints and so on. In this connection it seems plausible to introduce the notion of level of constraints.

Definition 4: Level of Constraint For any constraint $c \in C+$ or $C-$, this constraint is an object-level constraint if and only if both objects related by this constraint are single elements (not constrained pairs of elements).

For any constraint $c \in C+$ or $C-$, this constraint is a level-1 meta-constraint if and only if the objects related by this constraint are single elements or object-level constraints.

Iteration of the procedure applied in definition 4 leads us to the creation of an infinitely hierarchical set of levels of constraints. It also leads to the stratification of the procedure of computation of coherence. Let us recall that in order to partition the initial set of elements into the subset of accepted and rejected elements, all the constraints have to be defined at the outset. If we accept an extension of CaCS as provided by the definitions above, it becomes problematic to compute the coherence in the set encompassing elements related with different levels of constraints. Let us illustrate this point by the following simple example. Let the set E contain four elements e1, e2, e3 and e4. Let us also assume that (1) $<e1, e2> \in C+$, (2) $<e1, e3> \in C-$ and (3) $<e4, <e1, e2>> \in C-$. We have two levels of constraints here where constraints (1) and (2) are object—level constraints and (3) is a level-1 meta-constraint. It is first necessary to determine which of the objects related to each other by constraint (3) will be accepted and which will be rejected in order to establish whether on the object level the constraint (1) will eventually hold or not. This is because if, on the meta-level, the object $<e1, e2>$ were to be rejected, it would no longer be possible to state that this constraint related the two elements e1 and e2 on the object level. In such situation we would state that the element e4 attacked the constraint (1) successfully.

More generally, in such extended, multilayered CaCS it would be necessary to employ the following procedure of coherence computation:

1. Identify the number of levels of constraints in the initial set of elements E. Number them starting from 0 (object-level constraints) to n.
2. Construct a set E_n in which all objects are related by level-n constraints. Find the coherence-maximizing partition of E_n.

3. Construct a set E_{n-1} in which all objects are related by level-n−1 constraints. Introduce these constraints basic on the results obtained on the level n. Find the coherence-maximizing partition of E_{n-1}.
4. Continue the procedure until you reach the object-level set of elements.

Obviously, this procedure may seem overly complicated, also from computational point of view. It can be also criticized from a philosophical stance, because it introduces a stratified and not holistic view on the process of reasoning. However, although the proposal designed above should not be treated as a full-blown mathematical theory of meta-argumentation in CaCS, it shows that it is in principle possible to extend CaCS to encompass such type of argumentation.

The discussion in this section revealed that although the basic CaCS has several important disadvantages, it is possible to deal with them either on general level concerning possible extensions of CaCS, or on more concrete level, taking into account the peculiarities of legal reasoning. The results of the paper are summarized in the next Section.

12.5 Conclusions

The purpose of this paper was to argue for a plausibility of constructing of a model of legal judicial reasoning on the basis of CaCS, focusing on the problem of representation of legal arguments and conflicts between them in this framework. The philosophical discussion concerning CaCS was outside the scope of the paper. The results of the paper can be summarized as follows.

1. CaCS is a theory of coherence which possesses many attractive features (also on general level, but in particular as regards the project of basing a model of legal reasoning on it). However, it has also some disadvantages, discussed to some extent in the existing literature (and also in this volume). These problems were listed in this paper and referred to as the Structure Problem, the Constraint Definition Problem, the Relevance Problem, the Weight Assignment Problem and the Meta-Argumentation Problem. These problems were discussed in the context of an example concerning unstructured practical reasoning (Jazz Band case).
2. The problems indicated above can be dealt with and there are two basic procedures for achieving this aim: on the one hand, modifications and extensions of the basic CaCS theory, on the other hand, working on a structured model of legal reasoning within the abstract framework of CaCS. I focused on the latter technique; however, some problems seem to require extensions of CaCS.
3. The characteristic features of legal reasoning about norms—as a structured domain of knowledge—make it possible, in my opinion, to satisfactorily overcome the Structure Problem, the Constraint Definition Problem and the Relevance Problem. In particular, the existing jurisprudential work concerning the types of legal norms and arguments offers important insights how a CaCS-based model of legal reasoning can be constructed. The concept of legal paradigm

(Peczenik 1990) and the notion of legal story scheme[33] open the possibilities to overcome the Relevance Problem.
4. The problematic features concerning assignment of weights can be minimized if all the constraints are assigned approximately equal weight at the point of departure (in absence of very important reasons to the contrary).
5. The Meta-Argumentation Problem is the most challenging one for CaCS theory. In consequence, four possible options for dealing with this problem were outlined on the paper. The most ambitious technique involves a deep transformation of the basic CaCS in order to obtain Extended, Multi-layered CaCS theory. The development of cognate extensions in the field of AAF seems promising in this respect, but one should also note that CaCS is not a formalized theory as AAF and that can cause difficulties in elaboration of such extensions.

The open problems indicated above indicate two main directions of future research concerning CaCS-based model of legal reasoning: (1) formal, abstract work concerning the extensions of the basic CaCS theory and (2) careful development of definitions of constraint types and weight assignment procedures, possibly verified by empirical research.

References

Aarnio, A., et al. 1998. *On coherence theory in law*. Lund: Juristfölager i Lund.

Alexy, R. 2002. *A theory of constitutional rights*. Trans. J. Rivers. Oxford: Oxford University Press.

Alexy, R., and A. Peczenik. 1990. The concept of coherence and its significance for discourse rationality. *Ratio Juris* 3(1): 130–147.

Amaya, A. 2007. Formal models of coherence and legal epistemology. *Artificial Intelligence and Law* 15: 429–447.

Amaya, A. 2011. Legal justification by optimal coherence. *Ratio Juris* 24: 304–329.

Amgoud, L., et al. 2008. On bipolarity in argumentation frameworks. *International Journal of Intelligent* 23: 1–32.

Araszkiewicz, M. 2010. Balancing of legal principles and constraint satisfaction. In *Legal knowledge and information systems (Proceedings of the Jurix 2010 conference)*, ed. R.G.F. Winkels, 7–15. Amsterdam: Ios Press.

Bex, F., and B. Verheij. 2011. Legal shifts in the process of proof. In *Proceedings of the 13*th *international conference on artificial intelligence and law*, 11–20. New York: ACM

Dubois, D., and H. Prade. 2006. A bipolar possibilistic representation of knowledge and preferences and its applications. eds. I. Bloch, A. Petrosino, A. Tettamanzi, 1–10. *Fuzzy Logic and Applications, 6th International Workshop, WILF 2005, Crema, Italy,* 15–17 Sept. 2005, *Revised Selected Papers. Lecture Notes in Computer Science 3849.*

Dung, P.M. 1995. On the acceptability of arguments and its fundamental role in nonmonotonic reasoning, logic programming and n-person games. *Artificial Intelligence* 77(2): 321–358.

Dworkin, R. 1967. The model of rules. *University of Chicago Law Review* 35: 14–46.

[33] Advanced in the field of AI and Law by Bex and Verheij (2011).

Gordon, T.F., and D. Walton. 2006. The carneades argumentation framework—Using presumptions and exceptions to model critical questions. In *Proceedings of the First International Conference on Computational Models of Argument*, ed. P.E. Dunne, 195–207. Amsterdam: Ios Press.
Hage, J.C. 2001. Formalizing legal coherence. In *Proceedings of the 8th international conference on artificial intelligence and law*, 22–31. New York: ACM
Hage, J.C. 2003. Law and defeasibility. *Artificial Intelligence and Law* 11: 221–243.
Hage, J.C. 2005. *Studies in legal logic*. Dordrecht: Springer.
Hesselink, M. 2001. *The new European legal culture*. Denventer: Kluwer.
Joseph, S., and H. Prakken. 2009. Coherence-driven argumentation to norm consensus. In *Proceedings of the 12th international conference on artificial intelligence and law*, 58–77. New York: ACM
MacCormick, N. 1978. *Legal reasoning and legal theory*. Oxford: Oxford University Press.
MacCormick, N. 2005. *Rhetoric and the rule of Law*. Oxford: Oxford University Press.
MacCormick, N., and R. Summers (eds.). 1991. *Interpreting statutes: A comparative study*. Dartmouth: Ashgate.
McCarty, L.T. 1997. Some arguments about legal arguments. In *Proceedings of the* 6th *international conference on artificial intelligence and law*, 215–224. New York: ACM.
Modgil, S., and T. Bench-Capon. 2009. Metalevel argumentation. *Journal of Logic and Computation* 21(6): 959–1004.
Nielsen, S.H., and S. Parsons. 2007. A generalization of Dung's abstract framework for argumentation: Arguing with sets of attacking arguments. In *Argumentation in Multi-Agent Systems, Third International Workshop, ArgMAS 2006, Hakodate, Japan, May 8, 2006, Revised Selected and Invited Papers*, eds. N. Maudet, S. Parsons, and I. Rahwan, 54–73. Lecture Notes in Computer Science, 4766. Berlin/New York: Springer.
Peczenik, A. 1990. Coherence, truth and rightness in the Law. In *Law, interpretation and reality: Essays in epistemology, hermeneutics and jurisprudence*, ed. P. Nerhot, 275–309. Dordrecht/Boston/London: Kluwer.
Peczenik, A. 2008. *On law and reason*, 2nd ed. Dordrecht: Springer.
Pollock, J.L. 1995. *Cognitive carpentry: A blueprint for how to build a person*. Cambridge/London: MIT Press.
Prakken, H. 1997. *Logical tools for modelling legal argument: Study of defeasible reasoning in Law*. Dordrecht: Kluwer Academic.
Raz, J. 1992. The relevance of coherence. *Boston University Law Review* 72: 273. Also in Joseph Raz, Ethics in the Public Domain, revised edition, Oxford: Clarendon Press 1995, 77–325.
Sartor, G. 2005. *Legal reasoning, a cognitive approach to the law*. Dordrecht: Springer.
Sartor, G. 2010. Doing justice to rights and values: Teleological reasoning and proportionality. *Artificial Intelligence and Law* 18: 175–215.
Thagard, P. 2000. *Coherence in thought and action*. Cambridge, MA: MIT Press.
Thagard, P., and K. Verbeurgt. 1998. Coherence as constraint satisfaction. *Cognitive Science* 22: 1–24.
Yoshino, H. 1995. The systematization of legal meta-inference. In *Proceedings of the* 5th *international conference on artificial intelligence and law*, 266–275. New York: ACM.

Chapter 13
Ten Theses on Coherence in Law

Amalia Amaya

The aim of this chapter is to advance the following theses: (1) The concept of coherence in law may be best understood in terms of constraint satisfaction; (2) Coherence-based inference is an explanatory kind of inference; (3) There are three main operations whereby coherence may be built in the course of legal decision-making: subtraction, addition, and re-interpretation; (4) Epistemic responsibility is a pivotal component in a theory of legal coherence; (5) Coherentist standards of legal justification vary with context; (6) Coherence-based legal reasoning is a variety of reasoning about ends; (7) There are three main reasons why coherence is a value worth pursuing in law: epistemic reasons, practical reasons, and constitutive reasons; (8) The main motivation of legal coherentism is to provide a non-skeptical alternative to formalism; (9) The coherence theory of legal justification is psychologically plausible and this provides an argument in favor of this theory; (10) Legal coherentism is an agent-centered theory of justification. In what follows, I shall discuss in some detail each of these theses.[1]

[1]For a detailed statement and defense of these theses, see Amaya (2012, forthcoming). An earlier version of this paper appeared in Spanish in Amaya (2011).

A. Amaya (✉)
National Autonomous University of Mexico, Institute for Philosophical Research, Circuito Mario de la Cueva s/n, 4510 Ciudad Universitaria, Coyocan, Mexico
e-mail: amaya@filosoficas.unma.mx

M. Araszkiewicz and J. Šavelka (eds.), *Coherence: Insights from Philosophy, Jurisprudence and Artificial Intelligence*, Law and Philosophy Library 107,
DOI 10.1007/978-94-007-6110-0_13,

13.1 Legal Coherence as Constraint Satisfaction

The concept of coherence is a very slippery one. In the last decades, theories of coherence have been proposed in different domains, such as ethics,[2] epistemology,[3] the literature on practical reasoning,[4] discourse theory,[5] philosophy of language,[6] and philosophy of law.[7] These theories advance different views about how to determine when a set of elements, i.e., norms, discourses, works of art, theories, beliefs, etc. is coherent. Among the different concepts of coherence that have been defended in the literature, I find Paul Thagard's constraint satisfaction approach to coherence particularly interesting (Thagard 2000). This approach—and this is my first thesis—is extremely useful for defining the kind of coherence that is relevant for the justification of both normative and factual statements in law.

According to Thagard, the coherence of a set of elements is a matter of the satisfaction of a number of positive and negative constraints. These constraints establish relations of coherence—positive constraints—and incoherence—negative constraints—among the elements of a set. A coherence problem consists in dividing a set of elements into accepted and rejected in a way that maximizes the satisfaction of the constraints. A positive constraint between two elements can be satisfied either by accepting both of the elements or by rejecting both of them. A negative constraint between two elements can be satisfied only by accepting one element and rejecting the other. Thus, the idea is that we turn a set of elements into as coherent a whole as possible by taking into account the coherence and incoherence relations that hold between pairs of elements of this set.

This abstract characterization of coherence applies to a wide variety of problems. In order to apply this theory to a particular domain, it is necessary to specify the elements and relevant constraints. Thagard distinguishes six kinds of coherence: explanatory, analogical, deductive, perceptual, conceptual, and deliberative. Each kind requires different sorts of elements and constraints. Thagard has proposed theories for all these six kinds of coherence, which specify the relevant positive and negative constraints. For example, according to the principles of explanatory coherence, explanatory coherence is a symmetrical relation between hypotheses and evidence within a set; it arises out of relations of explanation and analogical relations between evidence and hypotheses; relations of contradiction and competition give rise to incoherence; and the acceptability of a proposition is claimed to be a matter

[2]On coherence theories of moral justification, see Rawls (1999), Goldman (1988), DePaul (1993), and Thagard (1998).

[3]See BonJour (1985) and Lehrer (2000).

[4]See Richardson (1994), Hurley (1989), and Thagard and Millgram (1996).

[5]For a review of the current state of coherentist approaches to discourse interpretation, see Hellman (1995).

[6]See Davidson (2001). See also Fodor and Lepore (1992).

[7]See, among others, MacCormick (1984), Dworkin (1986), Peczenik (1989), Aarnio (1998), and Hage (2004).

of its coherence with the rest of propositions within a set, some of which enjoy, nonetheless, a degree of acceptability on their own. According to Thagard, the solution of a particular coherence problem involves the interaction of different kinds of coherence. For instance, epistemic justification requires the interaction of deductive, explanatory, analogical, perceptual, and conceptual coherence.

The theory of coherence as constraint satisfaction, I would argue, may be successfully applied to give an account of legal coherence. Two kinds of legal coherence may be distinguished: factual coherence, i.e., the kind of coherence that is relevant to the justification of conclusions about disputed questions of fact in law, and normative coherence, i.e., the kind of coherence that is relevant to the justification of normative conclusions in law. More specifically, the suggestion is that one may develop a concept of coherence for the justification of conclusions about disputed questions of fact on the basis of Thagard's model of epistemic coherence, and a theory of coherence for the justification of conclusions about disputed questions of law on the basis of Thagard's theory of ethical coherence. Nonetheless, some modifications are necessary to take into account domain-specific features of legal reasoning.

Factual coherence results from the interaction of the same kinds of coherence that are relevant to epistemic justification with one major addition, namely, deliberative coherence. This kind of coherence is relevant to the justification of factual judgments in law given that there is an important practical dimension to epistemic reasoning in law. Explanatory coherence is the most important kind of coherence in a theory of the justification of evidentiary judgments in law. In addition to the positive and negative constraints established by the principles of explanatory coherence, it is necessary to add some constraints to account for the fact that the evaluation of explanatory hypotheses in law takes place within a highly institutionalized context. More specifically, the presumption of innocence may be treated as a constraint that requires that hypotheses compatible with innocence be given priority in being accepted and the reasonable doubt standard requires that the guilt hypothesis be accepted only if its degree of justification is sufficiently high to meet this standard.

Normative coherence requires the interaction of the same kinds of coherence that are relevant to moral justification plus another kind of coherence, namely, 'interpretative' coherence. This kind of coherence is necessary to give an account of the interpretative nature of legal argument. The principles of interpretative coherence are structurally analogous to the principles of explanatory coherence, except that positive and negative constraints hold between interpretative hypotheses and normative elements (i.e., precedents, principles, rules, etc.) rather than between factual hypotheses and propositions describing observations. Just as explanatory coherence is the most important contributor to the justification of factual judgments in law, so is interpretative coherence particularly important for the justification of normative judgments in law.

The theory of legal coherence as constraint satisfaction is attractive in that it allows us to formulate a number of criteria of coherence and thereby helps us overcome one of the main problems facing coherence theories in law, to wit, that they lack a precise account of the criteria of coherence and of how they should be balanced against each other. In addition, this theory provides us with the resources to give a unitary account of the role that coherence plays in the justification of both factual and normative judgments in law. This is not to say that this theory is without problems. To start with, the theory of coherence as constraint satisfaction does not give an account of the problem of how the set of elements over which the coherence calculation proceeds is generated, i.e., the problem of the input. Besides, it is also unclear how one may integrate the different kinds of coherence in order to give a solution to a legal problem, i.e., the problem of integration. Notwithstanding these problems, this theory provides a useful framework for developing a coherentist account of legal justification.

13.2 The Explanatory Nature of Coherence-Driven Inference

An important problem that any coherence theory of justification faces is that of giving an account of the process whereby one reaches the most coherent interpretation of a legal rule, the course of action that best fits with a set of values and objectives, the hypothesis about the disputed facts that best makes sense of the evidence available, or the scientific theory that best coheres with a body of observations. It cannot be explained—it might be argued—how a judge reaches the most coherent solution to a legal problem or what makes an interpretation of a work of art more coherent than another one is: these issues are but a matter of intuition. As Putnam put it, coherence, like jokes, "are not something we have an algorithm for, but something that we ultimately judge by 'seat on the pants' feel" (Putnam 1985, 132–133). But if this is so, then coherence theories are at a distinct disadvantage compared with alternative theories of justification that have the resources to give an account of the reasoning patterns that result in justified beliefs. Moreover, the purported lack of a theory of coherence-driven inference makes coherentism a non-starter as a theory of legal justification, for in public contexts, such as the legal one, it is imperative that decisions be backed by reasons rather than be the result of mere intuition. As opposed to theories of adjudication that rely on a clear description of the legitimate patterns of inference, e.g., the judicial syllogism, and theories of evidential reasoning in law that employ the resources of inductive logic, e.g., the Bayesian theory of legal proof, coherentism seems to lack any theory about how arguments from coherence work.

My claim is that coherentism, to the contrary, does have a clear description of the inferential processes that yield justified beliefs. Coherence-driven inference is a kind of explanatory inference. Therefore, we have the tools of abductive logic to give an account of the kind of inferences which, according to coherentism, confer justification. Coherence-based inference—and this is my second thesis—may be described as an 'inference to the best explanation', i.e., the most coherent explanation.[8] An inference to the best explanation in law consists of three main stages: (1) the generation or discovery of relevant elements—factual hypotheses and evidence, in the case of evidential reasoning, and interpretative hypotheses and normative elements, in the case of normative reasoning; (2) the pursuit, development, and refinement of a number of initially plausible decision alternatives; and (3) the evaluation and comparison of these decision alternatives with a view to selecting one of them as justified. Thus, an inference to the best explanation does not only work in the context of discovery, but it may also confer justification to its conclusions—because of its coherence-enhancing role—and it plays an important role not only in evidential reasoning in law but also in legal reasoning about normative questions.[9]

Inference to the best explanation leads us to accept as justified a hypothesis about the facts or the law that is most coherent among those that have been considered. Hence, this pattern of inference is first and foremost a process of coherence maximization. In the first stage, i.e., generation, coherence helps us narrow down the set of plausible hypotheses; hypotheses that blatantly incohere with background knowledge about the world and the law are excluded from consideration. Coherence also helps us generate new elements; the search for coherence stimulates asking questions which importantly aid the aim of inquiry. Asking what interpretative hypothesis could make sense of a body of precedents or what evidence would cohere with a given factual hypothesis is an effective way of identifying relevant hypotheses and evidence. The second stage, i.e., pursuit, in which each hypothesis is rendered as coherent as it can be, is critical to ensure that there is a fair evaluation of the alternatives. A number of coherence-making mechanisms—which I shall discuss in the next section—allow one to improve the alternative hypotheses about the facts and the law, prior to evaluating them. Last, at the third stage, coherence provides us with a set of criteria for comparing the decision alternatives so as to select one of them as justified.

Thus, coherence is not a question of intuition that cannot be subjected to critical analysis but the result of a process one may describe in detail by using explanatory reasoning. May coherentist reasoning be formalized? If coherence-based reasoning, as I have argued, is explanatory in nature, then it is highly unlikely that it may be formalized by means of traditional logical tools, given that explanatory relations cannot be reduced to syntactic or semantic relations, but pragmatic elements play a critical role in the generation and evaluation of explanatory hypotheses, and, thus, in judgments of coherence. Connectionist algorithms—such as those employed, for instance, by Thagard, computational models—like those used in studies on abduction in artificial intelligence, or belief revision formalisms—which we will examine shortly—are more appropriate to formalize the complex argumentative

[8]The literature on inference to the best explanation is extensive. The most detailed defense of a model of inference to the best explanation is Lipton's. See Lipton (2004).

[9]For a discussion of the role of inference to the best explanation in legal reasoning about facts, see Amaya (2009).

networks on which judgments of coherence depend. However, these formalisms, like any formalization, only have the resources to give an account of some aspects of coherence-based reasoning. Despite their limitations, they provide us with useful tools for better understanding the mechanics of coherence-driven inference.

13.3 Coherence-Making Mechanisms

How may one render an incoherent set of elements into a coherent one? Which mechanisms may be used to maximize the degree of coherence of an interpretative or factual hypothesis? As I said before, before evaluating the alternative decisions, it is necessary to improve and refine each of the hypotheses under consideration. Now, I would like to make a proposal as to how one may modify an alternative decision so as to make it as coherent as it can be. There are, I would argue, three coherence-making strategies, namely, subtraction, addition, and reinterpretation.[10]

Subtraction, which consists in eliminating some elements, is a well-known coherence-making operation. This operation is rather useful when reasoning about facts in law. For example, faced with contradictory testimony, a fact-finder may reach coherence by eliminating a belief in the credibility of one of the witnesses on the grounds that it conflicts with a hypothesis that is well supported by the available body of circumstantial evidence. Subtraction is also helpful for enhancing coherence when reasoning about norms in law. For instance, one may increase the coherence of an interpretative hypothesis that explains an important body of precedent and other relevant norms by ruling out as mistaken a precedent that is inconsistent with the principles underwriting such an interpretation.

Coherence may also be built by adding new elements. This strategy, which is perhaps less familiar, is also very useful in the context of legal reasoning (Klein and Warfield 1994). For instance, suppose that a legal decision-maker believes that the evidence at trial strongly supports a guilt-hypothesis. However, suppose that she also believes an expert testimony that conflicts with the hypothesis of guilt. There emerge, however, in the course of the trial, reasons for doubting the reliability of the method used by the expert. A fact-finder may increase the coherence of the theory of the case entailing the guilt of the accused by adding the belief that the expert testimony is not reliable. One may also use addition to enhance coherence when reasoning about normative issues. For example, one may increase the coherence of an interpretative hypothesis by adding a belief in an overarching principle that irons out the discrepancies between the proposed hypothesis and a relevant body of precedents.

---

[10]The taxonomy and definition of these operations is based on the operations distinguished in the belief revision literature. For an introduction to these formalisms, see Gärdenfors (1988). For a coherentist interpretation of these operations, see Olsson (1988). For applications of belief revision formalisms to law, see Amaya (2007).

Last, coherence may also be enhanced by a "reinterpretation" strategy, which amounts to eliminating one belief and replacing it by another.[11] For instance, incriminating physical evidence found in the house of the accused can be re-interpreted, in light of evidence of police misconduct, as decreasing rather than enhancing the coherence of the theory of the case entailing guilt. Similarly, one may re-interpret a body of precedent, which incoheres with a proposed interpretative hypothesis, in the light of an alternative principle so as to augment (rather than reduce) its degree of coherence.

These coherence-making mechanisms, i.e., subtraction, addition, and reinterpretation, enjoy a high degree of psychological plausibility. Holyoak, Simon, and collaborators have shown that legal decision-making is a process whereby decision-makers reconstruct the mental representation of the decision task so as to achieve a state of coherence at which the considerations that support the emerging decision are strongly endorsed and those that support the alternative decision are dismissed. Operations of addition, elimination, and modification of dissonant elements are pivotal, as these studies have shown, to reach a coherent representation of the decision problem.[12]

Now, if the production of coherence is at the core of decision-making and, more generally—as I will argue later—a constitutive part of human information processing then, there is a legitimate question as to whether the coherence built in the course of legal decision-making is either genuine or merely the product of an unconstrained tendency to construct coherence. For example, faced with a number of interpretative or factual hypotheses, legal decision-makers, in their effort after coherence, may manipulate the decision elements so as to secure that their preferred alternative is, by the end of the process, the most coherent one. Or they may ignore or underplay the relevance of disturbing evidence in order to preserve the coherence of their favored hypothesis. Thus, there is an important risk involved in coherence-based reasoning, namely, that of 'fabricating' coherence where there is none. In order to block ascriptions of justification to factual or interpretative hypotheses the coherence of which is the result of a defective process of belief formation, it is necessary to impose some limits to coherence building. It is possible—and this is my fourth thesis—to constrain the kind of coherence that generates justification by inserting a theory of epistemic responsibility within a coherence theory of justification. I turn now to discussing the relevance of judgments of epistemic responsibility to judgments of coherence and, thus, to legal justification.

---

[11]The term 'reinterpretation' is Conte's. See Conte (1988).

[12]For a summary of experimental results, see Simon (2004).

13.4 Coherence, Responsibility, and Virtue

Standards of epistemic responsibility are an essential element of a coherence theory of justification.[13] We humans have an outstanding ability to make sense of the world. Although individuals vary in 'mental agility', i.e., their tolerance for inconsistency, the ability and tendency to construe coherence is a critical feature of human cognition.[14] But then the following problem arises: how can we tell apart the kind of coherence that yields justification from the coherence that is the result of an unrestrained propensity to fabricate coherence? In other words, how may one distinguish the kind of coherence that is the result of prejudice, fantasy, or bias and that which results from our best efforts to achieve, as Rawls would put it, a reflective equilibrium among our beliefs, accepted background theories, and a set of relevant principles? In the legal context, this problem is also a serious one, for we do not want to attribute justification to beliefs about the law whose putative coherence is the result of personal adherence to moral principles that are unsupported by the relevant legal materials. Neither do we want to confer justification to beliefs about the facts under dispute the coherence of which results from systematic efforts at interpreting evidence so that it fits with a set of deeply entrenched but unwarranted beliefs (e.g., beliefs about the propensity of some racial groups to commit violent acts or the lack of honesty in some professions). Thus, it is necessary to determine the kind of coherence that generates justification so as to rule out as unjustified interpretative and factual hypotheses that, albeit coherent, are the result of defective processes of belief formation.

My proposal is as follows: a hypothesis about the facts or the law is justified if it could be the outcome of epistemically responsible coherence-based reasoning. The (interpretative or factual) hypothesis that an epistemically responsible legal decision-maker could have accepted as justified enjoys what I shall refer to as 'optimal coherence.' Thus, my suggestion is that legal justification is a matter of optimal coherence. For one to be justified in accepting a belief, an interpretation, a course of action, etc. by virtue of its coherence in the legal context, it is necessary to generate a number of alternatives and select the most coherent one in an epistemically responsible manner. That is to say, that an alternative decision is the most coherent one only gives one a reason to accept it as justified if one has carefully considered the relevant alternatives in the particular context and has evaluated their coherence in an epistemically responsible way. It is critical to note that a decision may be justified even if it is the outcome of an irresponsible process of coherence maximization, as long as an epistemically responsible legal decision-maker *could* have accepted it as justified by virtue of its coherence. Thus, the justification of a

[13]On the relationship between responsibility and epistemic responsibility, see Pryor (2001).

[14]The term is Festinger's. See Simon (1998, 549, 15 ff.).

decision depends on a counterfactual condition, not on a causal one. In contrast, a legal decision-maker is justified in taking a decision if the actual process of decision-making has been conducted in an epistemically responsible way.

Now, what is it for a legal decision-maker to behave in an epistemically responsible way? Two main accounts of epistemic responsibility may be distinguished: a 'deontic' approach and an 'aretaic' approach. Under a deontic-approach, epistemic responsibility is a matter of duty-fulfillment. One is epistemically responsible to the extent that one complies with one's epistemological duties, such as the duty to believe as evidence dictates or the duty to seek out more evidence about propositions which are less than certain on one's evidence.[15] According to the aretaic conception of epistemic responsibility, one is epistemically responsible insofar as one properly exercises a number of intellectual virtues, such as diligence, courage to face criticism, perseverance in following a line of inquiry, or open-mindedness.[16]

Perhaps, there is no need to choose among these alternatives. One could develop an irenic approach to the epistemic responsibility of legal decision-makers, which combines deontic and aretaic elements. On this view, legal deliberation about both the facts and the law requires compliance with certain epistemological duties as well as the exercise a number of intellectual virtues. I have defended such an approach elsewhere; however, I am not fully persuaded that this is a satisfactory theoretical position, as it puts together elements of very different philosophical traditions. In principle, given that the law aims at establishing standards of conduct that are minimally acceptable, rather than ideal models of conduct, a deontic approach seems adequate. However, there are some reasons why, I would argue, an aretaic approach may be preferable.[17] Virtue concepts have the advantage of greater richness than deontic concepts; a virtue approach does not reduce good epistemic practice to rule-following; and it allows us to put forward an ideal of legal agent according to which legal decision-makers do not merely aspire to avoid prohibited epistemic conduct, but to engage in epistemically valuable conduct. Nonetheless, I leave open the issue of which is the best way of defining standards of epistemic responsibility in the context of legal decision-making. The important point that I would like to emphasize is the need to complement a theory of coherence with a theory of epistemic responsibility—however it may be developed—in order to give a satisfactory account of legal justification.

---

[15]On epistemic duties, see Feldman (2002).

[16]The literature on epistemic virtues is extensive. The most influential version of virtue epistemology among those that take virtues to be character traits is Zagzebski (1996).

[17]For a defense of an aretaic approach to the epistemic responsibility of triers of fact—judges in their fact finding capacities as well as members of the jury—see Amaya (2008).

13.5 Coherence and Context

Context is essential when evaluating the coherence or incoherence of an interpretation, an action, a plan, or a theory. The process whereby coherence is constructed is, first and foremost, a process of contextualization. Margolis writes, "Context is the clue, however. Faced with an apparently non-coherent (not obviously coherent or incoherent) array of human thought and behavior or work, we search for a plausible or likely context of human purposes within which a given set of dreams, thoughts, plans, endeavors, theories, stories, paintings, statements, utterances, fears, commitments, hopes, or the like may be shown to be relevantly coherent or incoherent" (Margolis 1984, 23). Hence, the search for coherence is a search for a context in which one may make sense of a set of apparently incoherent elements. It is only when we have failed to make sense of a set of norms, propositions, etc. in light of a plausible set of interests, objectives, or beliefs that we abandon the presumption of coherence that governs processes of interpretation and make a judgment of incoherence.[18] In this sense, judgments of coherence are 'perspectival,' that is to say, a behavior, a hypothesis, or a discourse are coherent or incoherent relative to a point of view, a body of beliefs, or assumptions. However, and this is critical, the context of objectives, beliefs, etc. that is relevant to judgments of coherence is not given, but it is the product of the effort of the interpreter at preserving the presumption of coherence that guides the interpretation process.

A coherence theory of justification has to give an account of the way in which judgments of coherence, and thus, of justification, depend on context. The context-dependence of justification is a basic tenet of contextualism. In both ethics and epistemology, there have been defended several proposals according to which standards of justification vary with context.[19] The coherence theory of legal justification, I would argue, needs to be contextualized. That is to say, the coherentist standards of legal justification are not the same across contexts, but they are subjected to contextual variation. Now, what are the features of context that are relevant for fixing the standards of legal justification? And what is exactly that varies with context? Let us start by considering the first question.

There is no consensus about which features of context are relevant to justification. However, in the literature on contextualism, one may identify some features which, I would argue, play an important role in the justification of factual and normative statements in law.[20] Some of these features are as follows:

1. The stakes. When the costs of being wrong are very high, a stricter standard of justification is in order. For example, in most legal systems, standards of

[18]On the presumption of coherence, see Brown and Yule (1983, 234).

[19]See, among others, Annis (1978), Cohen (1986), Lewis (1996), and DeRose (1999). For contextualism about moral justification, see Timmons (1999).

[20]For an interesting proposal about which contextual factors are relevant to justification, see Williams (2001).

justification are higher in criminal cases, which involve serious consequences for the defendant, than in civil cases.

2. The role. Expertise and one's occupation also determine the severity of the standards that are appropriate in a particular context of justification. A higher level of scrutiny is required, for example, for the justification of a Supreme Court decision as opposed to a lower level court decision.
3. There are various goals that might be relevant in a particular context of justification, and relative to which a decision or belief might be properly characterized as justified. For instance, a decision about facts in law may be justified in light of the variety of goals that adjudication is meant to serve, while unjustified relative exclusively to the goal of truth-seeking—as happens in cases in which relevant evidence is rule out as inadmissible.
4. Methodological constraints. Standards of justification vary with the kind of inquiry that one is engage in (epistemological, legal, etc.). What is at stake here, as Williams puts it, is not so much the 'level' of scrutiny as the 'angle' of scrutiny (Williams 2001, 160). We can be more or less strict in setting up our standards of evidence within a particular field of inquiry, but some questions have to be set aside for us to determine whether a particular belief or hypothesis is justified in that specific field. For instance, to reason about facts in law, it is necessary to set aside skeptical hypotheses that would surely be relevant in the context of epistemological inquiry. And to reason about normative questions in law, rather than morals, one has to take the relevance of authority reasons for granted and exclude from consideration hypotheses which, while appealing from a normative standpoint, clearly conflict with the relevant legal sources.
5. The resources. The level of scrutiny that is reasonable in a particular context depends on the resources available. For example, in the context of legal reasoning, there are severe institutional and time constraints which put a limit to the kind of issues that may be considered before one accepts a decision as justified.
6. Dialectical features. Justificatory practices take place in a dialectical context that constrains what may be taken for granted and what, to the contrary, is a relevant alternative that needs to be ruled out for one's claim to be justified. The fact of mentioning or raising a possible defeator triggers a higher level of scrutiny. For example, an expert testimony may not be taken at face value as soon as doubts are raised about the credibility of the expert. Or a legal principle cannot be accepted as justified if its coherence with core constitutional values has been called into question.

The foregoing features—among others, this list is intended to be merely indicative, rather than exhaustive—are relevant to determine the severity of the standards of justification that is appropriate in a particular context. Hence, the question of whether a hypothesis about the facts or the law is justified cannot be addressed in the abstract, but it is necessary to take into account the gravity of the consequences of the legal decision, the institutional role of the decision-maker, the relevant objectives, the resources available, and the methodological and dialectical constraints characteristic of the particular context. These contextual features allow us to adjust the standards of justification and avoid the use of standards that are either too lax or too demanding.[21] But how—and I turn now to the second question raised above—does context fix the severity of the standards of legal justification?

There are three dimensions along which, I would argue, coherentist standards of justification may be may be lowered or raised: the threshold of justification, i.e., the degree of coherence required for justification, the domain of coherence, i.e., the set of elements the coherence of which is relevant to justification, and the constitution of the contrast set, i.e., the set of hypotheses within which one hypothesis gets justification by being most coherent. First, the degree of coherence that a hypothesis about either the facts or the law should enjoy in order to be justified depends on context. For example, a theory of the case may be coherent enough to justify a finding for the plaintiff in a civil case, even if it falls below the threshold of coherence required to find against the defendant in a criminal case.

Second, the domain of coherence also varies with context. For instance, in order to reach a justified decision in easy cases, it may suffice to seek coherence with, perhaps, a set a precedents and a relevant body of legal rules. However, in hard cases in which decisions carry serious normative consequences for the legal system, it seems necessary to expand the set of relevant reasons in order to make a judgment of coherence with a view to reaching a justified decision.

Last, the set of alternatives that legal decision-makers should take into consideration before picking one of them as justified depends on context as well. For instance, methodological constraints help configure the set of relevant alternatives. While the hypothesis that the defendant did not voluntarily commit the crime because he was, as we all are, deceived by a malign demon, might be relevant in the context of epistemological inquiry, it can be properly ignored in the context of a criminal trial.

To sum up, judgments of coherence (and incoherence) are context-dependent. A coherence theory of justification has to take into account that there is a contextual dimension to coherence judgments. To be sure, the introduction of contextual considerations into a coherence theory of justification makes it more complex and less precise. However, a contextualized version of coherentism has some reasons to recommend it. First, a contextualized approach to coherentism is more plausible from a psychological point of view than holistic versions of coherentism. Contextualized coherentism reduces the complexity of coherence computations insofar as it does not require agents to evaluate the coherence of the whole system of beliefs—factual or normative—but only the subset that is relevant in context. The contextualization of coherentist standards of justification also increases the

[21] Now, while the reasons for ensuring that we do not under-consider alternatives are pretty obvious, it may not be immediately clear why one should be concerned with not over-considering alternatives. Given our limited cognitive and institutional resources, as well as time constraints, it is important not to raise the standards of justification, unless there is a reason to do so. As Fogelin says, there are 'epistemic transaction costs' involved in raising a level of scrutiny, which, like most costs, we prefer not to incur. See Fogelin (2003, 123–124).

descriptive power of the theory, for legal decision-makers do not typically bring to bear their whole system of beliefs when solving a legal problem—as traditional, holistic, coherence theories assume—but only those beliefs that are relevant in the particular context. Besides, a contextualist approach to legal justification also has advantages from a normative point of view, in that it puts limits to the use of moral reasons when reasoning about normative issues in law and prevents beliefs based on inadmissible evidence from playing a role in evidential reasoning in law. Thus, the introduction of context in a coherentist theory of legal justification has some important advantages, even if it comes with a price in terms of the degree of precision that one may expect the theory to have.

13.6 Coherence-Based Reasoning and Reasoning About Ends

Coherence-based reasoning is a kind of non-instrumental reasoning. That is to say, coherentist reasoning allows us to reason about which ends are valuable and how to proceed when they come into conflict. According to the instrumental conception of practical reason, all practical reasoning is means-ends reasoning. Instrumentalism is problematic insofar as it places ends and values beyond the pale of reason. On this view, ends and values are fixed by individual preferences and constrain the space of deliberation, rather than being the subject of rational revision. When ends and values come into conflict, one should reduce those values to a common scale, in order to make a rational decision, or take the decision that seems intuitively best. As opposed to this reductive conception of the scope of practical reason, non-instrumental approaches hold it that it is possible to reason not only about what are the best means to achieve one's ends, but also about which ends are worth pursuing in the first place and how to solve conflicts among them.[22] Given that the law is responsive to a plurality of ends and values, legal decision-making often involves facing problems of value conflict. Thus, an instrumentalist conception of practical reason does not have the resources to guide legal decision-makers in their task. Coherentist methods significantly contribute to a better understanding of the patterns of inference whereby legal decision-makers may reason about ends and values in law.

There are several proposals about how coherence works as a standard of justification of practical inferences other than means-ends inferences. I will briefly discuss two proposals that are particularly interesting and, I would argue, useful in the context of law. First, Henry Richardson has developed a coherentist version of specificationism that is rather helpful for addressing problems of normative conflict (Richardson 1994). Some ends, such as 'happiness', a 'good constitution of a political body', etc., are too vague and indefinite to serve as starting points for means-ends reasoning. Specificationism holds that practical reasoning consists,

[22]For a brief but informative discussion of instrumentalism and its problems, see Millgram (2001).

at least partly, in specifying ends and norms.[23] Richardson has further elaborated the specificationist proposal in three important respects. First, Richardson provides a detailed definition of the operation of specification as a relation between two norms (or ends)—the initial one and its specification—that satisfies a number of semantic and syntactic conditions. Second, Richardson has proposed a criterion for telling apart correct (or rational) specifications from incorrect (or irrational) specifications. According to Richardson, a specification is rational as long as it enhances the coherence of the norms found acceptable upon reflection, where such coherence is a matter of finding or constructing mutual support among one's norms and ends and removing relations of opposition or practical conflict. Last, Richardson provides an additional reason for specifying ends: many of our norms conflict, but often one may remove the conflict by specifying them. As opposed to a conception according to which when two norms come into conflict one should either establish a lexical order between them or intuitively weigh and balance them with a view to determining which should prevail, Richardson holds that it is possible to satisfactorily address normative conflict by specifying the norms involved. Thus, according to Richardson, coherence-driven specification is a legitimate pattern of practical reasoning: practical reason is not merely instrumental, one may also reason about values and how to solve conflicts among them.

Another non-instrumentalist approach to practical reason in which coherence plays a fundamental role is that proposed by Susan Hurley (1989). Hurley advances an account of case-based deliberation that gives coherence a central role. According to Hurley, deliberation is first and foremost a process whereby one builds a theory that best displays as coherent the relationships among the several values that apply in the particular case. The fundamental claim of Hurley's coherentist account of practical reasoning is that there is a conceptual relation between the reasons that are relevant in a specific case and judgments about what to do all-things-considered: more specifically, the relationship in question is that of subject matter to theory. That is to say, a judgment about what to do 'all things considered' is right if it is favored by the theory that gives the most coherent account of the relationship among the specific reasons (such as moral values, legal doctrines, and precedents) that are relevant in the particular case. It is critical to note that these theories do not aim at explaining conflict away, which is, claims Hurley, an impossible task. The specific reasons for action that come into conflict in a particular case are not *prima facie*, i.e., reasons that may be shown not to apply, once one knows more about the problem at stake, and thus, that lack residual force. In contrast, Hurley holds that reasons for action are *pro tanto*, which come into genuine conflict and have residual force. For instance, consider a conflict between justice and clemency. It can be the case that an act is just but inclement and that such an act is right insofar as it is favored by the best theory about how justice and clemency are related to each other; the act may still

[23] The early pivotal papers on specificationism were by Kolnai (2001) and Wiggins (2001).

be inclement. In other words, the claim that there is a conceptual relation between specific reasons, i.e., *pro tanto* reasons, and all-things-considered judgments does not imply that conflict is eliminable.

In conclusion, coherentist methods, such as those proposed by Richardson and Hurley, provide us with the resources to reason about ends and values and, thus, expand the scope of practical reason beyond means-ends inferences. In consequence, the introduction of coherentist methods in law allows us to accord to reason in law a broader role than the role assigned to it by formalist and instrumentalist conceptions of law, which restrict patterns of practical inference to the rule-case judicial syllogism and the means-end one, respectively. Coherentist methods provide us with a way to reasoning about which ends and values are worth pursuing in law as well as how to proceed rationally when they come into conflict. This does not mean, however, that coherentism assumes a non-conflictual vision of law, as some critics of coherentism have argued (Raz 1992; Kennedy 1997). Quite the contrary. It is precisely because our legal systems are responsive to a plurality of values and because in modern societies there is a diversity of moral, religious, and political conceptions which impose claims upon the law that there is a need to appeal to coherence methods. Coherence does not eliminate conflict, but it gives us a way to proceed in the face of conflict. Thus, coherentist methods are a critical tool for realizing a primary function of the law, namely, that of solving conflict through argumentative means (Atienza 2006, 59).

13.7 The Value of Coherence

Why is coherence a value worth pursuing in the legal context? Which are the reasons why coherence should play an important role in the justification of judicial decisions? These are second-order questions, that is to say, questions about which arguments may be given in support of a coherentist standard of justification. There are three kinds of reasons, I would argue, why coherence should be sought in the course of legal decision-making, namely, epistemic reasons, practical reasons, and constitutive reasons.

The first kind of reasons—the epistemic ones—is the most controversial. Coherentist standards of justification are themselves justified if there are reasons for thinking that a legal decision-maker who accepts beliefs about the facts and the law as justified according to these standards is thereby at least likely to arrive at the truth. To be sure, one of the most debated issues in the coherentist literature is the question of whether coherence and truth are connected in the right way. And, as is well known, one of the main objections that have been raised against coherence theories of justification is that adhering to these standards of justification is not truth-conducive. In fact, some of the criticisms that have been directed against coherence theories stem—one way or another, from the problem of the truth-conduciveness of coherence. For example, one problem that coherence theories of justification face is that of ensuring that observational beliefs play that role that they ought to play in the formation and justification of beliefs about the world. In addition to the problem of the input or isolation, coherence theories do not provide any criterion for choosing among alternative sets of beliefs that are equally coherent. In light of these problems, coherentist standards of justification seem wholly inadequate as criteria of *epistemic* justification, that is, as criteria that help us search for truth.

To be sure, the problems of the input, isolation, and alternative coherent systems need to be taken seriously. However, although the relation between coherence and truth is problematical, coherentist standards of justification are not doomed to failure. In the coherentist literature there are a number of interesting strategies for showing that coherence and truth are properly connected. Laurence BonJour has given an explanatory argument to the effect that coherence is truth conducive. In his view, the best explanation of the coherence plus stability of a system of beliefs that meets the observation requirement (which guarantees that the belief system attributes high reliability to a reasonable variety of cognitively spontaneous beliefs) is that it corresponds (in the long run and approximately) to the external world (BonJour 1985). According to Thagard, (explanatory) coherence leads to approximate truth when the theory is the best explanation of the evidence, it broadens its evidence base over time, and is deepened by explanations of why the theory works (Thagard 2007). Other philosophers, like Keith Lehrer and Donald Davidson, have provided arguments that seek to establish a conceptual relationship between coherence and truth. According to Lehrer, self-trust, which plays a core role in his coherence theory of justification, allows us to establish a conceptual link between coherence and truth (Lehrer 2000). And Davidson establishes this conceptual connection by means of the concept of belief, as it is defined within his theory of interpretation (Davidson 2001).

To be sure these arguments, while compelling, do not conclusively establish that coherentist standards of justification are truth-conducive. However, in this respect, coherentism does not seem to be worse off than alternative theories of epistemic justification. After all, foundationalism—which is the main competing account of epistemic justification, has not succeeded either in conclusively refuting the skeptical hypotheses. Besides, coherence-driven inferences are defeasible: to require that it be shown that coherence is truth-conducive would amount to requiring that the problem of induction, which is hardly a distinctive problem of coherentism, be solved. In short, in order to show that coherence has epistemic value it does not seem necessary to prove the falsity of the skeptical hypotheses—which are, in any event, as troublesome for coherentism as they are for any other theory of justification.

In light of the foregoing arguments, and leaving radical skepticism aside, one may conclude that the prospects for showing that coherentist standards of justification are epistemically valuable are reasonably good. In the legal context, these strategies provide a plausible starting point for mounting an argument to the effect that accepting beliefs about the facts under dispute by virtue of their coherence leads us to accept beliefs that are probably true. In addition, it is worth mentioning that the problem of the truth-conduciveness of coherence is more acute for some versions of coherentism than for others. In the conception of coherence as constraint satisfaction that I have defended here propositions describing observations—evidence, in law—

have a priority in being accepted and thus, there are good reasons for believing that theories and hypotheses about the facts that cohere with those propositions (granted, of course, that our perceptual beliefs are not systematically mistaken, as the skeptic holds!) are probably true.

With regard to the theory of justification of conclusions about disputed questions of law, the connection between coherence and truth is much less problematical for two reasons. First, anti-realist or constructivist approaches to truth square well with coherence theories of justification. Indeed, the replacement of a conception of truth as correspondence by a definition of truth as coherence has been a common strategy to solve the problem of coherence and truth. And second, constructivist theories of the truth of normative judgments are, in principle, more plausible than realist theories. Thus, there does not seem to be any serious obstacles to analyzing the justification of normative judgments in law in coherentist terms.

In addition, there a number of practical reasons for pursuing coherence in the legal domain. Coherence is instrumental to several values that are central in practical reasoning and that are also important in the legal context. More specifically, coherence facilitates successful coordination, which is surely critical in a collective enterprise, such as law (Bratman 1987, 137; Richardson 1994, 152–158). Coherence also promotes effectiveness, for coherent plans of action tend to work better than conflicting courses of action or overlapping goals. Thus, a certain degree of coherence is indispensable to successfully advance law's project of regulating and transforming social life. Besides, coherence enhances the efficiency of plans of action, for it is more likely that there is a rational use of resources when one pursues a set of objectives that cohere with each other, and this is critical when it comes to public resources (Thagard and Millgram 1996). As is well known, coherence also aids the realization of values that are distinctive of the legal domain, such as the value of legal certainty (Moral 2003). Among other ways in which coherence promotes legal certainty is by facilitating knowledge of the law, for a coherent body of norms is more easily remembered and understood than a body of norms that fail to make sense as a whole. Last, a certain degree of coherence in legal decision-making at both the legislative and the judicial level is also pivotal for securing the social stability that the law aims to preserve (Alexy and Peczenik 1990).

Last, there are also constitutive reasons to value coherence in law.[24] Coherence plays a constitutive role in individual and political identity. A certain degree of coherence in individual and collective deliberation is necessary to be both a unified agent and part of a distinctive political community. When deliberating about the values and objectives that are relevant in a particular case, legal agents are also determining their own identity as members of a political community. Individual identity and group identity are not fixed—as Hurley has brilliantly argued—but they are the result of self-interpretation. Legal decision-makers are not free to disregard a concern for coherence because in so doing they would be refusing to determine their own identity as members of the political community to which they belong.

[24]Hurley (1989), especially Chap. 13.

The constitutive dimension of coherence in individual self-determination and group self-determination gives us a foundational reason for valuing coherence as a guiding standard in legal decision-making.

13.8 Coherentism as Anti-formalism

Coherentism provides, I would argue, an alternative to formalist conceptions of rationality, on the one hand, and skepticism, on the other. In the different fields in which coherence theories have been proposed, they have been advanced as an anti-formalist alternative to skepticism. The story, in general lines, goes as follows. Coherence theories in ethics, epistemology, philosophy of science, etc. have been proposed once attempts to provide a 'scientific' theory of rationality for those domains have failed. An easy—and relatively common—response to these failures is the skeptical one: in light of the insurmountable difficulties to give an account of justification in respectable terms—alias, in scientific terms—one cannot but accept that the justification of beliefs, norms, plans of action, etc. in these domains is doomed to failure and, consequently, that one cannot have knowledge in these domains. However, the apparent dilemma between formal rationality, on the one hand, and irrationality, bias, and whim, on the other, would only arise if formalism were the only possible model of rationality. Faced with the failure of attempts to model rationality after scientific rationality in a number of domains, the only viable response is not skepticism. Rather, the failure of these programs reveals that a formal conception of rationality is ill-suited to give an account of justification in domains other than science. Coherentism is then proposed as an alternative to scientific models of knowledge. This does not mean, however, that coherentism is a second-best strategy, which allows us to keep the illusion of knowledge alive despite the failure of formal models. Rather, coherentist proposals result from a firm conviction that these models cannot be appropriately applied in a number of domains and that there is a need to develop broader models of rationality that have the resources to give an account of our practices of justification.

I cannot go here into showing in detail that a similar motivation (i.e., to provide a non-skeptical alternative to formal theories) drives coherence theories in different domains. A few examples, I hope, should suffice to illustrate the point. In epistemology, given the serious problems facing the Cartesian project of grounding knowledge upon secure foundations, coherentism has been claimed to provide a non-foundational response to the problem of skepticism. Similarly, coherence theories in ethics aimed at providing a solution to the regress problem alternative to the traditional, foundationalist, one. Coherentist approaches to practical reasoning are meant to be an alternative to both formal models of practical inference (i.e., deductive models and, more recently, expected utility models) and intuition-based models of decision-making. In philosophy of science, coherentism also provides a middle-way between formalist approaches to the problem of theory-choice (e.g., Bayesianism) and skeptical ones. Similarly, in discourse theory, coherentism has been advanced as an alternative to formal models of discourse rationality, such as the cost-benefit model endorsed by relevance theorists and skeptical, subjectivist, approaches to discourse interpretation (Sperber and Wilson 1986).

In law, coherentism is also meant to be an alternative to formal models of rationality and, given the problems facing these models, a viable option to skeptical reactions. Coherence theories of law and adjudication aim at solving some problems of formal positivism: the troubling implications of legal positivism concerning the scope of judicial discretion, its difficulties to give an account of the role that moral reasons play in legal reasoning, a dissatisfaction with the conventional account of the sources of law, and a discontent with the limitations of the deductive approach to legal reasoning. As opposed to a conception of legal knowledge as a pyramid, a foundationalist view of legal justification, and a deductive model of legal reasoning, which are key elements of formal or classical legal positivism, coherentism advances a conception of legal knowledge as a raft, a coherentist account of legal justification, and a holistic approach to legal inference. The problems facing classical legal positivism do not necessarily lead us to accept the skeptical conclusions put forward by legal realism and (to a varying degree) the critical movements. Rather, it leads us to rethink the model of rationality that is apposite to law and to give a role to reason in law broader than the one accorded to it by formalist models.

In the context of evidential reasoning in law, coherentist theories of evidence and legal proof provide us with a non-skeptical alternative to Bayesian models. As is well-known, the Bayesian theory of legal proof—which, at least in the Anglosaxon world, still is the dominant model and which has an increasing influence in other legal systems—faces serious problems. To start with, this theory inherits all the problems of Bayesianism, as a general theory of evidence, e.g., the subjectivity of Bayesian calculus, the unavailability of the relevant probabilities, or problems of computational complexity. In addition, there are problems specific to the legal applications of Bayesianism, e.g., the Bayesian theory of legal proof does not give a satisfactory account of the presumption of innocence or the standards of proof. In light of these problems, coherentism aims at providing criteria of rationality for assessing conclusions about disputed questions of fact in law broader than those embedded in the conception of rationality as probabilistic coherence, which underwrites Bayesianism.

In conclusion, coherence theories across domains aim at providing a middle way between formal theories—which face, for several reasons, serious problems—and skeptical views. The success—and shortcomings—of the coherentist project should be assessed in the light of the objective of providing a non-skeptical alternative to formalism. Formalism, in its different varieties, assume, either implicitly or explicitly, that the so-called 'standard theory of rationality', i.e., the view that criteria of rationality derive from formal theories such as deductive logic, probability theory, etc., is correct (Stein 1996). This theory, however, is inadequate for several reasons. To start with, this theory ignores the substantive dimension of rationality, in that it only provides criteria of internal justification; it is overly idealized, given what we know about the psychology of reasoning; and it is too narrow, for a substantial part of what is involved in reasoning falls beyond the scope of application of these criteria of rationality. In addition, this conception has skeptical consequences, for most of what passes for argument in a number of domains is, in light of the formal standards of rationality, either irrational or arrational. Coherentism seeks to deliver a conception of rationality richer than the formal conception that is assumed in different fields of knowledge, including, to be sure, the legal one.

13.9 Coherentism and Naturalism

Coherentism enjoys a high degree of psychological plausibility and this gives it a distinctive advantage over competing accounts of justification. A drive towards coherence is an important feature of our psychological equipment. There is substantial psychological evidence that shows the relevance of coherence in our reasoning processes. Empirical studies strongly suggest that we find explanatory thinking natural: considerations of explanatory coherence are the engine that drives much inference in ordinary life.[25] Moravski has persuasively argued that cognition can be viewed as an activity that is directed towards the goal of achieving understanding, and that humans may be seen, in an important sense, as *homo explanans* (Moravcsik 1990, 213). Simon, Holyoak, and collaborators have shown that complex decision tasks, such as judicial reasoning as well as reasoning about evidence, are performed by building up coherence among a number of decision factors (Simon et al. 2001). In the context of legal fact-finding, these results support previous work by Hastie and Pennington that showed the relevance of standards of explanatory coherence in jurors' reasonings (Hastie and Pennington 1991, 519). That coherence plays an important role in the formation and evaluation of factual hypotheses in law has also been shown, in the context of judicial reasoning, by Wagenaar and collaborators (1993). Hence, the psychological plausibility of coherence-based reasoning in general and, more specifically, of coherence-driven reasoning in law has a solid empirical basis.

But—it might be argued—what is the relevance of these psychological studies to the project of developing a theory of legal reasoning? Legal theory and philosophy of law are, as is well know, normative disciplines. Theories of legal reasoning tell us how one ought to reason in law; they do not aim at describing the process whereby legal decisions are made. That coherence plays an important role in legal decision-making says nothing about which role it ought to play, if any, in a theory of legal justification. The objection is that I am committing the much discussed 'naturalistic fallacy'. However, this objection cannot take off the ground if one endorses a naturalistic approach to philosophy, i.e., the view that philosophy is continuous with science and, more importantly for our purposes, that there is a

[25]Lipton has interpreted Kahneman and Tversky's well-known results as indicating the presence of a strong proclivity to explanatory thinking, see Lipton (2004, 108–113).

continuity between philosophy and psychology. The separation between philosophy and psychology, between the normative and the descriptive, is of a quite recent vintage. Before the start of the twentieth century, and the advent of the analytical school, the study of mind and behavior was a central concern of philosophers. In the last decades, with the emergence of the cognitive sciences, the many interconnections between philosophy and psychology have been reestablished, and the standard view about the relationship between the normative and the descriptive has been reexamined. A trend towards naturalizing philosophy has been a main development in different branches of philosophy. In epistemology, there has been an increasing interest in work in cognitive psychology and the development of naturalized approaches to epistemic justification and knowledge has been at the center of the debate in the last years (Kornblith 1994). Naturalism is a popular approach in contemporary discussion about important questions in philosophy of science, such as the relationship between theory and observation or the social structure of scientific knowledge (Godfrey-Smith 2003). And one of the most important developments in moral theory in the last decades has been in the field of moral psychology.[26]

The naturalist trend, with few exceptions, has not taken off in the (more traditional) field of law (Leiter 1998). However, in what may be justly called, in light of their spectacular development, the 'era' of cognitive sciences, legal theory, I would argue, cannot but be responsive to the possible impact that results in cognitive psychology might have on its subject. In other words, it is necessary to 'naturalize' legal philosophy and rethink the relations between the normative and the descriptive. In the context of legal reasoning, there is an additional reason to endorse a naturalized perspective. The main objective of theories of legal reasoning is to ameliorate the legal practice. In other words, the development of a theory of legal reasoning should be at the service of improving legal decision-making—which is not to say that it does not advance purely intellectual interests as well, such as the progress of knowledge. Now, if this is so, then, even though the theory of legal reasoning should involve a great deal idealization, given its normative character, it is important that it does not idealize away of our cognitive capacities so much as to make it ill-suited to guide and regulate legal practice. The naturalist principle that 'ought' implies 'can' constrains the kind of theories of legal reasoning that one should aim at developing. Thus, a coherentist theory of justification, insofar as it builds upon ordinary reasoning processes, is well placed to advance the project of ameliorating the legal practice, which is, I would argue, a central one in legal theory.

To conclude, a theory of justification that gives coherence an important role enjoys, in principle, a high degree of psychological plausibility and this is a good reason to pursue the coherentist project, despite the many—and well known—problems facing these theories, as much in law as in any other domain. It is interesting to note, however, that even though the natural tendency towards coher-

[26]For an introduction to the central problems of moral psychology, see Sinnott-Armstrong (2007–8) and Doris (2010).

ence is, from a naturalistic perspective, a reason for adhering to coherence theories, it is also—as argued above—the source of one of the main problems of coherentism, namely, the fabrication of coherence. Coherence theories are objectionable in that they seem to attribute justification to beliefs, acts, decisions, etc. that result from epistemically defective processes. The challenge is, therefore, to develop a theory of coherence that is not only psychologically plausible but also normatively attractive. My own response to this challenge, as explained before, is to complement the theory of coherence with a theory of epistemic responsibility and thus to define legal justification in terms of optimal coherence. Although nothing prevents us from defining optimal coherence in terms of two independent conditions, namely, a condition of coherence and a condition of epistemic responsibility, the second, I would argue, may be understood as implicitly contained in the first one. Epistemic responsibility is not an alien component in the structure of a coherence theory of coherence; judgments of coherence and judgments of responsibility are intimately connected via the concept of agency, as I will argue in the next-and last- section.

13.10 Coherence and Agency

Coherentism puts the agent at the center of a theory of justification. There is a very interesting distinction in discourse theory between coherence *a parte obiecti* and coherence *a parte subiecti*, that is, between the coherence of a text as such and the coherence that the interpreter brings to a text (Conte 1988). It is the presence of the latter kind of coherence that accounts for judgments of discourse coherence. Coherence is the result of the effort of the interpreter: it is not a given property of a text, but it has to be built in the course of interpretation. Thus, a coherentist theory of justification is inextricably linked with an agent point of view, and this makes considerations of epistemic responsibility essential to justification. Hence, the introduction of the concept of epistemic responsibility in a coherence theory of justification is not merely an ad hoc addition, the objective of which is to remedy some of the problems of coherentism. Rather, responsibility may be viewed as an implicit—albeit underdeveloped—component of the coherence theory of justification.

Thus, a coherentist approach to legal justification reveals that there are important connections between judgments of responsibility and judgments of justification, between the properties of agents—the legal decision-makers who carry out their interpretative tasks in an epistemically responsible way—and the properties of the objects of interpretation—either the law or the facts. As opposed to traditional approaches to legal theory that focus on the properties that the legal system have or should have, coherentism is an agent-centered theory of justification. This does not mean that one should replace the analysis of the properties of legal systems by a 'jurisprudence of subjects' (Balkin 1993). But given that coherence is not merely a property of the objects but that the activity of the subject is critical to judgments of coherence, a coherentist approach to justification brings to light the relevance of features of the subject to attributions of justification. From a coherentist point of view, a theory of justification cannot neglect the study of the features of legal decision-makers that result in good decisions. In other words, from this point of view, it follows that legal ethics is a substantial part of a theory of legal reasoning.

A number of interesting lines of research opens up once one focuses on the subject—the legal decision-maker—who strives to find the most coherent solution to a problem of proof or a problem of interpretation in law. To start with, the question arises as to which is the most adequate way of spelling out the standards of epistemic responsibility of legal decision-makers. Are the deontic and the aretaic conceptions mutually exclusive? If they are not, how do the duties and virtues of legal decision-makers relate to each other? In addition, it is necessary to give a detailed account of the virtues that are relevant to legal reasoning. Are there any virtues *specific* to legal decision-makers? How do general virtues apply to the legal context? And what role do epistemic and moral virtues play in legal justification? These questions invite us to explore the possible applications of virtue ethics and virtue epistemology to legal theory. More specifically, these questions suggest the possibility of developing a neo-Aristotelian conception of legal reasoning. But these are issues that fall beyond the scope of coherence studies (and this paper) and are rather a research topic for another (future) investigation.

References

Aarnio, A., et al. 1998. *On coherence theory in law*. Lund: Juristfölager i Lund.

Alexy, R., and A. Peczenik. 1990. The concept of coherence and its significance for discourse rationality. *Ratio Iuris* 3(1): 130–147.

Amaya, A. 2007. Formal models of coherence and legal epistemology. *Artificial Intelligence and Law* 15: 429–447.

Amaya, A. 2008. Justificacion, coherence, and epistemic responsibility in legal fact-finding. *Episteme: A Journal of Social Epistemology* 5: 306–319.

Amaya, A. 2009. Inference to the best legal explanation. In *Legal evidence and proof: Statistics, stories, logic*, ed. H. Kaptein, H. Prakken, and B. Veheij. Aldershot: Ashgate.

Amaya, A. 2011. Diez tesis acerca de la coherencia en el Derecho. *Discusiones* 10: 21–64.

Amaya, A. (forthcoming). *The tapestry of reason: An inquiry into the nature of coherence and its role in legal argument*. Oxford: Hart Publishing.

Annis, D.B. 1978. A contextualist theory of epistemic justification. *American Philosophical Quarterly* 15: 213–219.

Atienza, M. 2006. *El derecho como argumentación*. Barcelona: Ariel.

Balkin, J.M. 1993. Understanding legal understanding: The legal subject and the problem of legal coherence. *The Yale Law Journal* 103: 105–176.

BonJour, L. 1985. *The structure of empirical knowledge*. Cambridge: Cambridge University Press.

Bratman, M.E. 1987. *Intentions, plans, and practical reasoning*. Cambridge: Harvard University Press.

Brown, G., and G. Yule. 1983. *Discourse analysis*. Cambridge: Cambridge University Press.

Cohen, S. 1986. Knowledge and context. *The Journal of Philosophy* 83: 574–583.

Conte, M.E. 1988. *Condizioni di coerenza: Ricerche di linguistica testuale*. Firenze: La Nuova Italia.

Davidson, D. 2001. A coherence theory of truth and knowledge. In *Subjective, intersubjective, objective*, ed. D. Davidson. Oxford: Oxford University Press.

DePaul, M. 1993. *Balance and refinement*. London: Routledge.

DeRose, K. 1999. Contextualism: An explanation and defense. In *The Blackwell guide of epistemology*, ed. J. Greco and E. Sosa. Malden: Blackwell.

Doris, J.M. (ed.). 2010. *The moral psychology handbook*. New York: Oxford University Press.

Dworkin, R. 1986. *Law's empire*. London: Fontana.

Feldman, R. 2002. Epistemological duties. In *The Oxford handbook of epistemology*, ed. P. Moser. Oxford: Oxford University Press.

Fodor, J., and E. Lepore. 1992. *Holism: A shopper's guide*. Oxford: Blackwell.

Fogelin, R. 2003. *Walking the tightrope of reason*. Oxford: Oxford University Press.

Gärdenfors, P. 1988. *Knowledge in flux*. Cambridge: MIT Press.

Godfrey-Smith, P. 2003. *Theory and reality: An introduction to the philosophy of science*. Chicago: The University of Chicago Press.

Goldman, A.H. 1988. *Moral knowledge*. London: Routledge.

Hage, J.C. 2004. Law and coherence. *Ratio Iuris* 17: 87–105.

Hastie, R., and N. Pennington. 1991. A cognitive theory of juror decision-making: The story model. *Cardozo Law Review* 13: 519–557.

Hellman, C. 1995. The notion of coherence in discourse. In *Focus and coherence in discourse processing*, ed. G. Rickheit and C. Habel. Berlin: DeGruyter.

Hurley, S. 1989. *Natural reasons: Personality and polity*. Oxford: Oxford University Press.

Kennedy, D. 1997. *A critique of adjudication (fin de siècle)*. Cambridge: Harvard University Press.

Klein, P., and T.A. Warfield. 1994. What price coherence? *Analysis* 54: 129–132.

Kolnai, A. 2001. Deliberation is of ends. In *Varieties of practical inference*, ed. E. Millgram. Cambridge: MIT Press.

Kornblith, H. (ed.). 1994. *Naturalizing epistemology*. Cambridge: MIT Press.

Lehrer, K. 2000. *Theory of knowledge*, 2nd ed. Boulder: Wesview Press.

Leiter, B. 1998. Naturalism and naturalized jurisprudence. In *Analyzing law: New essays in legal theory*, ed. B. Bix. Oxford: Clarendon Press.

Lewis, D. 1996. Elusive knowledge. *Australasian Journal of Philosophy* 74: 549–567.

Lipton, O. 2004. *Inference to the best explanation*, 2nd ed. London/New York: Routledge. 1st edn. 1991.

MacCormick, N. 1984. Coherence in legal justification. In *Theorie der normen*, ed. W. Krawietz et al. Berlin: Duncker and Humblot.

Margolis, J. 1984. The locus of coherence. *Linguistics and Philosophy* 7(1): 3–30.

Millgram, E. 2001. Practical reasoning: The current state at play. In *Varieties of practical inference*, ed. E. Millgram. Cambridge: MIT Press.

Moral, L. 2003. A modest notion of coherence in legal reasoning: A model for the European court of justice. *Ratio Iuris* 16(3): 296–323.

Moravcsik, J.M.E. 1990. *Thought and language*. London: Routledge.

Olsson, E. 1998. Making beliefs coherent. *Journal of Logic, Language, and Information* 7: 143–163.

Peczenik, A. 1989. *On law and reason*. Dordrecht: Kluwer.

Pryor, J. 2001. Highlights of recent epistemology. *The British Journal for the Philosophy of Science* 52: 95–124.

Putnam, H. 1985. *Reason, truth, and history*. Cambridge: Cambridge University Press.

Rawls, J. 1999. *A theory of justice*, ed. rev., Cambridge: Harvard University Press.

Raz, J. 1992. The relevance of coherence. *Boston University Law Review* 72: 273–321.

Richardson, H. 1994. *Practical reasoning about final ends*. Cambridge: Cambridge University Press.

Simon, D. 1998. A psychological model of judicial decision making. *Rutgers Law Journal* 30(1): 1–142.

Simon, D. 2004. A third view of the black box: Cognitive coherence in legal decision-making. *The University of Chicago Law Review* 71: 511–586.

Simon et al. 2001. The emergence of coherence over the course of decision-making. *Journal of Experimental Psychology: Learning, Memory, and Cognition* 27(5): 1250–1260.
Sinnott-Armstrong, W. (ed.) (2007-8). *Moral Psychology.* Cambridge: MIT Press.
Sperber, D., and D. Wilson. 1986. *Relevance: Communication and cognition.* Oxford: Blackwell.
Stein, E. 1996. *Without good reason: The rationality debate in philosophy and cognitive science.* Oxford: Clarendon Press.
Thagard, P. 1998. Ethical coherence. *Philosophical Psychology* 11: 405–422.
Thagard, P. 2000. *Coherence in thought and action.* Cambridge: MIT Press.
Thagard, P. 2007. Coherence, truth, and the development of scientific knowledge. *Philosophy of Science* 74: 28–47.
Thagard, P., and E. Millgram. 1996. Deliberative coherence. *Synthese* 108(1): 63–88.
Timmons, M. 1999. *Morality without foundations: A defense of ethical contextualism.* New York: Oxford University Press.
Wagenaar, W.A., P.J. Van Koppen, and H.F.M. Crombag. 1993. *Anchored narratives: The psychology of criminal evidence.* New York: St. Martin's Press.
Wiggins, D. 2001. Deliberation and practical reasoning. In *Varieties of practical inference*, ed. E. Millgram. Cambridge: MIT Press.
Williams, M. 2001. *Problems of knowledge.* Oxford: Oxford University Press.
Zagzebski, L. 1996. *Virtues of the mind: An inquiry into the nature of virtue and the ethical foundations of knowledge.* Cambridge: Cambridge University Press.

Index

M. Araszkiewicz and J. Šavelka (eds.), *Coherence: Insights from Philosophy, Jurisprudence and Artificial Intelligence*, Law and Philosophy Library 107,
DOI 10.1007/978-94-007-6110-0,

The manufacturer's authorised representative in the EU is Springer Nature Customer Service Centre GmbH, Europaplatz 3, 69115 Heidelberg, Germany. If you have any concerns regarding our products, please contact ProductSafety@springernature.com

Printed and bound by CPI Group (UK) Ltd, Croydon, CR0 4YY
30/09/2026
02225324-0007